Multiracial Child Resource Book
Living Complex Identities

MAVIN
FOUNDATION

MAVIN Foundation redefines diversity through innovative projects celebrating multiracial youth and families.

Multiracial Child Resource Book
Living Complex Identities

Maria P. P. Root
Matt Kelley

Editors

The *Multiracial Child Resource Book* is published by MAVIN Foundation, a 501 (c)3, nonprofit organization that is redefining diversity through innovative projects celebrating multiracial and transracially adopted youth and families. Your tax-deductible donation makes projects like the *Multiracial Child Resource Book* possible.

Editors	Maria P. P. Root, Ph.D. and Matt Kelley
Assistant Editor	Kimi Kawabori
Research	Philipp Aurand, Sashya Clark, Jonathan Higgins, Raymond C. Lam, Toni Sutton-Allie, Elaine Vega
Distribution	Sashya Clark
Art Direction	Chance T. Goldston
Design	HOTMETAL Creative, LLC and Kimi Kawabori
Proofreading	Kevin Allen, Kate Bokelman, Elizabeth Harrin, Hila Lenz, Catherine McDonald, Dan Tochen
Photography	Shawn Jezerinac and Paul Kawabori

ISBN 0-9729639-0-1
First printing, July 2003

For information, address:

MAVIN
FOUNDATION

600 First Avenue, Suite 600
Seattle, WA 98104
Phone: 206.622.7101
Toll Free: 888.77MAVIN
Fax: 206.622.2231
E-mail: info@mavinfoundation.org
Web: www.mavinfoundation.org

Printed in the United States of America

Dedication

This book is dedicated to the past, present, and future generations of multiracial youth.

To past generations, thank you for creating a template and often navigating this journey alone. For the current generation, thank you for being a constant inspiration for our work. For future generations, we hope you will play an active role in creating a more cohesive, multicultural society by redefining race and diversity.

Acknowledgments

A project of this magnitude required the generosity of many people and organizations.

First, we would like to thank our contributing authors and testimonial writers. We are grateful for their contribution of time and scholarship. We would also like to thank Kevin Minh Allen, James A. Banks, Russel Hare, Shawn Jezerinac, Nicholas A. Jones, Paul Kawabori, Todd Kwapisz, Amy McFarlane, Miranda Othberg, and Hunington Sachs for their considerable support.

Finally, thank you to our project funders: the Pride Foundation, the Ted Lord Allied Grant, the J.C. Penney Company Fund, Kinam Sohn and Eric Fredricks, Elsa and Patrick Higgins, John Cephas Martin, Jr., Gloria and Isamu Kawabori, Jennifer Poulson, Robert Poulson, Jonathan Higgins, and donations by MAVIN Foundation members for their role in making this project possible. We extend a very special thank you to the K&F Baxter Family Foundation for underwriting this project. It is through their generosity and vision that we are able to create this resource to help parents and professionals support the next generation of multiracial and transracially adopted youth.

Glossary[1]

The following terms appear frequently in this book and in various oral and written discussions on mixed race and transracially adopted people. The definitions provided here reflect the most common current usage.

Afroasian refers to people of African and Asian heritage.

Amerasian refers to anyone racially mixed of Asian ancestry. It is also a transnational term referring to racially mixed Asians in other countries. Subsumed under this term are Afroasian, Eurasian, and hapa (*hapa haole*). Amerasian originally referred to children of American and Asian national origin, usually fathered by White Americans. The term has been used broadly with children fathered by American servicemen in Asia.

Bicultural refers to a person who relates to two distinct cultures.

Biracial refers to a person whose parents are of two different socially designated racial groups, for example: Black mother, White father. In a less commonly used, but equally accurate meaning, biracial can also refer to someone who has parents of the same socially designated race, when one or both parents are biracial or there is racial mixing in the family history that is important to the individual. This use of biracial moves us away from requiring equal "fractions of blood" to recognize the prevalence of racial blending throughout American history. However, the social and psychological experience of the person who uses the term this way may be different from someone who is a "first-generation" biracial.

Bisexual usually refers to someone whose sexual desire and emotional attraction is oriented to more than one gender or sex. Someone can be bisexual in their sexual orientation and publicly declare any sexual identity such as bisexual, heterosexual, queer, transgender, or transsexual. Just as some people consider a biracial identity to reflect self-loathing or passing, a bisexual identity is similarly misconstrued by some.

Blood quantum is used primarily to establish the fraction or proportion of Native or Aboriginal heritage that a tribe may require for membership. This system originated out of the federal government's need for definition and restriction of tribal growth.

Culture encompasses the embracing, knowledge, and practice of traditions and values that span generations, though undergo change with the impact of historical events. Ethnicity is informed by the broader context of culture. For instance, being ethnically of Mexican heritage in the U.S. has shared and different meanings from being of Mexican heritage in Mexico because of the broader cultural context.

Ethnicity refers to self-identified membership in a group because of shared emotions, attitudes, and identification with values and history. It is a social identity that does not necessarily require a birth or adoptive parent of that ethnicity, but is usually passed on through the teachings of family and community. Thus, someone can be of Japanese descent and primarily identify as ethnically Hispanic if they were raised in Peru. Ethnicity can derive from racial identity and group membership, but is not synonymous with it. A person of African heritage can be raised in a White neighborhood and not ethnically identify as African American, but racially identify as Black.

Eurasian refers to people of Asian and White European heritage.

Hapa is a term derived from the Hawaiian language (*hapa haole*). Although it was originally used to designate someone who was partially a stranger or outsider—Hawaiian mixed with other national or racial heritage—today it is an inclusive term that designates someone of mixed Asian or Pacific Islander origin. Many people are broadening its usage to be more similar to Amerasian. For example, although hapa is more commonly associated with someone of Asian and White mixed heritage, increasingly people of Asian and Black heritage, Asian and Latino/a heritage as well as someone who is both Japanese and Korean are included. Some people are broadening its usage to encompass all racially mixed people, as well as Asian transracial adoptees.

Heterosexual refers to someone whose sexual desire and emotional attraction is primarily oriented to someone considered the "opposite" sex. This identity does not preclude attraction to or sexual experiences with persons of the same sex.

Homosexual refers to a sexual desire and emotional attraction primarily oriented to persons of the same sex. As a sexual identity, men identify as gay and women as lesbian or, in younger generations, as queer.

Hypodescent refers to a social system that maintains the fiction of monoracial identification of individuals by assigning a racially mixed person to the racial group in their heritage that has the lowest social status.

Interracial means involving or existing between two or more races. Some people use this term to describe multiracial people. However, this term is most often used to describe couples where each person is of a different race. For example, an interracial couple may produce a multiracial child.

Mélange, a French term for mixed, is a newer term used by many Black/White individuals to indicate being of mixed racial heritage with no racial designation.

Mestizo/a comes from a Spanish word designating racial mixing of someone with Indigenous and Spanish ancestry. It now has a broader meaning, referring to all people of mixed Latino ancestry. Because of shared Spanish ancestry, this term is also used among Filipinos and Filipino Americans to refer to light complexioned Filipinos or persons with one Filipino parent and one White parent. It is not necessarily considered a positive term, as it was derived from colonial racism and preference for light skin.

Métis/se is a French word that is most often applied to people of both Indigenous and French heritage in Canada. Historically, and in modern times, it has also been applied to anyone of mixed Aboriginal and non-Aboriginal ancestry.

Miscegenation refers to race mixing in intimate dating and sexual relationships. Thus, antimiscegenation means against intermarriage or against race mixing. The last anti-miscegenation laws were repealed in 1967 by a U.S. Supreme Court ruling in the case of *Loving* v. *State of Virginia.*

Mixed race refers to people who are of two or more racial heritages. This may be the result of their parents being of different heritage from one another or from race mixing in the grandparent generation.

Monoethnic means relating to or including one specific ethnic group.

Monocultural refers to people who claim or relate to a single cultural heritage.

Monoracial refers to people who claim a single racial heritage. It is also a system of racial classification that only recognizes one racial designation per person.

Mulatto/a, in its current usage, refers to someone who is of varying fractions of African and European heritage. Not all racially mixed persons view this as a positive designation. Its original meaning has negative connotations; many believe the word is derived from the Spanish *mulato* for mule, the infertile hybrid between a donkey and a horse. The suffix suggests a diminutive status. Arabic origins have been suggested for this term.

Multicultural means relating to, or including, several cultures.

Multiethnic means relating to, or including, several ethnic groups. Some people use this term interchangeably with the term multiracial, though these terms do not mean the same thing. For example, one person of Korean and White heritage may identify as multiracial or biracial, but only Korean American ethnically.

Multiracial refers to people who are of two or more racial heritages. It is the most inclusive term to refer to people across all racial mixes. Thus it also includes biracial people.

The **"one-drop rule"** originated as a way of keeping the White race pure. If a person had any African heritage, they were declared non-White and Black. This rule protected White plantation owners' financial interests. It is a little known fact that the "one-drop rule" was applied in the 1896 U.S. Supreme Court case, *Plessy* v. *Ferguson*, in which Mr. Plessy could not ride in a railroad car for White people because he was 1/8 Black. This rule has been applied to the border between White and all other racial groups to preserve White purity. For example, during WWII, persons of fractional Japanese heritage were sent to the internment camps.

Passing used be a term referred to persons, primarily of African descent, who were multiracial and could live their life as White if they disaffiliated with their relatives and the African American community. It is almost always used in a derogatory way when describing the motives or actions of multiracial persons. Ironically, many multiracial people do not wish to pass as White in contemporary time, but are perceived, and therefore "passed" as White unless they choose to reveal their racial or ethnic heritage.

Queer is a non-derogatory, inclusive word relating to lesbians, gay men, bisexuals, and transgendered people.

Race is a social designation and fabrication, the definition and boundary of which changes by country and even by generation. Racial classification was borrowed from the systematic classification of plants and animals to give this destructive concept scientific validity. Inferior personality and physical attributes have been attributed to persons colonized or perceived to be a threat to the group of people in power.

Racism reflects a combination of ignorance and prejudice. Combined, racism results in discriminatory behavior or attitudes towards a person because of his or her perceived racial group membership.

Transcultural refers to crossing, bridging, or transcending cultures.

Transgender refers to emotional and sexual attractions and orientations that can include both sexes and genders, as well as alternative genders and sexes. This sexual orientation and identity defies the conventional dichotomy between heterosexual versus homosexual. A transgenderist or transgendered individual may live their life being perceived as someone of a different sex than to which they were born, but usually without genital modification.

Transracial indicates movement across racial boundaries and is sometimes synonymous with interracial. This term is most notably used in the context of adoption across racial lines.

[1] *Adapted from Maria P. P. Root, ed.,* The Multiracial Experience: Racial Borders as the New Frontier, *pp.ix-xi. (Thousand Oaks, CA: Sage, 1996). Several terms were added or revised for definitions.*

Foreword

James A. Banks, Ph.D.

The nearly seven million people who indicated that they belonged to more than one racial group in the 2000 Census provide both challenges and opportunities to educators and other professionals who work with children and youth. The public recognition and affirmation of mixed race students that has occurred within the last several decades should compel educators to question existing racial categories and to ponder the meaning of race in 21st century America. As interracial marriages in the United States increase and current racial categories are continually challenged, race in America may become less significant in shaping the behavior of individuals and groups. Recent DNA evidence confirms that there are no significant biological differences among racial groups. Consequently, race is primarily a social construction, although it has significant and profound structural, economic, and political influences within societies and nation-states.[1]

The study of mixed race people provides rich opportunities for teachers to engage in fruitful discussions and dialogues among themselves and with their students about race as a social construction and the changing meaning of race through time. Students need to understand, for example, that racial mixture has a deep, rich, and complex history in the United States as well as throughout the Americas and the world. Teachers should help students realize that interracial relationships and biracial children born to these unions have a long history in the United States. Examples include the relationship between Sally Hemings and Thomas Jefferson,[2] the often silenced and denied Black heritages within White families,[3] and the mixed racial heritage of many eminent African Americans, such as Booker T. Washington and Frederick Douglass.

Whites and African Americans, Indians and Whites, and Indians and African Americans have produced offspring with mixed heritages since these groups first interacted in the Americas. The dominant racial and ethnic group in Mexico and throughout most of Latin America is racially mixed. The Mexican people, who are called mestizos, were created when the Spaniards colonized Mexico and produced offspring with Indian women. The Africans who were brought to Mexico added to its ethnic mix. Consequently, Mexican Americans are a racially mixed people. The legitimization of interracial mixtures in the United States is a rather recent phenomenon. However, interracial mixture itself is historic. This is an important distinction that needs to be understood by teachers and students.

Race is one of the main categories used to construct differences in the United States and in societies and nation-states worldwide.[4]

Racialization is a characteristic of both past and present societies. Groups with social, economic, and political power construct racial categories that privilege members of their groups and marginalize outside racial groups. Race is consequently a major variable used to determine the allocation of resources and benefits within societies. Powerful racial groups define their own characteristics as essential ones for attaining the benefits and rewards of society. Jacobson calls races "invented categories."[5] Omi and Winant state that the "determination of racial categories is an intensely political process."[6] Their theory of racial formation "emphasizes the social nature of race, the absence of any essential racial characteristics, the historical flexibility of racial meanings and categories and the irreducible political aspect of racial dynamics."[7]

Racial categories will continue to be contested as well as the very idea of race itself, especially by scholars,[8] as long as racial stratification and racialization exists within societies and nation-states. Teachers should help students to understand how racial categories have shifted over time and how established racial categories and groups have been deconstructed and new ones established. Several publications in the emerging field of White studies reveal how the multiple categories that were used to describe the races among White ethnic groups in the mid-19th century became one racial category in the 20th.[9][10][11] A monolithic White racial category emerged when the various White ethnic groups became culturally assimilated, racially identified as one group, and defined themselves in opposition to African Americans.[12]

With the arrival of the massive number of immigrants from Ireland in the 1840s and the waves of immigrants from Eastern, Southern, and Central Europe during the 1890s and the first two decades of the 20th century, Whiteness became a highly contested category. White ethnic groups who were established in the United States and who had social, economic, and political power defined the "huddled masses" of new immigrants as peoples of different races.

Jacobson describes these developments as "the fracturing of Whiteness."[13] Various groups of Whites became distinct races that were ranked, such as the Celtic, Slav, Hebrew, Iberic, Mediterranean, and Anglo-Saxon. The Anglo-Saxon was classified as the superior race. One writer stated that because of their "Celtic blood," the Irish threatened the American republic. Italians and Jews were

also defined as the Other near the turn of the century and experienced racial discrimination and hostility. Italians were often called "dagos" throughout the nation and "White niggers" in Southern states. In some parts of the South, Italians were forced to attend all-Black schools. In 1891, during the height of American nativism, 11 Italians were lynched after being accused of murdering the police chief of New Orleans.

The past teaches us several important lessons about the future of race in America. Racial categories and their meanings will keep changing, groups with power will construct race in ways that will benefit themselves and disadvantage powerless groups, and race is a powerful variable in the American conscience and in American society. Politicians are keenly aware of the power of race in America, as was revealed when the Republican Party's "Southern strategy" was uncovered in the debacle that led to the resignation of Trent Lott as the party's majority leader in 2003.

Research indicates that students are keenly aware of race and have internalized the misconceptions about race that are institutionalized within adult society.[14] However, many teachers find race an uncomfortable topic and consider themselves "colorblind."[15] Consequently, conversations about race in schools are often absent from the classroom and are confined to the playground and to other sites out of the gaze of teachers. Research also indicates that the colorblind perspective embraced by many teachers negatively influences their interactions with students of color and leads to the construction of school curricula that marginalize the histories and cultures of the diverse groups that make up U.S. society.[16]

The complex and multiple ways in which many multiracial students perceive their racial and ethnic identification challenge existing conceptions of race and many assumptions that educators, counselors, and psychologists make about race, ethnicity, and culture. Racial and ethnic identities are not fixed but are constantly changing, complex, and contextual, in part because of the interactions among groups within a society characterized by racial, ethnic, language, and religious diversity. Both mainstream White students and students of color are changed in these interaction processes.

An effective and thoughtful response to mixed race youths

requires that educational theorists, researchers, teachers, and other human service professionals rethink the meaning of race in American society and understand the extent to which it is a socially constructed idea that is often used to advantage some groups and to disadvantage others. Ashley Montagu calls race "Man's most dangerous myth."[17]

Theories and practices related to ethnic identity, ethnic culture, and the learning characteristics that theorists have associated with particular ethnic and cultural groups also need to be reconceptualized. These theories need to be problematized and reconstructed in ways that will enable them to provide insights into the identifications and behavior of students who identify with more then one racial or ethnic heritage.[18] Reconstructing and problematizing existing theories and research findings will be a challenge. However, this process will enable more complex and nuanced theories and explanations to be created that can guide effective practice. This book includes several informative articles that describe the identity development of mixed race children and youth that will help theorists and practitioners to reformulate existing theories.

Educational theorists, researchers, teachers, teacher educators, counselors, psychologists, and other human service professionals will find this informative and sometimes moving resource book useful as they attempt to reform schools, colleges, universities, and their practice to make them more responsive to the needs of mixed race children and youth. In his "Letter from the Birmingham Jail" Martin Luther King, Jr. wrote that "Injustice anywhere is a threat to justice everywhere."[19] Because the fates of all groups in society are tightly connected, educators and other human service professionals who promote justice and equality for multiracial children and youth are helping to liberate us all. ▌

Notes

1 J. A. Banks, ed., *Diversity and Citizenship Education: Global Perspectives* (San Francisco, CA: Jossey-Bass, 2004).

2 A. Gordon-Reed, *Thomas Jefferson and Sally Hemings: An American Controversy* (Charlottesville: University Press of Virginia, 1997).

3 E. Ball, *Slaves in the Family* (New York: Farrar, Straus and Giroux, 1998).

4 J. A. Banks, ed., *Diversity and Citizenship Education* (2004).

5 M. F. Jacobson, *Whiteness of a Different Color: European Immigrants and the Alchemy of Race* (Cambridge: Harvard University Press, 1998).

6 M. Omi and H. Winant, *Racial Formation in the United States: From the 1960s to the 1990s*, 2nd edition (New York: Routledge, 1994).

7 Ibid.

8 Ibid.

9 R. D. Alba, *Ethnic Identity: The Transformation of White America* (New Haven: Yale University Press, 1990).

10 N. Ignatiev, *How the Irish Became White* (New York: Routledge, 1995).

11 M. F. Jacobson, *Whiteness of a Different Color* (1998).

12 T. Morrison, *Playing in the Dark: Whiteness and the Literary Imagination* (Cambridge: Harvard University Press, 1992).

13 M. F. Jacobson, *Whiteness of a Different Color* (1998).

14 W. Stephan, *Reducing Prejudice and Stereotyping in Schools* (New York: Teachers College Press, 1999).

15 J. W. Schofield, "The Colorblind Perspective in School: Causes and Consequences," 4th edition updated, in *Multicultural Education: Issues and Perspectives*, ed. J. A. Banks and C. A. McGee Banks (San Francisco: Jossey-Bass, 2003).

16 J. W. Schofield, "The Colorblind Perspective in School" (2003).

17 A. Montagu, *Man's Most Dangerous Myth: The Fallacy of Race*, 6th edition (Walnut Creek, CA: AltaMira Press, 1997).

18 S. B. Heath and M. W. McLaughlin, ed., *Identity and Inner-City Youth: Beyond Ethnicity and Gender* (New York: Teachers College Press, 1993).

19 M. L. King, Jr., *Letter From the Birmingham Jail* (New York: HarperCollins, 1963/1994: original work published 1963).

Introduction

Matt Kelley and Maria P. P. Root, Ph.D.

If you look at classrooms and on playgrounds across the nation, you will see a growing number of children who do not fit into a single racial box. They are children who transcend simple racial categorization and whose lives straddle dual, and sometimes, multiple races and cultures. In cities like Seattle, Sacramento, and San Antonio, one in six babies born is multiracial. These children represent a rapidly growing population of Americans who draw from multiple racial groups and who are redefining how our society views race and diversity.

Although mixed race children and multiracial celebrities are becoming increasingly common, multiracial people in America are not a new phenomenon. The first laws in the Americas that prohibited sex or marriage across racial lines were enacted as early as 1661.[1] Their existence confirmed that people of different races were beginning to create families together. It was not until 1967 that the aptly named U.S. Supreme Court case *Loving* v. *Virginia* finally struck down the last of the anti-miscegenation statutes that remained law in 16 U.S. states. Incredibly, these horrible laws that lasted for over three centuries have been repealed for only 36 years.

Today, the vast majority of mixed race youth are loved and cared for by their parents and extended families. Although mixed race people are nothing new in the United States, what *is* new is that being multiracial is no longer the legacy of slavery and rape. During slavery, America bore witness to generations of African women who were raped by slave owners, and whose mixed race children inherited slave status since "one drop" of African blood classified them as Black. The "one-drop rule" was not only relegated to people of African descent. In the 20th century, Americans of even 1/16 Japanese heritage were considered Japanese and were among the 120,000 Japanese and Japanese Americans who were incarcerated in World War II internment camps.[2]

Census 2000 marked a symbolic end to the "one-drop rule" with a historic and long overdue change. For the first time in its 210-year history, the U.S. Census allowed people to check multiple races in 2000. It was also mandated that by January 1, 2003, virtually all agencies that received federal aid must allow for multiple race identification when requesting racial data.[3] Although the "one-drop rule" is no longer federal policy, its legacy remains. Many Americans of every race and culture continue to classify people according to the premise that people belong to only one race. Our society still operates under a pervasive system of monoracial bias that forces mixed race people to choose a single race identity on most job applications, heath care forms, and tests. Being forced to deny one or both of your parents' heritage is dehumanizing and can be traumatizing, especially when it is multiplied over the course of a lifetime. The hope and objective of this book is that the next generation of multiracial children will grow up unfamiliar with being forced to check "only one race."

What may help to facilitate this change is the multiracial baby boom. The unprecedented rise in interracial couples and mixed race children over the past few decades is resulting in a growing societal acknowledgment and acceptance of a mixed race identity. As more mixed race Americans identify with both the pieces *and* the "sum of their parts,"[4] America is responding by creating institutions that affirm these identities. Unlike prior generations, there is a growing body of resources that explain and affirm the mixed race experience. These resources range from children's books and community support organizations to mixed race campus clubs, scholarly anthologies, and national nonprofit organizations. Additionally, being multiracial today often means knowing and being aware of other mixed race people, celebrities, and the existence of support organizations. Today, millions of multiracial youth can navigate their mixed race journey with resources unavailable in the past.

We are fortunate that there is a wealth of people who are dedicated to exploring mixed race issues. Existing research has shown that many multiracial youth represent an "at-risk" population that deserves closer study. A 1998-2000 study by the Oregon Alliance of Children's Programs found that mixed race youth had higher rates of physical and sexual abuse than any other race. The same study also found that they were entering the Oregon juvenile justice system at unprecedented rates.[5] In the health care system, mixed race leukemia patients often cannot receive life-saving bone marrow transplants because of their unique heritages. Mainstream resources must be made available to the parents and professionals who work with mixed race children in order to help them to raise healthy and happy youth.

Fortunately, the *Multiracial Child Resource Book* will help parents and professionals accomplish this by offering the most exhaustive and up-to-date portrait of multiracial youth in America today. We were touched by the willingness and support of our contributors, and their generous contributions of time and scholarship. From

the start, it was obvious that the people involved in this project— from our chapter authors to our testimonial writers—recognized the critical importance of creating a comprehensive resource for parents and professionals about the mixed race experience.

This book provides a comprehensive resource to assist parents of multiracial youth, the professionals who work with them, and multiracial people themselves, to explore the multiracial experience today. The *Multiracial Child Resource Book* is a groundbreaking addition to the growing body of literature on the mixed race experience because it incorporates both recent research and cutting edge analysis by some of the nation's foremost experts on multiracial youth and identity development. For the first time, a book about multiracial youth includes both a developmental guide spanning from birth to adulthood, as well as multiple chapters on specific multiracial heritages, which include frequently overlooked mixed race populations, such as multiracial Pacific Islanders and Arab Americans. This research is accompanied by commentary from the true "experts"—young multiracial people themselves. Virtually every chapter is accompanied by a first-person testimonial from a mixed race young person or by their parents. Hearing their voices demonstrates the diversity and richness of what it is like to grow up mixed race in the U.S. In addition to profiling the mixed race birth family, the *Multiracial Child Resource Book* also recognizes the interface between multiracial identity and foster care and transracial adoption. This is but one example underscoring the book's inclusive and comprehensive approach.

As you read through this book, you will notice the diversity of tone and writing style among both our professional and testimonial writers. For instance, you may notice that inconsistent racial and ethnic labels are employed by chapter authors, our testimonial writers, and on the photos that separate the chapters. For example, some writers may choose to write "Black," whereas others prefer "African American." In every instance, we retained each author's terms because they reflect how they individually identify and what words they feel best describe their heritage. As you read through each chapter, we hope that this diversity of terms helps to expose the subjective and personal nature of racial and ethnic identifiers. Furthermore, we encourage you to read the book in its entirety. Each chapter provides a unique perspective into the mixed race experience. Even if your original impetus was to read about the specific experiences of children of both Asian and African American heritage, for example, each chapter provides important insight into the lives of multiracial youth. To best understand the diverse needs and experiences of multiracial children, readers should approach this book comprehensively.

Inevitably, groundbreaking books like this one will generate questions. "Isn't everyone mixed?" "Why do we need to create one more 'racial' group anyway?" "Isn't this divisive?" "If race is a social construct, doesn't recognizing multiracial people simply reinforce it?" These are all important questions. Although the mixed race phenomenon is not internationally unique—societies like Puerto Rico and Hawai'i are just two contemporary examples—the institutional recognition of a mixed race community on the U.S. Mainland is new. Second, the sheer number of people who chose to identify as mixed race in Census 2000 also represents something new. This book is a valuable contribution because it equips parents and professionals with tools they need to understand multiracial youth and to better serve them in everything from the classroom to family settings. These tools will help adults create nurturing environments that respect individual diversity that will ultimately contribute to a more supportive environment for *all* children. Finally, multiracial youth represent an exciting opportunity. As racial boundaries fade, the next generation of mixed race youth can offer their perspective of what it is like to identify with multiple groups of people, and to recognize that all of us hold a stake in each other's future. Despite our nation's painful history with race, our hope is that this book will encourage what could be a very exciting legacy: a generation of proud multiracial young people who can draw upon their experiences to advocate for progressive racial and social justice across all lines. ⧉

Notes

1 L. R. Tenzer, *A Completely New Look at Interracial Sexuality: Public Opinion and Select Commentaries* (Manhawkin, NJ: Scholars Publishing House, 1990).

2 P. R. Spickard, *Mixed Blood: Intermarriage and Ethnic Identity in Twentieth-Century America* (Madison, WI: University of Wisconsin Press, 1989).

3 Ibid.

4 T. Williams-Leon and C. Nakashima, ed., *The Sum of Our Parts: Mixed-Heritage Asian Americans* (Philadelphia: Temple University, 2001).

5 *The Oregon Alliance of Children's Program's Shelter Data Project.* (Salem, OR: Oregon Alliance of Children's Programs, 2000).

Jared
African American +
Caucasian

Elaine
Mexican +
Irish + Czech +
Jewish

Will
African American +
Caucasian + Blackfoot

Anita
Indian

Yasmin
Indian + African
American +
Caucasian +
Blackfoot

Alena and David
Mexican + Filipino +
Spanish + Italian +
Native American

...ardo
...an + Colombian

James
Black +
White +
Adopted

...ian +
...ese +
...uan

Michelle
Venezuelan +
Irish +
Chinese

Chris
Vietnamese +
Adopted

Section 1:
Multiracial "101"

Philipp W. Aurand

Age: 26

Racial/Ethnic Heritage: Black, German, Irish, Cherokee, and Indian

As the son of a White German mother and a multiracial Black American father, race identity and classification have been thought-provoking exercises for me. Growing up, I can't recall exclusively identifying with one specific race, yet I was fully aware of, and often proud of, being racially different. My identity was undoubtedly influenced by my mother's response to the limited "Black or White" race options on various documents. Instead, she would mark "Other" and affectionately write in "brown." Particularly on school enrollment forms, my mother was annoyed that equal consideration wasn't given to both people who had created her son. Brown skin and curly locks didn't quite fit the "White" box, while to check "Black" denied her contribution to my existence. Although neither of us was up in arms over the limited choices, we were definitely aware that something was missing.

My mother's rejection of Black or White labels in favor of brown demonstrated her valuing my entire heritage. Brown was a metaphor for an awareness, appreciation, and even celebration of multiraciality as being a reality unto itself. This was our reality regardless of trends or other people's levels of awareness. We were not going to let societal norms or ignorance influence our interpretation of racial identity.

Census 2000 marked an important shift in racial awareness in the U.S. I like the idea that multiracial people can "officially" indicate their entire heritage for the first time. I appreciate Census 2000 as a manifestation of a growing collective awareness around race. In the past, it was often dictated by surrounding influences, whether they be parents, friends, and communities, who had, at times, unwittingly downplayed and misunderstood multiraciality.

Looking back, as I continued to develop my biracial identity, I also downplayed components of my heritage. When I was 15 years old, I learned that I had Irish, Cherokee, and Indian ancestry on my father's side as well as African American. Despite this, I still primarily identified with my German and Black background. Perhaps I felt that it took enough effort to identify with two races, let alone four. In the past two years, however, I have come to fully embrace my multiethnic background.

Although I am aware that ideologies (particularly related to race) are slow to change, change is inevitable. Census 2000 is a compelling example. The ability to check "Black," "White," "American Indian," and "Asian," and having them all recognized, is a new experience. I feel that Census 2000 was an absolutely necessary development. Millions of Americans are embracing the option to "officially" acknowledge their multiple ethnicities for the first time. This change is an important development for racial consciousness in America.

Testimonial

Chapter 1

A Statistical Portrait of Children of Two or More Races in Census 2000[1]

Nicholas A. Jones, U.S. Census Bureau and Amy Symens Smith, U.S. Census Bureau

A growing number of Americans no longer identify solely as White, Black, American Indian, Asian, or Pacific Islander, but rather as a combination of two or more of these races. However, this is not a new phenomenon. In fact, early in our country's history, people were categorized as "mulatto," "quadroon," and "octoroon" to denote their mixed racial heritages, and while not widely known, individuals who wrote in terms such as "biracial" or "multiracial" were counted in the "Other" race category in recent decades. But Census 2000 was markedly different, as it was the first decennial census to allow respondents to self-report their multiple racial identities by selecting one or more races, and as such, marked a significant milestone for multiracial people.

In 1997, after a lengthy research process, the United States Office of Management and Budget (OMB) revised the standards used by federal agencies to collect, tabulate, and present information on race and ethnicity.[2] The federal government considers race and Hispanic origin[3] to be two separate and distinct concepts, and for Census 2000, the questions on race and Hispanic origin were asked of every individual living in the United States.[4] Perhaps the most profound change in these revisions was that of allowing respondents to report "one or more races" to indicate their racial identity.[5] This innovation came about after nearly 20 years of advocacy by interracial families, parents, and multiracial people, who questioned whether single race data collection practices accurately reflected the changing racial and ethnic diversity of the country's population. Thus, Census 2000 became the first decennial census to allow individuals to self-identify with one or more races, thereby enabling millions of Americans to report their unique multiple race identities and have them recognized and validated.[6]

Perhaps this opportunity for individuals to report more than one race in this new millennium will help to foster change in American society's long-standing racial ideologies. But in order to adequately position ourselves as educators, parents, researchers, and advocates, we must familiarize ourselves with the growing wealth of information about this previously unrecognized and under-researched "multiracial" population. To that end, this chapter sets the foundation by presenting a statistical portrait of the multiracial population, and in particular, multiracial children.

While some people report combinations of races to indicate their multiple-race identity, others often use generic terms such as "multiracial," "biracial," or "mixed." The U.S. Census Bureau uses the term "Two or more races" to refer to the population that reported more than one race. In this paper, we use the term

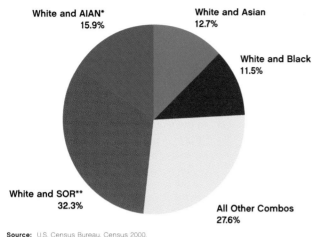

Source: U.S. Census Bureau, Census 2000.

Figure 1. Largest Multiracial Combinations: 2000.

* AIAN refers to "American Indian and Alaska Native"
** SOR refers to "Some other race"

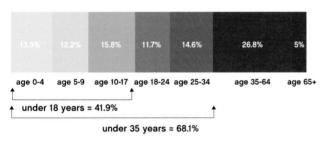

Source: U.S. Census Bureau, Census 2000.

Figure 2. Multiracial Population by Selected Age Groups: 2000.

"multiracial," which is commonly used by outside researchers to refer to this population. Data from Census 2000 provides new insights on the size and makeup of children who were reported as being of more than one race in the United States. These statistics illuminate the presence of multiracial people in American society, and enable us to recognize, discuss, and understand the depth and breadth of the contemporary multiracial existence. But in no way should this measurement be considered "the" multiracial population, or necessarily what it means to be "multiracial" in America today. Rather, this is a snapshot of the multiracial population in the year 2000, and a framework upon which we can base current and future discussions. For the multiracial population is a rapidly growing, complex meld of people and experiences, and as such may influence Americans' racial realities for years and generations to come. Therefore, it is hoped that the discussions in this book will serve to increase awareness and understanding of the important implications that multiracial children present to our society. While this information provides some answers, it also seeks to spark discussions and raise new questions for exploration.

Overall Multiracial Reporting in Census 2000

To begin, we answer the basic questions, "How large is the multiracial population?" and "What racial groups comprise this particular population?" In Census 2000, 6.8 million people, or 2.4 percent of the U.S. population, reported more than one race.[7] The multiracial population is not a homogeneous population, and contrary to popular belief, the "White and Black" combination is not the largest. The largest combination was "White and Some other race,"[8] numbering 2.2 million, and representing 32 percent of the total multiracial population. This was followed by "White and American Indian and Alaska Native," which represented about 16 percent, with 1.1 million. The third largest combination was "White and Asian," which represented about 13 percent, with 870,000. The fourth largest combination was "White and Black or African American," which represented about 12 percent, with 780,000 people. Together, these four combinations made up more than 70 percent of the total multiracial population (see Figure 1).

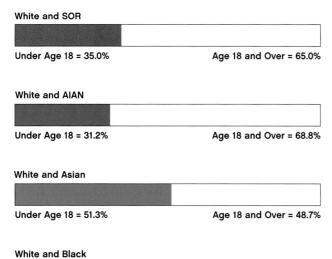

White and SOR

Under Age 18 = 35.0%   Age 18 and Over = 65.0%

White and AIAN

Under Age 18 = 31.2%   Age 18 and Over = 68.8%

White and Asian

Under Age 18 = 51.3%   Age 18 and Over = 48.7%

White and Black

Under Age 18 = 71.7%   Age 18 and Over = 28.3%

Source: U.S. Census Bureau, Census 2000.

Figure 3. Percent of People Under Age 18 for the Four Largest Multiracial Combinations: 2000.

Race Total Multiracial Children	Number 2,856,886	Percent 100.0
"White and SOR" children	772,663	27.0
"White and Black" children	562,914	19.7
"White and Asian" children	445,082	15.6
"White and AIAN" children	337,298	11.8
All other combinations	738,929	25.9

Source: U.S. Census Bureau, Census 2000.

Table 1. Largest Multiracial Combinations Reported for Children Under Age 18: 2000.

The Multiracial Population is Young

An examination of the race data by age distributions reveals that people who reported more than one race differ substantially in age from people who reported a single race. Overall, the multiracial population is much younger than the single race population (see Figure 2). About 42 percent, or 2.9 million, of the multiracial population was under age 18, compared with about 25 percent of the population reporting one race. Furthermore, nearly 70 percent of all multiracial people were younger than 35 years of age. Only five percent of the multiracial population was age 65 years and older in contrast to 12 percent of the population reporting one race. The young age distribution of the multiracial population may reflect recent societal changes, such as the rise in interracial marriages subsequent to the U.S. Supreme Court's 1967 *Loving* v. *Virginia* decision, which struck down prohibitions to interracial marriage, leading to an increasing number of multiracial children and growing acceptance of these identities.

The Multiracial Population is Diverse

The multiracial population is also heterogeneous with variations in the age distribution for these various combinations. For example, while only about one-third of the "White and American Indian"[9] population and of the "White and Some other race" population were under age 18, more than half of the "White and Asian" population, and nearly three-quarters of the "White and Black"[10] population were under age 18 (see Figure 3).

Of the children who were identified as being of more than one race in Census 2000, the four largest race combinations reported were: "White and Some other race" (27 percent), "White and Black" (20 percent), "White and Asian" (16 percent), and "White and American Indian" (12 percent). These four race combinations represented nearly three-quarters of the entire population of multiracial children under age 18 (see Table 1).

Where Do Multiracial Children Live?

Children in the four largest multiracial combinations are geographically dispersed across the United States. However, the geographic concentrations of each group reflect local racial composition, as illustrated by the following state and county

NUMBER "White and SOR" Children			PERCENT "White and SOR" Children		
Rank	U.S. Total	772,663	Rank	U.S. Total	27.0
1	California	247,060	1	Texas	48.2
2	Texas	100,636	2	New Mexico	47.9
3	New York	60,470	3	Arizona	38.9
4	Florida	37,052	4	California	36.8
5	Illinois	33,822	5	Illinois	34.1
6	Arizona	26,390	6	New Jersey	32.8
7	New Jersey	25,072	7	Colorado	31.1
8	Michigan	20,196	8	Idaho	30.6
9	Colorado	17,160	9	New York	30.5
10	Washington	16,009	10	Wyoming	29.7

Source: U.S. Census Bureau, Census 2000.

Table 2. Top Ten States for "White and Some other race" Children: 2000.

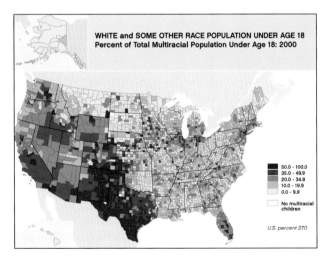

WHITE and SOME OTHER RACE POPULATION UNDER AGE 18
Percent of Total Multiracial Population Under Age 18: 2000

- 50.0 - 100.0
- 35.0 - 49.9
- 20.0 - 34.9
- 10.0 - 19.9
- 0.0 - 9.9
- No multiracial children

U.S. percent 27.0

Source: U.S. Census Bureau, Census 2000.

Figure 4. County Level Distribution of "White and Some other race" Children: 2000.

level distributions. First, we use top-ten ranking tables to compare the state level distributions of each multiracial combination by number and percent. Then, we use maps to depict the county level distributions of these combinations as a percentage of the total multiracial population in each respective county.

"White and Some other race" Children

California was by far the state with the highest number of children reporting "White and Some other race," followed by Texas and New York. However, Texas and New Mexico had the greatest percentages of their multiracial children reporting "White and Some other race." Seven states (Texas, California, Arizona, Illinois, New York, New Jersey, and Colorado) were represented in the top ten for both number and percent of children reporting "White and Some other race" (see Table 2). These concentration patterns may reflect the large Hispanic populations in these states.

Counties with the highest proportions of "White and Some other race" children were concentrated in Texas, and across several western states along the U.S.-Mexico border, as well as counties in southern Florida (see Figure 4). Other counties in the West with intermediate proportions of "White and Some other race" children included counties in southern Arizona, southern California, and an area spanning southeast Oregon, southern Idaho, northern Nevada, northwestern Utah, and southern Wyoming. Concentrations were also found in the remainder of Arizona, Utah, Nevada, northern California, and Wyoming, as well as counties in south and central Florida.

"White and Black" Children

California was the state with the highest number of children reporting "White and Black." However, West Virginia, Kentucky, and Ohio had the greatest percentages of their multiracial children reporting "White and Black." Two states, Ohio and Pennsylvania, were represented in the top ten by both number and percent of children reporting "White and Black" (see Table 3). This pattern may reflect the preponderance of Black and White population groups in these states.

The highest proportions of "White and Black" children were in counties in the South, Midwest, and Northeast (see Figure 5).

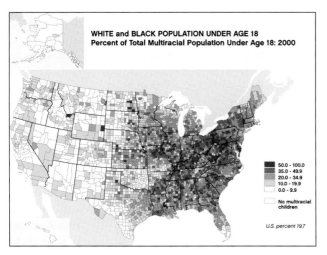

WHITE and BLACK POPULATION UNDER AGE 18
Percent of Total Multiracial Population Under Age 18: 2000

50.0 - 100.0
35.0 - 49.9
20.0 - 34.9
10.0 - 19.9
0.0 - 9.9

No multiracial children

U.S. percent 19.7

Source: U.S. Census Bureau, Census 2000.

Figure 5. County Level Distribution of "White and Black" Children: 2000

NUMBER "White and Black" Children			PERCENT "White and Black" Children		
Rank	U.S. Total	562,914	Rank	U.S. Total	19.7
1	California	67,782	1	West Virginia	49.8
2	New York	35,490	2	Kentucky	47.2
3	Ohio	33,673	3	Ohio	44.0
4	Texas	30,482	4	Indiana	41.4
5	Michigan	27,000	5	Pennsylvania	39.2
6	Pennsylvania	25,829	6	Iowa	37.6
7	Florida	25,613	7	Delaware	37.6
8	Illinois	23,920	8	Tennessee	36.8
9	Washington	19,380	9	South Carolina	35.5
10	Virginia	18,466	10	Missouri	34.3

Source: U.S. Census Bureau, Census 2000.

Table 3. Top Ten States for "White and Black" Children: 2000.

"White and Black" children showed the highest concentrations of the four multiracial combinations for counties in the Northeast and South. In the South, the majority of counties in all states had proportions of "White and Black" children above the national rate, especially counties in Kentucky and West Virginia. Midwestern counties in Indiana, southwestern Illinois, and Ohio also had proportions of "White and Black" children above the national average. Additionally, counties in the Northeast, primarily in Pennsylvania, showed high proportions of "White and Black" children.

"White and Asian" Children

California was by far the state with the highest number of children reporting "White and Asian." But Washington, New Hampshire, Hawai'i, and Virginia had the greatest percentages of their multiracial children reporting "White and Asian." Four states (Washington, Hawai'i, California, and Virginia) were represented in both the top ten by number and percentage of children reporting "White and Asian" (see Table 4).

At the county level, "White and Asian" children were the least geographically concentrated of the four largest multiracial combinations (see Figure 6). This population was nearly evenly dispersed across all regions of the U.S., which may reflect the heterogeneity of the Asian population itself. Not surprisingly, all of the counties in Hawai'i had high proportions of "White and Asian" children. Higher than average proportions of "White and Asian" children occurred in counties in Washington, Oregon, Idaho, southern California, Nevada, Utah, and Colorado.

"White and American Indian" Children

California and Oklahoma were the states with the highest number of children reporting "White and American Indian." However, Oklahoma and Montana had the greatest percentages of their multiracial children reporting "White and American Indian," followed by Alaska, South Dakota, and North Dakota. Two states, Oklahoma and Alaska, were represented in both the top ten by number and percentage of children reporting "White and American Indian" (see Table 5). These patterns may reflect the preponderance of American Indian and White populations in these states.

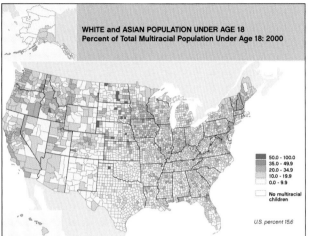

Source: U.S. Census Bureau, Census 2000.

Figure 6. County Level Distribution of "White and Asian" Children: 2000.

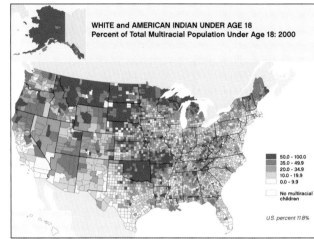

Source: U.S. Census Bureau, Census 2000.

Figure 7. County Level Distribution of "White and American Indian" Children: 2000.

NUMBER "White and Asian" Children			PERCENT "White and Asian" Children		
Rank	U.S. Total	445,082	Rank	U.S. Total	15.6
1	California	132,410	1	Washington	25.4
2	Washington	26,080	2	New Hampshire	23.9
3	Hawai'i	25,824	3	Hawai'i	23.5
4	Texas	20,837	4	Virginia	21.7
5	New York	20,351	5	Maine	20.8
6	Florida	16,567	6	Oregon	20.8
7	Illinois	15,776	7	Vermont	20.3
8	Virginia	13,446	8	California	19.7
9	New Jersey	11,666	9	Idaho	19.1
10	Michigan	10,554	10	Nevada	18.9

Source: U.S. Census Bureau, Census 2000.

Table 4. Top Ten States for "White and Asian" Children: 2000.

NUMBER "White and AIAN" Children			PERCENT "White and AIAN" Children		
Rank	U.S. Total	337,298	Rank	U.S. Total	11.8
1	California	54,076	1	Oklahoma	57.7
2	Oklahoma	36,762	2	Montana	53.2
3	Texas	17,754	3	Alaska	46.3
4	Michigan	16,306	4	South Dakota	45.0
5	Washington	16,229	5	North Dakota	43.5
6	Florida	10,557	6	Vermont	32.9
7	Oregon	10,537	7	Arkansas	31.1
8	New York	9,537	8	Maine	30.9
9	Ohio	9,506	9	Wyoming	29.6
10	Alaska	8,428	10	Alabama	25.9

Source: U.S. Census Bureau, Census 2000.

Table 5. Top Ten States for "White and American Indian" Children: 2000.

Counties with high percentages of "White and American Indian" children were concentrated in several distinct parts of the country (see Figure 7). One area, centered in Oklahoma, stretched into southeastern Kansas, southern Missouri, and northern Arkansas. Counties along the U.S.-Canadian border from Idaho to Michigan also had high proportions of "White and American Indian" children, as well as counties in Alaska. Additionally, western counties in Washington, Oregon, northern California, Idaho, Nevada, southern Colorado, and northern Arizona and Wyoming had intermediate proportions of "White and American Indian" children. Parts of Maine, New Hampshire, and Vermont also had intermediate proportions of "White and American Indian" children.

Future Considerations

This analysis of the multiracial population in Census 2000 provides a new look at racial diversity in the United States. The heavy concentration of children and young adults reporting more than one race in Census 2000 is a reflection of the tremendous increase in interracial marriages, the rise in multiracial births, and the increasing acceptance of multiracial identities over the last 35 years. If these trends continue, we may witness continuing large increases in the number of people who identify with more than one race.

Today's multiracial children and young adults reflect the results of America's recently evolving racial landscapes and human interactions. Society must do its best to recognize that these multiracial individuals represent a powerful new form of "diversity." We must strive to understand the needs of this population if we hope to actualize the potential contributions that multiracial people may make to our increasingly multiracial society.

Notes

1 Census 2000: This chapter is part of ongoing research on multiracial children and interracial families, and reports the results of research and analysis undertaken by Census Bureau staff. It has undergone a more limited review than official Census Bureau publications. This chapter is released to inform interested parties of research and to encourage discussion. The views expressed are those of the authors and do not necessarily represent the views of the U.S. Census Bureau. Please direct all correspondence to: Nicholas A. Jones, U.S. Bureau of the Census, Population Division, Racial Statistics Branch, Washington, D.C. 20233-8800, or e.mail nicholas.a.jones@census.gov. We appreciate the assistance and the insightful comments of Claudette Bennett, Kevin Deardorff, Campbell Gibson, John Long, and Trudy Suchan.

2 For additional discussion, please see: United States Office of Management and Budget. 1997. "Revisions to the Standards for the Classification of Federal Data on Race and Ethnicity." *Federal Register* (October 30). Washington, D.C. www.census.gov/population/www/socdemo/race/Ombdir15.html.

3 Hispanics may be of any race. The terms "Hispanic" and "Latino" are used interchangeably in this chapter.

4 The question on Hispanic origin asked respondents if they were Spanish, Hispanic, or Latino. The question on race asked respondents to report the race or races they considered themselves to be. Both questions were based on self-identification. For more information on these concepts, an explanation of the race categories used in Census 2000, and an overview of race and Hispanic origin populations at the national level, please see: Grieco, Elizabeth M. and Rachel C. Cassidy. 2001. *Overview of Race and Hispanic Origin: 2000.* U.S. Census Bureau, Census 2000 Brief Series (C2KBR/01-1, March 2001). Washington, DC. www.census.gov/prod/2001pubs/c2kbr01-1.pdf.

5 Other changes included terminology and formatting changes, such as spelling out "American" instead of "Amer." for the American Indian and Alaska Native category and adding "Native" to the Hawaiian response category. In the layout of the Census 2000 questionnaire, the Asian response categories were alphabetized and grouped together, as were the Pacific Islander categories after the Native Hawaiian category. The three separate American Indian and Alaska Native identifiers in the 1990 census (i.e., Indian (Amer.), Eskimo, and Aleut) were combined into a single identifier in Census 2000. Also, American Indians and Alaska Natives could report more than one tribe. Because of these changes, the Census 2000 data on race are not directly comparable with data from the 1990 census or earlier censuses, due, in large part, to giving respondents the option to report more than one race. Other factors, such as reversing the order of the questions on race and Hispanic origin and changing question wording and format, also may affect comparability. Therefore, caution must be used when interpreting changes in the racial composition of the U.S. population over time.

6 For additional discussion on multiracial reporting in Census 2000, please see: Jones, Nicholas A. and Amy Symens Smith. 2001. *The Two or More Races Population: 2000.* U.S. Census Bureau, Census 2000 Brief Series (C2KBR/01-6). Washington, D.C. www.census.gov/prod/2001pubs/c2kbr01-1.pdf.

7 In this chapter the term "reported" is used to refer to the response provided by respondents as well as responses assigned during the editing and imputation processes.

8 Census 2000 showed that the majority of people who reported "Some other race" were individuals of Hispanic origin, who provided write-in responses such as "Mexican," "Hispanic," "Latino," "Puerto Rican," and "Spanish." Overall, 90 percent of the 18.5 million people who reported "Some other race" alone or in combination were Hispanic.

Hideki
Japanese

Siri
European

Caetano
Japanese + European

Chad Thompson

Age: 16
Racial/Ethnic Heritage: African American and Caucasian

Generation Pride is the teen group for I-Pride, which stands for Interracial, Intercultural Pride. Our group meets at all I-Pride organized events, but we also get together outside of I-Pride for events we organize ourselves. I am the president of Generation Pride; it is my job to make sure meetings are organized and to mediate those meetings. I-Pride was founded in the San Francisco Bay Area in 1978, and is the nation's oldest group that brings together multiracial families. Thanks to I-Pride, the Berkeley school district was the first in the country to let students identify as "biracial" on forms asking about race. This was 22 years before Census 2000!

In the past, Generation Pride has had its fundraisers at I-Pride events and has used the profits earned from those fundraisers to go on outings. Though our members consist of teenagers from the ages of 13 to 17, we try to educate ourselves as well as have fun. Our most successful trip was to Los Angeles to visit the Museum of Tolerance and Disneyland. We saw the extraordinary exhibits on the Holocaust and the American Civil Rights Movement. These exhibits were fully interactive and I believe every single one of the members in attendance learned something valuable.

I've been asked to describe my feelings about being biracial many times. It has been a hard question for me to answer and I've never really felt I've answered it correctly. I think I have finally realized why.

I thought about this question and many others like it while I was at the Association of MultiEthnic Americans (AMEA) 2002 conference, held in Tucson, Arizona. I was scheduled to speak on a multiracial teen panel, so I wanted to be prepared to answer my questions clearly and truthfully. I was thinking about what I might say to the listeners at the conference when I came to the realization that being biracial wasn't a big deal for me. I then understood why answering questions about my feelings on the subject had been so hard to answer in the past. I would emphasize and exaggerate situations I had been in and feelings I had had so my answer would be a good one. In actuality, I usually feel the same as any of my other friends do about their racial or ethnic backgrounds. Though we talk about issues related to race, we don't concern ourselves with whether someone is part Black, White, or Asian. We all grew up in the Bay Area, in California, in the United States of America. I'm not put in very many situations where I feel awkward or uncomfortable about being biracial and I have been in even fewer situations where I was confronted violently because of being biracial.

I am not saying that my racial background doesn't affect me because it does. I'm simply saying it's not something I spend my time thinking about. In fact, for the first time, I only need to think deeply about my biracial background when I'm in a situation like this one, formally answering the direct question of "What is it like growing up multiracial?"

Testimonial

Chapter 2

The Evolution of the Multiracial Movement
Ramona E. Douglass

The formation of local grassroots organizations in the late 1970s and early 1980s, and the subsequent bonding of interracial couples, multiracial adults and transracially adoptive families[1] over issues of child-rearing, education, identity formation, and health created a cohesive mission from which a national advocacy movement emerged. It is my belief that understanding the birth of the multiracial movement in America requires that certain questions be explored and answered. For instance, how did the multiracial movement come into being, and in the process, overcome the challenges of nomenclature and diverse community experiences? What were the origins of the movement that brought these communities together in the late 1970s and early 1980s? What issues were significant enough to warrant the need to form national and regional multiracial advocacy groups across the country throughout the 1980s and early 1990s? What ideologies divided the multiracial leadership regarding the labeling/identifying of multiracial people on the 2000 Census? What constitutes multiracial communities of the 21st century? Finally, where is the multiracial movement focused today and what are its hopes for the future?

Since the exploration of each of these questions could easily be the basis for a chapter, my intent is to give readers an overview of the multiracial movement's history, its challenges and accomplishments. At the close of the discussion, there will be an introduction to a future possibility for multiracial people. What difference can be made in our society as a whole? What conversations need to be had across diverse racial and ethnic community lines that will transform our relationship to race as a nation and give our next generation of multiracial people a future worth living in?

Birth of the Multiracial Movement

Multiracial people and interracial relationships have been an integral part of America's history since the first European settlers arrived in the New World and established the first North American English colony in 1607. At that time, only White male settlers and Indigenous populations were present. The first ships that carried African slaves as cargo arrived 12 years later, and in that same year the first women of strictly European descent joined their White male counterparts in the tiny colony. This shortage of what was perceived as suitable women during the early development of the Americas resulted in widespread mixing of the races.[2] Those early relationships were not all voluntary. Many were formed out of rape, servitude, and denial of basic human rights. The offspring of those unions suffered the fate of the non-White parent in most instances, whether they were free, indentured servants, or slaves.[3]

There were brief periods in this early history when it was not deemed "immoral" or "unlawful" for different races to mix. But it was not until 1967 that the U.S. Supreme Court gave legitimacy to relationships between people of different racial backgrounds. The historic ruling of *Loving* v. *Virginia*[4] finally put to rest "the last vestiges of our nation's anti-miscegenation laws,[5] which had tarnished our historical growth and development..." since the 1600s.[6] It took another 12 years post-*Loving* before the first viable multiracial organization emerged in 1978 in San Francisco that is still in existence today—Interracial/Inter-Cultural Pride (I-Pride). Other organizations soon sprang up around the country, notably: Biracial Family Network (BFN) of Chicago in 1981; Interracial Family Circle (IFC) of Washington, D.C., in 1983; Multiracial Americans of Southern California (MASC) in 1987; Project RACE (Reclassify All Children Equally) in 1991, and Hapa Issues Forum (HIF) in 1992. Many other groups in key American cities came together for social interactions, political development, and networking of ideas on interracial living. By the late 1980s, the climate and conversations on race, specifically on mixed race, had escalated to a degree where a very vocal group of interracial families and multiracial adults decided that a national advocacy organization would be the best way to have their concerns and issues brought to the forefront of America's public consciousness. They were no longer satisfied with potlucks and picnics. Multiracial families with school-aged children and mixed race adults entering the job market would no longer accept people outside the community defining their cultural, ethnic, and racial affiliations.

The Formation of the Association of MultiEthnic Americans (AMEA)

On November 12, 1988, these pioneers in multiracial civil rights gathered in Berkeley, California, and called themselves the Organizing Committee of the National Association of MultiEthnic Americans. Out of that meeting, with 14 charter member organizations from across the country in attendance, AMEA was born. AMEA's first Executive Committee was elected with Carlos Fernandez (I-Pride),

president; Ramona Douglass (BFN), vice president; Reginald Daniel (MASC), secretary; and Sarah Ross (HONEY),[7] treasurer. Next, AMEA drafted a basic statement of purpose, defining itself as an educational organization that "promoted positive awareness of interracial and multiethnic people and families."[8] In the years between 1988 and 1995, AMEA's efforts concentrated on a) incorporating and obtaining 501(c)3 nonprofit status; b) testifying before Congress through its Political Action Committee (PAC) on the necessity for creating a multiracial/multiethnic category on all federal forms that requested racial data; c) creating an educational/legal advisory board with connections to prestigious institutes of learning; and d) forming strategic alliances with other national advocacy groups such as Project RACE and Hapa Issues Forum (HIF) to monitor local, state, and federal activities affecting interracial communities.

Accomplishments and Challenges on Issues of Race & Multi-Race

The period between the mid-1990s until the implementation of the 2000 Census saw the coming together and splitting apart of several factions within the multiracial movement. Alliances that were formed out of necessity between AMEA's President Ramona Douglass and Project RACE's Executive Director, Susan Graham, during the years 1994-1997 enabled our diverse communities to be considered a force to be reckoned with on issues of race and multirace. Graham, a European Jewish American woman who was interracially married with two African American/Caucasian children, and Douglass, a multiracial adult of African, American Indian, and Italian descent, represented major blocks of interest within the multiracial community. Project RACE systematically obtained multiracial category legislative victories in Ohio (Sub. H.B. No. 154 in 1992), and Illinois (S.B. 421-Public Act 88-71 in 1993). In 1994, a model piece of legislation, Senate Bill 149, was accomplished in Georgia that added a "multiracial" category not only to public school forms, "but to all state agency forms, as well as all employment forms and applications."[9]

By 1993, both AMEA and Project RACE had testified on behalf of the multiracial community at Congressional Hearings on Racial and Ethnic Standards. In 1994, Project RACE was asked to represent multiracial interests at a meeting of federal government agencies at the National Academy of Sciences in Washington, D.C. However, it was the appointment of AMEA's multiracial president, Ramona Douglass, to the 2000 Census Advisory Committee in December of 1995 that gave diverse multiracial/multiethnic interests a national forum in which to be heard by all branches of the federal government. Douglass' appointment to the Census Advisory Committee was soon criticized as endorsing a too "conservative" pace. Charles Byrd, editor of the Internet-based Interracial Voice, believed that too much time and energy was being wasted in self-explanation to traditional civil rights organizations and ethnic special interest groups such as the National Association for the Advancement of Colored People (NAACP), Mexican American Legal Defense and Education Fund (MALDEF), and the National Coalition for the Accurate Count of Asian and Pacific Americans. These organizations vehemently opposed the possibility of adding a multiracial category or any distinction for multiracial people on the 2000 Census. Byrd and others felt that a multiracial stand-alone category was more acceptable than any compromise that would only allow our community to check two or more boxes.

In June 1997, these ideological differences came to a head at the Third Multiracial Leadership Conference in Oakland, California. The participating organizations from across the country reached a consensus that a "check one or more box" format rather than a separate multiracial identifier would serve the highest community good. It would: a) allow for the celebration of diverse heritages; b) support the continued monitoring of existing civil rights legislation that impacted multiracial people directly; and c) it would also provide the most information for the accurate collection of racial/ethnic data for medical diagnosis and research. Of the organizations in attendance, only Project RACE rescinded its initial endorsement of the Multiracial Summit Statement. With that decision, AMEA and Project RACE ended their three-year strategic alliance. However, advocates of the "check one or more box" format found that their position was aligned with diverse organizations including the Japanese American Citizens League (JACL), the American Medical Association (AMA), and the federal Interagency Committee for the Review of Race & Ethnic Standards, which endorsed the implementation of that format on the 2000 Census race question.

What Constitutes the Multiracial Community in the 21st Century?

Census 2000's historic "check one or more" change resulted in nearly seven million Americans self-identifying with more than one race. Of the 6.8 million Americans who indicated two or more races on Census 2000, the actual number who identify as part of a multiracial community is still debated by federal health, social, and political agencies as well as community advocates of every hue and persuasion. Do multiracial people today even agree on racial/ethnic nomenclature? The answer is...not really. Some are wedded to non-race specific identifiers like "mixed" or "multiracial," which when used alone makes it impossible to distinguish what specific races actually apply. Because this would obscure much needed medical data for proper diagnosis and research on multiracial health is one reason why the single term, "multiracial," on the 2000 Census met heated opposition and obstacles both from within and outside this diverse community. Others have created or use terms unique to their specific racial mix. Some examples include "Blackanese," "Mexopino," or "Eurasian." Still others in the community have suggested that we abandon racial categories altogether and advocate for the adoption of legislation like the Racial Privacy Initiative (RPI),[10] sponsored by the controversial University of California Board of Regents member, Ward Connerly. Champions of RPI believe that passage of this Initiative on the California ballot in March of 2004 will help bring us closer to a colorblind society for subsequent generations of multiracial people.

Many multiracial and multiethnic Americans, unlike those who choose to identify solely with one race, remain unsure about whether or not to embrace their collective identity. The sheer diversity of the mixed race community also presents unique issues. For instance, the issue of hypodescent[11] resonates differently with Black/White multiracial people than with Asian/White and any other racial combination of multiracial people. For those who call themselves "hapa," (of mixed Asian or Pacific Islander heritage) instead of "multiracial," the ability to honor the heritages of both parents took precedence over the need to have a single multiracial identifier on Census 2000.[12] Similarly, for those who identify with both their Hispanic and non-Hispanic origins, common language and specific ethnic mix sometimes had mixed race Hispanics at odds with their non-Hispanic multiracial brethren on discussions and alliances around the Census race question.

Multiracial people are often asked by monoracial people how such diverse communities can ever be cohesive. These questions fail to recognize the diversity of "monoracial" communities. Who could say that there is not incredible diversity of shade, opinion, and experience among African Americans or Asian Americans? Despite the considerable diversity of the mixed race community, there is much that people who do not fit into one racial category share in our highly race-conscious society.

Future Possibilities

Post-Census 2000, multiracial advocates are left with the aftermath of their embittered battles over the race question. Inevitably, questions like, "What is next?" and "What is the new generation of multiracial leaders standing for in this decade?" arise. The answers are still forming. One thing is for sure: the face of the movement is changing. Dozens of multiracial student groups have popped up on college campuses from coast to coast. *MAVIN* magazine, which was founded by Matt Kelley in 1999 as a freshman at Wesleyan University, was created to help young multiracial people share their personal experiences. Today, it has become a national foundation addressing mixed race and transracially adopted issues. Annual conferences such as the Pan Collegiate Conference (held since 1996) and Hapa Issues Forum's regional conferences have helped to create annual focal events for mixed race college students. Most of these groups continue to celebrate the mixed race experience through art, poetry, composition, and other creative forms of self-expression. Many of these organizations are also incorporating the transracial adoptee experience into their mission statements. Although much of the campus organizations' focus remains on creating a social

Association of MultiEthnic Americans

The Association of MultiEthnic Americans' mission is to educate and advocate on behalf of multiethnic individuals and families by collaborating with others to eradicate all forms of discrimination. Founded in 1988, AMEA played a pivotal role in the U.S. Census allowing people to check "one or more races" on Census 2000 forms. Today, AMEA is committed to helping organizations comply with new federal guidelines on racial reporting and hosted the first national conference on the multiracial child in 2002.
Learn more:
www.ameasite.org

outlet to explore mixed race issues, many are also beginning to explore political and health issues, like holding bone marrow drives and fighting against anti-Affirmative Action legislation. At the MAVIN Foundation National Conference on the Mixed Race Experience held in April 2003, students representing dozens of mixed race student organizations came together to create a national coalition of mixed race student organizations to help shape the future of the multiracial movement. New national organizations like Swirl are also playing prominent roles in the movement. Following the lead of some of the movement's pioneers, this young generation is also expanding ties with other diverse communities.

As AMEA celebrates its 15 years of advocating on behalf of multiethnic people and families, the organization has shifted from its focus on census recognition of multiracial people. AMEA conducted its first highly successful conference honoring the multiracial child during the fall of 2002 in Tucson, Arizona. Today, AMEA is committed to assisting governmental organizations to comply with Office of Management and Budget (OMB) Directive #15 requiring organizations who receive federal aid and track race to allow for a "check one or more" policy. AMEA is working with newer organizations in order to see a generation of American children unfamiliar with the pain and confusion of "check only one race." What is apparent in all of these efforts is the necessity for our multiracial group leaders or representatives to continue to collaborate and dialogue with other communities. If we are ever to eliminate institutional racism in America, we must look to educate not only ourselves but the government agencies that tabulate people, the social services and health departments that categorize, diagnose, and treat people, as well as the general population that attempts to define us. We cannot know true freedom and the celebration of our diversity until we can be comfortable and supportive of every individual's right to choose in the matters of race and ethnic identity.

Notes

1 Families where the race of the parent(s) differs from the race of the adoptive children.

2 K. E. Russell, M. Wilson and R. Hall, *The Color Complex: The Politics of Skin Color Among African Americans* (New York: Doubleday, 1992).

3 Ibid.

4 Mildred Jeter and Richard Perry Loving's landmark interracial marriage case.

5 Laws against the mixing and co-habitation of different races.

6 D. Brown, "Making the Invisible Visible," in *The Multiracial Experience: Racial Borders as the New Frontier,* ed. M. P. P. Root (Thousand Oaks: Sage, 1996), 324.

7 Honor Our New Ethnic Youth (HONEY), Eugene, Oregon.

8 Excerpted from AMEA's mission statement (1988-1999).

9 S. Graham, Personal Interview, 1994.

10 American Civil Rights Coalition.

11 Term from the mythical "one drop of Black blood makes you Black" rule.

12 The California-based nonprofit organization Hapa Issues Forum (HIF) was at the forefront of this issue.

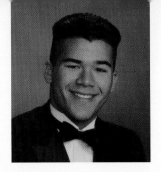

Rocky Kiyoshi Mitarai
Age: 24
Racial/Ethnic Heritage: Japanese and Caucasian

I was raised in Sonoma, California, a small, predominantly Caucasian town. I am Japanese and Caucasian. I remember my father telling me stories about my Japanese ancestry and how important it is. He told me that our family is from the samurai-class warriors who lived by a strict code of honor. The pride that my family instilled in me was challenged by many of my childhood experiences. The ensuing confusion made it difficult to come to terms with my mixed ethnicity.

Growing up, I had many experiences that made me question my racial identity. I remember a seventh grade project where students drew a picture of a man in a "rice picker's hat", buckteeth, and two slanted lines for eyes. The song written for the picture poked fun at narrow eyes and sushi. The entire class including the teacher laughed. I felt angry and ashamed. I heard what I now recognize as racist remarks throughout my life and started to accept them. Whenever I did protest the jokes, teachers told me that I shouldn't take things so seriously. It seemed as if I had an attitude problem and was making trouble.

Similar experiences strengthened my resolve to embrace my ethnicity. I remember accounts of my family's experiences during WWII in the internment camps, where they had to endure incredible hardships. Ironically, I felt a yearning to reconnect with my Japanese lineage while the Japanese Americans of my parents' and grandparents' era had tried to become more Americanized than ever in order to be accepted.

I started college at the University of San Francisco hoping to connect with my Asian peers. Asians usually hung out together in different cliques in which I wasn't welcome. I heard comments like, "Why do you try so hard to be full Japanese?" I was also told, "You shouldn't be in the Japan Club—you aren't a real Japanese." Another caustic remark was, "Eating rice today, huh? Are you getting in touch with your Asian side?" Rejection from my full Asian peers made me self-conscious and I tried even harder to gain acceptance.

One traumatic experience stands out. I was leaving a karaoke bar in San Francisco's Japantown. As a good luck charm, I wear a Chinese character on my necklace that says *fuku*, meaning "happiness" in Japanese and "good fortune" in Chinese. A group of Chinese and Vietnamese guys outside were staring at me and I heard one of them say, "Why is he wearing that necklace? He doesn't even know what it means." They followed me to my car and began to punch me. I fell down, and they started to kick me. At that point, I feared for my life. One of the guys yelled, "You see Bruce Lee movies and you want to be Asian, huh?" It didn't seem to matter that I was half Japanese.

After my violent experience I learned of the Hapa Issues Forum and found an outlet for my frustration. They related to my difficulties in coming to terms with my mixed race identity. I want people to understand that being multiethnic does not mean you have to identify with one or either culture(s). People may choose not to accept who I am because I am hapa, but this ignorance cannot change me. Nobody can take my heart and spirit away from me. I am very proud to be Japanese American.

—A longer version of this essay was originally published in "What's Hapa'ning: The Hapa Issues Forum Newsletter," and in *What Are You? Voices of Mixed-Race Young People*, by Pearl Fuyo Gaskins and published by Henry Holt.

Testimonial

Chapter 3

Patrolling Racial Borders: Discrimination Against Mixed Race People
Heather Dalmage, Ph.D.

"Is she part Black?" asked the imposing woman ahead of us in line at the Dollar Store. "Yes," I responded, not wanting to continue this conversation in an impersonal and public arena in front of my two-year-old daughter for whom the word race still meant, "last one to the porch is a rotten egg."

Raising her voice, the Black woman bent down toward my daughter's face and proclaimed, "We call that mulatto. Yes, indeed, you're a mulatto."

I felt strongly compelled to respond but was uncertain which piece should be addressed and how. Should I have begun to talk with this woman about the ugly origins of the term mulatto? Should I have addressed the dehumanizing and degrading aspects of categorizing other people (especially children)? I knew I was not going to let someone else impose the context of a race debate in front of my two-year-old. I left the store.

While such intrusions are not uncommon, more often they remain in the realm of the silent stare. A multiracial woman once said to me that being stared at was such a part of her existence that when it came time for her to perform in front of an audience she was very comfortable. Historically, in academic research and beyond, much emphasis has been placed on the ways multiracial people adjust to race in society. The assumption underlying

much of the analysis is that race is a concrete, objective, and static phenomenon. I propose that if we want to more fully understand multiracial experiences we need to "flip the script" and analyze why racial categories have been created in particular ways and why people who identify themselves with a single racial category feel the need and right to intrude upon, pass judgement on, and discriminate against multiracial people and their families.

Group Boundaries and Discrimination

Race thinking developed in the U.S. around and through questions of citizenship and resource distribution. The history of U.S. immigration and citizenship reflects a system deeply embedded in the protection of White privilege and the denial of rights to people of color. Colonization, slavery, genocide of indigenous people, the Chinese Immigration Exclusion Acts of the 1800s, the Bracero Program, internment camps, Jim Crow laws, and numerous other legally sanctioned forms of discrimination have been used to define and defend Whiteness by creating clear distinctions between White people and all others. When the distinctions seemed threatened, anti-miscegenation laws—those that denied people the right to marry across race lines—were enforced through penalties that included imprisonment, enslavement, and death. The primary threat was not the marriage itself but rather the fact that in the U.S. marriage legitimizes the offspring. If multiracial children were deemed legitimate, then all laws based on the separation of "the races" would be delegitimized. After three centuries of anti-miscegenation laws, in 1967, buttressed by the strength of the Civil Rights Movement, the Supreme Court ruled that interracial marriages must be recognized in every state. Unfortunately, multiracial families still face discrimination, and the children of these marriages are still expected to claim only one race.

While the Civil Rights Movement paved the way for the legal acceptance of multiracial families, it also created a new set of struggles for these families. The Civil Rights Movement included various groups struggling for liberation and self-definition such as the Young Lords, the Chicano Movement, the Black Power Movement, the Asian American Movement, and the American Indian Movement. Through these struggles, groups of color that had previously been on the defensive against White supremacist abuses began to define themselves for themselves. This meant that the distinction between insider and outsider was defined from *within* each of these groups rather than predominantly imposed from the outside by Whites. However, the way lines were drawn caused many problems for those who found themselves on the borders of racial groups, particularly those who were racially mixed. Moreover, the struggle for civil rights led to the passing of legislation meant to address and redress racism. The government needed a way to track compliance and by 1977 had agreed on four discrete racial categories; every U.S. citizen was required to check one. The census became a vehicle for protecting people of color against White supremacist abuse, *and* it strengthened the distinctions between racial categories. As a result, multiracial people, already discriminated against in a White supremacist society, became more susceptible to discrimination from all sides.

How "sides" are defined is a matter of history. Those people with whom we identify most closely, those with whom we share a history, a collective memory, and a collective way of knowing are generally considered our in-group, our side. For instance, a quick trip to the Gaza Strip makes the point clear.[1] Stone-throwing Palestinians do not have a natural or inherent disdain for the Jews at whom they throw the stones. Likewise the tank-driving Israelis are not genetically

driven to violence toward Palestinians. This particular conflict is driven by historical circumstances in which children are raised and through which they understand themselves and their world. The collective memories on each side are used to define the boundaries of in-groups. Often, as is the case in the Middle East, in-group cohesion is strengthened through the hatred of an out-group, those against whom in-group members define themselves. Moreover, each side knows itself in the negation of the other; for it is at the boundaries that identities are framed. In such a construction, little room exists for someone to be both Palestinian and Israeli.

The history of Whiteness and various forms of racism directed at groups of color has meant that in the U.S. being a member of one race—or one side—has immediately placed an individual as an out-group of the other. The greater the power imbalance between groups, the greater the emphasis on maintaining boundaries between sides. The boundaries are maintained on both the institutional and individual levels through various forms of discrimination. On an institutional level, discrimination occurs as an outcome of laws and the way society functions. For example, many children of color are denied equal access to education as a result of years of housing discrimination in a society in which a large portion of school funding is tied to property values through taxes. The segregated housing market ensures that children of color, particularly African Americans and Latinos, are disproportionately receiving an inferior education relative to White children. Discrimination and racism also play out between individuals. For instance, one student refuses to speak to another because she sat at the wrong lunchroom table. In this case, the discriminatory act is clear; the individual discriminator can be identified. Given that institutional mechanisms, from the housing market to the census, have functioned to keep lines between racial and ethnic groups clear and defined, multiracial children are facing unending demands to choose a side and stake a claim. In other words, demands are made that they adhere to the larger rules of race that guide U.S. racial thinking.

On all sides, border patrollers, or the race police, believe the color line is static and immutable, and thus they think they can distinguish between "us" and "them." Border patrollers claim that race is a simple concept, demand that others comply, and make their presence felt through various actions. The most common action, by far, is the stare. Other forms of border patrolling include probing and inappropriate questions. "What are you?" is one of the most common questions faced by multiracial people. Many times, however, people will not ask; instead they will begin to label a multiracial person. A friend of mine once told me that cab drivers assume she is whatever they are. Because border patrollers think they can determine "authentic" behaviors they also think they have the right to grant or withhold acceptance. Even when acceptance is not granted, individuals are expected to act in ways deemed appropriate; to do otherwise will provoke further patrolling.

All racial groups patrol the borders; thus, in addition to facing White racist abuse, multiracial people also face discrimination from their communities of color. Here I identify five broad areas of everyday life in which multiracial children are patrolled and face discrimination and demands to comply with existing racial rules.

1. Patrolling of the child's physicality:

All children tend to be conscious of appearance; however, not all children have to give conscious thought to the racial implications of their choice of hairstyle, make-up, weight and body shape, clothes, shoes, bags, and hats. Multiracial children do—they must because border patrollers on each side are watching and commenting. This form of discrimination can be very hurtful to multiracial children who must expend an inordinate amount of energy negotiating their appearance. For example, a Black-White multiracial woman I interviewed spoke of the devastation she felt as a child because her White mother did not learn to do "Black hair." As a result she faced relentless teasing from Black girls at school. Unfortunately, many parents, particularly White parents, do not understand the importance of hair and other physical markers to their child's ability to negotiate racial borders.

2. Patrolling linguistics:

Individuals who think that they can tell who is an "authentic" member of their race and who is not often listen intently to the use of language. Multiracial children are patrolled for their ability to "speak the language." For instance, a young multiracial student was granted acceptance by his Black peers only after he

Of Many Colors: Portraits of Multiracial Families
A traveling photo-text exhibition and book

Photographer Gigi Kaeser photographs and interviews 20 diverse American families formed through interracial relationships or transracial adoption. In a world where race is considered by many to be a formidable barrier between people, the families in this exhibit are celebrated as 20th century pioneers willing to risk disapproval and misunderstanding to find richness and value in diversity.

Learn more:
www.familydiv.org/ofmanycolors/

proved that he could play the dozens (or snaps, e.g., "Yo mama is so big..."). Once he could show that he understood the nuances of the language as it defines racial groups, then he was more accepted. Multiracial children are often bilingual; that is, they have the ability to comfortably converse as an insider with more than one racial group. Unfortunately, multiracial children who engage in bilingual practices are criticized as being wishy-washy and fake. Parents and teachers sometimes reinforce this idea by advising the child to "be yourself" thus implying that strong, certain, and clear-headed people speak only one way regardless of audience. In short, the message is that bilingualism is not acceptable and the child should choose a side. Such advice can be hurtful to a multiracial child for whom the ability to switch gears may be part of being her or himself.

3. Patrolling interaction with members of the out-group:

Here the border patrollers demand a denial of all connections to, or affections for, the racial out-group. While this most often occurs around the issue of dating and friendship circles, multiracial children are even pressured, at times, to deny their parents and relatives. Most multiracial children have been in conversations in which White people are portrayed as universally evil. In these instances, if the child says, "But my father and my grandparents are White, and they are not evil," her loyalties will be called into question; she risks becoming an outsider. Moreover, multiracial children who appear White are assumed by Whites to be an insider and are often subjected to White racist conversation. Multiracial children who speak out in these situations sometimes face the racist compliment, "Oh, we don't think of you as Puerto Rican, you're different, we think of you as White." In this case, the child is devalued, and those Whites giving the "compliment" assume White to be something highly valued and that they have the right to bestow an identity on another human being. The children expend much energy deciding how to respond to the patrolling and discrimination.

4. Patrolling geographies:

Here, I am using geographies to address the physical spaces individuals occupy in their lives. Because of the segregation in society, racial groups are often geographically defined. Children have little control over where they live, and yet they are held responsible by border patrollers for a street address that might place them on the wrong side of the race line. In addition, other geographies are patrolled including what school a child attends, choice of classes, choice of lunch room table, and how leisure time is spent. Multiracial children who might be comfortable sitting at several different (and racially defined) lunchroom tables may be reprimanded, "You are either one of us or you are not, you need to decide." A multiracial woman who attended high school in Manhattan recalled that White, Black, Latino, and Asian students each exited the school from different doors. Each day she left the school she was made aware that her choice of exit was being noted by others. In short, because all social spaces are raced, the spaces multiracial children occupy throughout the day carry messages to others about the child's loyalty to a particular side.

5. Patrolling of cultural capital:

Cultural capital is the resources individuals can draw upon to give them status and credibility in society. Given racial divisions in society, cultural capital is used by all sides to determine who is a loyal and credible insider. The cultural capital important among children as they become aware of racial categories includes taste in music, television programs, sports, and magazines. A multiracial man who grew up in the Bronx reported that in high school he loved the music of Barry Manillo but that he always hid the tapes and listened to that music when he was alone. His enjoyment of that music marked him "too White," and his Latino friends would have shunned him. Another Black-White multiracial young man remembered the difficulty he had with his Black friends when he joined the high school hockey team. He was given the label "White boy" for playing.

All children face patrolling; however, multiracial children face racial border patrolling in addition to the usual demands children place on each other for conformity. Some children are given (or assigned to) one racial group by parents and teachers and expected to comply. Unfortunately, too often parents and teachers dismiss border patrolling by invoking "colorblind" language. The children are told to avoid labeling themselves and that they are part of the human race. In many cases, however, teachers and some parents just ignore race altogether. In the silence, the children are left to fend for themselves. Fortunately, most multiracial children do successfully negotiate border patrolling; however, if parents and teachers were more aware of the unique forms of discrimination these children face, they might be able to reduce the burden.

While all sides patrol and police the boundaries of their racial communities, the reason for and consequence of the patrolling vary. Everyone who has learned about race, U.S. style, looks for clues about how to racially categorize others. Some White people need to take this step before they feel comfortable interacting with new people. They may sense that the color line is shifting and fear losing their racial status. Thus, until they can categorize others, they feel vague and uneasy about their own racial status and identity.[2] For people of color, the desire to make distinctions may concern a quest for allegiance and unity, a means to determine who is "us" and who is "them" politically, socially, and culturally.[3] Individuals who comfortably claim one racial identity or think that race is something that can be observed or uncovered with enough clues may feel confusion, anger, skepticism, concern, pity, hostility, curiosity, or superiority when they meet someone who does not seem to fit neatly into a preset racial category. These feelings play out through the course of interaction, and a multiracial person, regardless of how he or she identifies, must contend with the response of these individuals. For instance, Kimberly, a multiracial woman living in Manhattan, grew up being chastised by her parents and grandparents for not speaking "proper" English; in school Kimberly was taunted by Black students who insisted that she was trying to be White. As a person with racially ambiguous features, she receives many comments and stares from strangers. She is tired of hearing the same questions and comments and has also grown tired of defending herself:

> People come up to me and they'll say, 'Do you get confused between being Black and White?' I say, 'Well, yeah, you know, some mornings I wake up with this craving for fried chicken, and other mornings I just can't get the beat, I start

dancing and can't get the beat.' I want them to see how narrow-minded they're being. What do you think? One day I like fried chicken and the next I don't? It's not like that.[4]

Kimberly points to the thinking that underlies the unique discrimination faced by multiracial people. If it is believed that race is inherent to an individual and that race is a way to group people into discrete categories, then it stands to reason that multiracial people must have separate races compartmentalized within them. Depending on the mix, multiracial people are assumed to have a genetically programmed way of being that can cause, at the extreme, an "internal war." Responding to people the way she does, Kimberly externalizes the problem of race and, at the same time, gives others the opportunity to think about race in a more sophisticated manner.

Given the history of race politics in the U.S., multiracial people have been largely ignored and more generally subsumed under communities of color for statistical and research purposes. Thus, until recently, multiracial people have not had a collective voice and have had to negotiate border patrolling individually. The explosion of writings since the early 1990s has begun the process of documenting and creating a voice for multiracial people and their families. While multiracial children have many more resources available today than they did a generation ago, they still face a society that assumes and demands that people comply with racial codes of conduct—codes that have historically denied the existence of multiracial people.

Conclusion

In this chapter I have addressed a brief history of and social context for the discrimination faced by multiracial people in the United States. I have identified those who discriminate against multiracial people as "border patrollers." While the majority of this chapter addresses the individual outcomes of this discrimination, it is important to note that institutional forms of discrimination against multiracials maintain the framework in which border patrolling takes place. For instance, in the United States we have a segregated housing market and thus segregated schools. Stable, racially-mixed areas are few and far between. Thus, multiracial children often find themselves in situations in which they are the "only one" or one of a few. If their families live in predominantly White areas, then they will be the child of color in a White environment. If they are in an area that is predominantly of color, depending upon their own background and the background of the neighborhood, they will be labeled as different. Patrolling takes place on an individual level, the level of daily experience, the level that children are most likely to name and articulate. However, the fact is that border patrolling is the outcome of a larger system of racial injustice and segregation. Parents and teachers should be aware of the unique forms of discrimination faced by multiracial children and the White supremacist system in which that discrimination flourishes. ▮

Notes

1 For an elaboration of this point, see: J. Ferrante, *Sociology in a Global Perspective,* 4th edition (Wadsworth Publishing, 2001), Chapter 5.

2 For a wonderful analysis see: N. Gotanda, "A Critique of 'Our Constitution is Color-Blind,'" in *Critical Race Theory,* eds. K. Crenshaw et. al. (New York: New York University Press, 1995).

3 M. E. Dyson, "Essentialism and the Complexities of Racial Identity," in *Multiculturalism: A Critical Reader,* ed. D. T. Goldberg (Cambridge, MA: Blackwell Press, 1994).

4 H. Dalmage, *Tripping on the Color Line: Black-White Multiracial Families in a Racially Divided World* (New Brunswick: Rutgers University Press, 2000), 29.

Howard Family

Age: 6 (Nicole)

Racial/Ethnic Heritage: Japanese, Caucasian, and Native American

For the first four years of my daughter's life I thought very little about her multiracial heritage. I suppose that I didn't want it to matter. As a White male, race had never mattered for me and I naïvely assumed that my children would experience life the same way. It never occurred to me that my children were racially different from me, and, as a result, would experience life differently.

Race wasn't the only issue I rarely thought about; childhood cancer was another. One day Nicole stopped walking, saying her legs hurt. She started crawling to get around. The next day we took her to the doctor; before that day was over they told us Nicole had leukemia, a cancer of her bone marrow. Suddenly, both issues that I had avoided became forcefully relevant.

We immediately admitted Nicole to the hospital. Nicole's bone marrow was producing too many unhealthy cells, a condition that would eventually kill her. To get a transplant a patient needs a compatible donor.

We struggled to understand and accept what was happening. Our next step was to search the National Marrow Donor Program (NMDP) Registry. Despite the extensive registry, there wasn't a match for Nicole. As a multiracial person, Nicole was an unusual patient. Whereas Caucasians make up almost three-quarters of potential donors, the number of people of color is critically small. Since people are most likely to find a match with someone of a similar heritage, Nicole will likely need a donor who is mixed race: both Asian and Caucasian.

Unable to find Nicole a match through the NMDP, we put our hope in finding a donor ourselves. Dozens of family members, neighbors, and even strangers began helping us by organizing donor registration drives and helping us fundraise to pay for Nicole's medical costs. It was difficult to raise awareness about an issue most people rarely talked about: race, and, specifically, mixed race. I learned how decades of being forced to check "only one box" had discouraged multiracial Americans from acknowledging their mixed race heritage. I also learned that few doctors realized that their multiracial patients had unique medical needs. It seemed daunting to have to change a vast healthcare system that didn't recognize that people like my daughter even existed. Then we contacted MAVIN Foundation. In response, they started their MatchMaker Bone Marrow Project, the only national program dedicated to mixed race donor recruitment and education. Together, we have registered nearly 6,000 people and helped educate people about the need for mixed race donors.

Today, Nicole's cancer is in remission, thanks to a new drug called Gleevec. We don't know how long the medicine will last or the long-term side effects, but we are grateful for every healthy moment. Over a year has passed since Nicole's diagnosis and we still haven't found her a donor. We need people to host bone marrow registration drives and we need financial support to continue our efforts to increase hope for people facing life-threatening diseases. A year ago, I myself was in the dark. Today, I'm fully committed to educating others about this pressing need. I hope that you will join me.

Testimonial

Chapter 4

Health Issues Facing Mixed Race People

Cathy Tashiro, Ph.D., RN, MPH

Approximately seven million people checked more than one racial category in the U.S. Census 2000,[1] an event that could have potentially far-reaching consequences for how we think about population health. In the United States, health statistics are analyzed according to the standard racial categories used in the census. Now, for the first time, data must be analyzed based on the numerous racial combinations selected by census respondents. Hopefully, this will focus attention on the existence of people of mixed heritage and move us toward thinking more critically about the meaning of racial categories and their relationship to health risks.

Unfortunately, the use of racial categories to track health and illness differences between populations, while important for gauging health disparities, has probably reinforced belief in the genetic homogeneity of the "races" for both the general public and healthcare providers. Too often, analyses of "racial" differences in population health outcomes, such as the differences between Black and White infant mortality rates, fall prey to inappropriate genetic explanations, neglecting the effects of racism and other environmental factors on health outcomes,[2] although increasingly, such analyses are subject to criticism.[3]

It is no accident that medicine is prone to biological explanations

for racial differences in health status. The history of medical science is tainted by numerous examples of flagrant bias, unprincipled experimentation, and reinforcement of unscientific beliefs in racial hierarcy.[4] The acknowledgement of the existence of people of mixed race can be a genuine challenge to established views about the biological basis of race so commonly found in the health research literature. However, thus far, the full implications of the changing racial landscape have been slow to enter the health literature, and discussions of people of mixed race have tended to focus on the data management problems they represent. Meanwhile, people of mixed race continue to face inappropriate and potentially harmful assumptions by health providers based on their presumed racial identities.[5]

I would like to provide a personal example of this. I recently had the disquieting experience of visiting a dermatologist's office because I was concerned about some skin lesions on my face. The doctor looked at me and laughed. "Asian women don't get skin cancer." I replied, "Actually, I'm half Asian, and my mother is of Irish descent with extremely fair skin." His response was, "Asians don't get skin cancer." We continued in this circular exchange for a few more rounds, until I finally gave up, thinking, "Just get me out of here and I'll never see this guy again." It seems remarkable that this physician, who probably had years of highly demanding and specialized training, was unable to see beyond my phenotypical appearance, which to him indicated that I was Asian. Not to mention that he was even wrong about Asians not getting skin cancer! Such misconceptions can obviously have serious consequences. If we are evaluated as if our risks are confined to those associated with our most visible "race," at best we suffer from incompetent care, and at worst, from potentially life-threatening misdiagnosis and treatment. My interviews with other people of mixed race have yielded similar stories of their encounters with the medical system and real confusion about what their health risks are.

Like my experience with the dermatologist, mixed race people are often viewed as if they only consist of the most "colored" aspect of their racial ancestry. In my case, as a woman who is of Asian and Irish ancestry, I was seen as Asian. If we are to understand why mixed race people are frequently treated as if their most subordinate race eclipses every other aspect of their ancestry, we must take a brief look at history. For most of recorded U.S. history, Whiteness has been a prerequisite for full citizenship rights, and the color line dividing Whiteness from people of color has been maintained most vigorously. Arguably, the United States has had the most conservative definition of Blackness, with its use of the so-called "one-drop rule," or rule of hypodescent, by which anyone with a "drop" of African ancestry had to be considered Black or Negro.[6] This policy reached its height during the Jim Crow years of legalized segregation and inequality in every aspect of life. As a result, the population we now call African American is quite diverse, and it is estimated that as much as 30% of the African American gene pool comes from non-African sources.[7]

While this extreme definition of color as "one drop" was not applied as strictly to other minority groups, there are cases of denial of citizenship to people of mixed Asian descent and the invocation of a kind of "one-drop rule" in times of crisis, such as the internment of anyone with essentially a "drop" of Japanese ancestry during World War II. Racial hierarchy and the view of color as a kind of contaminant, outweighing everything else in personal identity, are widespread in our history and popular beliefs, and health professionals are not immune to these associations.

Thus, in my belief, the number one health issue facing people of mixed race is societal ignorance about what race is and what race is not, and the assumptions by healthcare professionals that flow from their misconceptions about race. So let us first talk about what race is. Race is a social category, not a biological one. Our racial categories are imprecise and have fluctuated throughout our recorded history[8] based on factors like ideology, prevalent social beliefs about race, political expediency, and claims from various groups to be counted. Considering global comparisons can help put into perspective how limited our categories are. For example, a person of mixed European American and African ancestry considered "Black" in the United States might be considered "White" in some Caribbean nations, based on skin color and social class, and "Coloured" during apartheid South Africa.

It is undeniable that some diseases are more prominent in certain populations than others. Yet the key question is whether they are "racially" related. For example, in the U.S., sickle cell anemia is commonly considered to be a "Black" disease. In reality, the global distribution of Hemoglobin S, which is responsible for sickle cell, covers not only parts of Africa, but areas of Asia, the Middle East, and Southern Europe as well. The Hemoglobin S global distribution corresponds with geographical areas of high malaria, and it is hypothesized that sickling of the red blood cells evolved as a protective response to malaria.[9] The population distribution of sickle cell and other inherited traits such as lactose intolerance (inability to digest milk sugar) do not correspond neatly to our traditional racial classifications.

Studies have confirmed that there is more genetic variation within so-called racial groups than there is between them. Differences between members of the same population account for over 80% of genetic variation.[10] In addition, so-called race mixing is not new in our country; populations considered to be White, Native American, and African American have been interbreeding practically since they first encountered each other. Even constructed census categories like "Asian" include significant genetic differences among and between subpopulations.[11][12] These differences within populations are compounded for people of mixed race, who are an extremely diverse group, amplifying challenges such as finding matching bone marrow donors. People of color in general have more difficulty finding matches for stem cell and bone marrow transplants, and African Americans in particular are harder to match because of their genetic diversity. Finding unrelated donors for anyone is difficult, but particularly complex for people of mixed race, given their diverse heritages. That is why innovative programs like MAVIN Foundation's MatchMaker Bone Marrow Project, which recruits multiracial donors to the National Marrow Donor Program, are so significant in that they provide vitally needed diversity to the pool of potential donors.

The State of Research on People of Mixed Race

Trying to determine the health risks of a mixed race child can be daunting, given the minimal research that has been done on people of mixed race. The few existing health studies have tended to raise more questions than provide answers. They have focused on infants because the race of parents is recorded on most birth registries, thus making it possible to identify the child as mixed. For example, a study of race and birth weight in mixed Black-White babies found that infants of Black mothers and White fathers were of lower birth weight than those of White mothers and Black fathers.[13] While initially the low birth weight rates for both groups of biracial babies appeared to be higher than those for Whites, after controlling for other variables, the rates for the babies with White mothers and Black fathers were close to those of infants with two White parents. The infants of Black mothers and White fathers still had higher rates of low birth weight than those with two White parents after controlling for other potential influences. The authors were not able to explain this trend conclusively, but they hypothesize that the factors involved are nongenetic and probably related to the life experiences of the Black women having these biracial babies, particularly the chronic exposure to the stress of racism.

Some population differences are more clearly identified as having a genetic basis. For example, East Asians tend to have higher bilirubin levels than Whites at birth, which can result in jaundice in the newborn. A recent study compared bilirubin levels in Asian, White, and mixed Asian-White newborns.[14] The study found that the mixed infants were more likely than the White babies and less likely than the Asian babies to be diagnosed with

Nicole

Luke

Quito

MatchMaker is MAVIN Foundation's innovative national program to diversify the pool of bone marrow donors through mixed race donor recruitment and education. As the only national program of its kind, MatchMaker is the best hope for mixed race leukemia patients like Nicole, Luke, and Quito. Since its founding in 2001, MatchMaker has registered nearly 4,000 new potential life-saving donors to the National Marrow Donor Program Registry!

Learn more:
mavinfoundation.org/match maker.html

jaundice. However, only the infants of full Asian parentage had high enough levels to require treatment. Interestingly, the mixed infants were more likely to have elevated levels when the father was Asian, not the mother.

Clearly, much more research is needed on people of mixed race that looks beyond statistical data to the complexities of their lives and influences on health and illness. Now that people of mixed race will be identified in the data, it will be increasingly possible to do research on people of various ages, without having to rely on parental statistics to infer that they are mixed. One such study has looked at birth outcomes of mixed race mothers.[15] The authors conclude that no clear patterns emerged for these mixed race mothers as a whole, and that the population of people of mixed race is extremely heterogeneous, therefore impossible to definitively categorize as a group.

Conclusion

So, given the diversity of people who are of mixed race, can conclusions be drawn about their health risks? I think it is difficult, and potentially harmful to do so, given that research on people of mixed race is in its infancy, and that people who are mixed form such a diverse group. Clearly, it is important that much more research be done on a variety of mixed race populations.

Given the current state of knowledge, the most important bit of advice I have for parents and professionals caring for mixed race children is to be constantly vigilant about your assumptions based on the child's appearance. None of us are immune to the common beliefs and associations of our society regarding race. Advances in molecular biology are showing us that the genes controlling factors like skin color and hair texture are pretty insignificant when compared to the vast array of our genetic complexity. Yet we continue to make sweeping assumptions based on those factors and what "race" they place a person in. For healthcare providers, I would advocate a kind of "universal ancestry precautions," analogous to the universal precautions for infection control stimulated by the HIV/AIDS epidemic, which advocate that healthcare workers employ proper infection control techniques with all patients they encounter, not just singling out those whom they might deem to be "at risk." Do not get me

wrong; I do not mean to imply that race represents infection. But like infection, one's ancestry may not be visually apparent. These universal ancestry precautions would assume that anyone might have any so-called "racial" ancestry whatsoever somewhere in their background. This would force us out of a false sense of security that we can predict health status and risk based solely on racial phenotype, which can have life-threatening consequences. It would force those of us in the health professions back to the tried and true arts of healing based on thorough psychosocial and health assessments that recognize the totality of those whom we serve. This can only be good medicine for all of us.

Notes

1 E. Schmitt, "For 7 Million People in Census, One Race Category Isn't Enough," *The New York Times* (13 March 2001), A1, A14.

2 E. Van den Oord and D. Rowe, "Racial Differences in Birth Health Risk: A Quantitative Approach," *Demography* 37(3) (2000), 285-298.

3 R. Frank, "The Misuse of Biology in Demographic Research on Racial/Ethnic Differences: A Reply to Van den Oord and Rowe," *Demography* 38(4) (2001), 563-567.

4 N. Krieger, "Shades of Difference: Theoretical Underpinnings of the Medical Controversy on Black/White Differences in the United States, 1830-1870," *International Journal of Health Services* 17(2) (1987), 259-278.

5 C. Tashiro, "Mixed but not Matched: Multiracial People and the Organization of Health Knowledge," in *The Sum of Our Parts: Mixed Heritage Asian Americans*, eds. T. Williams-Leon and C. L. Nakashima (Philadelphia: Temple University Press, 2001), 173-182.

6 F. J. Davis, *Who is Black? One Nation's Definition* (University Park, PA: Pennsylvania State University Press, 1991).

7 J. L. Graves, *The Emperor's New Clothes: Biological Theories of Race at the Millennium* (New Brunswick, NJ: Rutgers University Press, 2001).

8 No more than two consecutive censuses have used exactly the same racial categories. See: D. Goldberg, *Racial Subjects: Writing on Race in America* (New York: Routledge, 1997).

9 J. E. Bowman and R. F. Murray, *Genetic Variation and Disorders in Peoples of African Origin* (Baltimore: The Johns Hopkins University Press, 1990).

10 G. Barbujani, A. Maggini, E. Minch, and L. L. Cavalli-Sforza, "An Apportionment of Human DNA Diversity," *Proceedings of the National Academy of Sciences of the United States of America* 94(9) (1997), 4516-4519.

11 T. L. Bugawan, J. D. Chang, W. Klitz, and H. A. Erlich, "PCR/Oligonucleotide Probe Typing of HLA Class II Alleles in a Filipino Population Reveals an Unusual Distribution of HLA Haplotypes," *American Journal of Human Genetics* 54(2) (1994), 331-340.

12 L. Geng, et. al., "Determination of HLA Class II Alleles by Genotyping in a Manchu Population in the Northern Part of China and its Relationship with Han and Japanese Populations," *Tissue Antigens* 46(2) (1995), 111-116.

13 J. W. Collins and R. J. David, "Race and Birthweight in Biracial Infants," *American Journal of Public Health* 83(8) (1993), 1125-1129.

14 S. Setia, A. Villaveces, P. Dhillon and B. A. Mueller, "Neonatal Jaundice in Asian, White, and Mixed-Race Infants," *Archives of Pediatric and Adolescent Medicine* 156(3) (2002), 276-279.

15 K. E. Heck, J. D. Parker, C. J. McKendry and K. C. Schoendorf, "Multiple-Race Mothers on the California Birth Certificate, 2000," *Ethnicity & Disease* 11(4) (2001), 626-32.

Bill of Rights for Racially Mixed People
Maria P. P. Root, Ph.D.

I HAVE THE RIGHT...

Not to justify my existence in this world.

Not to keep the races separate within me.

Not to be responsible for people's discomfort with my physical ambiguity.

Not to justify my ethnic legitimacy.

I HAVE THE RIGHT...

To identify myself differently than strangers expect me to identify.

To identify myself differently from how my parents identify me.

To identify myself differently from my brothers and sisters.

To identify myself differently in different situations.

I HAVE THE RIGHT...

To create a vocabulary to communicate about being multiracial.

To change my identity over my lifetime—and more than once.

To have loyalties and identification with more than one group of people.

To freely choose whom I befriend and love.

Alexis
Mexican + Caucasian

Madison
Mexican + Caucasian

Section 2:
Identity and Development

Chapter 5

Racial Identity Development and Persons of Mixed Race Heritage
Maria P. P. Root, Ph. D.

Contemporary thinking on racial identity development stems from the intersection of psychology and the racial pride movements of the 1960s and 1970s. The racial pride movements catalyzed solidarity within race and further reinforced notions that one must identify with a single race. Ironically, these movements reinforced the mechanisms that maintained notions of racial purity.

The history of race in the United States, and specifically the "one-drop rule" to reinforce hypodescent, provides a key to understanding how psychological models evolved in a way that has excluded the reality of many mixed race persons. The "one-drop rule" specifically ensures that multiple racial heritages will be reduced to a single heritage. Hypodescent determines the race or ethnicity a person of multiple heritages is assigned. Specifically, a person is to assume or is assigned the heritage that has the lowest social status. Historically, a person of White European descent who also descended from a parent of color was always assigned the racial status of the person of color.

Thus, racial identity theories are really monoracial identity theories and have excluded an explanation for how people come to identify with more than one race. They have been very useful for understanding some of the processes by which people moved from a naïve stance in understanding racial discrimination in the U.S. to a sobering reality that race operates as a critical variable in social relationships, to an even more complex understanding of race and humanity.[1][2][3] These theories tell the story of the effects of the overt and insidious trauma of racial discrimination, violence, and maltreatment. Historically, persons of color have had a universal vulnerability to racism's impact. A critical stage in racial identity theories is the retreat into the racial community for refuge and the learning of pride by knowing one's history.[4] This is where contemporary identity theories are failing, not all, but many multiracial people.

We must separate contemporary mixed race experiences from historical experiences of mixed race.[5] Before the repeal of the last anti-miscegenation laws in 1967, more than 10 states still had laws against intermarriage.[6] Racial identity was constructed through a combination of the "one-drop rule" and hypodescent. A multiracial person could only be one race; mixed race identity had to be kept private. Persons born after this period of time through approximately 1980 were still subjected to these rules, but the rates of intermarriage had increased, so they were not so isolated in their experience. Persons born after 1980 started to come of age and are coming of age during a time of public discussion of mixed race, several mixed race persons in the public eye, and an unprecedented change in the U.S. Census recording of race in 2000, which allowed a multiracial person to be multiply identified. They did not have to "choose one" or check "other."

In this chapter, Root's *Ecological Framework for Understanding Racial Identity* provides a framework for understanding the complexity of racial identity development. The model looks at invisible factors affecting identity as well as the common influences we presume. Developed in the 1990s, the model was based on approximately 10 years of research on multiracial people. Each influence illustrated will be explained so that the complexity of the identity process is unraveled and applied to understanding why people, even within the same family and with the same parents, can have different identities.

Background "Invisible" Context
• Regional and generational history of race and ehnic relations
• Gender and sexual orientation
• Class

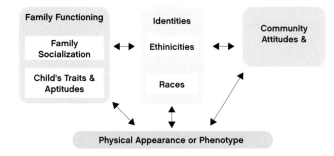

Racial Identity Options for Mixed Race People

At this point in time, the community of color with which a mixed race person may identify may not provide the automatic acceptance provided for most persons of color. Mixed race persons are put to "racial authenticity tests" and often subjected to stricter standards of conduct than other people because of the history and the mechanisms appropriated in the racial pride movements to create a refuge from the daily assaults of racism.

Multiracial declarations of identity are often misunderstood. Furthermore, lack of a single correct racial identity for mixed race persons adds to misunderstanding the fluidity and situational nature of some persons' public racial identities.

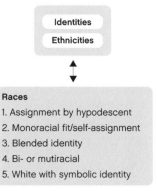

Five types of identities emerge from the research on mixed race persons. The identities are affected by the generation into which a mixed race person is born.[7] Generation determines whether or not there is an option to publicly declare a mixed heritage and how it will be understood or misunderstood. For older generations, monoracial identity, the result of either assuming a social assignment according to the "one-drop rule" and hypodescent, was the only option.[8] Younger generations may now publicly identify as multiracial and even refuse to break identity down into racial categories or declare bi- or multi-racial identities with elaboration on the various racial and ethnic heritages. The newest identity to emerge is "symbolic Whiteness."[9] This identity appears to reflect identification with a class lifestyle and values, or a lack of exposure to an ethnic background with which one identifies. A person can be well-adjusted holding this identity if he or she has the temperament to withstand other persons' opposition to such a declaration or has another salient identity.[10] These identities might be related to some aptitudes such as gifted musician, athlete, or student.

Influences on Racial Identity

Since the mid 1990s, multiracial persons started to propose identity models to help understand pathways and influences affecting identity. Root's *Ecological Framework of Racial Identity Development* is the longest standing of these new multiracial models and is presented here to help multiracial people, their parents, educators, healthcare workers, and policy makers understand the complexity that gives rise to the various identities of multiracial people by generation. Four "invisible" influences are important for understanding how mixed race identity exists differently for children and young adults now than in previous generations.

Geography and Generation

A geographical region's and generation's history of race and ethnic relations provides a critical format for understanding what identity options are available and how relations are transacted. For example, in the 2000 Census, the southern states of the U.S. had the fewest people declaring more than one race, even though this part of the U.S. has a significant history of mixing.[11] However, much of this mixing was in the context of slavery and not by choice. Combined, the western states had the highest proportion of multiple race declarations. This region repealed laws against intermarriage earlier than the southern states and has the most diversity of ethnic and racial groups in the country. Three longstanding interracial family grassroots groups originated in California. Generationally, younger people declared themselves with multiple races and were declared by their parents similarly in much greater number than persons over 30 years of age.[12]

Sexual Orientation

Sexual orientation provides a context in which the politics of race may be minimized or sexualized. Minority sexual identities such as lesbian, gay, bisexual, and queer have been considered "White" by many communities of color. Racial minorities have had a difficult time seeking refuge in their racial or ethnic community because of rejection of their sexual orientation.[13] More opportunities for affiliation and acceptance are found within the White community. Thus, individuals working to understand their sexual identity may encounter similar aspects of disenfranchisement or the need to deny certain aspects of their identity in order to have acceptance and inclusion in the community of color. Even within the sexual minority communities, identities such as bisexual have similarly mixed receptions with many of the individuals in these communities considering bisexuality an "inauthentic identity" or confused state.[14]

Gender

Gender plays prominently in race relations. Three significant issues arise. First, whereas men have historically been the persons who had more power and freedom to choose their mates, women's freedom to choose their mates has increased.[15] Women's freedom to choose their mates has resulted in more interracial and interethnic unions. Who ethnically, racially, and culturally socializes a child must be a more conscious choice or effort in multiracial families; traditionally it is assumed women will do this. Second, for persons of mixed race, the gender dynamic operates as the race of the male partner seems to more powerfully assert something about the race of the female partner. Thus, fewer assumptions are made about the mixed race man who dates a White woman than about a mixed race woman who dates a White man. Twine's[16] study of young women attending the University of California found that these young biracial Black-White women were consciously choosing to date African American men, partly as way of declaring and affirming their African descent or heritage. Whereas they might still identify as mixed, these women anecdotally reported a reduction in racial authenticity testing when they dated Black men than if they had a White partner. Third, mixed race sons and daughters are sometimes mistaken as the sexual partners of their parents as they grow older because of the lack of acknowledgement of healthy interracial families, and the failure of people to observe family resemblances when color and other racialized features are part of the picture.

Class

Lastly, class is one of the overarching contexts for understanding how race is experienced. In the U.S., very narrow assumptions are made about the classes within which a person of color resides. It is often assumed that a person of color comes from a working class or an unemployed class. One of the newest identity options is a symbolic White identity that appears to be a stand-in for a class and lifestyle marker. With this identity, one's other ethnic or racial heritages are not hidden, but the individual experiences more detachment from them and finds them an interesting part of his or her heritage. These individuals have often grown up in families where they have been taught that one race is not better than another and that race is a fairy tale. They often have little knowledge other than acquired written information on the minority side of the family, have had little contact with the non-White side of the family, and are much loved by the White side of their family. For some mixed race families that have been able to afford good schools and nice neighborhoods, their mixed race children may share more in common with other children of middle or upper middle-class values within and across race than children who are of working-class families regardless of race. Unless the family has sought to live in an upper middle or upper-class neighborhood that is within a rare ethnic or multicultural enclave of similar families, their children will most likely attend school and live amongst White peers.

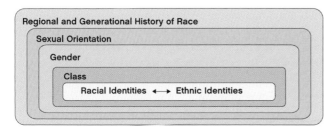

Family Functioning

The quality of the emotional sustenance and stability that a family provides seems to be key to how a child negotiates many aspects of his or her developmental years, with racial identity being just one aspect of his or her development. Emerging research demonstrates that when the family is destabilized by one or more of the following variables, identity resolution may become more difficult: inconsistency of parental emotional

availability due to personality, mental illness, or substance abuse; lack of extended family acceptance; significant losses and disruptions through untimely deaths, bitter divorces, or moves; lack of a sense of belonging, love, and acceptance within the family; and the presence of trauma due to violence, physical, sexual and mental abuse, or neglect.

When any combination of these variables are present, young children, who start to internalize the racism of society, may attempt to make sense of difficult situations based upon the irrational notions of race that surround them.[17] Thus, if a Chinese American parent repeatedly breaks promises to materially provide for their child because of a gambling addiction, this child may think that promise-breaking is inherent to being Asian or Chinese and reject this aspect of his or her heritage. Likewise, a child may reject any White identification if a parent has been emotionally and mentally cruel or dominating; he or she may think that this is part of being White. Without intervention to help children and adolescents sort through these issues, they are left to their own devices. Their idiosyncratic interpretations will often be influenced by the racial system.

Family Socialization

Family socialization takes place within the context of family functioning. Bitter divorces or estrangement from a parent or one side of the family affects possible influences of family socialization. A child is more likely to have a chance to integrate different aspects of his or her heritages if both sides of the family are available and respect for different worldviews is communicated.[18][19][20] Family socialization to ethnic identity includes the languages spoken in the home, the parents' identities, birth countries of the parents as well as their children, given names, spiritual traditions, racial socialization, and the family's sense of its racial identity. With the latter variable, a multiracial family can identify and exist within a monoracial community—of color or White—or avoid discussion of racial or ethnic identity. The latter choice confuses children.[21]

Despite whatever racial or ethnic labels parents supply their children, there is no guarantee that their children will end up identifying this way.[22] However, it is important to supply labels to even provide acknowledgement of the connection to racial or ethnic heritages and open the door to discussion.

Traits and Aptitudes

Family socialization and the family's functioning can be experienced and negotiated differently by children in the same family. Temperament, social skills, coping skills, special talents or gifts, health, physical attractiveness, and academic aptitude or difficulties color the family and the inner world of a child. For example, some children have been deemed particularly resilient or invulnerable children.[23][24] It is not to say that they are unmarked by adverse family circumstances, but that they have a determination and confidence often coupled with something that is outwardly appealing about them that attracts other people to them. It may be academic, athletic, or social giftedness. It may be physical attractiveness and social skills. But these traits and aptitudes may increase the likelihood of adults outside of immediate family providing more attention, approval, or guidance to them. These children are often deemed easier children within a family. Being teased about being of mixed race or called names will not hurt such a child to the degree it will a

sibling who is very shy and sensitive to rejection. This sibling is not as socially attractive in an immediate sense. If children have any health or academic difficulties, a difficult family environment (including a divorce) will make their internal lives more difficult. The path to resolving personal racial identity may be difficult and take longer. Despite a child's resilience to stress and trauma, research indicates that multiple traumatic experiences erode this resilience.[25] The intersecting environments of family functioning, family socialization, and traits and aptitudes are illustrated.

Community Socialization

Although the family ultimately has the greatest influence on a child's development, the communities within which the child interacts socially have significant influence on both the family and its children. With a child's attendance at church and entrance into school, other adults outside of the family are introduced and have the potential to impact the child's experience of him or herself. As children grow older, peer influence becomes more important. During the pre-teen and adolescent years, peer influence often supercedes parental influence. The attitudes that adults and other children convey about race become difficult when a child's family does not talk about race or racism. When other persons' ideas about race and racial identity are different from the family's ideas or the child's ideas, the family needs to anticipate conversations and provide a place in which to have them. Learning how one is perceived as a person of mixed race heritage, depending on the identities that one is given by the family or declares oneself, results in a multitude of reactions. These reactions provide practice for negotiating identity in familiar communities. This practice becomes especially important for the adolescent who, moving into his or her young adult years, leaves home and moves to a new community. Prior to this move, his or her racial identity has been negotiated through older siblings, parents, aunts, uncles, grandparents, and friends of the family "passing on the word" about this child or family's racial identity or orientation.

For families living in military communities, being a military family becomes an important identity. Certain behaviors and expectations are socialized. There are unique aspects of being part of a military

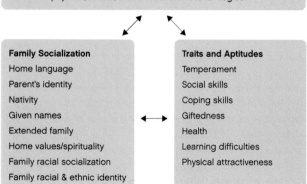

Family Functioning
- Consistency of parental availability
- Extended family acceptance
- Losses and disruptions to family life
- Sense of belonging, acceptance, and love
- Violence/physical, sexual, mental abuse/emotional neglect

Family Socialization

Home language

Parent's identity

Nativity

Given names

Extended family

Home values/spirituality

Family racial socialization

Family racial & ethnic identity

Traits and Aptitudes

Temperament

Social skills

Coping skills

Giftedness

Health

Learning difficulties

Physical attractiveness

Community Attitudes & Racial Socialization
- School/work
- Community (e.g., church, athletics, recreational groups)
- Friends
- New community

family. For example, many children who grow up in military families experience multiple moves during their school years. Living abroad in military communities may deflect some of the salient aspects of racial socialization present in civilian life in the U.S.A.

Physical Appearance

Physically mixed appearances often result in both adults and children asking questions such as, "What are you?" Despite declarations, some children, as well as adults, are met with responses such as, "You don't look it," "You can't be," or "Are you sure?" These responses indicate how folklore, as well as reality, are attached to how a mixed race person appears to others. Because a continuum of physical appearances exists within each group that overlaps between racial groups, persons of contemporary mixed heritage are often confused for persons of different races and ethnicities from which they originate. This confusion often informs a child of the irrational logic of race. However, without help to see this illogic, a child may not come to this conclusion. Physical appearance, particularly at this moment in history is a social facilitator or barrier to racial group acceptance.

Because of a history of racism and classism that has resulted in colorism within groups,[27] [28] [29] some families show favoritism towards lighter-skinned children. The process is quite irrational. In a study by Jacobs using wooden dolls of different shades, he found that young children had to learn to distort their perception of skin color in order to accurately identify their race or their parent's race according to social standards.[30] Relatives, strangers, and even parents may derive their opinions of family resemblance based on skin color rather than on the combination of features a child possesses.

Racial features and scanning observe more than skin color.

Coloration includes skin, eyes, and hair color. Identification and misidentification is also based upon eye and nose shape, hair texture, and body proportions.[31] Standards of beauty, particularly for girls and women, use a Western European or Scandinavian prototype as a reference. In pursuit of this ideal, many teenagers and women of Asian descent seek eyefold surgery. African American girls and women seek to straighten their hair or use skin lighteners.

Phenotype, or physical appearance, interacts with all dimensions of the *Ecological Framework* discussed. Family descriptions of twins or siblings, one who looks White and one who looks like a

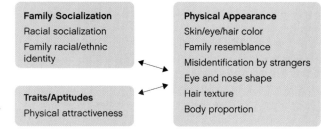

Family Socialization
Racial socialization
Family racial/ethnic identity

Traits/Aptitudes
Physical attractiveness

Physical Appearance
Skin/eye/hair color
Family resemblance
Misidentification by strangers
Eye and nose shape
Hair texture
Body proportion

person of color or mixed, result in anxiety over the different experiences these children will have and how these experiences may set up comparisons between them or affect them adversely. Thus, family functioning, family socialization, and a child's traits and aptitudes become important. Parents may need to be particularly attuned to the attitudes conveyed toward mixed race children in the various environments in which they play, learn, and work.

Summary

The Ecological Framework for Understanding Racial Identity provides an affirmation of the real environments that shape multiracial identity. We are typically aware that family and community influence the social and emotional environment of a child. However, with multiracial children we need to look at the influences within family that can derail identity. There are multiple sources of confusion and dysfunction that will make life harder. These experiences may become "color-coded" if the child's distress is not discerned and addressed. Similar dysfunction within important community environments such as teasing and discriminatory attitudes may also make identity resolution more difficult. Temperament and attractive or unattractive features of a child also affect their life experiences. Acknowledgement of the role of a child's traits and aptitudes has been missing in all previous models of racial identity development.

We seldom acknowledge that contexts such as regional histories, generation, and class are a significant backdrop to racial identity. Sexual identity issues and gender issues figure prominently in how these identities are negotiated.

Lastly, phenotype is important, but does not totally determine how persons will identify themselves. It will predict some of the life experiences a child is likely to have based upon the communities in which she or he is raised, the part of the country in which she or he lives, his or her social attractiveness, and the family socialization to understand others' reactions to their appearance and its congruence or incongruence with their declared identity.

Identity is fluid. It is a means to understand oneself within the context of social relations and one's worldview. Thus, it can change over time. Children can start out labeled as mixed by their parents. They might later acquire a biracial label and elaborate that they are of Asian and African descent. As young adults, they may travel to Africa, returning in love with African culture and identifying with their African roots and all things African or African American. Alternately, they may find themselves feeling very congruent with Japanese American culture and always add to their ethnic identification the racial designation that they are Black, too, to recognize this part of their heritage and explain their appearance to inquisitive eyes. And later yet, they may find that they indulge all aspects of their heritage, watering one set of roots when it needs it more for sustenance.

We have entered complex times. Being a multiracial person is possible, and coexists with beliefs that such an identity is temporary or misinformed. This tension is necessary for growth and understanding. With nurturance and dialogue most persons of contemporary mixed race heritage find an identity that works for them. Although this identity may be different in different situations, this is normal and adaptive as long as a core sense of values and relational attachments are sustained.

Notes

1 W. E. Cross, Jr., *Shades of Black: Diversity in African American Identity* (Philadelphia, PA: Temple University Press, 1991).

2 J. E. Helms, *Black and White Racial Identity: Theory, Research, and Practice* (New York: Greenwood Press, 1990).

3 T. A. Parham and J. E. Helms, "Relation of Racial Identity Attitudes to Self-Actualization and Affective States of Black Students," *Journal of Counseling Psychology* 32 (1985), 431-40.

4 W. E. Cross, Jr., *Shades of Black* (1991).

5 M. P. P. Root, "From Exotic to a Dime a Dozen," in *Women and Therapy*, eds. A. Gillem and C. Thompson (New York: Haworth Press, 2003).

6 P. R. Spickard, *Mixed Blood: Intermarriage and Ethnic Identity in Twentieth-Century America* (Madison, WI: University of Wisconsin Press, 1989).

7 M. P. P. Root, *Women and Therapy* (2003).

8 M. P. P. Root, "Resolving "Other" Status: Identity Development of Biracial Individuals," in *Diversity and Complexity in Feminist Therapy*, eds. L. S. Brown and M. P. P. Root (New York: Haworth Press, 1990), 185-205.

9 M. P. P. Root, "Experiences and Processes Affecting Racial Identity Development: Preliminary Results from the Biracial Sibling Project," *Cultural Diversity and Mental Health* 4 (1998), 237-47.

10 M. P. P. Root, *Cultural Diversity and Mental Health* (1998).

11 U.S. Census Bureau, 2002.

12 U.S. Census Bureau, 2002.

13 K. M. Allman, "(Un)Natural Boundaries: Mixed Race, Gender, and Sexuality," in *The Multiracial Experience: Racial Borders as the New Frontier*, ed. M. P. P. Root (Thousand Oaks, CA: Sage Publications, 1996), 277-290.

14 B. A. Firestein, ed., *Bisexuality: The Psychology and Politics of an Invisible Minority* (Thousand Oaks, CA: Sage Publications, 1996).

15 M. P. P. Root, *Love's Revolution: Interracial Marriage* (Philadelphia, PA: Temple University Press, 2001).

16 F. W. Twine, "Heterosexual Alliances: The Romantic Management of Racial Identity," in *The Multiracial Experience: Racial Borders as the New Frontier*, ed. M. P. P. Root (Thousand Oaks, CA: Sage Publications, 1996), 291-304.

17 M. P. P. Root, *Cultural Diversity and Mental Health* (1998).

18 M. P. P. Root, *Love's Revolution* (2001).

19 F. Wardle, *Tomorrow's Children: Meeting the Needs of Multiracial and Multiethnic Children at Home, in Early Childhood Programs, and at School* (Denver, CO: Center for the Study of Biracial Children, 1999).

20 B. Wehrly, K. R. Kenney and M. E. Kenney, *Counseling Multiracial Families* (Thousand Oaks, CA: Sage Publications, 1999).

21 M. P. P. Root, *Love's Revolution* (2001).

22 M. P. P. Root, *Love's Revolution* (2001); and *Cultural Diversity and Mental Health* (1998).

23 E. J. Anthony and B. J. Cohler, *The Invulnerable Child* (New York: The Guilford Press, 1987).

24 N. Garmezy, "Children Under Stress: Perspectives or Antecedents and Correlates of Vulnerability and Resistance to Psychopathology," in *Further Explorations in Personality*, eds. A. Robin, J. Arnoff, A. Barclay, and R. Zucker (New York: Wiley, 1980).

25 E. J. Anthony and B. J. Cohler, *The Invulnerable Child* (1987).

26 T. K. Williams, "Prism Lives: Identity of Binational Amerasians," *Racially Mixed People in America*, ed. M. P. P. Root (Thousand Oaks, CA: Sage Publications, 1992), 280-303.

27 C. H. Arce, E. Murguia, and W. P. Frisbie, "Phenotype and Life Chances Among Chicanos," *Hispanic Journal of Behavioral Sciences* 9 (1987), 19-32.

28 C. C. I. Hall and T. I. C. Turner, "The Diversity of Biracial Individuals: Asian-White and Asian-Minority Biracial Identity," in *The Sum of Our Parts*, eds. T. Williams-Leon and C. L. Nakashima (Philadelphia, PA: Temple University Press, 2001), 81-92.

29 K. Russell, M. Wilson, and R. Hall, *The Color Complex: The Politics of Skin Color Among African Americans* (New York: Harcourt Brace Jovanovich, 1992).

30 J. H. Jacobs, "Identity Development in Biracial Children," in *Racially Mixed People in America*, ed. M. P. P. Root (Thousand Oaks, CA: Sage Publications, 1992), 190-206.

31 C. C. I. Hall, "Asian Eyes, Body Image and Eating Disorders of Asian and Asian American Women," *Eating Disorders* 8-17 (1995).

Connor
Japanese + Caucasian + Native American

Yasmine
Libyan + Chinese + Irish

James
African American + Japanese

Chapter 6

My Quest for What My Identity Is
Pearl Fuyo Gaskins

I didn't even realize that I was biracial until maybe ninth grade, because I started feeling the pressure to assimilate with a certain racial group. You had Black here, Whites here, Asians over there—I liked all of the people, so I didn't want to do that. I guess that was the beginning of my quest for what my identity is and I don't think I've reached the pinnacle yet.

Miriam, 15, German-American mother, Filipino-American father

Miriam was one of 80 mixed race teens and young adults I interviewed over a period of two-and-a-half years. They grew up in cities, suburbs, rural towns, and military bases, in places as diverse as Hawai'i, New Jersey, and Alabama. Their racial and ethnic backgrounds reflected the many ways of being racially mixed, including hapa, Creole, Black Seminole, "Blackanese," Mestizo, and "Blatina." Some preferred traditional labels such as African American, Asian American, and Native American.

Interview excerpts, essays, and poetry from 45 of these folks were compiled into a book: *What Are You? Voices of Mixed-Race Young People* (Henry Holt, 1999).

"Quest" is the word Miriam used to describe the work she was doing to explore her racial identity. It's an apt metaphor. Racial identity is not static. Most of the people I talked to described their racial identity as constantly evolving. Although discovering who you are and where you fit in can be more complicated for multiracial young people, I found that most of my interviewees eventually found a racial identity they were comfortable with.

For some people, this important work starts at a very tender age with the realization that they are "different" in the eyes of other people. Acts of prejudice and exclusion can still trigger painful emotions decades later. For example, Brian from Cupertino, California, now 23, recalled what he called a "formative experience" in early grade school. Brian, whose mother is Asian American and whose father is European American, said he was unjustly accused of stealing by classmates.

"They called me names, like 'Chinaman,' and did the slanty-eyes thing," said Brian. "I was like, why are they all picking on me? Later on, I saw that I was being singled out specifically because of the way I look...I had no idea that I was half, or that I was part Asian, mixed race, biracial, or anything. I was just myself—and suddenly, that was wrong."

Despite experiences such as this, Brian, like most of the people I interviewed, said that race was not a front-burner issue during elementary school. Of course, the experience of each person is unique and depends on many factors, including the level of tolerance for difference in their community, attitudes of family members, and even the mixed race person's physical appearance. And on conscious and unconscious levels, young children absorb and internalize messages about race that they encounter in the world around them.

But in general, people reported that as pre-teens they were not caught up with trying to observe race and figure it out. For example, many said that friendships were easily formed across color lines. It is not until they hit adolescence that race and racial identity move to the front burner for many mixed race children, as well as their peers. As might be expected, adolescence is when many of the people I interviewed reported wrestling most deeply with issues of racial identity.

One of these people was 14-year-old Chela of Oakland, California. Her father is African American and her mother is European American. Being biracial was a non-issue in elementary school, she said. But that soon changed. "In junior high, people always wanted to know—what was I?" said Chela. "In seventh grade, when I was 12 and 13, I was sort of still trying to figure it out."

Mixed race teens—and all teenagers—have a lot to figure out because they are faced with a multitude of new challenges. Social cliques and dating become important as teens move away from their families and increasingly turn to their peers. As a result, the teenage years, especially the middle school years, are often marked by brutal peer pressure. It may be tough for a teenager to assert his or her mixed race heritage if his or her peers don't support that.

Looking back to his high school years, Kevin, 24, who has a Black Indian mother and an African American father, described the enormous power his friends had over his racial identification. "If I would mention something about going to the Seminole Nation or about being mixed," he said, "people would be like, 'You're Black, that's it.' I'd be like, 'Oh, okay,' because my friends were telling me this...I think a lot of my identity was shaped by people in high school because teenagers are always looking for acceptance and they just want to fit in. All I wanted was to not be seen as different. It was horrible."

Adolescence is also the time when the brain's cognitive engines are jump-started. Armed with new tools of critical thinking and complex reasoning, many racially mixed teens discover new insights about the world and their place in it. For example, Saladin, 22, of Arab American and European American heritage, said he started to ponder the idea of race in high school.

"I read Malcolm X and a lot of different stuff that had to do with race and racism," said Saladin, "and I think I started trying to figure it out. There were different things that happened during high school...a lot of ugly racism came out around the Gulf War....In the media, Saddam Hussein was portrayed as a fanatic, or a terrorist, and that was linked to the fact that he is an Arab. Seeing that stuff started to make me think more consciously about the fact that I am an Arab."

Like Saladin, many people were deconstructing race and concluding that race was not a valid way to categorize people. Chela worked out a theory with her biracial friend Tanna. "Being biracial isn't hard because we're confused about our racial identity," she said. "It's hard because everyone else is confused. The problem isn't us—it's everyone else." What a brilliant insight! It's important for racially mixed young people to make the leap from "there's something wrong with us" to "there's something wrong with society." Many of the people I talked to had come to this conclusion.

The late teens to the early 20s was the period when most of the people I interviewed embraced their mixed race heritage and began to actively explore their identity and their cultural roots. College students took ethnic studies and social science classes. They wrote poetry and research papers about mixed race issues. Many went abroad to meet overseas relatives for the first time, study different cultures, and learn foreign languages.

Large college campuses are diverse, giving students the chance to interact with people of racial and ethnic groups they previously had no contact with. For many of my subjects, these new interactions brought both positive and negative experiences that helped shape their racial identity. For some, college was their first chance to interact with other multiracial people. They set up Web sites, organized student groups, and traveled to conferences.

College is not the only place where identity development occurs. When people are 18, 19, and 20, they are also joining the military and taking jobs out of high school. Young people are very mobile. Psychologist Maria Root says that just moving from one community to another can force racially mixed people to renegotiate their racial identity as the way that people view or categorize them changes.

The most exciting aspect of my research came about by accident. Tracking down and interviewing 80 young people took several years because I had to squeeze it in on evenings and weekends. The slow pace was frustrating, but it allowed me to follow several people over time.

One of these people was Miriam. When I first spoke to her, the 15-year-old Las Vegas native was disconnected from her Filipino roots. She described herself as "a little brown girl growing up in a completely White family." She lived with her biological mother, who was German American, and a European American stepfather. She never met her Filipino biological father. She told me: "I don't feel a connection to Filipinos. If I was in a crowded room and I was looking for a connection with someone, I wouldn't go up to an Asian person, because I've never been around the culture. I don't know anything about it."

A year later, I talked to Miriam again after she received a scholarship and attended the Filipino American Women's National Conference. The experience changed her life. "Overnight, all this Filipino stuff started happening to me!" she said. "I had never been surrounded by so many Filipinos in my life!...It was like, 'Wow, this is me!' But still, I was like, 'This is not me. I feel so White.'" After she went home, she was "still mulling it over." Then she attended a school dance and decided to say hello to a first-grade classmate who was Filipino. "She introduced me to all of these Filipino people. Then all the sudden, I was asked to the prom by a Filipino guy and I became friends with his friends. So now I have a whole group of Asian friends who I hang out with all the time...now, most of the time, I feel, 'I'm a part of this. I'm Filipino.' It's becoming more a part of me every single day."

It's not unusual for multiracial people to immerse themselves in different surroundings as they experiment with culture and race. They may shift back and forth between different racial groups and identities. Root says this is a natural thing to do in order to find out where you fit and who you are.

Serving Children in Biracial/Bicultural Families

This video and training manual, developed by the Oakland, California-based Childcare Health Program, is designed to assist childcare providers to integrate activities and materials that focus specifically on biracial and bicultural children into existing multicultural curricula. It is also intended to help childcare providers assist multiracial children with the important task of developing positive racial and cultural identity.
Learn more:
www.childcarehealth.org

But what struck me is the lack of support—even opposition—many multiracial people encountered during this process. For example, Miriam's friends asked her, "What's up with this whole Asian thing? Are you trying to be Asian?" Other people heard similar comments from their friends and family members. But my subjects didn't let the lack of validation stop them.

Another person who I followed over time as she struggled with identity issues was 19-year-old Maya, who is African American and European American. When I first interviewed her, she was a freshman at an East Coast college, hundreds of miles from home. She described the difficulty of choosing a racial label. She shifted back and forth between Black and biracial.

"I definitely want to be accepted as Black by the Black community," said Maya. "I don't want my friends to think I'm trying to be better than them or different. But at the same time, I am different. I have another experience that's a little bit different because I was raised by a White person. So that's a very important part of who I am and I can't really ignore that and deny that fact."

About 18 months later, I caught up with Maya again. I was wondering if she would be the same tentative, conflicted girl I had spoken to earlier. Was I surprised! Maya had grown up into a self-confident and determined young woman. She was involved in student government and politics. She had some amazing insights about her transformation.

"I think I wasn't sure who I was before," said Maya. "I was a little confused because I couldn't separate who I was from how other people viewed me, and I think that's something all adolescents and young people go through on some level."

"For a while I think I was consumed with the racial aspect of my identity. When I thought about what made me who I was, I used to think that it largely had to do with race. Although I still see that as an important factor, I don't see it as a confusing factor anymore. I have found so many other things at this stage in my life that have helped me direct my identity like: What will my career be? What type of person do I want to be? What's my spiritual base? What can I offer to the world or to my community?"

"And I realize that race, to me, is more something that I react to and deal with on the outside than something that I create for myself. I think what's clearer for me today is that my internal identity has to do with all those other things I talked about—my goals, my spiritual ideology, etc. Being biracial or being Black really doesn't have a lot to do with those things."

Some people I interviewed were confused and conflicted about their racial identity, as Maya was initially. But they did not stay stuck there. The people who were grappling with identity issues eventually resolved them in a healthy way. Difficult experiences lead them to a deeper understanding of themselves and the world.

This chapter introduced you to some of the developmental issues that influence racial identity. On the following pages, you will find chapters that cover specific periods of a child's life. The authors—researchers and child development experts—discuss how typical developmental issues are shaped by the multiracial experience and vice versa.

Monique
African American + Italian +
Irish + Adopted

Todd
Caucasian

Brian
African American + Italian +
Irish + Caucasian

Stephanie, Doug, and Emma Smith
Age: 3 (Emma)
Racial/Ethnic Heritage: African American and Caucasian

We moved to Seattle in 1994. We first visited the city the summer before when we became engaged, and were entranced by the long, languid summer days, and the pristine natural beauty surrounding the city. Our overly-idealized view of the Northwest was only heightened by the riots that had torn L.A. apart. Those were difficult times for everyone in L.A., and especially for an interracial couple.

After having worked to ensure that our families would be respectful and tolerant of our relationship, a definite task with Doug's White relatives, we sought an external environment to match. We decided that for us to be comfortable and to raise a family, we would not settle in a city that was too large since those cities are often starkly segregated and the gap between the "haves" and "have-nots" too wide to make our fitting-in comfortable. Nor would we settle in a small town; traditions there frequently run too deep and the concept of "diversity" can be too foreign. We had no desire to take on the burden of educating an entire community on what being an interracial couple and family meant. That simply wasn't for us. Here we found a relaxed and accepting atmosphere that made it possible to begin our marriage on the right footing.

Years later, in April of 2000, we had our first child, Emma. From the moment we knew of her arrival, both of our families were thrilled with the news. For my family, Emma was the first grandchild. In Doug's family at that time, she was the youngest of three. Our parents, but particularly our mothers, arranged parties and trips to Seattle to keep us

company, and call after call arrived anxiously waiting for her birth. Emma is a wonderful, happy, and well-adjusted child. Her familial experience is one that all children, biracial or not, should have: a multitude of people love her unconditionally. She is comfortable visiting my extended family in Los Angeles as well as Doug's in Minneapolis. At nearly three, she is too young to notice racial differences. Our combined family runs the entire gamut of skin tones and hair colors. Emma's complexion is a mélange of us all. By all early indicators, it seems that her experience growing up biracial will be a good one. She now has new cousins from Doug's brother who are half "Minnesotan" and half Sri Lankan. As her parents, we nonetheless feel compelled to constantly expose and educate her on every aspect of her heritage.

On the surface, it may seem we were quite different with little common ground on which to build a life together: he born and raised in a White, Protestant family in the North, and I in a Black, devoutly Catholic family in the South. What we soon learned, however, was that despite the obvious differences, there was so much we and our families had in common: a great respect for education, a love of family life and travel, a belief in the humanity of all, and, not to be overlooked, an appreciation for good food.

It would be untrue to say we have not at times faced resistance to our love and marriage, both from people close to us and from others we don't know. For the most part, however, people have been supportive.

Testimonial

Chapter 7

Birth to Three Years: Parental Issues

Mary Murchison-Edwords

I am African American and my husband of nearly twenty three years is White. In January 1983 we started the Interracial Club of Buffalo (I.C.B.) as a support group and social organization for interracial families, mixed race people, and families who had adopted transracially and/or internationally. At the time we formed the club we were unsure whether or not we wanted to have children of our own. The group, however, represented a good opportunity for us to meet and interact with others who were raising their own mixed race children. And, through that experience, we became comfortable with the idea of parenthood.

In July of 1984 after giving birth to our first daughter, Livia, I experienced my first racist incident as the parent of a mixed race child. It was during my maternity stay at the hospital. Having been invited to participate in basic baby care lessons, including a class on how to bathe a newborn, I was bathing my baby. A White nurse looked me directly in the eye and began making a series of insensitive comments, although she thought she was being nice and talking socially to a friend. "Your baby is so bright and doesn't look anything like you," she said. "She must favor your husband." "You must have some White in you for her to turn out so White looking." "At least Daddy knows it's his." "Maybe next time you'll have a Black one."

I was already feeling the pangs of the baby blues and wondering how I was going to keep my little one alive, so this woman did not help matters. In a strange sort of way, however, she helped me to become stronger and a better advocate for my child. When your child is small, he or she cannot speak for him or herself. You have to do it for them. So I decided then and there I would use these negative situations as an opportunity to help inform and educate people—no matter what race, color, or ethnicity—about interracial families and multiracial people.

Just before I checked out of the hospital, a different White nurse brought a special form that had something to do with the baby's birth certificate and asked only me to sign, not my husband. Without talking to either of us, she had written in the baby's race as Black on the form. I told her I wasn't going to sign it unless she changed it to mixed race or multiracial. I explained that we were raising our child with an appreciation for all of her heritages and would not let one take dominance over the other; racial identity is an important issue and parents of mixed race children should address it from birth. I said for my child to be identified as Black was disrespectful to her White father and disregarded his existence. The nurse said she could not make the change I requested but would compromise by crossing out Black

Does Anybody Else Look Like Me?: A Parent's Guide to Raising Multiracial Children
Donna Jackson Nakazawa,
Perseus Publishing, 2003

Drawing on psychological research and input from more than 60 multiracial families, *Does Anybody Else Look Like Me?* addresses the special questions and concerns facing mixed race families today, explaining how they can best prepare their multiracial children to make their way confidently in our color-conscious world. From simple scripts to help children gracefully react to insensitive comments at school, to advice on guiding older children toward an unflappable sense of self, *Does Anybody Else Look Like Me?* outlines for parents how, exactly, to deflect the objectifying and discomforting attention multiracial children so often receive. Full of powerful stories and expert counsel, parents in mixed race families will find understanding and insight here as they strive to raise their children in a changing world.

and replacing it with "mother is Black" and "father is White." Apparently, my stance made an impression on her because when I had our second daughter 19 months later at the same hospital, she remembered.

Because I have a dark complexion, hair, and skin and my children look White, I have frequently been questioned about my legitimacy as their mother. This is an issue for all parents who appear physically different from their children. Complete strangers, usually older White women, have come up to me and asked things like "Are you the babysitter?" or "Are those your real kids?" When my youngest daughter, Julia, was eight months old, her hair became bleached blonde by the sun. One evening I was holding her in my arms and browsing in a store when an Asian American man came up to me and asked if I had dyed her hair. I simply said no that my baby's hair was natural and she was biracial.

As my girls got older I made it a point to do things that reinforced their multiracial heritages and made them feel comfortable about themselves. I also helped start a monthly playgroup for mixed race children. It is important for these kids to know they are not alone and that there are others like themselves.

By the age of three most children are cognizant of racial and color differences among people. They look at these differences with curiosity and not in a negative way. It is the adults in their lives who teach prejudice and racism. To help ensure my children would appreciate all of the colors of the rainbow, I enrolled them in a racially diverse nursery school program. I also provided them with a variety of multicultural toys and books. Whenever I came across such items, I would buy them whether or not they reflected our family's racial mix. Our collection grew to include Crayola multicultural crayons (skin, hair, and eye colors of the world's population), pencils, paint, washable markers, construction paper, modeling clay, dolls, puppets, and an interracial family puzzle (Black father, blonde White mother, tan mixed race daughter, family dog) manufactured in the Netherlands. In *Through My Window* by Tony Bradman and Eileen Browne (Silver Burdett Press, 1986), Jo, a little biracial girl, stays home sick from school and her White father takes care of her. Her Black mother wanted to stay, but she has to go to work. A sequel to this book, *Wait and See* was released two years later (Oxford University Press, 1988). In Mary

Hoffman and Jennifer Northway's *Nancy No-Size* (Oxford University Press, 1987), Nancy, a mixed race child, questions her status as a middle child. She is neither tall and dark like her older sister nor light and small like her baby brother. Her mother is Black and father is White. Sarah Garland's *Billy and Belle* (NAL Publisher, 1992) is illustrated with an interracial family (Black father, pregnant White mother, biracial son and daughter) preparing for the arrival of a new baby. Networking with interracial families and other groups helped me to discover these books and other resources.

One of the primary arguments cited against interracial marriage by so-called well-intentioned people is that the children of these relationships will be confused about their identity and not accepted by either race. Even my mother said to me that my children would hate me for bringing them into the world. But once I had my babies, she became a good grandmother. Had my relationship with her remained difficult, I would not have had second thoughts about keeping them away from her. It is important for mixed race children to be raised in a loving and positive environment. They do not need to be exposed to people, particularly family members, who are racist and intolerant.

To properly prepare our children to deal with society and its pressures, we have to be tough and act as their advocates during these early years. Friendship with other interracial families or participation in interracial groups can help significantly in this effort.

Did you know?

According to Census 2000, multiracial youth are disproportionately young:

Percentage of the single race population between the ages of birth to three years old: **5.4%**

Percentage of the multiracial population between the ages of birth to three years old: **11.3%**

Gloria Gstirner-Domingo
Age: 4
Racial/Ethnic Heritage: Indian, Portuguese, and Austrian

My four-year-old daughter Gloria was born in Calgary, Canada. Her father, whose racial background is South Indian and Portuguese, was born in London, England and raised in Canada. I was born and raised in Austria, and consider myself Austrian-Canadian, although I currently reside in Seattle. My first language is German, and in an effort to raise Gloria bilingual I only speak German to her. She is becoming familiar with German culture; currently her favorite show is a German cartoon called *Biene Maja*.

We are dealing with the dynamics of four different countries in our family—Canada, the U.S., India, and Austria. Balancing this definitely keeps us on our toes. We also try to incorporate as much diversity as possible into our lives; our home library celebrates a wide range of occasions like Chinese New Year and Martin Luther King Day. It is important to us that Gloria grows up understanding not only where she came from, but also valuing diversity of all kinds.

Gloria goes to a predominantly White private school, and I have a feeling that she was welcomed because they were looking to increase the diversity in their school. I have become increasingly invested in her schooling because I feel that they do not address racial issues enough, and have facilitated a few workshops on racism in our society. This has come out of my own personal experience with racism. I grew up with a lot of ingrained, unconscious racism that I didn't address or realize existed until I got my masters in counseling. I recognized how much I judged my husband's parents, and came to

understand that it was cultural bias. I want to change things. I want my daughters to grow up in a society where they are accepted, respected, and allowed to be strong women.

Having a multiracial child and my own upbringing has made me sensitive to how people perceive race. This even goes for people in my own family. I noticed this underlying racism in my family's reaction to my husband. They would make unflattering generalizations about Indians, but then always add that my husband was different. He was accepted by my family, but it was as if they accepted him but not where he comes from. In turn, my husband's family welcomed me, but religion was a huge factor. His parents wanted to make sure the girls were raised Catholic, and have always been persistent in this regard. With his side of the family there is more of a religious than racial focus.

Gloria is somewhat aware of her skin. She has said that mama is White, papa is brown, and she's brown, too. I don't think that she really gets it yet. When she was younger, people would always tell me (they were usually White) that she had such a nice tan in the middle of winter. No one thought she could be mixed race. Eventually, I got annoyed and would say, "No, she doesn't have a nice tan, her father is of color." Gloria has always stood out. People tell me all the time how cute and striking she and her younger sister are, never quite realizing that she is multiracial and unique. My hope for her is that she grows up able to accept herself for who she is and not feel pressure to choose one race to identify with.

Testimonial

Chapter 8

Developmental Needs of Children Between 4 to 7 Years Old

Rosa Hernández Sheets, Ph.D.

A majority of the scholarship on multiracial identity focuses on how adolescents and adults identify self and how they are categorized by others.[1][2] This body of work acknowledges the presence of multiraciality; however, it does not show parents and teachers how to address the needs of young multiracial children. The purpose of this chapter is to examine the developmental needs of four- to seven-year-old multiracial children. I begin with a brief overview of the cognitive and social skills children develop during this time period. Next, I discuss the social experiences of dual heritage children and explore how they may affect social development. I conclude with suggestions to promote children's social competence.

Cognitive Development

We know that four-year-olds are quite different from seven-year-olds and that children change significantly—physically and cognitively—during this growth period. At this age, children (1) learn to classify objects and people, (2) experience a rapid increase in language ability, (3) understand concrete concepts (e.g., a truck, man, flower), (4) have limited understanding of abstract ideas (e.g., truth, justice, racism), (5) display egocentric behaviors (they are self-centered), (6) have difficulty interpreting events from someone else's point of view, and (7) focus on one perceptual aspect of an event (e.g., length or number, not both).[3]

Children's racial, ethnic, and cultural heritages influence their process of socialization, which determines what particular cultural knowledge (e.g., language, conduct codes, and information) they acquire. Young children also begin to understand their personal and group status within the greater community (society). They are able to discern mutuality of perception—agreement in the way one perceives self and the way one is perceived by others. For young children, lack of shared perceptions in settings outside the home can be stressful and harmful.

Social Development

As children expand their cognitive skills, they also develop socially. During this age children develop social competence—the ability to make and keep friends—and self-discipline skills—the ability to generate their own thoughts, feelings, and actions, which helps them control and monitor the behavior needed to learn new information and achieve personal goals.[4][5] Children's social skills allow them to function capably and comfortably in multiple settings. For example, Jaime (age five, Filipina American mother and Mexican American father) comments after

Black, White, Just Right!
Marguerite W. DeVol, Concept
Books, 1993

(From *Booklist*.) A mixed race child
celebrates the rich inclusiveness
of her life in a joyful picture book.
Mama's face is chestnut brown,
Papa's face turns pink in the sun,
the child's a little dark, a little light,
"Just right!" Each double-page
spread shows how members of
the family are individuals with likes
and dislikes, hobbies and habits
that move beyond stereotype.
Mom orders vegetarian; Dad
orders ribs and bagels; the child
likes it all. Mom does ballet; Dad
dances to rap. Mom likes African
masks; Dad goes for modern art;
the child loves the Egyptian part
of the museum. Each page has a
rhyming refrain that ends, "just
right." In keeping with the upbeat
text, Trivas' energetic gouache
illustrations are full of movement
and affection.

the first month of school, "I'm one of those kids who like school.
Everybody likes me and I like everybody." Arthurleen, a preschool
teacher, describes Crystal's social behavior (age four, African
American mother and Mexican American father): "She joins
playgroups easily. She has lots of friends. Crystal is happy,
outgoing, and always in control of her actions." Both Jaime and
Crystal display positive social behaviors.

Advocates of self-discipline point out that children's perception
of self and their capacity to self-apply strategies to control, adapt,
and adjust their behavior to meet social and academic demands
affect subsequent school success.[6] Children who believe that
they are able to maintain and sustain self-control have a sense
of self-efficacy—a belief in one's capabilities to learn or perform
behaviors at acceptable levels. Their ability to respond to the social
standards present in their environment and to control their behavior
to meet individual, family, and group needs are characteristic of
their development and socialization process.

It is also important for children to have friends. Friends support
children's emotional development, create opportunities to develop
social skills, facilitate comparisons necessary for identity development,
and foster a sense of group belonging. Children who have friends
are generally more cooperative, emphatic, socially competent,
self-confident, and less lonely. The following vignette, followed
by a short description of Lisha and Sabrina, offers a brief
analysis of the children's and teacher's behavior and demonstrates
the importance of friendships at this age:

Vignette: Born in October

Lisha (White mother, Black father) and Sabrina (White mother,
Black father) were in different kindergarten classrooms. They
became friends on the playground. Lisha sat next to Sabrina in
the cafeteria during lunch. She asked if Sabrina could come to
our classroom during rainy day recess—a 20-35 minute period,
which happened frequently in the rainy Pacific Northwest. One
rainy day lunch recess Sabrina brought paper to the table where
I was organizing children's folders. Lisha carried two baskets of
crayons; one held people colors, the other regular crayons.
Chatting happily, sometimes including me in the dialogue, they
drew body outlines, hair, facial features, and clothes. After coloring

tiny lips red, Lisha found her people color, "seashell," and filled out the skin areas in her face, arms, and legs. Sabrina, unfamiliar with people colors, tested different colors. Finally, she selected "fawn." Lisha said, "Oh! Your color's pretty." Sabrina, answered, "That's because I'm Black and White." Lisha replied, "Me too! Me too! I'm Black and White, too!"

I cautiously asked Sabrina, "Sabrina, how do you know you're Black and White?" She replied, "Because I was born in October. My sister was born in April and she's White." [Sabrina's mother has remarried and the new infant sister is monoracial White.] Lisha announced, "Me too, me too! I was born in October just like you." Sabrina smiled, "I already know that." They finished coloring, put their pictures inside Lisha's desk, went to the activity area, and took out trays of Legos.

Lisha and Sabrina

Five-year-old Lisha's birthday is on March 8th. She lived with her mother and had minimal contact with her father who lived in a different city. In the classroom, Lisha had the opportunity to self-select peers for social and work groups, engage in collaborative learning experiences, and freely interact with other children. While not excluded in the classroom, she did not have a close friend or a small group of friends; rather, she easily joined and was invited to different social and work groups. During recess she and Sabrina were "best friends." Lisha did not have behavioral or academic problems.

Sabrina, age six, celebrated her birthday on October 12th. She lived with her mother, stepfather, and little sister who was born in April. She did not have any contact with her father. In Sabrina's classroom children were required to remain in their seats, work independently and quietly, follow directions, and participate in whole-group teacher-directed instruction. Sabrina's teacher reported that Sabrina had a tendency to "talk," did not consistently complete her seatwork, and often had difficulties "following directions and staying in her seat." For a kindergartner, Sabrina experienced significant disciplinary actions. She was often removed from the classroom (standing outside at the wall near her classroom), was repeatedly sent home for not following teacher directives, and received an official

one-day suspension for crawling under the table and unplugging the computers in the computer lab.

Analysis of Child Behavior

Through their art, crayon selection, and conversation, both Lisha and Sabrina expressed racial awareness and skin color differentiation. Lisha's willingness to share Sabrina's birthday and biracial identity appeared to confirm a close friendship with Sabrina. While they gravitated toward each other on the playground, it was Lisha who preserved and maintained the relationship. Lisha had more opportunity to select friends. While this close relationship might be based on Lisha's and Sabrina's recognition of shared racial markers (e.g., skin color, hair texture) and biracial identity, in this setting, factors such as teachers' classroom management, disciplinary and instructional behaviors, and having a 'status of one' in their respective classrooms may also be consequential.

Analysis of Teacher Behavior

There is no way to know why the close friendship between Lisha and Sabrina emerged; however, I maintain that my knowledge of how young children select friends, the importance of these relationships to their social and cognitive development, and my understandings of the factors involved in children's friendship choices (e.g., racial heritage, gender, language, interests) helped me recognize the importance of this self-selected friendship bond. This information prompted me to respond in ways to support this relationship. For example, I asked the principal if Sabrina's mother might give permission to transfer Sabrina to my classroom. This request was denied. I offered to help during Sabrina's "time-outs," so these daily punishments were sometimes served in my classroom. When she came, Sabrina joined Lisha's group and the other children accepted her as Lisha's "best friend." Sabrina's teacher appeared to be more concerned with the children's ability to function in a group (e.g., cooperation, compliance to room standards) and less concerned with social skills leading to the development of close interpersonal relationships.

Children are most often attracted to peers of the same gender and often express preferences for friends from the same racial and ethnic background. Since multiracial children are perceived by other children and teachers as having a single racial and ethnic heritage of color, this monoracial association affects their friendship selection. For example, I found that young children (ages five to seven) knew that they were "mixed," but this identity dimension did not necessarily limit cross racial relationships; however, "race" was a factor in friendship patterns for older multiracial children (ages eight to 10).[7] Older multiracial children had to "prove" and project a single ethnic or racial loyalty to make and keep friends.

Implications for Multiracial Children

Scholarship points out that the emerging social skills of four- and five-year-olds are often linked to their need to have a playmate.[8] Preschoolers and kindergarteners confer and withdraw the status of friends at will according to general compatibility, variable moods, and the nature of the present activity. At this stage, comments such as "Will you be my friend?" "You're not my friend!" or even "I hate you!" are not literal expressions of emotion but rather perceptions of the momentary prospects for play. Although children may experience disappointment and even anger at a rebuff during playtime, such feelings generally reverse at the next positive encounter. At this age, children use friendship to facilitate bonding and promote access to play.

Around ages six to seven, children's friendships acquire a more sophisticated and lasting content. At this age children need to be successful socially, understand the reciprocity of friendship, experience increased peer influence, and detect their own and others' social status. Friends are nice, exchange resources and services, share activities, and maintain a relationship over time. Children at this stage share secrets, things, and promises with their friends. They may also choose to terminate friendships if they perceive that a friend refuses to help, ignores their needs, and/or destroys feelings of trust. These feelings and experiences provide the groundwork for the mutual respect and responsibility that characterize mature friendships.

For multiracial children, friendship also seems to be influenced by their dual racial background and by their awareness of this heritage. Memories of multiracial adolescents in my research showed that most felt as if they "always knew" they were multiracial;

however, by age three or four they sensed that they were perceived by relatives, teachers, and peers as having a single racial and ethnic heritage of color. While they remembered preschool and kindergarten as relatively race-free, most of them reported incidents that appeared contradictory. For example, Lavong stated, "I didn't think about race then. We all played together and got along." Later she wrote, "I didn't want my mom to come and walk me home from kindergarten because she was Chinese and everybody thought I was Black." Tia, adopted as an infant by a White family, recalled those early years, "We played with everybody, went to birthday parties and stuff. Nobody stressed about race." Yet, she added, "When I was little, I always wanted blue eyes and blond hair. I knew my biological mom was White, but no one would believe that my real mom could be White. They thought I was just Black, and I felt Black, too." Another student Landle said:

> Mostly little kids get along. I remember playing with all races. When I was little, I looked Chinese, but I didn't know how I looked, plus I thought I was White. My mom was White, my step-dad was White, my sisters were White, blond blue-eyed and everybody pretended I was White. I never knew or saw my real Dad.

When asked to describe the first time he became aware of his multiracial background, Landle said, "I always knew. I was only in kindergarten when kids started making fun of me. They used to chant 'Ching Chan Chong.' I never told anybody."

Children with Asian or Black and White heritages remembered feeling that they were perceived as Asian or Black in Grades 1-2.[9] They believed that everyone, Asians, Blacks, and Whites, categorized them as people of color. Most had Asian and Black friends, felt accepted and comfortable in their respective Asian or Black social groups, and neither sought or avoided White friendships. While at age six and seven children may be aware of race and can experience the stress of rejection, it is important to note that due to their cognitive development they have a very limited grasp of the abstract idea of racism. For example, Lecia explains, "I played with Black kids. I only played with Whites when I was around my cousins. They used to call me 'n-----.' The Black and the White kids thought I was Black. I felt Black. But then of course I knew my mother was White." Morris, White-Asian (Chinese American) moved from the city to a rural farming town in the middle of first grade. He relates:

We moved and I went to an all-White school. I hated it. I wanted to move back to the city. I missed my Asian friends. I hung out with Mexicans who could hardly speak English. White kids didn't accept me as White, even though they could see my mother was White. I was seen and felt like a minority.

The racial and ethnic categorization by self and others appeared less traumatizing for multiracials with a heritage from two racial groups of color. They reported feeling embraced by their peers in both racial and ethnic groups. During the primary grades they remembered friendships in both of their racial groups as well as friendships with Whites. It appeared that their clearly defined "minority status" decreased racial identity dissonance. For example, Lucy reminisced:

The Black kids knew I was mixed because I had long hair. The Mexicans knew I was Black because I had dark skin. Whites just thought I was a minority. But it really didn't matter. I had Mexican and Black friends. I had Asian and White friends too. My very best friend lived next door. She was African American.

In the cases where rejection occurred, they were able to act on rather than control and conceal their emotions. They remembered support from friends. Tammy, whose mother was Mexican American and father African American, laughed as she recalled a particular incident: "I was in second grade and this Mexican girl told me I couldn't be her friend because I was Black. I told her I didn't want to be her friend because she was fat. We [Tammy and other Mexican American friends] didn't play with her for weeks."

Promoting Social Competence
Although family, church, and community are important sources for developing friendship, for most children, school is a primary place to acquire a sense of social group belonging and to practice the skills necessary for making and keeping friends. At all developmental levels, children exhibit varying degrees of success at making and keeping friends. The skills required for positive social interaction come naturally to some children and prove more challenging for others. When children have difficulty establishing friendships, it is important for parents and teachers to understand the situation at hand as well as other possible sources for the problem. *There is a distinction between children who do not have friends because they lack social skills and those who are targets of bias, prejudice, and discrimination.* In the case of the former, guided activities and deliberate interventions can help children practice sharing, overcome shyness, control aggressive tendencies, and/or meet other challenges. When children are excluded because of differences in skin color, appearance, language, social class, gender, ability level, or other factors, it is the adult's responsibility to intercede with reassurances to the victim, corrective guidance to peers and witnesses involved, as well as appropriate interventions to understand causes and minimize reoccurrences. Children who consistently isolate themselves or who display excessive aggression may require referral to a specialist.

Since children's conceptualization of friendship may differ from adults, sometimes parents and teachers make decisions and/or comments that may not be realistic or appropriate. For example, when teachers do not acknowledge how status (e.g., the only multiracial child in the classroom) affects social opportunities, ignore the needs of isolated children, or minimize the stress caused by constant peer harassment and rejection, they may fail to use available resources to help children develop social competence. They might believe in forcing friendship patterns, and say: "In this class we are all friends." Children realize that is not the case. Everyone does not play together. From a child's perspective, it is impossible for everybody to be "friends."

Friendship connections, by nature, are mutually selected constructions; therefore, failure to provide an authentic context with freedom to choose friends, may ultimately deny children the opportunity to form emotionally binding relationships. Rejected children may be ignored or forced into uncomfortable interactions rather than be given opportunities to self-select groups during collaborative work and play activities. The following suggestions promote positive social encounters:

1. Acknowledge children's dual heritage. Children report that parents and teachers are not aware of the pressures inherent in their dual heritages—"My parents don't know what I go through, they're not mixed" and "Teachers don't have a clue." Sometimes the issues affecting young multiracial children are not necessarily associated with how they are labeled and categorized or with societal issues of racism and discrimination; rather, they rest with parents' and teachers' inability to recognize and respond to their developmental needs. Parent and teacher failure and/or unawareness of children's social needs may inadvertently subject multiracial children to experiences and actions that interfere with their social and cognitive development.

2. Recognize when discriminatory or exclusionary behavior is harmful and intervene by providing models and opportunities for forging friendships. Discuss how diverse skills (motor, artistic, academic, and musical) and attributes (race, ethnic heritage, language, socioeconomic status, class, and gender) that children possess influence their ability to form and maintain friendships. Give children opportunities to self-select friends for various activities.

3. Encourage children to notice and appreciate their own physical traits and those of others. Discuss how people may have simultaneous individual identity and group membership in one or more racial and ethnic groups. Value racial and ethnic diversity characteristics (e.g., compare and contrast skin colors and affirm the beauty of all of them). Explain why children's physical traits may be similar and/or different from family members. Provide hand-held mirrors for children to inspect their own faces and a large mirror at child level so they can see themselves full-size with their friends. Examine the curriculum, classroom climate, and home environment for indirect messages about race and implicit judgments regarding racial markers (e.g., in books and posters, watch for patterns of association between light- or dark-colored characters, and traits perceived to be positive or negative). Include a variety of materials in shades of brown and black in your art projects, room decorations, and other resources.

4. Acknowledge the importance of friendship to the social and cognitive development of children. Discuss what friends do and what friendship means. Have children draw themselves playing with friends, label, and display them. Discuss what it feels like when a playmate moves away (e.g., make a going-away friendship book to give to children who are moving, invite to a going-away lunch). Prepare skits and role-plays in which friends are an emotional and cognitive resource (e.g., offering hugs, sharing resources, having fun together, translating, explaining school norms, etc.).

Understanding the cognitive and social developmental skills of four-to seven-year-olds and awareness of how these competencies may be displayed by multiracial children can help parents and teachers play a significant role in their development. Well-designed, appropriate activities in the home, community, and school can create conditions and provide opportunities for children to grow cognitively, practice social skills, and develop self-discipline. A way to assess children's growth and competence is to observe their behaviors and interactions with others. The degree to which children are happy and comfortable in their home and school setting, feel liked or disliked, and exhibit competence in controlling their behavior can serve as a barometer of growth and adjustment. Changes or lack of change in children's behavior can assist you in planning and modifying particular intervention strategies.

Did you know?

According to Census 2000, multiracial youth are disproportionately young:

Percentage of the single race population between the ages of 4 to 7 years old: **5.7%**

Percentage of the multiracial population between the ages of 4 to 7 years old: **10.1%**

Notes

1 M. P. P. Root, ed., *Racially Mixed People in America* (Newbury Park, CA: Sage, 1992).

2 M. P. P. Root, ed., *The Multiracial Experience: Racial Borders as the New Frontier* (Newbury Park, CA: Sage, 1996).

3 J. Piaget, *The Origins of Intelligence in Children*, trans. M. Cook (New York: International Universities Press, 1952).

4 W. W. Hartup, "The Company They Keep: Friendships and Their Developmental Significance," *Child Development* 67 (1996), 1–13.

5 B. J. Zimmerman and D. H. Schunk, eds., *Self-Regulated Learning and Academic Achievement: Theoretical Perspectives* (Mahwah, NJ: Erlbaum, 2001).

6 Ibid.

7 R. H. Sheets, "Friendship and Multiracial Identity Formation: Can Friendship Cross Colors?" in *Working with Mixed Heritage Students, PreK-12: Connecting Development with Practice*, ed. K. Wallace (Westport, CT: Greenwood Publishing, in press).

8 Hartup, *Child Development* (1996) and Sheets, *Working with Mixed Heritage Students* (in press).

9 Sheets, Working with Mixed Heritage Students (in press).

Yasmin Devon Sansguiri Adams
Age: 8
Racial/Ethnic Heritage: Indian, African American, Caucasian, and Blackfoot

As the mother of a multiracial child, I am simultaneously curious, apprehensive, and appreciative of how my daughter's racial ambiguity will affect her life's journey. I am South Asian American, born in India, and her father is African American with Caucasian and Blackfoot ancestry. Yet most people cannot tell what Yasmin's racial makeup is. I wonder how her "undeterminable" appearance will affect her self-identity and her interaction with society.

So far, Yasmin rejects classification. She signs her homework "Yasmin S.A. Devon," taking her middle name, Devon, as her last name, and reducing both parents' last names to middle initials. She is currently interested in her own self, not in the sum of her parts.

However, society might differ with her on this. Recently, Yasmin's good friend told her about a girl he met, commenting that she was Black like Yasmin. A stunned Yasmin replied, "I'm not black—I'm not even brown!" She knows the literal colors but is not yet aware of their racial synonyms. It may take some time before she understands the concept of racial identity, even as others attempt to determine hers.

Because of her racially ambiguous appearance, Yasmin might not face as frequently the stereotypes that most South Asian Americans and African Americans deal with. Many people don't identify her as being of multiple races at all, and those who do often cannot identify what those races are. Since we have the same skin, hair, and eye color, some people who meet both of us conclude that Yasmin is full South Asian American.

However, once people meet her dad, I suspect they no longer view Yasmin as being multiracial—they may simply label her as African American. Similarly, her father is said to be Black and not mixed race, despite his Caucasian and Blackfoot heritage, because of the "one-drop rule" predominant in the U.S. Having said that, these dynamics could change during her life, due to her changing appearance or self-identity, or conversely due to society's changing views about racial identity.

As Yasmin enters her teens and then adulthood, she might encounter some resistance to her mixed race heritage. For example, if she joins the South Asian Club or the African American Club on her college campus, will the club members wonder why she has joined? Will she continually have to explain her name or appearance? Or will that even bother her—will she simply see it as an organic part of life?

I suspect that as Yasmin grows older, she will become increasingly interested in learning about one or more of her backgrounds, in an attempt to connect with her heritage and to cement her identity. So far I have taught her about South Asian culture and Hinduism, just as her dad has exposed her to Civil Rights and Christianity. On the other hand, she might distance herself from one or more of her backgrounds, perhaps in response to society rejecting her in those roles.

In all, Yasmin will encounter many unique circumstances on her life's journey. While Yasmin might experience some frustration or pain, she and others like her are critical to the evolution of familiarity, understanding, and acceptance in our society. Hers is very much a multiracial story, and I feel very honored and hopeful to play a part in it.

Testimonial

Chapter 9

Mixed Race Youth Between 8 to 11 Years Old
Peony Fhagen-Smith, Ph.D.

Children between the ages of eight and 11 years old undergo major developmental changes. I will review the major changes in cognitive and social functioning along with a review of self-understanding during the middle childhood years. This will be followed by a discussion of the role of race and ethnicity in self-development among multiracial/multiethnic children between the ages of eight and 11 years old. I will conclude with a discussion of the impact of family socialization on racial and ethnic self-development.

Before proceeding, I would like to pose a simple problem. Based on what we understand about children's cognitive and social development, imagine how biracial children from three different age groups would respond to the statement, "Describe yourself." Throughout this chapter, I will use the following responses to illustrate various points concerning identity development during the middle childhood years. A five-year-old from a qualitative study on biracial children and racial identity by Christine Kerwin and her colleagues stated, "I would say that I was brown and I had a lot of hair and that it was curly and that…I would be wearing jeans…I would tell you that I would be at my house swinging on my tire swing."[1] In the same study, a nine-year-old stated, "I have a complexion between White and Black and it's sort of light brownish, goldenish color."[2] Finally, a 15-year-old, whose mother is Japanese American and father is Jamaican, labels herself AfroAsian and states, "How can I consider myself either/or?"[3]

Cognitive and Social Changes

Middle childhood is a period marked by important cognitive changes. The new cognitive capacities that develop during this period include becoming more logical, deliberate, and consistent, i.e., cognitive operational thought. Children become more capable of thinking through actions and their consequences. They are able to engage in concentrated acts of deliberate learning with no tangible rewards; they keep in mind the points of view of other people in a wider variety of contexts.[4]

Socially, children's conceptions of friendship develop from an emphasis on participating in joint activities to an emphasis on sharing interests, building mutual understanding, and creating trust.[5] Social differentiation in peer groups creates preference patterns for who likes to spend time with whom. Physical attractiveness is a major factor in popularity. However, relevant social skills, such as making constructive contributions to group activity, adopting the group's frame of reference, and understanding social rules also play an important role in popularity.

Holt Heritage Camp

Holt International Children's
Services is the world's largest
adoption agency. Holt Heritage
Camp offers a fun and safe
environment for international
adoptees to share their common
experiences; learn about the
culture, traditions, and history of
their birth countries; and support
one another. At Holt Heritage
Camp adoptees immerse themselves in self-discovery with fellow
adoptees, which encourages
positive mentoring and friendships
that promote healthy identity
development. Camp occurs at
three locations across the country
each summer.

Learn more:
www.holtintl.org

Participation in peer groups is important to later development
because it fosters the ability to communicate, to understand others'
points of view, and to get along with others: social perspective
taking. As children begin to participate in peer groups, their
relationship with their parents undergoes significant changes. Parental
control shifts from direct to indirect methods such as reasoning,
humor, appeals to self-esteem, and the arousal of guilt.

The ability to coordinate differing attributes of the self into
higher order concepts is a major advance of the middle childhood
period.[6] Children may now recognize themselves as smart, which
is a higher-order trait label, based on success in math and
science, and also dumb, another higher-order trait label, based
on being less successful in English and social studies.[7] This
aspect of self-development can be extended to developmental
changes relative to ethnic and racial concepts of self. In the
beginning of this chapter, three responses to the inquiry
"describe yourself" were given. The five-year-old child's
response included only one descriptor that centered on the color
of their skin. In contrast, the nine-year-old child's response
included a more elaborate description that included both racial
terms and color (e.g., "I have a complexion between White and
Black and it's sort of light brownish, goldenish color."). The
terms White and Black are higher-order race labels. While children
in middle childhood begin to use higher order race labels, the
possible continued use of color descriptors indicates a transition in
social cognition as they wrestle with racial and ethnic identity.
By early many adolescents shed their need to use color descriptors and
simply rely on higher-order race labels such as AfroAsian or biracial.

The Self, Race, and Ethnicity

Based on the work of several researchers,[8] there is a suggestion
that race and ethnic self-representations undergo cognitive
developmental changes similar to other aspects of self-representations.
By age 10, children are able to use racial and ethnic categories to
classify themselves (racial/ethnic self-identification) and other
people (racial/ethnic classification) accurately and reliably.
Furthermore, by middle childhood children understand the
permanence of their ethnicity and/or race, called ethnic/racial
constancy, and have developed feelings and preferences for their

ethnic/racial group membership(s). Racial/ethnic self-identification, racial/ethnic classification, racial/ethnic constancy, and racial/ethnic feelings and preferences are all components of a racial/ethnic sense of self that provide a cognitive foundation for forming a racial/ethnic identity.

As children rely on social comparisons for formulating views of the self, race and ethnicity invariably will play a role. Race and culture can be prominent components of the self for multiracial children due to differences and similarities in physical appearance and cultural behaviors with children from majority and other minority groups. Two dimensions of racial self-representations may become prominent during the middle childhood years: racial salience and racial evaluation. Racial salience describes the extent to which race is a major part of how a child views himself; for example, if asked to describe themselves, children include racial markers in their self-descriptions. Many children younger than seven do not use racial markers to describe themselves and instead use color terms. Racial evaluation describes the positive, negative, or neutral feelings a child has about his physical appearance and the extent to which a child feels positively, negatively, or neutral toward his own racial/ethnic groups.

Equally important to consider are children's ethnic self-representations. Ethnic behaviors, values, preferences, and beliefs may influence not only children's social comparisons, but also personal and interpersonal relations with peers, parents, relatives, and others. A heightened consciousness of characteristics of the self that influence interpersonal, along with cognitive development, may propel ethnicity to a new level of consciousness for children. Two independent components of ethnic self-concept are also suggested to be prominent during the preadolescent and early adolescent years: ethnic feelings and preferences and the use of ethnic behaviors. Ethnic feelings and preference describe a child's preferences for things related to one's cultural backgrounds. The use of ethnic behaviors describes the degree of engagement in culturally relevant behaviors.

Biracial children may oscillate between strong identification with one parent's cultural background. For example, a child with a Japanese American mother and a Jamaican father may first strongly identify with his Japanese heritage and take on a hyper-intensified Japanese identity. After several months or even a year he may take on a hyper-intensified Jamaican identity. It may not be until the end of middle childhood or the beginning of adolescence that a more equal identity is developed that encompasses both cultural backgrounds. While children's ability to use multiple racial descriptors is present during middle childhood, establishing an ethnic identity is more complex and depends on the composition of one's "multiracialness" (i.e., African American/Irish American vs. Chinese American/Puerto Rican).

Parental Influences

Although Boykin and Toms' conceptual framework of child socialization was developed with African American parents in mind, their framework is applicable to all parents of color including parents of multiracial children.[9] Parents of multiracial children negotiate three different realms of experience: mainstream, minority, and cultural. Thus, socialization of race and ethnicity fall within three categories; socialization in the mainstream of American society or mainstream socialization, socialization linked to proximal cultural context, called ethnic socialization, and socialization concerning racial minority status (i.e., racial socialization). Each of these aspects of socialization has been conceptualized differently, but is strongly related.

Stevenson describes the concept of racial socialization as "the process of communicating messages and behaviors to children and adolescents to bolster their sense of identity given the possibility and reality that their life experiences may include racially hostile encounters." As a consequence of living in a majority/minority stratified society, where being a multiracial individual can mean being treated differently, an important part of parenting is teaching children to cope with racism, prejudice, discrimination, and "biracialism." Biracialism is a term I use to describe acts of discrimination or racial insults that are unique to the biracial experience. For example, being stared at intently on the train because someone cannot figure out whether or not you are your child's mother or the nanny, telling someone you are Jewish and being asked what the conversion process was like when in fact you were born to a Jewish mother, or a monoracial person of color thinking that you must think that you are better/

prettier/smarter because you are part White. Parents of multiracial children can act as a buffer between their children and society, and racial socialization can function as a filter of societal information about racial status. Racial socialization can also entail explanations of majority and other minority groups' discrimination and hostility as a way to steer children's causal attributions regarding discrimination toward healthy development.

Intricately related to learning how to handle racism and discrimination is developing ways of gaining or maintaining access to majority cultural and social institutions for services, employment, power, etc. This is labeled mainstream socialization.[10] Mainstream socialization includes learning to develop a bicultural orientation.[11] A bicultural orientation encompasses accommodating to majority (i.e., White/European American) culture's beliefs and behaviors as a way to function adaptively in mainstream society, along with retaining characteristics of one's own culture. That is, a person learns to function optimally in more than one cultural context and to switch repertoires of behavior appropriately and adaptively as called for by the situation. Many multiracial children, who are raised by a White/European American parent, may develop a bicultural orientation with more ease.

The final realm of socialization, ethnic or cultural socialization, entails fostering a positive orientation toward one's own cultures and acceptance of one's ethnic group memberships. Ethnic or cultural socialization also encompasses the transmittal of "group patterns of values, social customs, perceptions, behavioral roles, language usage, and rules of social interactions that group members share in both obvious and subtle ways."[12] Multiracial children's ethnic or cultural socialization will depend on their parents' own racial and ethnic identities. Racial, ethnic, and mainstream socialization processes include specific verbal behaviors, mainly specific statements regarding race; modeling of behaviors; and exposure to specific objects, contexts, and environments. Through these mechanisms of learning, children acquire and internalize the values, attitudes, and behaviors promoted by their parents and families.

One might ask how is a positive racial and ethnic sense of self developed? What are the mechanisms that promote or inhibit this development? Howard Stevenson proposes a model of self

development that incorporates the role of racial and ethnic socialization. He suggests an interpersonal theoretical view of self-development, called the extended self. The extended self view defines self-development as evolving from interdependent and interpersonal processes.[13] The extended self is buttressed, supported, and alienated by the messages and interactions that one experiences in the family, which is surrounded by other socializing agencies. Stevenson points out that the family may be the most important institution for most children, who are building selves and identities in several domains: gender, sexual, racial, personal, and cultural. Furthermore, he contends that the teaching of survival and cultural pride will have a major impact on racial and ethnic self-development.[14]

Family, peer, community, and broader cultural contexts provide images and messages about what it means to be multiracial, which shape the selves of multiracial children. An extended self becomes mature when it is bolstered by various environmental systems that are proximal to the family (e.g., peer, community). The buffering process is essential for challenging those images and messages that are oppressive and negative, and reinterpreting them into a culturally empowering manner. Stevenson suggests that a mature and healthy racial and ethnic sense of self cannot develop without the buffering process that racial and ethnic socialization can provide.

Conclusion

The cognitive and social changes that occur during the middle childhood years are major and contribute to major changes in racial and ethnic self-understanding. Children during these years move beyond describing themselves and others based on color and begin to use racial descriptors to describe themselves. For biracial children they cognitively coordinate seeing themselves as falling into multiple racial categories. Furthermore, with the ability to compare themselves and others socially (i.e., social comparison), ethnic identification becomes more prominent. Biracial children begin to develop ethnic feelings and preferences for their cultures and perhaps take on hyper personas that embody their view of how a person of their cultural backgrounds should behave. Therefore, I suggest that it is during middle childhood, when parental influence shifts from direct to indirect methods such as reasoning, humor, appeals to self-esteem, and the arousal of guilt, that racial, ethnic, and mainstream socialization is critical. This is exemplified in the following excerpt from a newspaper article.

> Ashley White-Stern, 17...was raised in the Jewish faith of her mother. But her Black father exposed White-Stern to African American culture as well. So she had a bat mitzvah at 13 and a year later participated in a rites-of-passage ceremony inspired by African traditions. Last December, she participated in a Kwanzaa celebration at Phillips Academy, then visited old friends at Temple Israel in Boston. For her, race has never been an issue. "My parents always told me I was both," says White-Stern, who wears her hair in skinny braids that snake past her shoulders.[15]

Did you know?

According to Census 2000, multiracial youth are disproportionately young:

Percentage of the single race population between the ages of 8 to 11 years old: **6.0%**

Percentage of the multiracial population between the ages of 8 to 11 years old: **9.1%**

Notes

1 C. Kerwin, J. G. Ponterotto, B. L. Jackson, and A. Harris, "Racial Identity in Biracial Children: A Qualitative Investigation," *Journal of Counseling Psychology* 40 (1993), 221-231.

2 Ibid.

3 V. E. Jones, "A Rich Sense of Self," *The Boston Globe* (29 February 2000), A1, A7.

4 J. H. Flavell, P. Miller, and S. Miller, *Cognitive Development* (Englewood Cliffs, NJ: Prentice Hall, 1993).

5 D. R. Schaffer, *Social and Personality Development* (Pacific Grove, CA: Brooks/Cole, 1994).

6 S. Harter, "The Development of Self-Representations," in *Handbook of Child Psychology: Social, Emotional, and Personality Development, Volume III,* eds. W. Damon and N. Eisenberg (New York: Wiley, 1998), 553-617.

7 Ibid.

8 S. Harter, M. E. Bernal, G. P. Knight, C. A. Garza, K. A. Ocampo, and M. K. Cota, "The Development of Ethnic Identity in Mexican-American Children," *Hispanic Journal of Behavioral Sciences* 3-24 (1994), 12.

9 A. W. Boykin and F. D. Toms, "Black Child Socialization: A Conceptual Framework," in *Black Children: Social, Educational and Parental Environments*, eds. H. P. McAdoo and J. L. McAdoo (Newbury, CA: Sage, 1985), 33-51.

10 J. S. Phinney, B. T. Lochner, and R. Murphy, "Ethnic Identity Development and Psychological Adjustment in Adolescence," in *Ethnic Issues in Adolescent Mental Health*, eds. A. R. Stiffman and L. E. Davis (Newbury Park, CA: Sage, 1990), 53-72.

11 A. O. Harrison, M. N. Wilson, C. J. Pine, S. Q. Chan, and R. Buriel, "Family Ecologies of Ethnic Minority Children," *Child Development* 61 (April 1990), 347-362.

12 Ibid.

13 H. C. Stevenson, "Theoretical Considerations in Measuring Racial Identity and Socialization: Extending the Self Further," in *African American Identity Development*, ed. R. L. Jones (Hampton, VA: Cobb and Henry, 1998).

14 Ibid.

15 V. E. Jones, "A Rich Sense of Self," *The Boston Globe* (29 February 2000), A1, A7.

...hael
...bino + Dutch

Kanna
Japanese +
German +
Irish +
Austrian

...thy
...panese + German +
...rean + Irish +
...erto Rican

Philipp
Black +
German +
Irish +
Cherokee +
Indian

Samantha Derr

Age: 11

Racial/Ethnic Heritage: African American, Caucasian, and Native American

At school when kids used to ask me if I was White, I always knew I was multiracial, but I was confused about why anybody really cared. Eventually, I began to understand the history of how being White or Black used to make a big difference in what kind of life you could have. Now, it still matters but mostly because people can't let go of how it used to matter and how hurtful those things were. Whenever I see that there are a lot more Black people who are really poor, I feel uncomfortable about it because those Black children aren't getting raised as well as other kids are and I think it is seriously affecting their future. It can also affect other children around them, like at school, because sometimes they are really mean.

My Dad and his family are Black, and my Mom and her family are White. Both of my parents are part Native American (a very, very small part). On my Dad's side, I have southern American culture that respects their African heritage. On my Mom's side, I have both southern American culture as well as English culture. So I have three races and three cultures I identify with.

My parents have never said anything to me about being multiracial, but told me that no matter what color you are, to always have self-respect and respect for others. Some people in my family have told me that I'm lucky, but I think they meant that I look good, not that I will get more respect because of it. I just call myself tan. I never really take that much time to think about it. If someone asks me if I'm White, I just say, "No, I'm tan." I never really wanted to make a big deal about it because it doesn't matter what color you are, it just matters what you're like on the inside.

They've always said that if somebody makes fun of you, even if it's not about color, you should just ignore them. When I was very little, I would say, "Sticks and stones may break my bones, but words can never hurt me." So as long as they didn't physically hurt me, I can still ignore them. Also, my mom told me that people who make fun of other people usually are trying to make themselves feel better by putting others down.

I wish I could have a book that is in the school library about people who are multiracial so I could relate to other multiracial kids. I would like it to show other people that it's not as different as they think. It would be so cool if there were magazines and TV shows that had multiracial people like me in them. They are all usually Black or White. I have never known any group that is just for people who are multiracial. But in school, there was this thing we had to fill out on what we thought about our teachers. We had to check either White, African American, Hispanic, or multiracial, so I got lucky on that one.

Testimonial

Chapter 10

The Identity Development of the 11- to 14-Year-Old Multiracial Youth

Donna Jackson Nakazawa

Between the ages of 11 and 14, young adolescents embark upon the difficult task of achieving a clear sense of identity: to know and understand themselves as individuals, as well as to discover their own unique place in society. By trying out and freely experimenting with different roles, young adolescents struggle to find an identity that seems tailor-made for them. This process of finding their unique place in society helps them gain a sense of who they are, a sense of self that will serve as a bridge between the childhood they have only recently left behind, and their future as an adult, which awaits them.[1]

During this struggle for an identity, to find out where they "fit in," young adolescents worry whether anyone else is like them and if the feelings of confusion they feel are normal (i.e., Does anyone else feel the angst I feel? Does anyone else out there understand me?). Young adolescents have only recently, between the ages of nine to 12, gained a deeper grasp of the factors that define racial and cultural identity, as well as a fuller awareness of racism in its historical and societal context. These questions of "Is there anyone else out there just like me?" and "Where do I fit in?" increasingly begin to be informed by race: for the young adolescent, racial sameness is now a central marker for assuming that someone is similar to them, that someone will

understand them.[2]

But while monoracial adolescents can assuage their fears of not fitting in by befriending other adolescents who are "just like" them, for multiracial youth, this search to find one's identity is inherently more complex. For them, there is a heightened aspect to "feeling different," since they often are racially unique in their school and/or community setting.

This desire to find others who are racially like them, and who therefore understand them, is but one of several factors that make the middle school years particularly difficult and confusing for the young multiracial teen. Like all very young teens, they are now much more independent from their parents than they were at nine, 10 or 11. Being more independent, they are more likely to keep any angst they do feel about not fitting in, due to their multiraciality, inside—which may only intensify their confusion and fear. For the first time they are paddling out alone, straight into a sea of shifting friendships and emotions.

As they move away from their family as a primary source for information and reassurance and closer to their friends as a primary source of information and acceptance, their interactions with friends take on a new intensity; peer opinion assumes paramount importance in their lives. It is no surprise, then, that the emotional

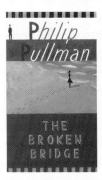

The Broken Bridge
Philip Pullman, Random House
Children's Pub., 1994

(From Kirkus Reviews) Ginny's peaceful life in a Welsh village with father Tony is disrupted when it's revealed that she has an older half brother, Robert, also 16. Her mother, she's been told, was a Haitian artist who died soon after her birth; now Ginny also learns that Robert's recently deceased mother—not hers—was Tony's wife, a discovery that casts doubt on the little Tony has said about her origins. Already struggling for self-identity as a teenager, a gifted artist, and almost the only dark-skinned person she knows, Ginny is drawn into a search for a past now gradually revealed as far more convoluted than she imagined, with enough woe to explain Tony's reticence and enough surprises to keep readers guessing. Ginny is less concerned with being Black than with realizing herself as an artist; as such, she is sharply realized, an intelligent, and creative observer. Great for ages 12 and up.

world of the early adolescent is full of distractions and anxiety about what others think of them.

Meanwhile, there is much else that's new to think about, too: gushing hormones are kicking in, with the attendant heightened emotions, bodily changes, and self-consciousness, and issues of dating and race are surfacing for the very first time (e.g., "If the White kids date the White kids and the Black kids date the Black kids, and I'm Black and White, who will I date?"). Because kids this age now put so much emphasis on their social life, new and more intense cliques are being quickly created, with kids often separating out according to shared interests, such as football, track, chess, and similarities (race, cultural background, socioeconomic status). As young teens begin to form groups increasingly divisive by race in a way they did not in prior years, multiracial young adults often find that even their oldest friendships are subject to suddenly change. The seas are shifting. This intense confluence of wholly new changes within oneself and amidst one's social group can be extraordinarily difficult for any early adolescent to navigate, but especially for the multiracial youth who so often feel they do not fit in anywhere racially.

Yet during these years, as kids enter a new middle school setting, the multiracial youth is faced with having to make tough choices about where they feel they do belong. Suddenly plunged into a larger school teeming with new students, they, like all teens, must struggle to quickly find their place.

In general, most teens, once they do find a group where they feel they fit in, are quick to wrap themselves in that cloak of identity. But in the process of trying to better identify who they are, they often reject all that they are not, including those who differ from them racially. Moreover, adolescents who are insecure about their own identities may exaggerate these differences in order to help boost their own sense of self-worth and prove their solidarity to their group.[3] For instance, those in a clique of White lacrosse players may put down the Asian chess players as a way of underscoring their place in their own group. But what of the multiracial Asian/White child who plays on both the lacrosse team and who is in the chess club? Where does this multiracial child fit in? How can he choose one racial group, when he is both?

Consider the words of a Black Vietnamese adopted young

adult, who, looking back, recounts that "Being 12 and 13 in junior high was the toughest time in my life. We left elementary school and went into a bigger group in junior high. Everyone started dividing up and you had to choose which table you wanted to sit at in the cafeteria. All the kids were choosing where they wanted to be so they wanted me to choose, too. It was like, Black, Asian, or White, which is it? The Black girls would come up, touch my hair, and say, 'What are you?' Both the Black kids and the White kids would say things like, 'You look like a door hit you in the face.' I didn't date and I felt really ugly. The whole process was just weird and it made me feel awkward and different. It was very hurtful."

Many of the young multiracial interviewees, with whom I have spoken for my book, report that as kids in middle school begin to form cliques divided along racial lines, they feel pressured to choose one racial group and distance themselves from their other racial heritage. But again, herein lies a paradox for the young multiracial teen: on the one hand, understanding one's entire, authentic racial identity is a critical part of overall identity development, and yet many teens feel pressured to identify with only one of their racial heritages in order to "fit in." It is for this reason that the majority of young adults I have interviewed report that the early period of adolescence is the most difficult phase of their lives.

A Black/White teen commented on eighth and ninth grade, saying, "They were the hardest time for me. It's a time when you really want to belong and you need to have a group where you know you fit in. But I looked different, and I felt torn. Because I hung out with the White kids at school, the Black kids in my neighborhood felt I was not accepting of them and the Black community. I spent half my time at school playing one role as part of that White world and half my time at home hanging out with the Black kids. I felt that no one got me because I was more complicated. The worst part is that I never got to be all of myself at the same time."

Mixed race adolescents often feel even more acutely than monoracial teens do that no one, not even parents or close friends, really understands the unique situations they face or the intrapersonal conflicts they experience. Since they are so overtly

confronted with the question, "Where do I fit in?" they have to consider the question of their identity in a more conscious way than do monoracial youth and think hard about making distinct identity choices. They do not have the luxury of choosing a social group without consciously thinking through that identity choice, and what it says about who they are and are not.

Nevertheless, weaving one's way through this labyrinth of identity, friendships, and emotions, while integrating one's experiences into a positive sense of identity, is a task the adolescent in a mixed race family must face. Although pressures to choose one racial identity are most intense during the adolescent years, many young people are able to successfully maintain a multiracial self-concept.

For instance, the Black Vietnamese transracially adopted young woman who spoke earlier recounts that by twelfth grade, she came into her own. She explains, "I just got this mentality that I wasn't going to be pressured into choosing; something in me said, 'I'm not going to play this game.' If I liked someone, I was going to be friends with them, no matter what race they were or what clique they were in. I thought, 'I don't care if you don't like me if I hang out with the Black people, and I don't care if you don't like me if I hang out with the White kids.' I don't know where I got that strength that I just wanted to be me, to be friends with whomever I liked, but it gave me a lot of sense of self. Then by twelfth grade, I realized that my friends were getting along great. I was very conscious that these were two races hanging out together and I sometimes had to remind one person of one race of the humanity of the person of the other race. I felt this role was very important and I'm sure it strengthened my sense of who I am today."

What allowed this young multiracial woman to have what she calls "that strength" of self not to choose despite enormous peer pressure? Like all of the multiracial youth I have interviewed who have achieved a healthy multiracial identity, this young woman had such a strong foundation laid for her by parents, who included all her racial heritages into her multiracial identity from the earliest stages of her development; extreme pressure to identify with only one of her racial heritages felt inherently wrong to her. In addition, she grew up in an inherently multiracial setting where multiracialness was, reassuringly, considered the norm: her parents had eight children—six of whom were not only adopted but multiracial. Furthermore, her parents had a wide circle of other multiracial families as friends, providing her with a large number of multiracial role models amidst a diverse community and home life.

Less fortunate are those kids who were not prepared by parents from the earliest ages with an open dialogue regarding being multiracial, and who were thus left vulnerable as they entered adolescence. In some circumstances, these are children for whom the issue of race was sometimes negotiated by their families social status, to the degree that race did not seem to arise as an issue during childhood, and thus their parents did not feel the need to address it. In other circumstances, children were pressured to "pass"[4] rather than to identify as multiracial, or the topic of race was neglected entirely. Inevitably, these kids later faced a substantial shock as they entered adolescence and experienced hurtful dating and peer situations, making it much harder for them to emerge from adolescence intact. Adolescents in this latter group sometimes relate that their experiences during these years are too painful to talk about even today. Some state they have not recovered from the painful experiences of middle/early high school, even as they move on toward college. These under-prepared kids tend to see the problem as partly within themselves, rather than as being within those around them. Indeed, if a child's multiracial identity has been addressed in their early years through ongoing conversation and dialogue, and by inclusion of all their cultures, then the child is far better prepared to successfully complete adolescence and achieve a healthy multiracial self-concept.

This is not a simplistic or easy task. It may include undergoing authenticity testing with peers, such as being asked to do a hyper-caricature of one racial aspect of oneself in order to convince others one really is Black "enough" or Asian "enough." Nevertheless, even while experimenting in this way, young adults who have been successfully prepared begin to feel that such a "one-race" role is artificial and inappropriate, out of synch with who they really are. They simply must stretch toward a more whole sense of self. As they do, many report they become

secure enough about who they are that they are able to have a racial identity potentially described as fluid; they may describe themselves as biracial in some situations, with some groups, and as Black or Asian in others. But whatever they might call themselves, or whatever the context of the situation they are in, they are still solidly sure of who they are.

If they have succeeded at developing a healthy multiracial identity during these years, they feel quite good later in life about their ability to have navigated these dramas, and about their ability to not affiliate with only one racial group. Many report feeling especially good about having become a bridge between different groups of people who might not otherwise have come together. Often, they express great pride and confidence about this role. Looking back from their twenties, some report a feeling of moral achievement, to be able to stand in a place where they are able to have empathy for all. As one Black, White, and Jewish multiracial 19-year-old reflects in retrospect, "I think being multiracial has allowed me to see things from both sides of the color line, opening my mind to differences of all types so that I don't prejudge anything or anyone. It has allowed me to see love for what it really is, which is something I think a lot of people miss out on." Others report feeling an enhanced authenticity as individuals, as they make choices to be surrounded by people who they like for who they are, and who also like them for who they are.

How can we help our multiracial adolescents to succeed in navigating their way through the confusion of early adolescence as they search out their identity? In addition to the importance of laying the groundwork early on for an ongoing dialogue regarding a child's multiracial identity, it is also critical that a child is exposed to a diverse community, school, and/or neighborhood setting. For instance, one Black/White young adult who did not report suffering through her early adolescent years says, when looking back at her early teen experience, "We always had all these wonderful families and friends, through an interracial family group my mom co-founded, coming in and out our door; I met families who were all kinds of crazy combinations. So even though I went to a predominately White school, I never felt I was the only one. Even though my girlfriends at school weren't mixed, I grew up in a very mixed world. I never felt alone." Like other healthy multiracial youth, this young woman was able to see the problem as being with the "other" children rather than within herself.

What happens when a child does not come of age in a diverse setting? It certainly makes a tremendous, and positive, difference for multiracial children who do not have the advantage of growing up in a diverse community if their parents establish a wide-open forum for discussing their children's multiracial identity. But it is less apparent whether establishing such an open dialogue about being multiracial is sufficiently helpful enough to overcome the clear disadvantage of not having other children around who are racially like oneself. I have certainly interviewed some multiracial youth who seem to prove that very aware parenting can ameliorate, to a large degree, the negative effects of not growing up in a multicultural/multiracial community, but more research needs to be done to adequately answer this question.

Ideally, multiracial adolescents will have both: aware parents who are fully involved in the process of helping their children to understand their multiracial identity from a very young age, and a diverse setting in which to come of age.

It is also important to be aware of the role gender plays during these critical developmental years. Multiracial girls may experience more difficulty during adolescence, on the one hand, because they are viewed as "exotic" in a way boys are not. However, interestingly, a number of multiracial adolescent girls, having grown up in a post-feminist age without the consciousness of female objectification that was a central dialogue of the feminist generation, report they enjoy being valued for their exotic uniqueness. One young woman phrases it this way: "I think it's much easier to be a mixed girl than a mixed guy. There is a positive stereotype that being mixed makes you exotic and beautiful and it plays into that fantasy men have. Guys don't have that beauty issue to help them. Everyone I hear talking about mixed girls always says, 'Oh, they're so hot!'" When asked if she was disturbed by that objectification, she replied, "Is that objectification? It may be, but I'll take it!"

Being different in the sense of being exotic, however, may be a double-edged sword for mixed race girls: if they are desired, they may feel at some point in their maturation they are only being pursued for superficial reasons, because they do look exotic; if they are not desired, they may feel they are not being pursued for superficial reasons, because they look different.

On the other hand, multiracial boys who are heavily involved in sports may hold the advantage of being able to solidify their sense of belonging because of the camaraderie engendered by being part of a sports team. This camaraderie often extends beyond racial lines. However, they may have to work harder to prove themselves among the majority White population both academically and later on within the work setting than do multiracial women, as long as women are viewed as less threatening than men in terms of academia and the workplace.[5]

It seems, in sum, that navigating social peer relationships, dating relationships, and one's relationship with oneself is intensely challenging for the young multiracial adolescent between the ages of 11 to 14. It is only by careful preparation as parents and professionals that we can lay the foundation for them to feel comfortable with their own identity, and to thus journey successfully throughout these early adolescent years and into adulthood.

Did you know?

According to Census 2000, multiracial youth are disproportionately young:

Percentage of the single race population between the ages of 12 to 14 years old: **4.3%**

Percentage of the multiracial population between the ages of 12 to 14 years old: **5.9%**

Notes

1 E. H. Erikson, "Identity and the Life Cycle: Selected Papers," *Psychological Issues Monograph* 1 (1959).

2 L. Derman-Sparks, C. T. Higa, and B. Sparks, "Children, Race and Racism: How Race Awareness Develops," *Bulletin* 11(3 & 4) (1980), 8.

3 F. Wardle, *Tomorrow's Children: Meeting the Needs of Multiracial and Multiethnic Children at Home, in Early Childhood Programs, and at School* (Denver, CO: Center for the Study of Biracial Children, 1999).

4 Wanting a child to "pass" refers to a parent's hope that others within their community will erroneously assume that their child is *all* Black, or *all* White, or *all* Asian, rather than multiracial.

5 M. P. P. Root, "Resolving "Other" Status: Identity Development of Biracial Individuals," in *Diversity and Complexity in Feminist Therapy*, eds. L. S. Brown and M. P. P. Root (New York: Haworth, 1990), 185-205.

Bernardo
Mexican + Colombian

Fred
Japanese +
Afrian American

Michelle
Venezuelan +
Irish + Chinese

Alex Mitra
Age: 16
Racial/Ethnic Heritage: Mexican and Filipino

My racial heritage is Filipino and Mexican, but I identify as mostly Mexican. Growing up, there were a few times I wasn't sure if I was Asian or Pacific Islander, but besides that, I have never really felt confused about my racial identity. I just felt like being a minority because I don't like being a part of a mainstream crowd.

Where I live, there are mostly Asians and White Irish elderly people. At school, I've been called "tanned Asian", Chinese and all this other stuff. I don't know if they think I'm Chinese because of my eyes. Some people think Filipino because my nose is kind of flat. When they hear I'm Mexican they say, "Whoaaa!" Not many people think I'm Mexican, and I'm cool with it. I don't really care if people don't know I'm Mexican. They'll find out sooner or later.

Growing up, I went to two different schools. In the Mission area of San Francisco, I interacted with mostly Latinos, who were the majority. In the Sunset neighborhood, there is a big Chinese and Japanese population. Changing back and forth is just interesting, watching how each ethnicity views each other. The Asians think the Mission is all rough, tough, and so dangerous, while the Latinos think the Asians are just another crowd so they don't really care about them. I felt offended by it so I would stand up for my other ethnicities or my other homies saying, "Chill, you don't know about it, so don't go there. You're just talking trash about something you don't know so just shut up." Most of them would be surprised, because I am usually more playful and don't come on strong like that, but I feel really strongly about people not being stereotypical.

My parents did not really talk about my being multiracial since my school is really racially tolerant and there's not much discrimination. They taught my younger brother and older sister about our background, and basically let us decide how to identify on our own. Because we spoke Spanish in the home, we were brought up mostly Mexican. I wish my parents had taught us more about our Filipino culture, and especially the language, Tagalog. When you learn the language, you also learn the culture. I barely know anything about Filipino culture, but my sister constantly tries to find out more about the Filipino side of our family.

I do remember having to check only one box on racial forms, and it sort of felt like you were just shutting one part of yourself out. But you just decide, "Ok, it can be like that, but later I want to find out more about that side and check both."

In school, multiracial people were not really discussed. I guess they just thought that we'd know about it. If someone was more than one race, they thought we wouldn't make a big deal about it. I'm fine not having them teach me about it because personally I don't think there is much to teach; multiracial people have more customs to teach than monoracial people. There's different customs and languages, that's all.

Testimonial

Chapter 11

Identity Development Issues for Multiracial and Multiethnic Youth 15 to 17 Years Old

Karen L. Suyemoto, Ph.D. & Juanita M. Dimas, Ph.D.

The development of a positive sense of identity is the primary developmental task for 15- to 17-year-old youth. Identity here refers generally to a sense of self, an answer to the question "Who am I?" As adolescents master cognitive and emotional skills enabling greater abstraction, hypothetical thinking, and self-awareness, they explore different perspectives, experimenting with various ways of thinking and feeling, and considering possible values, preferences, choices, and behaviors. Eventually, this experimentation and evaluation leads to the development of an idea of self or "central personal identity." Although this central personal identity is constantly changing, it provides a general answer in a given moment to "Who am I?" against which new ideas, behaviors, and values can be considered.

Part of what sets this group apart from 11- to 14-year-olds is greater cognitive abilities, allowing 15- to 17-year-olds the ability to consider more complex solutions or answers to their questions, as well as to the questions that other people pose to them. Greater cognitive abilities also allow for more independent decision making among these soon-to-be adults. Increased social independence and the associated increase in the number of social contexts (e.g., access to new social venues available in high school such as dances or school events, the ability to travel

independently to events and experiences farther away made possible by driving) also mean more contexts in which to consider the meaning of being multiracial. Dating is an especially important context that sets this group apart from 11- to 14-year-olds. Particular issues related to racial/ethnic acceptance and exclusion, and gender identity (masculinity and femininity) in relation to intimate relationships are frequently experienced for the first time in high school, although these issues may continue into adulthood.

The greater cognitive abilities and social contexts also encourage 15- to 17-year-old multiracial youth to begin to consider the *integration* of identities, exploring the complex ways that multiple contexts and multiple identities—such as racial and ethnic identities, gender identity, and identity related to sexual orientation—shape their experiences. Which specific identities are most salient to a particular adolescent will relate to the ways in which the individual, the family, the community, and the society see that adolescent in relation to what is dominant, "average," or most common. While each specific identity can be *discussed* as if it is separate from all others and from the central personal identity, it is important to remember that this is not the way identities are *lived*.

For example, Sue, a 16-year-old girl, whose mother is European

American (White) and whose father is second-generation Chinese American, may have a racial identity as multiracial, an ethnic identity as Chinese, an identity as a girl or woman, an identity as a lesbian, and an identity as an artist. While we can discuss each of these identities separately, it is important to remember that Sue lives them as a whole—for example, her Chinese identity will affect her experience and identity as a lesbian, and both of these identities will affect her identity as an artist; Sue lives her life as a multiracial Chinese European American lesbian young artist. This means that any generalizations made in discussing racial and ethnic identities in multiracial youth need to be carefully applied, with particular attention paid to other identities and experiences. Because gender, race, and ethnicity are paid so much attention to in the U.S., it is particularly important to consider the three of these together rather than separately. The stereotypes applied to a multiracial boy of African descent will not be the same as those applied to a multiracial girl of African descent, and the ways in which they will be differentially treated will affect the development of their identities.

Multiracial adolescents frequently have to create positive racial and ethnic identities without role models who can help them understand how to develop these identities as a multiracial, multiethnic person. In monoracial families, adolescents at least have the model of their parents. The identity explorations and experiments of multiracial adolescents may be different than monoracial adolescents because they do not fit well into how people generally understand race and ethnicity.

In the United States, most people think of race and ethnicity as the same thing. A person who "looks Black" (race) is usually assumed to be African American (ethnicity), with certain cultural experiences and knowledge. Similarly, a person who "looks White" is usually assumed to be "American" (meaning European American) with cultural experiences and knowledge reflecting the dominant American culture. But multiracial adolescents may not clearly "look" like any specific race. And their cultural experiences may not be the same as the way they may look. For example, the first author has several multiracial friends who, according to their experiences with others, "look White." But their identities and cultural experiences are as Indigenous People and Asian Americans. They

have had to develop their racial and ethnic identities from experiences that do not fit the general social view of what race and ethnicity mean and how they relate. The multiracial adolescent may therefore find it more difficult to find a sense of belonging among their peers. While all adolescents are unique, the social importance of race and ethnicity in the U.S. means that not fitting in to ideas about race and ethnicity can also have implications for feelings of belonging more generally. This then has implications for general identity development, as the sense of belonging offered by adolescent peer groups enables the adolescent a place of safety from which to experiment with new behaviors and identities.

Each major racial group has its own ideas about ethnicity and race and its own views of multiracial people within its group, so the experience of multiracial adolescents within particular ethnic and racial groups will vary (see sections in this book on specific heritages of multiracial children and youth). But all multiracial adolescents challenge the general social assumption of racial separation. And most multiracial adolescents are developing their ethnic and racial identities in relation to more than one group. The cognitive abilities and new social experiences of 15- to 17-year-old multiracial youth generally raise the questions of "Who am I?" "Who do others see me as?" "Where do I belong?" and "Who do I want to be?" to new levels, often leaving these youths trying to negotiate multiple and often contradictory responses from both within themselves and from the significant people in their lives.

"Who am I?"
Trying on Different Labels and Identities

Multiracial adolescents may experiment with different ways to answer "What are you?" Trying on different labels is a way to explore the increased possibilities made clear by more advanced cognitive skills and to begin to differentiate the personal and social meanings associated with the different options. Sue (the example introduced earlier) may try various labels for her racial and ethnic identities such as "Chinese," "Asian," "multiracial," or "American." She may distance herself from racial and ethnic identities generally, denying that these are the identities and categories that are important to who she is, even as others try to pressure her to racially categorize herself. Thus she may say she is an artist or a student. She may also more actively resist racial categorization, answering "What are you?" with responses that point to the assumptions being made, such as "I'm human."

Considering Multiple Identities and Identifying as Multiracial

Multiracial adolescents may explore how they may have multiple identities in relation to multiple ethnic and racial groups. For example, Sue may identify as Chinese American, as European American, as Asian American, as multiracial, and as American. She may resist a single identity or a single group for identification. Alternatively, she may choose a single identity such as, Chinese American. But this does not mean that she necessarily rejects any part of her family or heritage. She may also identify differently in different contexts. Sue may also actively identify as multiracial. This may involve a temporary idealization of stereotyped ideas of multiracial people. For example, Sue may identify as multiracial and feel proud and special because she is "exotic." But multiracial adolescents may also actively identify as multiracial without accepting stereotypical views. This may involve seeking out multiracial role models through the media, through literature and narratives written by multiracial people, or through social groups or Internet discussions. They may begin to explore how race and ethnicity are commonly understood in the U.S., leading to a better understanding of their own experiences of difference and exclusion.

"Who do others see me as?" and "Where do I belong?"

It is the social experience of difference and others' responses to this difference that *most* characterizes racial and ethnic identity development in multiracial 15- to 17-year-olds.[1] The frequent question "What are you?" and the request to "Check One Box Only" reflect people's need to racially categorize. The constant demand to address these requests is one reason why racial and ethnic identity development is so important for multiracial adolescents. Thus, the question "Who am I?" is explored most during this developmental stage through the exploration of the questions "Who do others see me as?" and "Where do I belong?" Multiracial youth aged 15 to 17 explore these questions in a variety of ways in relation to themselves, their families, and their peers.

Frequently Changing Self-Perceptions and Attitudes Towards Others

The ways in which multiracial adolescents feel about their own race and ethnicity and about family, peers, and particular ethnic groups or heritages rarely remain the same over time. Sue may at times see being multiracial as a positive thing and sometimes she may want to "pass"[2] as monoracial. She may feel positively about her parents' racial and ethnic heritages, or she may be angry that they are who they are, or that they brought her up in a particular way. She may value Chinese culture or she may want to be "only American." She may also feel all of these things at once. In addition, Sue's attitudes and feelings may not always be what her behavior reflects. For example, she may feel positively about her family's Chinese heritage, but simultaneously act "more American" with her peers in response to their expectations. Some multiracial adolescents describe that the ways in which they see themselves at school are very different than the ways they see themselves at home. Developing a positive sense of identity will mean eventually integrating these contexts. This does not mean that identity will not change with different contexts, but rather that the adolescent does not have to feel that she is being only part of who she is.

Struggling with Family Meanings of Race and Ethnicity

Sometimes there may be unresolved issues about race and ethnicity within the immediate or extended family that affect the identity development of multiracial adolescents, such as familial discrimination. These questions and struggles may have always existed, but older adolescents (15 to 17) may be more willing than younger adolescents to make waves by actively questioning, challenging family understandings and/or breaking implicit taboos about what things will and will not be discussed. Even without obvious issues, multiracial adolescents frequently struggle with the meanings of their identities in regards to their relationships with individuals in their families as newly developed cognitive abilities of this developmental stage make these meanings more recognizable or salient to these adolescents. In addition, the

What Are You?: Voices of Mixed Race Young People
Pearl Fuyo Gaskins, Henry Holt, 1999

What Are You? is the result of Pearl Gaskins's years of in-depth interviews with 80 mixed race young people. In their own words—which are at times defiant, humorous, and insightful—they address issues such as dating, family life, prejudice, and racial identity. Combining interviews with poems, essays, and insights from experts, *What Are You?* reveals what it means to be living proof that America's ideas about race make no sense. The book includes an extensive bibliography, resource guide, and photographs of young people who contributed.
Learn more:
www.whatareyou.com

increased independence and attempts to define themselves separately from the family may increase the salience of questioning family meanings of race and ethnicity as they explore whether they will accept and claim these meanings for their own.

If Sue identifies more as Chinese, does that mean she cares less about her European American mother? If she refuses to identify as Chinese, how will her father feel? As a young woman, how does Sue negotiate how to identify with her mother as a woman, but one who is not Chinese American? Parents and extended family need to accept multiracial children as actively being a member of all cultures and multiple races. This can be challenging at times for parents whose own families of origin are monoracial or monocultural.

Monoracial and monocultural families may be more likely to emphasize the ways in which the family is similar and the children are like the parents in order to emphasize family cohesion and connection. Within a multiracial and multiethnic family to recognize and encourage identification with all ethnic, cultural, and racial backgrounds requires a recognition that family connection is rooted partly in difference: one's children are simultaneously similar to and very different than oneself. All the different parts together make the whole. For example, Sue is similar to her mother because both are women, yet different because her mother is not Chinese. However, the family would not be the same if Sue were not part of her mother and part of her father. The various family members are connected to each other not in spite of but partly because of their differences.

Actively Learning About Personal and Family Histories
Learning about the multiple ethnic and racial heritages of families can be one way that multiracial adolescents begin to understand themselves within social contexts. This kind of exploration can help provide a sense of belonging to the family and to a history of people that led to the current experience. Understanding how and why parents chose to marry may be part of creating models of dealing with being outside of social expectations related to race and ethnicity.

Negotiating Social Pressure
Multiracial adolescents may be pressured by their peers to

choose a single racial or ethnic identity or to exaggerate some behaviors seen as necessary to fit in with others. They may try to "pass" in order to decrease difficult feelings of exclusion or difference. They will need to deal with how others treat them and their expectations in relation to ethnicity and race. The pressure to pass may be subtle and may not include outright rejection or exclusion. For example, Sue's high school teacher may separate the class by perceived ethnic groups for a class exercise and include Sue in the White European American group, although Sue identifies herself as Chinese; Sue's teacher may also place her friend Jason who is multiracial of African descent in the African American group. Sue and Jason may respond by trying to be more like how others perceive them (e.g., to pass as White or as monoracial African American).

Peer groups are very important at this age and multiracial adolescents will want to find some way to belong. The social groups multiracial adolescents try to be a part of may encourage them to behave in ways that make them more similar and less different. For example, like many monoracial minority adolescents, Sue may try to immerse herself in her ethnic heritage and ethnic social groups. However, this may be difficult if the Asian group does not want to accept her because she is multiracial. The Asian group may actively reject her or they may accept her conditionally. She may be expected to "act more Chinese," to prove that she is culturally knowledgeable, to passively allow or even participate in putting down White European American culture, race, or people, and/or to deny or downplay her White European American racial or cultural heritage. Similarly, a White European American peer group may reject Sue because she is visibly a person of color. Like the Asian group, even if she is accepted by the White group, Sue may be expected to act more culturally European American, to passively endure racism (like jokes or comments) by other clique members or to deny or downplay her Asian ethnic and racial heritage. Multiracial adolescents who belong to more than one racial or ethnic minority group may also be expected to choose only one and may have similar experiences of being expected to deny or denigrate part of their heritage or to value one group over another. Sue and other multiracial adolescents will need to make constant decisions about whether they submit to or

resist these social pressures. They may make different decisions at different times and in different contexts as they explore the meaning and consequences of different approaches for their self-view and for their social relationships.

Dealing with Dating Taboos

For many multiracial 15- to 17-year-olds, the beginning of dating presents new challenges to their developing racial and ethnic identities that did not exist for them as younger children. As young children, interracial friendships may have been common place; however, interracial dating continues to be less common. For multiracial individuals, this means that they will almost always be in the minority, as it is often unusual for a multiracial individual to have the possibility of dating another multiracial individual of their same backgrounds.

Multiracial individuals frequently report that beginning to date brings up strong reactions in others about their multiracial status and background. Many teens of today's world think that race is not that much of an issue for them personally. They may know that race matters intellectually, but they somehow feel that their experience will be different, that their actual experience will not be affected by what is common to others like them. They may have a sudden and emotional awakening when subtle or not so subtle racial exclusion or stereotyping occurs around dating. This is often a critical moment when the ways in which others see them shift in a fundamental way as suddenly racial background is important, when before it was not: before they were accepted in various friendship circles, but now suddenly they are not acceptable for dating.

An example of this is Eileen, a Latina Irish girl who has always been popular in school but does not have a steady boyfriend. For school dances that traditionally involve the boy asking the girl, she finds that she is the last among her friends to get asked, although many others in her group are also single. Eileen is included on group dates, but seems to have difficulty being asked on solo dates. It is likely that Eileen is experiencing racial exclusion. Part of what can make these experiences particularly difficult is that in many cases it is impossible to know that this is the reason, particularly if race has not been a social issue in the past in relation to friendships. Eileen is then at risk for believing that there is something wrong with her individually that makes boys avoid dating her.

Dating also raises issues related to the interactions of late adolescents' multiple identities such as race, ethnicity, gender role, and sexual orientation, among others. Sue's identity as a multiracial Asian American and her identity as a lesbian may not integrate well in her social experiences. The few lesbians she knows are likely to be mostly White European American (depending on where she lives and goes to school) and, like the heterosexual youth described above, may unconsciously or consciously choose to date girls like them. Her issues related to developing racial and ethnic identities may not seem important or relevant to her lesbian friends, who are seeking connections around their difference as lesbians. Similarly, her Asian American friends (or her multiracial friends, if she has such a group) may not accept her lesbian identity. Sue will have to negotiate how each group defines not only the connecting group identity (lesbian or Asian American or multiracial), but also that group's judgments about other oppressed or stigmatized groups or statuses (race or sexual orientation) and Sue's membership in both groups.

Gender stereotypes applicable to particular racial or ethnic groups or to multiracial individuals may also become particularly salient in relation to dating. For example, negative stereotypes of African American men may become suddenly applied to a multiracial adolescent in ways that are new to him and that exclude him from dates with either African Americans or European Americans; or the exotic stereotype may lead to particular kinds of expectations of dating for a multiracial person of Asian descent. Multiracial teens may internalize these stereotypes or try on various different roles in healthy ways while they explore their options. For example, as a 13-year-old African American Korean boy, Sue's friend Jason had friends from many different ethnic backgrounds and paid little attention to stereotypes of African American men specifically. But as a 15-year-old, Jason began to hang out mostly with African American friends and did not date at all. When Jason was 16 he began to date and to present himself to girls in ways that specifically reflected his peer group's idea of African American masculine heritage. When he

was 17, Jason dated only Asian American girls, although he continued to consciously present himself in what he viewed as particularly African American ways. In this example, Jason's multiracial identity is being shaped in relation to his identity on the cusp of becoming a man and as a heterosexual. Jason is experimenting with different ways of connecting these identities in different social relationships. The complex issues of identity and exclusion that can arise for the first time for multiracial 15- to 17-year-olds entering the dating world are often just a glimpse of what is yet to come in the next life stage. For example, while interracial dating is less common than interracial friendships, it is often more acceptable than interracial marriage.

Recommendations for Teachers and Parents: Contributing to "Who do I want to be?"

When multiracial adolescents encounter adjustment difficulties, it may or may not be related to being multiracial. On the other hand, the experience of being multiracial and multiethnic may affect or shape the ways in which other challenges are met or addressed. Thus, while it is important to avoid assuming that any problem is rooted in race or ethnicity, it is also important to be knowledgeable about the issues and willing to explore possible connections. Research shows a relationship between ethnic identity and adjustment. Multiracial college students who asked the questions "Who am I?" and "What are my choices?" and who actively explored their options, and who made deliberate choices, choices and commitments to some identities and meanings, had more positive self-esteem, regardless of the specific choices they made, than those who made choices without exploring their options, or who had not made any choices. It is the process of search and commitment, rather than the final kind of identity that is most important. Supporting the process of exploration, evaluation, and choice is therefore a primary goal of those seeking to support multiracial adolescents.

Parents and teachers can help multiracial adolescents develop positive racial and ethnic identities in a number of ways:

1. Examine monoracial assumptions. Parents and teachers can help by making language inclusive and avoiding assumptions that people have only one identity or racial or ethnic reference.

Opening discussions about issues related to seemingly monoracial school/community groups and clubs may also be important.

2. Provide role models. Providing role models to multiracial adolescents can help them develop their own understanding and sense of belonging. Researching media figures, providing age-appropriate readings, and finding age-appropriate Web resources are some ways to find multiracial role models. Multiracial social/community groups are emerging across the country.

3. Help adolescents understand the social context of race and ethnicity, including the monoracial nature of this social context. This can help multiracial adolescents recognize that feelings of difference and exclusion are based in rigid ideas about race and racial purity and not related to any shortcoming of who they are as people. Teachers can help address peer exclusion and social pressures for multiracial adolescents by helping *all* students understand race and ethnicity, not just students of color. Parents can help adolescents understand how race can affect intimate relationship choices and how people can internalize race-biased ideas about who is suitable or desirable to date.

4. Understand identity development as a process and identity as a changing thing. Parents and teachers need to understand (and be tolerant of) the significant and frequent changes in adolescents' attitudes towards themselves and others. Parents and teachers can encourage multiracial adolescents to explore and learn about all of their ethnic and racial heritages, as well as the history and heritage of multiracial people within their referent groups.

5. Accept multiple (possibly simultaneous) identifications. Parents can communicate that they will accept and care about the adolescent regardless of how he or she chooses to identify (e.g., if he or she chooses to identify as similar to only one parent, or as multiracial and not similar to either, or simultaneously similar to both) and regardless of the race or ethnicity of their friends or partners. Parents and teachers can communicate an understanding of multiple identities and the importance of context.

Multiracial adolescents will need to negotiate the social challenges and categorizations of a historically segregated monoracial, monocultural society. This negotiation and the understanding that their experiences of exclusion are based in problematic ideas of race, rather than in themselves, are greatly facilitated by some understanding and preparation for these challenges by parents and teachers. Although kids are generally resilient, the issue is finding the environment and resources to help all children thrive to their greatest potential.

Did you know?

According to Census 2000, multiracial youth are disproportionately young:

Percentage of the single race population between the ages of 15 to 17 years old: **4.3%**

Percentage of the multiracial population between the ages of 15 to 17 years old: **5.5%**

Notes

1 G. K. Kich, "The Developmental Process of Asserting a Biracial, Bicultural Identity," in *Racially Mixed People in America*, ed. M. P. P. Root (Thousand Oaks, CA: Sage, 1992), 304-321.

2 To "pass" as something or someone that you are not, usually to avoid negative consequences and/or for some gain. For example, "That Black man often passes as White." See G. R. Daniel, "Passers and Pluralists: Subverting the Racial Divide," in *Racially Mixed People in America*, ed. M. P. P. Root (Thousand Oaks, CA: Sage, 1992), 91-107.

Matt
Korean + Norwegian +
French + German +
Irish + English +
Russian + Greek + ?

Toni
Black + Indonesian +
Native American

Antonio
Filipino + Spanish +
Norwegian + Honduran

MiXeD at the University of Washington and hi'brid at Seattle University

MiXeD and hi'brid are MAVIN Foundation-sponsored student organizations at the University of Washington and Seattle University dedicated to exploring the mixed race and transracial adoptee experience. We are two of nearly 50 similar organizations on college campuses across the U.S. and Canada that have sprung up over the past 20 years in response to a multiracial baby boom. In the single year since our founding, both organizations have hosted speakers, events, bone marrow drives, and other activities. This year, we worked together to host the MAVIN Foundation National Conference on the Mixed Race Experience.

It makes sense that college is often the first time that many of us have actively explored the meaning of being mixed or adopted across racial lines. As students venture away from the comfort of their families, friends, and hometowns for the first time, it's natural to explore new identities. A college campus may be more or less diverse than the neighborhoods where we grew up. It may be more or less common to be mixed race or transracially adopted. But the fact that it is different, combined with our often newly-gained independence, often helps us reevaluate how we perceive ourselves.

College is a defining time, and although our respective experiences vary as much as our diverse heritages, we've also recognized shared themes. One theme is simply the result of our blurring lines of race and ethnicity on a campus and in a society that still forces people to identify monoracially. In our group meetings, we discuss how this assumption impacts our lives and informs our decisions to seek resources to celebrate who we are as multiracial and transracially

adopted people.

In our meetings, it is always interesting to see the divergent opinions that exist, and to witness the varying reasons why people attend. Since heritage organizations are popular on many campuses, students have great opportunities to explore different communities. Some of us choose to identify with all, only one, or even none of our ethnicities. Some of us reject outside definition, embrace it or remain unsure. The experience of figuring out one's identity can prove daunting to people who may have grown up feeling they are the "only ones" trying to contemplate and come to terms with their unique backgrounds.

Multiracial organizations provide a platform for students to explore myriad aspects of the multiracial experience. We have learned many students have never had a supportive environment to consider race and negotiate their racial identities. Interacting with people who share similar backgrounds can be simultaneously eye-opening, empowering, and cathartic.

Clubs such as MiXeD and hi'brid aren't confined to multiracial and transracially adopted people exploring their identities. Many students just want an avenue to discuss various issues and exchange ideas with other students. Their own lack of knowledge related to multiracialism has made them curious and eager to acquire more information. Multiracial clubs on college campuses validate the mixed race experience and help to generate curiosity with individuals who may otherwise never have given the idea much thought.

Testimonial

Chapter 12

Contextual Factors Affecting Identity Among Mixed Heritage College Students

Kendra R. Wallace, Ph.D.

This chapter explores contextual influences on identity development among mixed heritage college students from an anthropological perspective. The transition from high school to college represents a rite of passage for young adults, many of whom are leaving their families and communities for the first time. Freshmen and sophomores acclimating to campus environments continue to be engaged in the development of their social identities through their interactions with peers, yet often apart from family.

Mixed heritage students face unique identity issues within the microclimate of the college campus, where interethnic and interracial group relations take on a heightened intensity.[1] The common emphasis placed on group solidarity within higher education contexts can be particularly significant for mixed heritage students, whose experiences within a collective provide vital learning opportunities that inform how they will identify with the community.[2] Mixed heritage youth may encounter biases within their heritage communities due to their minority, majority, or multiple ancestries. They may also experience cultural clashes, which can impact their sense of legitimacy and belonging within the group. Furthermore, identity politics at work on college campuses may direct opportunities for identification and participation within a community. The next section provides a brief overview

of the theory framing this chapter, followed by a discussion of common processes affecting the identity development of younger mixed heritage college students.

Theoretical Framework

The approach to mixed heritage identity taken in this chapter draws heavily from sociocultural theories of human identity and development. Such theories help us explore more precisely the individual, flexible, and yet collective nature of social identities. Specifically, these theories allow us to approach identity development as a joint social activity that emerges out of a negotiation process between the individual and the reference group.

First, it is important to make a clear distinction between ethnicity and race and between ethnic and racial identity, even though these concepts can clearly influence one another. The terms race and ethnicity are often used synonymously out of confusion or for theoretical ease, but they are built upon fundamentally distinct ideas. An ethnic group is a social group whose members share ancestry and specific cultural features based on common geographic, national, and sometimes religious origins. A racial group is perceived as having a common biological heritage, umbrellas multiple ethnic groups, and determines membership socially (ascription) according to appearance (phenotype), by racial ancestry (genotype) or both.[3] However, race is socially constructed and has no basis in science, although it remains an important social marker and structuring force of identity.[4]

Ethnic *identity* is the dimension of a person's sense of self that develops out of an understanding of one's membership within an ethnic group, and the meaning that the membership conveys.[5] Ethnic identity also involves the individual's acquisition of the cultural and linguistic features representative of a group.[6] Racial *identity* refers to that part of a person's self-concept that is grounded in her/his experiences as a member of a broadly perceived racial group. Race plays a dominant role in racially segregated societies, where the imposition of racialized identities overshadows the intricacies of cultural differences. Nonetheless, racial and ethnic identities are developed along a two-way street; that is, these identities are not merely imposed by outsiders, but collectively worked out both by the individual and the group.

Often left unexamined, however, is the role of culture and how it influences ethnic identity, which requires a consideration of enculturation. Enculturation is a process that involves transmitting (by the group) and acquiring (by the individual) complex cultural frames of reference which guide how and why we do what we do, and how we see ourselves.[7] Gee's Discourse theory helps us to think more concisely about the relationship between ethnic identity formation and enculturation. A Discourse is like a cultural framework that consists of the specific building blocks, such as knowledge, ideas, worldviews, behaviors, etc., common to a group of people.[8][9] Such frameworks are shared yet flexible, guiding people's interactions and helping to maintain group boundaries by penalizing individuals who stray too far from its course, most often by labeling these individuals as outcasts, misfits, eccentrics, or other such derogatory titles.

When applied to the study of mixed heritage identities, Gee's discussion between *acquired* and *learned* cultural frameworks is particularly useful. A child acquires her primary framework, or culture, *unconsciously* as she grows up within a specific ethnic group, and it is within this community where a person's core social identities are established. Such an apprenticeship process allows the child to master the framework inadvertently and become culturally fluent within the group over a sustained period of time.[10] For example, how a person talks, turns a phrase, gestures, positions the body, wears clothes, interacts, evaluates the world, and sees herself socially all reflect a particular cultural framework that is shaped over time by the evolving life-ways of the sponsoring ethnic group/s.

By contrast, a secondary cultural framework is one that is consciously learned at a later age, outside the home in public arenas such as schools, churches, and other social organizations. Since a secondary framework is learned consciously, it is more difficult for newcomers to achieve a native-like fluency in it. For example, schools in the United States tend to project mainstream cultural frameworks in what is valued in the curriculum, what kinds of interactions and behavior patterns are expected from students, the desired form and use of language, how intelligence is displayed and perceived, how schooling and teachers should be viewed and approached, and how schoolwork should be handled in the home.

The cultural framework concept is important for understanding how cultural fluency affects students' participation and identification with their heritage groups, especially within minority communities. We cannot presume mixed heritage individuals grow up participating equally within all of their heritage communities, since where they are raised and by whom they are raised are quite variable, even within the same family. This means that students will come to college with varying degrees of cultural fluency in their heritage communities. Some may be newcomers to a group and will have to consciously learn the culture if they are to participate successfully in it; others may be novices who are unevenly proficient at the culture and must work at becoming more fluent; and a few may have had opportunities to become fully fluent in each culture. Depending on their experiences, how mixed heritage students identify with their heritage communities will range from the symbolic to the more "lived" or concrete.

Finally, college entrance can be considered a "critical learning period," or what George and Louise Spindler refer to as a time of cultural compression.[11] As they make this major life transition, mixed heritage youth leave their families to enter a social context in which the expectations and roles related to group membership are especially concentrated. Cultural legitimacy and loyalty can become increasingly important in such spaces, where these students' physical appearance, interactional style, or ancestry can stigmatize them as foreign, culturally suspect, or even invisible to other group members. The imposition of group norms of identification and solidarity are often employed, reinforced, and challenged on college campuses, encouraging new dimensions of growth in the developmental trajectories of students' ethnic and racial identities.

Identity Themes

The following section explores core themes related to ethnic and racial identity formation among mixed heritage students in college, and draws upon the experiences of university students in northern California.[12] The students cited are undergraduates or graduates attending Lakeside University, a private institution located in a suburban community in the San Francisco Bay Area. The San Francisco Bay Area boasts one of the most significant populations of mixed heritage individuals: slightly more than twice the national average.[13] Of the approximately sixty-five-hundred undergraduates at Lakeside, the University reports a student body that is 51 percent European American, 24 percent Asian American, 11 percent Latino American, eight percent African American, five percent "Other" and two percent Native American Indian.[14]

As students enter into campus life, they may come to realize that their mixed heritage can affect how they are perceived and welcomed by their peers. Students may encounter questions about their backgrounds by curious people, or by those trying to determine if they are group members. Mixed heritage students also may experience testing by peers within their heritage communities, ranging from the subtle to the overt, from the innocuous to the acrimonious. Such testing takes place in many ways and serves to reinforce the group's borders and core identity as members seek to establish varying degrees of cultural citizenship among those who can lay claim to membership.[15] At issue are the loyalty and legitimacy of mixed heritage students, who may be seen by their minority peers as culturally "suspect" because of their physical appearance (looking unrelated to the

group or "mixed"), mixed ancestry, non-traditional name, and/or lack of cultural fluency (acting, sounding, or somehow seeming "different").

Within minority communities, in particular, students may find that looking "mixed" affects their peer relationships. Amanda Wilson[16], who is Jamaican and Chinese American, recalls learning quite explicitly about the politics of skin color and hair within the African American community:

> [My] freshman year... [I heard comments like] "those girls who think they're White," and "those European-looking girls" and I was sitting right there... Immediately when I got to college I wore my hair in a bun every day because I didn't want to feel like... starting off on the wrong foot with anybody...And also the light-skinned thing...always added to the hair...

Still other students who are more ambiguous in appearance may be completely invisible within a minority community unless their parentage is made explicit. For Marta Elizondo (who is Italian, German, and Mexican American) and Sandy Zubaida (who is Iranian and European American), their names provide a vital connection to their minority heritage:

> I get asked [what I am] all the time... [but] a lot more...in the Latino community than anywhere else... Probably because I'm fair skinned and because of the way I dress and stuff, too, I'm not typical[ly] Mexican. If they see my name then I'm [seen as] Latina right away...[Marta]

> There was an announcement [for] a Persian club meeting... so I decided I'd go...This guy was looking at me the whole time like "You're in the wrong room!" I had to leave early...and he said, "Wait! What's your name?" I told him and he [asked], "Are you half? What are you?" I think he was full (Persian). [Sandy]

Too often, mixed heritage students who are part White are

presumed to be "of color" and, therefore, readily identified with and by their minority heritage community. This assumption overlooks the experiences of many students, including those of diverse minority heritage.

Mixed heritage status may also influence how warmly students are received by their peers, as Elizondo and Jocelyn Saghal, who is Swiss and East Indian, illustrate:

> Well, there's a...definite Latina faction [in my program]... And I normally do identify with the Latina culture. But this group has pushed me somehow on the outside and part of it I'm feeling is my mix[ed heritage]...Sometimes I have the feeling that I don't have the full experience of being full Latina...[Elizondo]

> Last year I went to a South Asian [group]; I'd never been to one. But I really didn't feel welcome in that group at all. It's very subtle...very insidious, that [message], "Well, you're not pure Indian. You haven't lived [in India] for a long time." That's really problematic for me [to] feel like [they're thinking], "Both parents have to be Indian," or "You can't really claim this, 'cause you're not really Indian." [It was] just very subtle things, [like] not being welcome in their conversation, body language, and innuendoes. [Jocelyn]

Despite how they identify, students may find that they must prove their cultural citizenship because their mixed heritage makes their authenticity questionable in the eyes of their peers.

In addition to physical appearance, name, and racial heritage, peers within minority heritage communities may also pick up on the more subtle markers of ethnic identity related to the group's shared cultural framework. How a student acts, dresses, or sounds are all cultural elements that can have heightened importance within ethnic group participation on college campuses. If they are fluent, or relatively fluent, in the group's cultural framework, mixed heritage students may find themselves unconsciously shifting how they interact to match the style of their peers. But students who are not as culturally fluent may feel pressure to consciously change their behavior in order to fit in or prove their citizenship. Realizing the important role that language plays in ethnic group membership, Donna Tesh, who is White and Panamanian, describes trying to alter her dialect:

> My roommate tells me I'm terrible at [code switching] because I didn't grow up speaking Black vernacular or anything like that. I grew up in a white-bread type of area... I don't really try [anymore]. But there [were] definitely times, mostly during my college years, where I would veer a little bit in that direction. It was more a thing of when I would see people and think about what they were thinking about [me]...how I dress or how I act.

Some mixed heritage students may enroll in courses to learn a heritage language that wasn't spoken at home, or unknowingly or knowingly attempt to code-switch to a non-standard dialect when talking with their peers. In sum, the level of cultural fluency that students have within their heritage communities can facilitate or hamper their peer relationships. Newcomers may feel the need to prove their citizenship, even emphasizing some aspects of their identity while playing down others, in order to establish a sense of efficacy and belonging. More culturally fluent students may not feel an identical sense of pressure to prove their authenticity or loyalty.

Within the mainstream, part White students may find their mixed heritage to be a source of curiosity. Sandy Zubaida, introduced earlier in the chapter, feels that Whites often inquire about her "unusual" last name and her "interesting eyes," the two features that suggest she isn't only White. Females, especially, are likely to have their mixed ancestry explicitly sexualized as they are praised and validated for their "exotic" looks. For part White students who are more clearly "of color," rigid standards of Whiteness can prevent them from being viewed as White by their mainstream peers regardless of their cultural experiences or racial heritage. But these seemingly inflexible standards of Whiteness are also misleading, as noted by Kay Meki, who is Japanese and European American:

You know, you're [with your] friend, you're in a car and an Asian driver drives by and the[y] say something like "Nip driver!" They kind of look at you. They say that without even thinking, and then they kind of look at you...and then [say] "Oh, but you're ok, you're not like them."

Some part White students note that they feel their White peers relegate them to a middle ground, not White and not quite a "real" minority, sometimes in the guise of implicitly racist comments, like the one above. Finally, mixed heritage students may be designated the resident ethnic expert by their White peers, or by White faculty. Spotlighting a lone student for their ethnic heritage is unfair for anyone, but it can be particularly awkward for mixed heritage students, some of whom may not feel qualified to speak for the group because of their multiple ancestries.

Dating can be politically-charged, as well, raising complex issues of identity and allegiance for some mixed heritage university students. If a person is perceived as dating "outside" of her or his ethnoracial group, there can be various implications depending on the sociohistorical relationship and relative statuses of the involved groups. Students may find a lack of support from friends and family members alike if they choose to date someone who is seen as from a lower ethnoracial status, as Marta recalls:

When we were in high school, my sister started dating a Black guy and my dad had a fit. My sister and I were very, very surprised and upset because we had been taught all this time that there's no barrier, or whatever. This, coupled with the fact that both my parents were [in a] mixed marriage, and my grandparents were [a] mixed marriage. And here my dad was doing the same hypocritical thing that my grandfather had done to my parents! There was a Black guy that I was playing volleyball with, and I remember my dad being very edgy about that, too, like, "Well, are you going out with him?" But I thought that very strange when all these years we had been brought up to counter that.

Peers from minority communities may view a mixed heritage

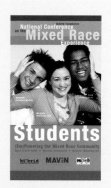

Multiracial Campus Organizations and the Pan Collegiate Conference on the Mixed Race Experience

Since 1996, multiracial students from across the country have converged annually to celebrate the mixed race experience. Organized and attended by students representing some of the nearly 50 mixed heritage student organizations on campuses from coast to coast, the pan collegiate conference provides a unique forum for students to connect and share their experiences. In 2003, students converged in Seattle to create a national coalition of student organizations to help shape policy and guide the mixed race student movement.

Learn more:

www.mavinfoundation.org/conference

member who dates outside a particular community as demonstrating a lack of commitment to, or low regard for, the group regardless of the person's heritage or ethnic upbringing. Such assumptions about an individual's motivation can lead to increased testing and marginalization within the community. Heterosexual mixed heritage students, especially females, also may find that who they date, or specifically, the ethnoracial background of who they date, is of great interest to their single heritage peers, especially within minority communities. Here, community surveillance of students' romantic lives can take on increased importance to the maintenance of the group depending on the ethnoracial status of the partner and, implicitly, that of their prospective children.

Conclusion

The pronounced emphasis of ethnic and racial group membership on many campuses can make college a critical period for learning about the politics of identity for all students. Peer interactions are critical avenues through which students continue to shape their ethnic and racial identities. Especially for mixed heritage students, peer interactions invite opportunities for cultural compression as members of the heritage community work to reinforce its boundaries. Such compressions may have a marginalizing effect, making clear that a student's mixed heritage matters within mainstream and minority communities. Furthermore, the relative fluency students have in the cultural frameworks of their heritage communities can profoundly affect their sense of efficacy and belonging within these groups. The advent of multiracial and ethnic student organizations on university campuses over the past two decades has created a critical space for mixed heritage individuals in which to address these issues. Not only do these student organizations provide an opportunity for mixed heritage students to meet and discuss pertinent identity issues, these groups also establish a visible forum in which to address interracial and ethnic topics impacting the social, political, and curricular life of the broader campus.

Mixed heritage students are an incredibly diverse population and we must take great care in our attempts to understand their experiences. Uncovering trends in student attitudes or ethnic

and racial identification become insightful only when we can understand the experiences and the emotions cultivating them. This chapter tries to show how identity development is imbedded in the social relations of schools. Educators and administrators, therefore, must consider the formal and informal curriculum, as well as the climate of campus relations in their efforts to create contexts that are critically supportive of all types of human diversity. ▌

Did you know?

According to Census 2000, multiracial youth are disproportionately young:

Percentage of the single race population between the ages of 18 to 20 years old: **4.3%**

Percentage of the multiracial population between the ages of 18 to 20 years old: **5.4%**

Notes

1 S. Hurtado, J. Milem, A. Clayton-Pederson, and W. Allen, "Enhancing Campus Climates for Racial/Ethnic Diversity: Educational Policy and Practice," *The Review of Higher Education* 21(3) (1998), 279-302.

2 R. Miller, "The Human Ecology of Multiracial Identity," in *Racially Mixed People in America,* ed. M. P. P. Root (Thousand Oaks, CA: Sage, 1992).

3 R. M. Burkey, *Ethnic and Racial Groups: The Dynamics of Dominance* (San Francisco: Benjamin Cummings Publishing Company, 1978).

4 M. Omi and H. Winant, *Racial Formation in the United States: from the 1960s to the 1980s* (New York: Routledge and Kegan Paul, 1986).

5 J. S. Phinney, B. T. Lochner, and R. Murphy. "Ethnic Identity Development and Psychological Adjustment in Adolescence," in *Ethnic Issues in Adolescent Mental Health*, eds. A. R. Stiffman and L. E. Davis (Newbury Park, CA: Sage, 1990), 53-72.

6 R. M. Burkey, *Ethnic and Racial Groups* (1978).

7 H. F. Wolcott, "The Anthropology of Learning," in *Education and Cultural Process,* ed. G. D. Spindler (Prospect Heights, IL: Waveland Press, 1987), 26-52.

8 A Discourse with a capital "D" is a set of values, attitudes, ways of doing and living in the world that is shared by a social network, as opposed to small "d" discourses that are "connected stretches of conversation." See: J. P. Gee, *Social Linguistics and Literacies: Ideologies in Discourses* (New York: Falmer, 1990), 142.

9 J. P. Gee, *The Social Mind: Language, Ideology and Social Practice* (New York: Bergin & Garvey, 1992).

10 J. Lave and E. Wenger, *Situated Learning: Legitimate Peripheral Participation* (Cambridge, UK: Cambridge University Press, 1990).

11 G. Spindler and L. Spindler, "Do Anthropologists Need Learning Theory?" in *Education and Cultural Process,* ed. G. D. Spindler (Prospect Heights, IL: Waveland Press, 1987), 53-69.

12 The stories presented here were gathered from in-depth, expressive autobiographical interviews with nine college students of first-generation mixed heritage. At the time of the interviews, each participant was at least twenty-one years of age and, therefore, able to speak concisely about their initial college experiences.

13 U.S. Census Bureau: "Ranking Tables for Counties by Race Alone, Race Alone or in Combination, and Two or More Races Populations." Summary File 1, PHC-T-14. 2000.

14 Demographic data for graduate students were not available for the year when this study was conducted.

15 The term "cultural citizenship" is borrowed from the work of Renato Rosaldo, but here its use is not a reference to issues of diversity and difference in relation to nationhood.

16 Please note that I have attempted to retain the ethnic styles of the subjects' names through the pseudonyms selected.

Cindy Howe
Age: 25
Racial/Ethnic Heritage: Korean and Black

My parents met when my father was in the U.S. Army and stationed in Korea. He was 27 and my mother was 17. My mom thought that the U.S. was the land of milk and honey, but my father's low rank and wages forced her to clean officer's houses to support us. Cultural differences and my father's infidelity made their marriage impossible—they separated when I was only one year old.

This initial disruption was the first of many. I moved nine times and attended eight different schools. Between the ages of 1 and 4, I don't know where I lived or who took care of me. I know that I went to kindergarten in Idaho with my dad until he tried to put me into foster care. My mother intervened and put me on a plane to live with my Korean "Auntie." I wouldn't see my mom again for almost 20 years. When I was 10, I moved to Germany to live with my father again. His wife hated me and always told me that she would kill me. When I overheard him tell my stepmother that he was being deployed to the Persian Gulf, I told a teacher about my stepmother's abuse and threats. In a way, I put myself into foster care. My dad simply signed the papers and didn't fight to keep me. At 14, my stepmother died and I moved back in with him. Our relationship was turbulent and I moved out to live with my boyfriend. When his abuse broke my collarbone, I drove to Seattle—as far from him as I could. Four years after moving to Seattle, I got a call from an Atlanta hospital that had found my father sick and homeless. His hypertensive vascular dementia, a condition he developed during the Gulf War, had worsened. At 21, I became his legal guardian.

Growing up, neither of my parents ever talked about identity issues. Preoccupied by the disruptions in my life, I never talked to them about being multiracial or about how much I suffered alone. I've always been surrounded by people who had low expectations for me. Going through many difficult situations in my life has made me realize that I don't want to repeat my parents' mistakes. Honestly, with everything they did I'm trying to do the complete opposite in order to stay out of trouble. Despite all of the disruptions, I am a resilient woman. Today I have an American Ethnic Studies degree from the University of Washington and am the first person in my family to graduate from college. It's funny how when kids turn out well a lot of the credit goes to the parents. I don't agree with that. Sometimes they get credit for something they didn't do.

When I heard the sparse mention of Black accomplishments in high school, I felt a little pride. I didn't start really having a dialogue about being multiracial until college. As an adult, I have been able to explore and pursue multiracial books and organizations, even working at a multiracial nonprofit organization. Today I am appreciative of the resources available to multiracial people and families and am proud to have contributed to them. I am hopeful that parents and educators will seek out these resources to offer multiracial kids, what every child needs—a home free of major disruptions, and parents and professionals who are equipped to address their needs.

Testimonial

Chapter 13

When and How Families Can Disrupt Mixed Race Identity

Shelly Tomishima, Ph.D.

The family is generally the foundation of one's environment while growing up, regardless of racial or ethnic background. Most people depend upon their families to provide for them and to teach them about a variety of things in life, including values, socialization, and culture. Many interracial families do a terrific job providing for and teaching children. However, other interracial families may encounter obstacles that make negotiating mixed race identity difficult for young people. Although this chapter specifically focuses on disruptions in mixed race families and their impact on mixed race children's identities, it does not necessarily assert that dysfunction is more prevalent in mixed race families than in the general population.

The family can be pivotal in helping to shape the children's identities. It can have a positive impact by helping children to understand the racial system in which we live, to raise children in ways that make them feel good about themselves, and to bolster their resilience to adversity.

Despite the fact that most children are raised in families that don't have multiracial role models, research has demonstrated that eventually, children develop ways of understanding and coping with racism that not even their parents understand. Although mixed race parents often seek advice on how to raise the children culturally, they often overlook the fact that their children's mixed race identity will develop over time and is not just a one-time decision about what cultures to expose them to.

This chapter will specifically look at the variables within the family that were found to have a significant impact on biracial/biethnic identity development, including familial reaction to interracial marriage, familial strife, parental identities of the dominant caretaker, siblings, extended family, and familial reaction to biracial offspring. Each of these variables within the family context will be described and an example of its impact on mixed race identity development will be provided. The examples provided are just one person's account of how his or her mixed race identity was impacted. The information provided is not intended to reflect all mixed race people's experiences, but to provides guideposts to assist others in understanding how some may experience the process of mixed race identity development. The information given is based upon research conducted by Tomishima[1] and is corroborated by findings emerging from the contemporary research on mixed race.[2][3]

Familial Reactions to Interracial Marriage

The families' reactions to an interracial marriage were often the first obstacle for participants' parents, as interracial couples, to overcome. Participants revealed the prejudices in the White and non-White sides of their families.

A few participants revealed that their parents eloped because the familial reactions to the interracial marriages were so profound. Hyumne explained why her parents eloped:

> My mom's parents totally protested, so my parents eloped. Once I was born, their relationship was somewhat impaired, but I don't think my mom's parents ever felt completely comfortable with my dad. I learned later that my father's mother wasn't happy he was going to marry a Caucasian, but I never heard her say anything about my mom.

Families of color often encouraged marriage within their culture. Tomiko related what occurred between her mother and her maternal grandmother: "Her mom used to always tell her, you have to marry Japanese, you have to marry Japanese."

On the other hand, White families were also frequently opposed to interracial marriages. Rian said that her White grandmother did not like her Japanese father. "We kind of think my grandma's a little bit prejudiced against my dad."

In some cases, neither side of the family was in favor of the idea of an interracial marriage. Hapa said: "My Chinese grandfather muttered for days something to the effect of, '400 million Chinese men in the world and she has to marry a White guy?!'" Hapa also admitted,: "My White grandparents weren't too happy either." Although families may adapt over time and learn to eventually accept interracial relationships, many interracial couples appear to continue to initially experience racism and prejudice within their families.

Familial Strife

One of the most surprising and significant findings was patterns of strife in these interracial families. Without exception, all of the participants revealed significant conflict within their families, including divorce, conflict due to racial remarriage, addiction, an absent parent, and abuse.[4] Moreover, participants frequently reported multiple types of familial strife within each family. For example, one participant reported that his father was abusive, an alcoholic, and largely "emotionally" absent, which profoundly impacted his life and identity development.

The most striking aspect of the familial strife theme among participants was that they reported these issues, but most were hesitant to elaborate on them. The most frequent issue that occurred in these families was divorce. However, it was unclear if the rates of divorce in interracial families differs substantially from those of the general public, and more research is needed to compare rates of divorce.

Having an absent parent, physically or emotionally, was also a common experience. As a result, one participant said:

> At an early age, I learned to be responsible for my life and decisions. I have regrets about that and the moments when advice could have saved me from bad decisions, but I am also a mentally stronger person for it.

Occasionally, a parent was absent because he or she was a workaholic. In most cases of workaholism, the father was the workaholic.

People discussed the impact of having one parent as their dominant caretaker. MJ talked about how it was being a Black/White racially mixed male raised by his White mother:

> I grew up basically around a bunch of women, my mom, her twin sister, and my aunts. I've never seen my dad. I never met my dad until recently. I found out where he lives...and saw some more pictures besides the one picture I've always had of him. And also, my grandma. So I grew up around...a bunch of White women in the middle of Black neighborhoods.

Rosie clarified how being raised by her Mexican father impacted her gender identity: "I think like a man. I think sometimes I feel like a man, but I can't let anybody think that I am vulnerable, or that I have needs...It is really hard for me to cry in front of other people."

Several participants reported that various family members were alcoholics (e.g., mother, father, grandfather, and aunt). Another issue that occurred in mixed families was abuse (i.e., participants described the abuse that their parents endured). Furthermore, one participant reported that her father was a "grumpy anger-holic."

Two participants talked about how race was an issue and caused conflict during a remarriage within the family. One participant shared: "Then...my mom remarried an older Black man who, because of his own experiences with racism, hated anything White, including me most of the time."

Despite all of these issues being disclosed, it became unclear if there is a higher rate of family strife within interracial families or if the rates of strife were just comparable to those observed in the general population. Being a mixed race family does not necessarily mean that strife is going to occur. It simply means that the family may have different obstacles to consider, address, and overcome in the family's and children's development. The resulting impact that the familial strife has on a mixed race child may depend upon the supports around the child and how the child interprets familial incidents (e.g., "Dad is grumpy because grandma and grandpa don't like that mom and I look different" versus "Dad is having a bad day at work"). Supportive parents may assist children in making sense of what is going on in their families, in avoiding misinterpretations, and in derailing their mixed race identity. In addition to parents being supportive of the children's identity process, their own racial and ethnic identity may play a role in the youths' identity process.

Parental Identities

When talking about their families, participants reported that their parents' identities impacted their own identity development. Frequently, participants with one White biological parent talked about their non-White parent and his or her racial identity (or lack thereof). A variety of experiences impacted participants' parents, including having an "American" identity, having a Jewish identity, experiencing feelings of shame, being punished for speaking their native languages, and an emergence of

Counseling Multiracial Families
Wehrly, Kenney & Kenney, Sage Publications, 1999

Counseling Multiracial Families addresses a population that has been neglected in counseling literature. It includes a history of racial mixing in the United States, the special needs and strengths of multiracial families, the challenges of interracially married couples, and the social and cultural issues related to parenting multiracial children. Biracial identity development research is translated into counseling practice with children, adolescents and adults in multiracial families.

parental identity as an adult.

Hapa commented on how his parents identified primarily as American and how that affected him:

They were definitely American. All those cultural differences were just amusing little anecdotes to be melted away. I basically grew up without race in my home. I was not made to be ashamed of what I was; it just wasn't supposed to be a big issue. So most of my culture has been acquired as an adult. My mother now tells me that she wishes they had given me a Chinese name and some more culture.

Aisha talked about the impact of Judaism in her father's life and her life:

Probably if my father had identified as White, and not Jewish, I'd do the same. But he very consciously brought Judaism to the forefront of his life when I was about 10 years old. In doing so, he brought it to the forefront of my life, too.

Rian provided a moving story about how her father was punished for speaking his native tongue.

When my dad was growing up...my grandpa didn't want [him] to learn Japanese, because of...World War II and...all the negative experiences they had, as my grandparents, because they are second generation.

Alma illustrated the feelings of shame that her father carried throughout his life:

I found out that my dad didn't really want to speak Spanish in the house. He got out of the barrio. He moved away from his family. He wanted a new life, and basically he never realized as a kid that he was a minority.

Despite themes of shame, embarrassment, and an initial push to move away from their minority culture, some participants discussed how their parents later came back to embrace their cultures. Alma portrayed how her father's identity as a person of color is now emerging as an adult: "My dad lately has kind of come, through the emergence of my identity, he has done the same. I think...I made him aware of the fact that he has repressed that part of him for so long." In spite of parents' impact on youths' mixed race identity, participants also discussed differences between themselves and how their siblings racially identify themselves.

Siblings

Two participants revealed that they have siblings whom racially identify in a different way than they do. In both cases in which siblings were discussed, they shared that their siblings identified as White. Hapa noted how his sister identified: "My older sister identifies as White for all intents and purposes." In the following explanation, Rian first disclosed how she identified herself on applications. Then she depicted how her sister's identity differs from the rest of the siblings in her family:

Now I just do Japanese American and that's been kind of hard in my family, because I have an older sister, she looks...she doesn't look as much Japanese as I do, but uh, she claims more White than we do. And the rest of our family, we kind of get upset with her.

Mixed race people often lack parental role models on how to negotiate their racial identity, but siblings often do not provide role models for the identity that would be congruent for a younger sibling. In addition to the immediate family members, relatives in the extended family also may be influential on a youth's identity development.

Extended Family

When asking about extended families, participants discussed and contrasted both sides of their extended families (both the non-Caucasian White and the White sides of their families).

Several participants mentioned that interactions with each side of their extended families were very different. Bill explained:

> [They are] very, very, very dissimilar. On my mom's side, I had one uncle, [and] two cousins, and they are all just... as White as can be...[My dad's side is] completely different....there is a park over here...and we rented the park out, because we had to. [There were] 200 and something people in the family. My dad...is the third youngest out of like...15 or 16 I think. I mean, we just have a ton of...aunts, uncles, cousins, whatever, and it is just amazing, at least in that way...We kind of jokingly...[say that] my brother and I are like chalk and sand [(laughs)], when we go to these things.

A few participants indicated that they had "adopted" family members, which were actually close friends of the family. Aisha illustrated how she broadly defined extended family:

> My extended family includes family members outside of my immediate core, as well as people that have been adopted into our family over the years. I love family. I feel like they hold pieces of my past that I can't remember because they cared for me when I was little and did their best to raise me. They continue to "raise" me by supporting me with phone calls and birthday cards, invitations to come and visit, appearances at my special events, like graduations and wedding receptions.

Aisha also revealed how there was racial segregation within her family: "The flip side is that there is not a single person on my mom's side who is not Black or a single person on my dad's side who is not White."

Different sides of the family may impact mixed race identity based upon a wide variety number of variables, including where the family lives, what part of the extended family is close to them, the neighboring cultures and communities, the nature of familial relationships (e.g., a close relationship between

Love's Revolution: Interracial Marriage
Maria P. P. Root, Ph.D., Temple University Press, 2001

In the last quarter of the 20th century, interracial relationships and marriages have steadily multiplied. In *Love's Revolution: Interracial Marriage*, more than 100 vignettes give a contemporary view of committed interracial relationships. Through interviews with more than 175 people, Maria P. P. Root identifies the changes over the last 25 years that have allowed the interracial landscape to flourish. In her book, she documents how families function like businesses: some like small franchises, while others are like corporate empires. She also offers ten truths about contemporary interracial relationships.

maternal grandmother and mother versus strained relationship between paternal grandparents and father). In addition to the extended family's reactions to the interracial marriage, families also have to deal with the family's reactions to the mixed race children.

Familial Reactions to Biracial Offspring

An interesting pattern emerged with regard to how families reacted toward the biracial/biethnic participants as the offspring of interracial marriages. Without exception, all of the Black/White participants reported being shunned by their White grandparents, at least initially. MJ explained what occurred to him in his family:

> My [White] grandfather shunned my mom and me because he was pretty racist in his upbringing, um, but through the years he got over that and accepted me and my mom...and put my mom back in his will. So he went through a lot of change, but I know he was pretty disappointed when I was first born, as I was the first of many biracial children to be born in the family.

The remainder of the participants (Asian/White, and Latino or Latina/White) clarified that their families generally reacted toward them with love. Alma said: "As far as my other grandparents, they were just like the typical grandparents. Always loving, never...the Mexican-ness in me was never addressed. It just didn't exist." This pattern warrants additional research to determine if the process of Black/White mixed race people is distinctly different in comparison to other racial mixes.

Conclusion

Our families indeed impact our early experiences and likely shape our subsequent identity development. However, interracial families often have unique experiences as a result of having to deal with the reactions of the people of different races within their families. As previously noted, familial strife, what parent raises a child, and his or her identity impacts the children's identity development. In addition, the extended family's reactions to the marriage and mixed race offspring may impact the youth's mixed race identity, with some siblings even identifying differently. Although some of the variables contributing to biracial/biethnic identity development are beginning to be identified, additional research is needed to develop further understanding of the contributions of these variables, their possible interaction, and how they may affect mixed race identity development.

Notes:

1 S. A. Tomishima, *Factors and Experiences in Biracial and Biethnic Identity Development*, Dissertation. University of Utah (2000).

2 G. Kich, "The Developmental Process of Asserting a Biracial, Bicultural Identity," in *Racially Mixed People in America*, ed. M. P. P. Root (Newbury Park: Sage, 1992).

3 M. P. P. Root, "Experiences and Processes Affecting Racial Identity Development: Preliminary Results from the Biracial Sibling Project," *Cultural Diversity and Mental Health* 4 (1998), 237-247.

4 The sample that this qualitative study was based on included 15 participants and may not necessarily be reflective of the mixed race population at large.

Michael Alto
Age: 19
Racial/Ethnic Heritage: Filipino and Dutch

If I could choose one word to describe myself, I would choose the word different. "Different" not only describes my multiculturalism and sexual orientation, but also describes my family and my early childhood. Ever since I was younger, my life has defied all forms of conformity. The sense of being different and the feeling of not belonging have been difficult on my confidence and self-esteem, but it has made me a strong and independent individual of whom I am proud today.

During my childhood, while still forming my identity, my family was always a source of intrigue for me. My father was Filipino and my mother identified as biracial because she was part Dutch. Looking at my family, I noticed a variety of skin shades and facial features. My father had the darkest skin of all of us, while my mother was very fair. My sisters and I ranged from White to a tanned brown. Some of us had dark and flat noses, while the rest of us had lighter hair and fine noses. This was my first significant realization of my cultural heritage.

An important outlet that helped me explore my cultural identity was the Filipino American Association of the Tri-Cities. As a folk dancer for four years, I performed at public and cultural events. Though all the other kids were Filipino, and I identified as Filipino and Dutch, I still felt like the odd one out because I looked different. Nevertheless, I welcomed the feeling of belonging to a group.

During my first semester of college, I joined the Filipino American Students Association on campus and though the members of the group were very nice, I still didn't feel a part of the group. However, I immediately felt welcomed and comfortable around the Gay, Lesbian, Bisexual, Transgendered, and Allies Program (GLBTA). Dealing with my sexual identity was increasingly becoming easier now that I was in college. I made the choice to be "out" roughly about second semester of that year. I made the decision to "come out" to my mother and sister Carol during Christmas break, and the experience was very joyful and positive. I am still wary of telling others in my hometown because I have always been a source of gossip in the Filipino community there.

I was not always comfortable with my sexuality. I realized that I was attracted to other boys during eighth grade, and the feeling only grew stronger as I moved on to high school. Because high school was not a very positive experience for me, as it was extremely religious and a small school, I did not feel comfortable coming out, yet I knew that some people suspected that I was gay. The key indicator was the fact that girls were always chasing me, but I showed no interest in them.

Now that I am in college, I feel liberated in that I can express myself better. I am more confident of my cultural and sexual identity. Recently, I was selected to go to a nationwide conference at the University of California-Davis addressing LGBT issues in the college environment. I hope to bring back programs that my college will use to promote awareness about the LGBT community. In addition, I want to be a "voice" for all those multicultural students who identify as LGBT because the LGBT community is underrepresented by students of color.

Testimonial

Chapter 14

On Growing Up Queer[1] and Hapa[2]
Wei Ming Dariotis, Ph.D.

Unfortunately, the title of this chapter is completely misleading. I did not grow up identifying as either queer or as hapa (an Asian or Pacific Islander American of mixed heritage). I did not know these words, and in fact, neither term was as widely used back then (in the 1970s) as they are now.

I did not recognize either of these identities as my own. While I had a good grasp on who I was, "Wei Ming Dariotis," I did not understand the mixed heritage my name implied; I did not know what I was. I did not have any clear sense of my identity as a unitary whole. Instead, my childhood and adolescence were filled with the intense demands other people made on my identities. When I was asked the ever-present, "What are you?" question, I knew the questioner was curious about my racial identity, while my heterosexuality was always assumed (yet another reason to cut short my long hair). Heterosexuality was so fixed as a normative identity that I never considered the possibility of being anything but heterosexual until I was in college. Many people of mixed heritage struggle with their racial or ethnic identity just as much as most people struggle with sexuality during adolescence. Adolescence is, for most, a time of intense identity flux, but for lesbian, gay, bisexual, transgender (LGBT) mixed heritage youth, it can be even more confusing as others constantly question our identities, without ever offering an option that is inclusive of all that we are.

We often think of identity in a biological sense as predetermined, given at birth (or even before birth as science seeks genetic tags for queerness and society talks of bloodlines). *But biology is not identity*. One's genetically determined gender may be indeterminate, or may be different from the gender one chooses or is culturally assigned. One's "race" or ethnicity cannot be determined by biology, because these have everything to do with culture, and how human societies construct ideas of race and ethnicity.[3] Biology is not identity. Nor is phenotype, or physical appearance, an accurate marker of identity. While many LGBT people have taken to a kind of LGBT-identified behavior or fashion as a way to self-identify, there is no sure way to identify someone's sexuality just as there is no sure way to identify someone's "race" or ethnicities. The biological focus on identity fails to consider that what really shapes our identities is *context*—particularly the contexts given by family and community. These contexts are what create, shape, and, in some cases, support our identities.

Of Contexts and Continuums

Recently, I spoke on the now annual "Gay Panel" offered by the faculty at my old high school. Speaking to a roomful of high school sophomores, I explained that I had not perceived myself to be bisexual until I was in college. This realization of my bisexual identity coincided with my self-discovery of an Asian American identity. Coming from situations, time periods, or cultural backgrounds where LGBT identity was not considered a valid option, many of the other panelists similarly did not "come out" until later in life. A young student asked us if we wished we had been told earlier that we were lesbian, gay, bisexual, or transgender. My response was that, rather than wishing I had been told I was bisexual or queer, I wished that lesbian, gay bisexual, and transgender sexuality was taught as part of the continuum of human sexuality, so that I might have considered my identity in a more holistic way. I wish we were given all the options, and allowed to choose for ourselves what we were, at that moment—with the possibility of that identity being adjusted or changed over time. The problem is, people have a very fixed notion of sexual identity. Not only are we limited to heterosexuality, but once we have established an identity, we are tied to it—any change leads to accusations of being inauthentic or fake. Bisexual and transgender people are particularly susceptible to this accusation, as is anyone whose sexual identity has changed over time (i.e., the bisexual who is told he/she is "really" gay; the transgender person who is told she is not "really" a woman).

Similarly, racial identity in the United States is constructed in a purely binary oppositional structure, with no examples of the possibility of mixed heritage identities. As queer mixed heritage youth, we are provided no sense of how to adopt a mixed, multiple, or even shifting identity. We are not given the option of a mixed heritage identity. Rather, we are forced to either choose from among our parents' ethnic heritages, or we may adopt an intermediate identity—Native American, Latino, Filipino, Puerto Rican, etc.— that approximates a sense of our mixed heritage (whether we realize this at the time or not).[4] We often choose these alternate identities because others will not accept our mixed heritage as a valid identity. In the words of Maria Root's seminal "Bill of Rights for Racially Mixed People," all mixed heritage people should "have the right to identify...differently than strangers expect [them] to identify [and]...differently in different situations." To this, I would add that we have the right to alter our identities over time—precisely because they are not fixed in biology, but exist within the contexts of our families and communities, which

we can see shifting everyday, hopefully towards accommodation of newly recognized identities.

"I have the right to freely choose whom I befriend and love"
-from The "Bill of Rights for Racially Mixed People" by Maria P. P. Root

Why the need to assert this right? Because mixed heritage people are often called upon to prove group loyalty by whom we choose to date and befriend—as though this defines our identities. And to some extent this is true, our relationships create our communities, which provide the context for our identities. But we should not therefore be limited in whom we can choose as partners and friends. Anne Lundbom, a 21-year-old bisexual, bi-gendered (female identified) woman of Filipino and Swedish/White American heritage, describes herself as "multiracial because I have to acknowledge that I am both—White and Filipino, at the same time...I cannot just say that I am a person of color because that would be wrong, inaccurate to say. I think it is about being as honest and accurate as you possibly can be." There is powerful pressure on mixed heritage youth to choose one or the other side definitively. Queer mixed heritage youth occupy an even more tenuous position, as the logic of ethnic nationalism[5] often disparages homosexuality as much as heterosexual dating outside the ethnic group—particularly "dating White." In as much as homosexuality is also often seen as a "White disease," queer mixed heritage youth of partial European ancestry are often perceived as traitors to the group identity. Lundbom describes this phenomenon in her analysis of the connections between her sexual and ethnic identities, saying, "it's fluid, I'm able to relate a little bit to both sides. I'm the bridge because I'm so in between everything in every direction. If I'm bisexual then I'm still safe; if I'm not super fem and not super butch then I can hang out with everybody. Which means that I have enemies on both sides, as well."

Queer sexuality within communities of color has often been suspect because it can be perceived as undermining group cohesiveness. The acceptance of LGBT youth of color has proceeded through activist and social organizations, such as AQUA (Asian Pacific Islander, Queer and Questioning, Under 25, Altogether) in the Bay Area, which supports queer Asian and Pacific Islander American youth. However, even in these organizations, LGBT mixed heritage youth may find it difficult to gain acceptance. Where is a youth of mixed Chinese and African American heritage supposed to go? In an Asian Pacific Islander group, a person of this mix may be perceived just as Black. In an African American group, the social codes the youth has learned from within Chinese American culture may be misunderstood. While doing a Web search for resources available for mixed heritage queer youth, I found that, while there are organizations that specifically address the needs of African American, Asian American, Latino, and Native American LGBT youth, the section of the Youth Resource Web site denoted as "cross cultural" contained only an article on interracial dating within the LGBT community. Anne Lundbom, responding to her experiences with Bay Area queer API groups, says, "I think when it comes to groups that are just one thing—Asian groups, or queer groups—they need to understand broader issues—you don't have to work on them, but [you should] know what is going on."

Hapa Issues Forum, MAVIN Foundation, AMEA, I-Pride and other organizations dedicated to mixed heritage issues have in the past been very heterosexual in focus. This has been very much due to the framing of our issues within an "interracial dating/marriage make mixed babies" paradigm. But now, many leaders of mixed heritage organizations are themselves adults of mixed heritage, and we are developing our own sense of ourselves as human beings existing along multiple axes of identity, including both race and sexuality. Thus, we are finally in a position to consider LGBT sexuality as an important component of our mixed heritage communities—not only as a corollary to the boundary-crossing transgressivity of racial mixing, but also as a way of being that provides a healthy challenge to heterosexism within the mixed race anti-racist movement. Only recently, in 2001, the San Francisco Chapter of Hapa Issues Forum organized the first hapa contingent for the San Francisco Queer Pride March. Beyond recognizing the lived reality that many mixed heritage people are also queer, this solidarity refocuses our identity away from biological fixity and towards the fluidity, focusing instead on heritage, families, and communities. Asian and Pacific Islander

Illustration by Jolie Harris

Split at the Root: A collection of works by multiracial queer youth

As a student at the University of Puget Sound in Tacoma, Washington, Jolie Harris began the "Split at the Root" project as part of her senior thesis. The project aims to collect works by multiracial queer youth to publish as an anthology. Her hope is that queer youth of mixed heritage will read the anthology and feel connected by the common themes expressed by others who are "split at the root." She also hopes that the anthology will bring to light issues of diversity within the queer community and various ethnic communities.

transracial adoptees, in particular, are becoming increasingly commonplace within the larger LGBT community, and many LGBT parents adopt internationally. Recognizing our common experiences as mixed heritage people within an LGBT context allows space for addressing the issues and needs of all members of our community.

All Grown Up

We do not grow up as lesbian, gay, bisexual, transgender and as hapa or mixed heritage, we are rarely given these identities unconsciously or "naturally" by our (possibly) monoracial and (perhaps) heterosexual parents. Therefore, we can only come to an understanding of ourselves within these broader, more fluid identity categories through the active support of our families and communities. Organizations dedicated to LGBT youth, and to mixed heritage youth, must recognize the need to encompass both mixed heritage and lesbian, gay, bisexual, and transgender identities within their communities. Below, I offer some preliminary questions to consider when thinking about what kind of services to offer and how to go about doing so:

• What are the most difficult issues specific to LGBT multiracial youth?
• How do these issues differ from those of monoracial queer youth? Or heterosexual multiracial youth?
• How do their mixed heritage and LGBT identities intersect?
• What services need to be provided to LGBT multiracial youth?
• What kinds of barriers are there to these youth accessing services?
• What kind of community is available to LGBT multiracial youth?
• Given that the multiracial movement is fairly heterosexual in both context and content, what place is there for LGBT youth in the multiracial movement? Or, what can LGBT youth teach the multiracial movement?
• Given that the LGBT movement is both White-dominated and monoracialist (in much the same way as are other aspects of our society), what place is there for mixed heritage LGBT youth? Or, what can LGBT mixed heritage youth teach the LGBT movement?

These questions are only meant to be taken as a starting point. Developing community support around emerging identities is a lengthy process with no clear end in sight. This process is, however, critical to the survival and growth of LGBT communities, communities of color, and the multiracial movement. Those groups on the margins of our communities can provide invaluable perspective. If we do our job right, and now, LGBT mixed heritage youth of the future may well be able to grow up with a clear sense of all the identities available to them, and they might even be free to create a few more that we cannot yet imagine. ▌

Did you know?

Here is a well-known multiracial person who has identified as also being Lesbian, Gay, Bisexual, or Transgendered:

Greg Louganis (Diver, Olympic gold medalist)

Notes

1 Queer is a political identity with which I, as a bisexual woman, feel comfortable. However, not all people who are lesbian, gay, bisexual, or transgender feel comfortable or identify with the term "queer."

2 Hapa is a Native Hawaiian word meaning "part" or "mixed." During the period of European colonization, it was used in the phrase "hapa haole," referring to those people who were of both Native Hawaiian and European American heritage. It has since been adopted within the larger Asian Pacific American community, especially on the West Coast, to refer to people of any mixed heritage Asian or Pacific Islander (APIs) (including Eurasians, Afro-Asians, Native-Asians, Latino-Asians, mixed APIs, and API transracial adoptees).

3 There is, according to biologists, only one human "race." To refer to multiple "races" is therefore inaccurate. However, the lived, social reality is that the current dominant system divides humanity into approximately five distinct "races": white (European), yellow (Asian), brown (Latino), red (Indigenous), black (African). I have listed them by color to emphasize the constructed nature and absurdity of these categories, and the fact that they exist within a hierarchy. It is the fact that these "racial" categories are hierarchical that makes mixed heritage such a dangerous and transgressive thing. The only way to maintain the hierarchy is to maintain the distinctions between the different levels.

4 Note that each of these ethnicities, and many others, are examples of current ethnic identities emerging from a past historical mixing of several different groups.

5 "Ethnic Nationalism" as I'm using it here relates to the Black Power Movement of the 1960s and 1970s and Yellow Power Movement of the 1970s, and the ideology that the heterosexual male is the apotheosis of the ethnic nation. Congruently, female sexuality is jealously guarded for the exclusive use of the heterosexual ethnic man, and queer sexuality is seen as suspect, a tool of the White man used to destroy the community-as-nation.

Maya Rovelstad
Age: 3
Racial/Ethnic Heritage: Mexican and Puerto Rican

Three and a half years ago Maya was born in Texas in the very hot month of July. We were fortunate enough to be present at her birth and to spend two weeks with her birthmother and maternal grandfather. I am not sure who was more nervous when we first met, but we were all grateful for the chance to get to know one another. I now know that Maya got her great sense of humor from her grandfather and her delight in climbing and speed from her mother! Since then we have visited and continue to talk regularly. I am convinced that the connection will enable Maya to better understand who she is as she grows. And I know the contact has been of comfort to her birthmother.

Still, Maya, who is Puerto Rican and Mexican, will grow up with Caucasian parents and an older sister who was adopted from Peru, likewise also in an open adoption. Because both our daughters are of color they will share many experiences: the experience of growing up with parents who don't look like them, of living in a Euro-centric world where racism is built into the system, and likely the experience of "not fitting" into the neatly-drawn boxes of this society. They will likely share an experience in the community of adoptive families in which there appears to be a lack of understanding of the challenges transracial adoptees may face. After all, it is very easy to go through life as a White person without ever having to consider what life is like if you are not White. Unfortunately, it is not yet a requirement for prospective adoptive parents to pass "Race Issues 101." On the positive side, they will hopefully share the knowledge that regardless of how a family comes together, there is no difference in the love that family members have for each other. I also hope they will know that our diversity is our strength.

What they won't share is the complexity of being of mixed ethnicity. The pre-occupation with fitting everyone into a system of Black and White will add another challenge to Maya's life. To provide her with an opportunity to develop cultural competency and to establish authentic connections to her cultures of origin is even more difficult. Still, I hope that through personal relationships and cultural experiences, Maya will be be able to take pride in who she is and feel good about her specific make-up. Maya is already noticing eye and hair color differences. She is convinced that people with green eyes can see at night, though her dad doesn't seem to confirm that theory! Her beautiful tight curls attract a lot of attention and so far she says she likes the comments. Of course, at three she is met with nothing but smiles and she misses the inquiry that at times follows as to "what she is."

We are already talking about both race and adoption in our family. We will continue to do so both at home and in our community. In our school district we are working at implementing multicultural education and in our community we continue to raise awareness of equality and justice. After all, how can we fully support our children if we are not willing to work to change the things that make their lives difficult?

Testimonial

Chapter 15

Domestic Transracial[1] Adoption and Multiraciality[2]
By Gina E. Miranda, Ph.D., C.A.P.S.W.

Occupying the social status "transracial adoptee" or "multiracial" challenges the very core of many cherished beliefs and taken-for-granted assumptions of how race, family, and culture are lived in the United States. As transracial adoptees, we defy the notion that all children are parented by persons with whom they share a racialized group membership and cultural heritage. We are made aware that in the U.S., when physical appearances and heritages among family members do not match or when its constellation drifts from the biological mother-father parenting norm, the possibilities for our healthy development within these contexts occasions disproportionate public concern and professional debate. Through classroom assignments (e.g., family trees/genealogies), compulsive stares that accompany family outings, or polite interrogations from strangers, neighbors, and friends, we and our families are routinely put on notice regarding the degrees of our difference.

As multiracial adoptees with White parents and a range of racialized appearances, many theories, both academic and folk, regarding how an identity is developed may not fully represent our realities. Not all of us have had access to our birth cultures through immersion experiences or relationships that existed in the context of our daily home life. Knowledge about our cultures of origin sometimes remained separate from us during childhood because of our adoptive parents' choices, or forever unknown due to missing information at the time of our conception, birth, or because of inaccurate information within our case files. Some of us were placed for adoption because of our mixed racial heritage.[3] [4] [5] All of these facts of our beginnings and circumstances of our adoptions can facilitate an acceptance or rejection of our known/unknown biological origins, shape our interactions with others assumed to be similar, and complicate the paths we take in putting together the pieces of our identity puzzle across the life course. Some search for this biological connection and locate their birth families. For others, we socially construct our kinship network to include relationships and experiences that affirm us and, in turn, become reflections of our identities into adulthood.

Multiracial children, however, have been an overlooked population within most transracial adoption studies. Their needs have also been ignored by the child welfare system,[6] a system that continues to lack a detailed and uniform method for recording and reporting the biological racial heritage of children in its care. Therefore, after first reviewing the literature one might conclude that this population comprises an insignificant proportion of children adopted transracially. Yet despite missing data from national statistics, a closer read of transracial adoption research provides some evidence that bears noting. Given the lack of data and research on other populations of mixed race adoptees, the following discussion will draw from research involving those with Black-White parentage (hereafter referred to as biracial). The relevance of these findings to multiracial adoptees with other racialized backgrounds will be noted as the multiracial literature on non-adopted populations permits.

Biracial Children and Transracial Placement

It is rarely acknowledged that biracial children have often dominated the sample populations within transracial adoption research dating back to some of the first and most extensively referenced studies in the United States. As Table 1 below indicates, two recently published studies on transracial adoption outcomes continue this trend with samples that are over 70% biracial.

Early adoption literature indicates that this population of mixed race babies is most representative of the first transracial adoptions involving infants of Black descent in the U.S.[7] [8] Indeed, what is known about transracial adoption outcomes for "Black children" is largely reflective of the experiences of biracial adoptees.[9] Yet these facts and any possible analysis of unique factors associated with multiraciality and identity work are over-shadowed largely because of two unyielding socio-political realities.

First, with few exceptions, the polarized discourse surrounding transracial adoption practice has narrowly framed the debate and resulting research to pursue two overarching closed-ended questions: Is transracial adoption good or bad, and can White parents raise children of color to have high self-esteems and positive racial identities? Research has responded by focusing on assumed culturally universal factors of well-being (e.g., academic achievement and self-esteem) and has historically relegated its investigation of racial identity to decontextualized and mutually exclusive racialized preferences (e.g., friends and dating partners) and single racial label use.[10] Disproportionately, these studies focus on outcomes for children of Black descent. When adoptees score well on self-esteem and school achievement measures and follow socially prescribed norms by matching their racialized biology with the "correct" racial labels (interpreted as their identity) transracial adoption is deemed a success. Though skeptics remain, few studies have attempted to explore more dynamic and fluid conceptualizations of identity development

for this population. Even fewer have pursued the complexities of this process for multiracial adoptees.[11] Unfortunately, the politics of transracial adoption have held this entire field of research an intellectual hostage; in nearly 30 years of scientific inquiry few transracial adoption studies have strayed from these master domains.

Secondly, it should not be surprising that this body of research mirrors the society in which it is conducted, a society that categorizes anyone with any Black heritage under the "one-drop rule" as Black. In addition to the existential hazards this poses to an individual's identity development in society, it is problematic because transracial adoption research has historically had an implicit goal, and an explicit societal expectation, of assessing White parents in their abilities to transmit so called "healthy racial identities" to their adopted children. Existing research has not fully appreciated the diversity of racialized heritages and physical appearances within its own samples, a diversity that arguably is central to understanding the findings related to outcomes of racialized identity development. In fact, the very definition of "healthy identity" and the processes of its development for multiracial adoptees remain unexplored territory. Our inability to fully and directly access this research in ways that have substantial relevance for the majority of participants within many of these studies ultimately limits the ability of parents and

Study	Percentage of biracial transracial adoptees in sample*
Grow & Shapiro (1974)	82% biracial (90% described as light skinned)
Zastrow (1977)	95% biracial
McRoy & Zurcher (1983)	73% biracial
Simon, Alstein, & Melli (1994)	Phase 4 study: 68% biracial**
Vroegh (1997)	78% biracial
Patton (2000)	73% biracial
Simon & Roorda (2000)	71% biracial

*This is an underrepresented list—only studies on domestic transracial adoption providing racial heritage data for biracial adoptees are included. **Data on biracial adoptees not provided for earlier phases of study.

social workers to make informed decisions throughout the adoption and parenting process. Collectively, these two realities have left the field of child welfare and individual adoptive parents with a conceptualization of "needs" among transracial adoptees within often simplistic, monocentric, and decontextualized frameworks.

Given recent shifts in how the nation officially categorizes race and the burgeoning field of multiracial literature, it is timely to extend this social movement and discussion of identity development to acknowledge the various ways in which one's racialized biology and racial appearances mark a significant group of multiracial persons whose racialized identity work does not occur in biological family systems. The purpose of this final discussion is to begin this shift in exploring the responses of adult biracial adoptees in their advice to future and current adoptive parents of biracial children.

The information and quotations used in this final section are drawn from dissertation research that includes a series of in-depth interviews with 15 adult biracial adoptees who were raised in the northern U.S.[12] Representing myriad physical appearances, most (n=13) were women, and all participants were between the ages of 21 and 32. This study covered a broad range of topics with participants, including questions about their adoption stories, how they were racially socialized in their families, and lessons they had learned about race and culture into adulthood. It is hoped that presenting an extremely limited selection of findings related to parenting advice will begin a conversation that can branch out to more deeply explore the diversity of experiences with identity work among the population of transracial adoptees who have multiracial heritage.

Insider Wisdom on Transracial Adoptive Parenting and Biraciality

In the long run, I feel like I have this HUGE gift, to be able to relate to people...to both worlds. Nobody's getting over one on me! (Female adoptee, age 30)

I think...it's taken a lot of intrinsic motivation on my part to really develop me. Just pulling things from friends and reading books, and just...walking around in my own skin. And I *still* struggle with it, okay? I still

Pact: An Adoption Alliance

Pact is a nonprofit organization begun by two adoptive parents in 1991. Since its inception, Pact has been dedicated to the mission of providing the highest quality adoption-related services to children of color, their birth parents, and their adoptive parents. Pact also works with adoption professionals to facilitate adoptions and to initiate programs that better serve clients raising children of color. Top priority is given to programs especially designed to support and inform adopted children and adopted adults of color. Importantly, Pact goes beyond traditional adoption services by offering extensive post-placement opportunities for all families raising children of color, providing informative and essential education, connection, and support.

Learn more:
www.pactadopt.org

have people calling me red bone and a half-breed. But…really…I've had to rely greatly on myself." (Female adoptee, age 28)

And you know, I'll be 80 years old, and I'll still be figuring things out. You know? Never really be able to figure things out. Never REALLY be able to explain it to my friends *exactly*. (Male adoptee, age 28)

If nothing else was clear among this population, it is that life presents opportunities to change and rework who one is in relationship to shifts in society, life events, and changes in family composition. All stories were filled with negotiating and renegotiating the importance of race and transracial adoption across the life course, and an understanding of one's own story particularly in relationship to those of other adoptees and multiracial people. This is a unique dimension of the identity development process for this population, as there are no "cultural traditions" or wisdoms that fully speak to the reality of their experiences. Although some referred to the generation of transracial adoptees who were adopted in the 1960 and 1970 as "our generation," and that "we were some of the first," there is no collectivity of elders to seek in gaining cultural wisdom of being a transracial adoptee. Or perhaps, the elders are in the making and are now only in their 30's and 40's. Therefore, among these respondents, developing one's identity was understood as a lifetime journey often forged on one's own, ideally with the support of parents, friends, and the families they created along the way.

One of the adoptees who described her parents' approach as supportive in culturally grounding her identity development particularly in the Black community states, "…in order to know…I had to be IMMERSED in that. My parents didn't take me *outside* of the African American culture. They didn't stick me completely in it, though, and leave me either. They were there with me, and we would talk through things, and we *ALL* learned things." This statement reminds parents of the importance of being open to one's own growth and change in order to meet the needs of a transracially adopted child. For biracial and other multiracial adoptees, this can require highly pro-active parenting

in making connections and developing relationships that may not be naturally occurring in any community. It may also require parents to develop a more sophisticated understanding of diverse historical and contemporary racialized dynamics in the communities of color that represent their children's birth cultures.

Many adoptees described their White parents as unaware of existing skin tone politics and racial litmus tests[13] within the Black community. One adoptee recalls her experiences after her parents enrolled her in a more diverse high school so she could develop friendships with Black peers. Not having prior exposure to a Black community, she felt she could have been better prepared:

I DEFINITELY did not get that. I mean, it was like I was sent to school to fend for **myself**! You know!? My parents had no idea—but that's what it was. It was like being thrown into a cage of lions, and like, here—okay—good luck! Hope you make it out okay—if you haven't been beat up by the end of the day! And THAT, that scars. That left huge **scars**—and I see it come out now.

Certainly all adoptees' childhood experiences in a Black community were not solely negative, and as adults, five claimed this cultural context exclusively as where their greatest comfort lies. Yet, it is telling that the language used to describe some experiences in both White and Black communities was often reflective of war terminology and living in hostile environments. Many talked about the "survival skills" they needed or the "armor" and "ammunition" required in "fending" for themselves during times when their parents were not around, or able, to protect them in either predominantly Black or White contexts. This finding is consistent with research involving non-adopted multiracial populations beyond Black-White who also report having to deal with racism and racialized interactions in myriad cultural communities. Experiencing challenges to legitimize one's identity and cultural insider status in specific cultural contexts is not an uncommon phenomenon, even for multiracial adults.[14] [15] [16] Consequently, White adoptive parents must appreciate that despite their love for their children, the world will not consistently respond in kind to a child who is both mixed race and transracially adopted. It would behoove both social workers and parents to be aware of these within-group dynamics and not assume that a child's racialized biology alone will facilitate a reciprocal bond or automatic acceptance between those who share this heritage. In fact, these findings suggest transracially adopted multiracial children must develop additional skills beyond coping with racism to negotiate their multiply othered statuses as adoptee, as transracial adoptee, and as multiracial. Among these skills is the ability to anticipate the inevitably inconsistent reactions that their politicized social statuses and often racially ambiguous appearances evoke across different contexts.

Clearly, parents cannot prevent a child from experiencing racism, colorism, and racial litmus tests, nor do all multiracial adoptees require the same cultural or racial socialization. Yet, choices parents make in their neighborhoods of residence and the environments they provide for their children do set the parameters of their children's racial and cultural worlds. In so doing, they establish the boundaries of a child's early ecological competencies, and ultimately, a child's confidence to survive and thrive within those contexts. Most of the adoptees in this study (n=13) believed it was important to live in substantially diverse communities and for parents to find additional ways of incorporating an adoptee's birth cultures into the family's identity and daily life. Missing these experiences was not damaging to their future success within mainstream White society. It was damaging, however, to their sense of competence and acceptance in predominantly Black communities, into adulthood. It is highly probable that other groups of multiracial adoptees lacking ongoing and immersed exposure to their birth communities of color would also render similar outcomes.

Feeling confident in one's communities of origin is important for adoptees not because all biracial persons, for example, must feel comfortable around all persons of Black decent, but because developing these relationships and cultural connections allows the adoptee to truly "choose" and construct an identity that is grounded culturally and affirmed experientially. If being biracial/multiracial means one has choices in how to identify, then transracial adoptees who are multiracial have a right to

Whale Talk
Chris Crutcher, Greenwillow Books, 2001

Geared towards a teenage audience, *Whale Talk* is a witty portrayal of high school's delicate social hierarchies. Centered on a high school's new swim team, the book is narrated by T.J., an adopted, Japanese-Caucasian-Black headstrong teen who is wise beyond his years. Vying to change a school athletic program that places greater value on letterman jackets than the heart and soul of each athlete, T.J. creates a swim team of people like him—misfits. Although his crew develops into a respectable team, what is more important is the long bus rides that offer each student important time to share the pain that makes them who they are. Great for ages 12 and up.

have ongoing access to immersion within their birth cultures so they have something tangible, beyond racial labels, to choose from. Ideally, this requires parents to not only be learning along with their child, but be facilitating that competence within their child. As one adoptee who was raised in a Black community comments:

> As a parent you need to be willing to integrate the community, don't make your CHILD do that. And that's what my parents did. That's why my experience is so different. Because you're supposed to be able to handle that as an adult, don't throw that on your child. The biggest mistake I see adoptive parents make is that they think that's all we need—love—and a few cultural events each year, a Black book...a few token friends of color. I think it comes from...the parents' sense of being comfortable or uncomfortable within that, then I think they give the tools to the biracial person that they need to survive. I grew up in a family where we didn't look like each other, and it was respected—celebrated. We didn't have to hide it—the best and worst of both worlds.

Ultimately, child welfare practitioners and others involved in the adoption process bear initial responsibility for ensuring that potential adoptive parents gain this knowledge and cultural competence early on and most definitely prior to placement. This requires social workers to engage in critical conversations about race and culture with adoptive candidates to explore potential intrafamilial racism including their own racism or colorism, and any assumptions they may endorse about multiracial people. These conversations must transcend the monocentric frameworks typically applied to understanding the needs of transracial adoptees to recognize the unique racialized experiences for children who are multiracial. Arguably, child welfare professionals must themselves be trained in providing racially sophisticated services to potential adoptive parents, and sanctioned to make placement decisions that reflect the short and long term best interests of each child. Achieving this objective is problematic for many reasons. Among them is the fact that the child welfare system continues to operate primarily under monocentric methods of racial categorization and monocultural understandings of racialized biological heritage. It is hoped that this chapter and others within this book will offer a strong argument for the need to support the child welfare system and social workers in pursuing a knowledge base that advances how the profession addresses issues of race and culture for any adoptee, but for transracially adopted children of mixed heritage in particular.

This can begin by utilizing existing multiracial literature, theory, and research to construct more culturally relevant frameworks for conceptualizing and understanding the needs of multiracial children. In so doing, the enduring politics of the transracial adoption debate and of multiraciality can be repositioned and understood as powerful contextual factors salient to the lifetime identity work of multiracial adoptees. Certainly, their best interests are served when child welfare professionals and adoptive parents attend to issues of race and culture in ways that reflect its complexity in the world in which each adoptee will live. Indeed, any future discussion of the best interests of this population must begin and end with the voices and acquired wisdom of those adoptees who are now adults and have lived this experience.

Did you know?

Here are some well-known people who are both multiracial and adopted:

Greg Louganis (Diver, Olympic gold medalist)

Dan O'Brien (Athlete, Olympic gold medalist in the decathlon)

Notes

1 It is widely acknowledged that "race" is a biological fiction. Racialized language and labels without capitalization are used in this paper to recognize this *and* its unyielding reality as a socially constructed dimension of daily life in the United States. Therefore, "transracial adoption" in this paper refers to parents racially designated "white" adopting children of "multiracial" heritage born in the U.S.

2 Multiracial and mixed race will be used interchangeably as pan-racial labels to refer to people whose parents claim different racialized group memberships. For a more detailed discussion on the limitations of language in the U.S. in research on adoption, race, and racialization of identities see: G. E. Miranda, *Mixed Feelings: Stories of Race, Kinship, and Identity Among Biracial Adoptees*, Dissertation. Madison, University of Wisconsin, (2002).

3 For testimonies involving mixed race adoptees who report being surrendered for adoption by their white mothers due to their black heritage see: S. Patton, *Birthmarks: Transracial Adoption in Contemporary America* (New York: New York University Press, 2000). See also Miranda, *Mixed Feelings* (2002).

4 Miranda, *Mixed Feelings* (2002).

5 Regarding increased foster care placement of mixed race children with white biological mothers, see: G. Folaron and P. M. Hess, "Placement Considerations for Children of Mixed African American and Caucasian Parentage," *Child Welfare* 72(2) (1993), 113-125.

6 G. Folaron and P. M. Hess, *Child Welfare* (1993).

7 D. Day, *The Adoption of Black Children* (Massachusetts: Lexington Books, 1979).

8 For a discussion of past transracial adoption research and the treatment of mixed race children of black-white descent in child welfare systems past and present see: Miranda, *Mixed Feelings* (2002).

9 Given the continued unmet demand for healthy white infants among the majority of adopters who themselves are white, other populations of mixed race children with white heritage (e.g., latino/white, asian/white, native american/white) may also represent a higher number of placements with white parents.

10 For a more detailed critique of transracial adoption research and measures of race and racial identity see: Miranda, *Mixed Feelings* (2002).

11 Miranda, *Mixed Feelings* (2002).

12 Ibid.

13 Litmus tests refer to the political nature of being mixed race or "light skinned." In this case, within the black community the biracial person's so called "authentic blackness" is tested. Transracial adoptees and multiracial persons are particularly vulnerable to these litmus tests when their racialized appearances or their cultural behaviors are understood to be "white." For a discussion of racialized behaviors and the history of race as performative in the black community see: J. M. Favor, *Authentic Blackness* (Durham, NC: Duke University Press, 1999).

14 P. F. Gaskins, *What Are You? Voices of Mixed-Race Young People* (New York: Henry Holt & Company, 1999).

15 C. C. O'Hearn, ed., *Half and Half: Writers on Growing Up Biracial and Bicultural* (New York: Random House Books, 1998).

16 M. P. P. Root, ed., *The Multiracial Experience, Racial Borders as the New Frontier* (Thousand Oaks, CA: Sage Publications, 1996).

Zak Heaton

Age: 19
Racial/Ethnic Heritage: Korean and African American

Although I don't really know why my parents decided to adopt, I know they saw a picture of me when I was two months old and I flew over from Korea three months later. I was adopted when I was five months old from an orphanage in Inchon, Korea and am the biological son of an African American GI and a Korean mother. My parents told me that I was adopted when I was growing up so I knew where I was coming from, and they made it a point to never treat me any different than my four brothers.

Most people accepted my family, even though I grew up in a predominantly White neighborhood. I do remember how strangers would check us out when they saw us together, but it wasn't that bad. Of course, I encountered discrimination, but it never really was a big problem; people in Seattle are pretty open-minded. Because my family has always embraced and supported me in whatever I have done, I've never felt strange or different growing up.

My parents and brothers have been very supportive of me and helped me learn about my heritage through going to Korean cultural events and celebrating Martin Luther King's birthday at our local community center every year. I also created a word for being both Black and Asian: Blasian. But, I guess I don't really know what it means to me to be Black, Korean, and adopted. I guess it means I'm different from everyone else.

Over the years, my parents have asked me if I wanted to figure out who my birth parents were. They have always been supportive and open surrounding that issue. Right now, finding my birth parents is not important to me, but I don't know, I may want to someday.

I have four brothers and we are all very close in age: I am the youngest and the oldest is 24. We are close and were always active in sports, and grew up competing against each other in basketball, wiffle ball, and foosball, or our favorite past time, the bowling-ball shot put. I like competition, and I'm on the University of Washington swimming team. I have been swimming since I was one and began competitive swimming at seven. Another passion I have is art—I drew a huge graffiti mural on a wall in my backyard, and am going to draw more now that I'm in college. This is my first year in college and I am thinking about pursuing a degree in International Studies.

I like my experience. I think that when you're mixed you obviously look different to others and I take pride in that. I also think being mixed makes you good looking because you are unique. Otherwise, I don't think I'm different than anyone else.

Testimonial

Chapter 16

International Adoption of Mixed Race Children
Susan Soon-keum Cox

For intercultural or interracial families, bridging more than one culture, race, ethnicity, and identity can be a delicate balance. For children adopted internationally, achieving that delicate balance can be even more complex and is part of the life-long journey of adoption.

In the 1950s, when families in the United States began adopting mixed race children from Korea, they planted seeds of change that continue to engender a new racial multiplicity across the American landscape. The modern era of international adoption began following the Korean War when Harry and Bertha Holt, from Creswell, Oregon, saw a film about orphaned children in Korea. The children, born to Korean mothers and United Nations soldier-fathers were unwelcome in Korea; their mixed heritage was unaccepted in their birth country. Believing that these children could be loved and raised by non-Korean families, the Holts worked to pass a bill in Congress allowing children to immigrate to the U.S. for the purpose of adoption. In 1955, the Holts adopted eight biracial children from Korea.

In the 1970s, approximately 2,000 children were adopted from Vietnam. The first adoptions from Korea and Vietnam shared the distinction of war. As in Korea, many of the first generation of adoptees from Vietnam were fathered by foreign soldiers. These children of Vietnamese mothers and American soldiers came to this country with the added burden of coming from a war that was divisive and painful. For the adoptees who were Black Korean or Black Vietnamese, there was the added indignity of being seen by others in their birth countries as racially Black. This overlooked the strong connection adoptees felt toward their birth heritage to both their birth countries and their birth parents, despite the reality that most of them did not know or remember them.

Since then, worldwide approximately 200,000 children have been adopted internationally. Each year, U.S. families adopt approximately 125,000 children. Of those children, approximately 20,000 are adopted from abroad.

In the late 1970s, international adoption began from India, Thailand, the Philippines, and Latin America. The children adopted from these countries were rarely of mixed racial heritage. This also became true of the next generation of children being adopted from Korea, thus changing the profile of international adoptees significantly. There is no formal source of data regarding the racial profile of the nearly 20,000 children adopted internationally each year, but placements of mixed race children today are rare.

When families in the U.S. began adopting children internationally, the concern of assimilation was given priority over connection to birth culture and identity. "Fitting in" and "belonging" was considered the measure of success. That was nearly five decades ago, and those children have grown up and assimilated. In communities throughout the U.S., they became a part of the culture and identity of their adopted families and communities. Often isolated in rural communities, that first generation of international adoptees grew up not knowing another person who "looked like me." They identified themselves with the lives they were living, not the lives they were born to.

As thousands of Korean children were adopted by White families throughout the United States, it was impossible to ignore the differences of race and heritage between the children and their families. It was also very controversial. In those early pioneering days, it was considered by many to be a crazy social experiment. Adoptive parents were advised to "Americanize" their children as quickly as possible.

Particularly for some of the early adoptees, some parents insisted they were "not really Korean" since their birth fathers were not Korean and mostly Caucasian. The early adoptees from Korea rarely, if ever, had opportunities to be exposed to anything regarding their Korean heritage including others who looked like them. This made acknowledging or claiming the Korean part of them more difficult than accepting and embracing it. This reality clashed sharply with the truth that adoptees saw reflected in the mirror, or the sometimes deliberately cruel observations made by others reminding them that they were different. Although they could learn to fit in, they were not truly the same.

I was nearly five years old when I was adopted by a family in rural Oregon. Like many other children adopted during that time, my mother was Korean while my father was not. Although I was only half Korean, my face clearly reflected my mother and I was considered "Oriental" although my Korean passport identified me as Caucasian. Not only was I the only Korean in my family, I was the only Asian in the little town where I grew up. The only language, food, and customs I knew were not Korean. My parents, who were eager to do what was best for me, followed the practice of the day which was to help me be "like them" and everyone else around me.

It was not long before I felt I was my parents' daughter in every way. I never doubted their love or connection to me. They were simply my mom and dad. However, the outside world does not always recognize the emotional connection of family, but sees the obvious differences of race. People often inquired, "Who are your real mom and dad?" Amazingly, strangers I did not know felt no restraint questioning me from the time I was very young. This is a question all interracial adoptive families must prepare to address. In the beginning, the adoptive parents will have to respond, and later, the adoptees themselves will face this task. The answers must always consider the boundaries of dignity and comfort for the child beyond the curiosity of the person inquiring. Adoptees and their families do not "owe" a response to intrusive questions.

International adoptive families may also be required to answer questions like, "Why are you bringing these foreign kids here?" or similar negative reactions to other countries and cultures. A truth of interracial families is that they are always visible and often that requires them to validate the "realness" of their family.

The true emotional relationships between adoptive parents and their children of another race and culture are not affected by those differences. However, the reality is that interracial families look different, and that often means others hold the belief that the relationships are different, that they are not as "real." Parents adopting a child of another race and culture must assume early on the role of advocating for their family since they will be called upon to validate it, often to people they have never met before.

Within the context of daily living, adoptive parents, and adoptees themselves, can put aside that they do not look like they belong in their adoptive family. Families are defined by far more than physical appearance of family members. However, as families go out into the community, and particularly as the children enter their school years, those differences may be confronted constantly in this new environment. Any pretense that adoptive families might have that their family "is not different" quickly disappears in the reality of what their children face every day.

What adoptive families must learn is to separate the feelings and connection of family from the differences of culture and identity between parents and children, and prepare to meet the challenges that sometimes can be truly painful as well as joyful. This includes meeting the challenges children will face from their school experience. Educators extend the parents' role as advocates for internationally adopted children by being informed of the unique differences without creating an environment that makes the child feel uncomfortably different and awkward.

Children of a different race and culture provide wonderful opportunities to incorporate a personal perspective in teaching others a broader global perspective. However, it is critical not to make adoptive children feel displayed for the benefit of others. Incorporating an international adoptee's birth culture into class should be done in the same manner that any other child's birth culture or ethnicity would be incorporated.

In elementary school, family tree projects can create anxiety for adoptive families, as their family history is obviously different and more complex. Fitting their family into a typical family tree assignment, particularly since it begins in another country, is confusing at best. Furthermore, many international adoptees of mixed heritage do not know the racial background of one or both parents. Educators must be sensitive to any awkwardness this might present and give adoptees the freedom to create a tree that they believe reflects them, although it might not fall neatly into the guidelines of the assignment. Some children will simply choose their adoptive family's history; others may show their beginnings in another country as a graft or as an entirely different family tree structure. These choices should belong to the child as a way to own and share who they feel they truly are.

Parents of international adoptees are generally Caucasian and have never personally experienced the challenges their child will confront because of race. Schools can play a significant role in keeping parents informed of how their children are seen by their classmates and alert them to issues that may become negative. From an early age, adoptees are often protective of their parents and do not share these issues with them because they do not want to hurt them, they do not believe they will understand, or worry their parents will over-react to the situation. Parents need to be aware of the reality these issues may present for their children and look for opportunities to discuss them.

Like all children, international adoptees are sheltered and protected

Vietnamese Adoptee Network (VAN)

VAN seeks to maximize the Vietnamese adoptee experience in a caring, supportive environment by networking them to other Vietnamese adoptees and community resources. VAN was established following a 25-year Vietnamese adoptee reunion in 2000. For the first time in many Vietnamese adoptees' lives, they were reunited with other adoptees at the first-ever Reunion of the First Generation of Vietnamese Adoptees, in Baltimore, MD. The Reunion provided the catalyst to start VAN. Many of the founding members realized that the time had come for the torch to be passed on to the adoptee community, and that the stewardship of their history and future direction should be in their hands.
Learn more:
www.van-online.org

by their parents. They see and experience the world through the protected filter of their environment of family and friends who love and care about them. As adoptees get older and more independent, parents lose their ability to always effectively shield and protect their children from the outside world.

An adoptee's race and identity become particularly significant during adolescence when issues of dating begin to emerge. As classmates experience the typical struggles of their independence and identity, adoptees have the added complication of being a different race from their adoptive family and often the community around them. There may be changing nuances in relationships with classmates and friends. Friendships that have been comfortable and close may become distant and awkward. As international adoptees begin dating, issues of race and identity become amplified. This is especially hurtful and confusing when adoptees suddenly see themselves as "different" and "other" because they are treated that way by friends they have known and associated with since childhood. This is a period when an adoptee's self-esteem and confidence can be deeply affected.

International adoptees generally have fewer opportunities to discover who they are in terms of their ethnicity and heritage. Their adoptive parents and family must be committed to embracing not only their child, but their child's ethnicity and culture. Parents must provide opportunities for their children to explore, learn and find the balance of who they are and where they fit in both their birth and adoptive cultures.

International adoptees have a growing number of resources available to help them learn about and stay connected to their birth culture. These include culture camps, homeland tours, international adoption conferences, books, publications, and television programs. Recently, the Internet has become a significant resource for both adoptees and their parents.

Ethnic celebrations are being established and take place in many regions of the country. Ethnic communities have begun to extend their support to adoptees through community programs and church activities. This often includes holiday celebrations, and cooking and language classes. An important resource for international adoptees, local ethnic communities may sometimes have conflicting biases about international adoption. Particularly

as adoptees mature, it is natural to gravitate to others who "look like me." This can create unique complications. It is not uncommon for adoptees to begin dating someone of their same race and learn that the parents and family of the person they are dating do not approve of them because they are adopted. It is a painful reality for adoptees to experience divisions not only of race, but of culture.

International adoptions are also affected by current events and circumstances in the birth country, both positive and negative. India, Vietnam, Guatemala, Korea, China, Romania, and other countries have reacted to events like the Olympics, World Cup Soccer and other sporting events, the accidental bombing of the Chinese Embassy by the U.S., national elections when the official U.S. policy has been in conflict with the ruling party in the other country, incidents involving U.S. military, economic sanctions, visits by high level government officials, media stories, and most recently, Severe Acute Respiratory Syndrome (SARS).

Circumstances and world events affect international adoptions and directly touch the children adopted from those countries. Parents, teachers, and others involved with adoptees need to be aware of images and stories and the potential impact on international adoptees. It is necessary to help them understand the situation as well as prepare their own response if that becomes necessary.

I was in the fifth grade when there was a hostile incident between North Korea, South Korea, and the U.S. I was stunned and hurt when my classmates accused me of "stealing their ship." I was too young to know what they were even talking about and much of what they had learned and said was influenced by their parents. It was a painful experience I still remember.

In 1999, the Gathering of Korean Adoptees was the first event to bring international adult adoptees together for the first time. Attended by over 400 individuals from the U.S. and Europe, for a surprisingly large percentage, it was the first time they had interacted with other international adoptees. Research by the Evan B. Donaldson Adoption Institute confirmed that while most considered themselves to be well adjusted as adults, that issues of race and identity were often a struggle.[1]

In 2000, at the Reunion of the First Generation of Vietnamese Adoptees, about 250 adoptees came together to share their common experiences. It was evident that while most of them felt deeply connected to the U.S., like the Korean adoptees of the first generation, they also felt deeply connected to their birth country. For both groups of adult adoptees, issues of race and identity were infinitely more significant than issues of adoption.

Research by the Evan B. Donaldson Adoption Institute shows that growing up in the, 1950s and, 1960s, most Korean adoptees considered themselves to be White.[2] As adults, this changed dramatically and most now think of themselves as Korean or Korean American. When asked which was a more significant issue for them, race or adoption, overwhelmingly, the issue was race. Particularly as adoptees become adults and independent from their adoptive families, they are defined not by adoption, but how others see them. An adoptee's ability to balance issues of race and identity is crucial to how she or he feels about herself or himself.

As international adoptions become more commonplace, it has become generally accepted in this culture and society. Adoptees' adaptation into their adopted communities makes it easier for societies to overcome their prejudices as people come into close contact with others who look different but are socially members of their society. International adoptees born in a number of different countries now speak with the local accent and express the mannerisms that identify them as a member of their adopted community.

To review, parents and educators should keep the following six points in mind when working with multiracial international adoptees:

1. Interracial families are always visible and the outside world may only see the obvious differences of race, rather than the emotional connection of family. Parents must make a consistent, special effort to embrace their child's ethnicity and culture by seeking out resources.
2. Parents and children should eventually be prepared to advocate for their family to strangers with prying questions. However, they do not "owe" a response to these intrusive questions. Local ethnic communities, too, may have conflicting biases about international adoption.
3. Parents of international adoptees are generally Caucasian and have never personally experienced the absence of White

Voices From Another Place: A Collection of Works from a Generation Born in Korea and Adopted to Other Countries
Edited by Susan Soon-keum Cox, Yeong & Yeong Book Company, 1999

Voices is filled with emotionally charged testimonials, artwork, and moving poems that document the diversity of the Korean adoptee experience. "Mirror," written by an adoptive mother and also one of the most poignant essays, explains how the author feels disconnected from her daughter because of her Korean features. This feeling of distance between mother and daughter is a kind of metaphor for the book; it exemplifies the limbo that many adoptees feel between their families and society, and between their birth and home countries.

privilege. As adults, most adoptees feel that issues of race are more significant to them than issues of adoption.

4. Educators must be sensitive to the awkwardness of some class projects that assume monoracial birth families, such as family trees. Furthermore, although children of different races and cultures provide opportunities to teach others, adoptees should not feel displayed for the benefit of others.

5. Educators can play a significant role in keeping parents informed of how their children are seen by their classmates.

6. An adoptee's race and identity become particularly significant during adolescence when issues of dating begin to emerge. As adoptees get older and more independent, parents will lose their ability to always shield and protect their children from the outside world.

It is not possible to always have the answers or be able to prevent or protect children from the hurts and slights of a world that does not always acknowledge differences and diversity as blessings. Individuals of any race or culture, including international adoptees, do not outgrow the longing to be connected and have a sense of belonging. Everyone needs to know they are part of a larger community with other unique individuals who are "just like me."

Notes

1 M. Freundlich and J. K. Lieberthal. *The Gathering of the First Generation of Adult Korean Adoptees: Adoptee's Perceptions of International Adoption* (New York: The Evan B. Donaldson Adoption Institute, 2000).

2 Ibid.

Zachary Gorba

Age: 12

Racial/Ethnic Heritage: Samoan, European, Asian, and African

I entered the Washington State foster care system in 1995. I am Samoan and European mostly. My dad also had Asian and African, but I identify myself as Samoan and African.

I don't know how my parents met. I don't know my dad. I know what his name is! I can see my mom, though, about once every two to three months. I have three sisters and two brothers, one is my stepbrother. I am the oldest. Every two months or so, I can see them. None of them are in foster families, they are with their parents. I have been in out-of-care placement for four and a half years now. I remember being in about five homes, but I don't remember much about the neighborhoods. Usually there are not many Black people at my schools.

Being multiracial means "mixed," I guess. It's not really good or bad, it just is what it is. I don't think race really matters when it comes to foster care. I've met lots of other kids in foster care and they are mostly mixed. Foster care to me means a place to live, a family. When I think of my future adoptive family, I have no preference of who they are...whether they're White, Black, or mixed. All of my foster families except one were White. The others were Black. It just doesn't matter to me, though.

I haven't really been curious about being multiracial before. Multiracial issues have never been really talked about before at my schools. I don't do much around my heritage...why is there so much focus on heritage? I don't really know other kids with my background so I've never had conversations about it before and I'm not really curious about other heritages necessarily either.

No one has ever made any assumptions about my race before. I've never experienced discrimination or racism. I haven't had to pick any boxes on a form yet about my race. I don't even really know what I'll say yet when race comes up as a topic with my own kids.

Testimonial

Chapter 17

Multiracial Youth Within the Foster Care System
Melissa Wolfe

Foster care is a complex system that mystifies those of us who not only become a part of it but those outside of it as well. The system is designed to be a safety net for vulnerable children but has developed a tragic reputation for being a destination for unwanted and unloved youths. Most communities hear more about its fallacies than tales of triumph and successful permanent placements, which do indeed exist within it each and every day. Historically, foster care was publicly acknowledged as a place where troubled children ended up, but in reality, children become a part of the foster care system because of a lack of an appropriate caretaker, often punctuated by abuse, neglect, and/or abandonment of the child. When children's essential needs for healthy development in a safe home cannot be met, they are taken into the care of the state government's child welfare system.

Multiracial youth are a part of the growing number of ethnic minority children who are often overrepresented in foster care.[1] Minority children represent more than 60% of the foster care population, but only 20% of the U.S. population.[2] As the number of children in the foster care system rises,[3] so do the specialized needs of those in its care and the need to work more closely with communities in helping these children find permanent, nurturing homes. Foster care experience is unique because it varies by the individual from child to child, both based on the circumstances of how the child came into the system and also the effect of being in the system. Once in foster care, however, these youths have an increased risk of experiencing homelessness, unemployment, incarceration, unplanned pregnancies, and health problems.[4] [5] [6]

Racial Disparities

Race has always been one of many factors in determining whether a potential permanent home is truly in the best interests of the child. Historically, matching racial backgrounds of the youth to the racial background of foster and adoptive families was the accepted norm. Unfortunately, available families have not kept up with the growing population of the ethnic diversity of the foster care population. In many states, children of any color, including multiracial children, are labeled "special needs," along with those who are older than eight years of age, have mental or physical disabilities, or have a sibling also in foster care. Special needs children are categorized as such because it is statistically harder to find adoptive homes for them. Although there is insufficient data to accurately assess if it is harder to find a permanent home for multiracial children, these youths continue to be labeled "special needs" by many states if they are members of at least one ethnic minority group.

In 1994, federal legislation was passed to address the racial disparity in foster care.[7] The Multi-Ethnic Placement Act (MEPA) was designed to ensure that children were no longer denied a chance at being considered for a permanent home solely on the basis of their race or ethnicity. The intention was to stop the waiting process and to get children out of the system as soon as possible so they could reach safe, permanent homes of any kind. Other goals included attempting to increase recruitment efforts aimed at finding more families within communities of color and eliminating discrimination. An amendment followed two years later, called the InterEthnic Placement Act or MEPA II, which further clarified how child welfare agencies need to make a concerted effort to recruit families representative of the races of the children in foster care.[8] The intent is to ensure that race is not an impediment for either children or families in child welfare practices. These Acts were significant steps in alleviating previous challenges with adoption placement practices and promoting acceptance of multiracial families, but it is still left to the professional opinion of case workers to determine the importance of race in a child's life and subsequent foster care placement.

Despite this legislation, it remains challenging to learn specifically about the multiracial child's journey through the child welfare system. It is complicated by the lack of information on the multiracial foster care population. It is still common to find demographic information with categories such as "Unknown" or "Other."[9] Not only are multiracial children in a completely non-descriptive category, but it also encourages some to select only one ethnicity.

Foster care is also not a culture easily visible in our communities. Historically, foster care and adoption experiences were kept hidden and private as if they reflected negatively on the child personally. People may not wish to reveal their exposure to foster care also because it is a very personal experience and, as one can imagine, it is not easy to speak of separation from family members particularly if abuse, neglect, or abandonment has occurred. The confidentiality issues surrounding those exposed to foster care offer few opportunities to reveal to the general public how multicultural foster families and children are forming. It is becoming more widely accepted to see members of the same family with different or mixed ethnic backgrounds, but how these families and their communities address multiculturalism can affect how the multiracial child views his or her own identity, as well as ethnicities which may or may not be a part of his or her foster family's.[10]

Transracial Adoption

With more mixed race children entering into the system, transracial adoptions are increasing.[11] How can we help multiracial foster youth become individuals with a strong sense of racial and cultural identity? Although race is only one of many aspects contributing to personal identity, there is a need to understand more widely the aspects of racial heritage impacting child development. Transracial adoption has highlighted this need with its surrounding controversy over the past few decades.

Proponents of transracial adoption contend that "racial matching" policies of foster children and adoptive families prevent placement of children of color. It is also inherently discriminatory to make decisions on the sole basis of race. Foster youth miss chances of being in a permanent home sooner and prospective adoptive families are deprived of the opportunity to adopt a child. Opponents of transracial adoption, on the other hand, contend that adoptive families are not able to help transracially adopted children develop the ability to deal with racial issues and experiences outside of the home. Families may not be able to appreciate or help their children explore their racial identity and heritage when they have no previous experience doing such with themselves or with the particular cultures their adopted child is a part of.

For a multiracial child, it is equally uncertain whether a family with mixed ethnicities will better serve that child's needs. Each child and family is unique in what they bring to a family environment. Each child in the foster care system has individual needs that must be met by potential permanent placements. Few will argue that ethnic heritage should not be a factor in this significant decision, and efforts continue in the child welfare community to find ways to nourish multiculturalism in foster care youths and their families.

Issues Affecting Multiracial Children and Families

How we evaluate the importance of cultural heritage in a child's development is becoming a greater challenge as we face a dramatic conversion to more ethnically diverse communities. Foster care youth have a unique setback to overcome as transitioning families and homes interrupt their personal development process. Cultural awareness and understanding are delayed as children taken into the system face more perilous situations of losing family members, receiving inconsistent health care, transferring schools, and losing other things that most children have the privilege of taking for granted, such as having a reliable place to go to for holidays. For those who never find a legal permanent placement, many are released on their own by age 18. They leave state care without essential knowledge and appreciation for their multiracial identities, and potentially little awareness even of how to pursue further exploration of them.

Foster care is a cultural experience in itself and each child within it must adapt to it. Foster care becomes part of their personal history and may even replace what semblance of family history they have—a history that should be filled with information about their relatives and themselves.[12] They miss stories about previous generations including who their ancestors were, what ethnicities they are, how they met, where they lived, what their personal accomplishments were, and what happened to them. There may be no traces of heritage beyond a foster youth's own memories or beyond what their state case file documents.

Children who enter foster care are also immediately placed into a position of powerlessness. They are placed into a system that can create feelings of having no control over their future or themselves as individuals. They must live in an organizational structure that enforces how a dominant culture exists and how they are not part of it. This experience puts these youths at an immediate disadvantage in embracing cultures as equally influential and important. How do we empower these children who have lived in an accepted form of oppression? In order for us to nourish a positive multicultural experience in the world, we must ensure that multiracial experiences are positive.

One of the systemic goals of foster care is to support reunification of children with their birth families and relative caretakers when appropriate. Foster care can be extremely disruptive of identity when suddenly youths are placed with families of different races,

Casey Family Programs

On any given day there are more than 500,000 children living in foster care across the U.S. Although most will eventually be reunited with their birth families, approximately 125,000 of these children have no plan for reunification and little prospect for adoption. Originally, foster care was the safety net for children whose parents were ill or had died. Today's foster children have complicated needs; most have been abused or neglected, often by parents suffering from alcohol or substance abuse problems. A disproportionately large percentage of foster kids are multiracial. Casey Family Programs provides an array of services for children and youth, with foster care as its core. Casey services include adoption, guardianship, care by extended family, and reunification with birth families. Casey is also committed to helping youth in foster care make a successful transition to adulthood.
Learn more: www.casey.org

religions, values, and other cultural differences. Being mindful of the cultural environment children are coming from can be helpful in learning more about who they are already and how to provide more helpful advocacy and support as they mature. With a biracial child, if the foster placement is representative of only one of the child's ethnicities, behaviors and values of the family could dramatically affect how the child will eventually develop attitudes toward their other ethnic heritage.[13]

Fostering Multiculturalism

Each foster family placement is different and each may represent the first time a family has had to address any multicultural issues or the first time the child is in a home of a dominant culture unlike any previously experienced. Nourishing personal growth in multiracial children today will lead to more understanding and supportive multiracial families and communities in the future. We must learn to acknowledge the different ways families are formed, and how foster care and adoption are an integral part of how our community takes care of children in need. Helping our foster care youth develop into unique and capable adults involves personal commitment. We must understand how each foster child, through no fault of his or her own, has involuntarily become a part of a system that has limitations on helping his or her realize their potential. It is our choice to support this at-risk population by learning to accept and strengthen families in all their differences including blood relations and ethnic backgrounds.

Although there have been significant strides toward helping educate and support multiracial children and families in recent decades, social service providers, parents, advocates, and all adults are important role models for youth to learn about being multiracial in a society of racial inequality. We must determine how much impact growing up in a home with or without diverse cultures affects not only the child, but the entire family unit and the family dynamic. This responsibility involves more than just awareness of differences but analyzing our own belief systems, as well as those of all the individuals a foster child may be exposed to. If we do not, we risk failed placements. We risk more disruption for these at-risk children and only bigger challenges in the future of how to support our expanding multiracial communities.

We need to create family environments that promote exposure to all the different aspects of a child's heritage and the ethnic heritages the child is not a part of. It is important for children to understand and accept cultural differences and to think about their own beliefs in relation to others. A multicultural education consists of learning about customs, language, communication styles, holidays, traditions, foods, clothing, hairstyles, and religious practices, among other differences. As an adult role model, do you have awareness of these differences between cultures and do you encourage education about them?

Multiracial children in the foster care system need to learn that their ethnic heritage is an important part of their identity as individuals. Give them an opportunity to say what ethnicities they identify with and what that means to them. Encourage these youths to learn what their ethnic heritages are and understand how being placed in out-of-home care will expose them to different cultures and belief systems. Find out how important matching racial heritages of their foster care placements is to them and why. Encourage their self-discovery of multiculturalism and your own in the process.

Conclusion

Foster care has forced society to look at the definition of family in new ways. It is no longer simply blood ties that create a family, but the presence of love, acceptance, and nurturance. The image of family is changing and racial characteristics are visually bringing this new definition outside of the privacy of our homes. Children may no longer look exactly like their parents or caregivers, and it is important to learn to adapt to different faces, colors, and cultures within a family unit. Children are raised by extended relatives, different foster families, single parents, same sex parents, and an array of adult figures; all of these people can provide intricate family support systems. As mentors, parents, relatives, friends, advocates, and professionals, we all contribute to the culture within our communities and how all children growing within them will identify themselves in the future. Multiracial children are drawing much needed attention to past challenges of the foster care system but are also leading us to accept a new responsibility as a culturally diverse and accepting society. We must evaluate our own perceptions of family and expand them if necessary to ensure that multiracial foster youth are accepted and raised as unique contributors to our community. As we focus more efforts on understanding the impact of being a multiracial child, we must not forget the individual cultures behind this label. Acknowledging multiple ethnic heritages should mean more than just accepting a new category of "multiracial." This description will easily become as indefinable as the category of "Unknown" and we will accomplish little in our efforts at impacting our youth with positive cultural identities. We have a momentous responsibility because for those children who remain within the foster care system for the remainder of their childhood, the only family support system they may experience is the community of all of us.

Notes

1 U.S. Department of Health and Human Services, Administration for Children and Families, Administration on Children, Youth and Families, Children's Bureau, Adoption and Foster Care Analysis and Reporting System (AFCARS).

2 P. A. Curtis, G. Dale, Jr. and J. C. Kendall, eds. *The Foster Care Crisis: Translating Research into Policy and Practice* (Lincoln, NE: University of Nebraska Press, 1999), 84.

3 U.S. Department of Health and Human Services, Administration for Children and Families, Administration on Children, Youth and Families, Children's Bureau, Adoption and Foster Care Analysis and Reporting System (AFCARS).

4 W. Blome, "What Happens to Foster Kids: Educational Experiences of a Random Sample of Foster Care Youth and a Matched Group of non-Foster Care Youth," *Child and Adolescent Social Work Journal* 4(1) (1997), 41-53.

5 C. W. Harlow, *Profile of Jail Inmates 1996* (Washington, D.C.: U.S. Department of Justice, Bureau of Justice Statistics, 1998).

6 N. P. Roman and P. B. Wolfe, "Web of Failure: The Relationship Between Foster Care and Homelessness," *Public Welfare* 55 (1995), 4-11.

7 D. Brooks, Devon and A. Bussiere et. al, *Adoption and Race: Implementing the Multiethnic Placement Act of 1994 and the Interethnic Adoption Provision* (San Francisco: Stuart Foundations, 1997).

8 Ibid.

9 P. A. Curtis, G. Dale, Jr., and J. C. Kendall, eds. *The Foster Care Crisis: Translating Research into Policy and Practice* (1999).

10 H. Fogg-Davis, *The Ethics of Transracial Adoption* (Ithaca, NY: Cornell University Press, 2002), 20.

11 D. Brooks, Devon and A. Bussiere et. al, *Adoption and Race* (1997).

12 *It's My Life: Summary of a Framework for Youth Transitioning from Foster Care to Successful Adulthood* (Seattle: Casey Family Programs, 2001), 25.

13 H. Fogg-Davis, *The Ethics of Transracial Adoption* (2002).

Tuvaelagi
Samoan +
African American

Jon
Caucasian +
Filipino + Spanish

Mariko
Japanese? +
Filipina? + Adopted

Bernardo
Mexican + Colombian

Elana
Austrian

Antonio
Filipino + Spanish +
Norwegian + Honduran

Cindy
Korean + Black

Anu and Gloria
Indian + Portuguese +
Austrian

Ravi
Indian +
Portuguese

Brigette
Japanese + Irish

Section 3:
Specific
Multiracial
Heritages

Chapter 18

Issues and Experiences of Racially Mixed People
Maria P. P. Root, Ph.D.

Physical appearance and assumptions about racial group belonging shape the myriad of experiences that people of racially mixed heritage share. People of mixed ancestry, whether of an immediate interracial parentage or a generation or two removed, are the object of many people's fears: fear of the unknown, fear of the in-between.

Fear and prejudice are additives in the formula for racial discrimination, which ranges from the unconscious to the conscious. For example, we experience unconscious fears when our racial parentage is discovered to be something other than what an acquaintance or stranger initially thought. Subsequently, we are treated differently. For example, a young biracial woman of African American and German parentage told me that her White fifth-grade teacher was critical of her classroom performance even though she was a good student. Her German mother requested a parent-teacher conference. The next day at school the teacher inappropriately remarked, "I didn't know your mother was White." After this sequence of events, the young woman remembers herself as an 11-year-old girl seeking to understand why her teacher had stopped being critical and started praising her. Nothing about her performance had changed, except that her teacher now knew she had a White mother. When she brought this up to her parents, her mother and father used this experience

as a teaching point about racial prejudice and its irrational realities in this country. The White supremacist literature conveys the conscious display of displaced fear of the unknown in its hatred of mixed race people. Some groups' missions include eradication of mixed race people, the harbingers of a "mongrel race," and the people who make them. Until recently, the legal system of racial classification also did everything to eliminate recognition of the in-between and unknown.

Whereas a small minority of people thinks in this extreme, misperceptions of mixed race people abound between the extremes. These misperceptions of multiracial people and their origins arise largely because we have an unresolved history of racial maltreatment of people of color, privilege by White and light skin color, and a long history of trying to prevent interracial marriage and its production of children in which the irrationality of privilege by color was so apparent.

No rational logic guides or predicts why mixed race people should experience the things they do. Anecdotally, the most frequently shared experiences across groups are the "What are you?" question and the insistence, confusion, and/or distress that people have when a mixed race person identifies differently than they expect, for example, biracial Asian-Latino, Black and

White, or African-Indian. More recently, young people of mixed descent are inadvertently transgressing the hypodescent and "one-drop rules." Some declare they are White because they did not know this centuries-old rule. Most of these young people are not trying to pass as White and may not know what this means. However, this old narrative is frequently misapplied to this latter identity. All of these declarations are an issue only because people have come to believe the fairy tale of race.

The myriad of irrational experiences confronting multiracial youth complicates racial and ethnic identity development as well as a sense of social belonging, attractiveness, and esteem. It makes what is often an assumed or invisible process lengthier, more conscious, and/or more labored. Parents and other significant adults want to help navigate a racial concourse with which they are not entirely acquainted. In multiracial family support groups, both White parents and parents of color who have looked at their own experiences and observed the experiences of their children conclude they do not share the same experience and need more information on how to guide them and walk with them through the parts of the journey they can.

Whereas there are commonalities in the mixed race experience, such as being questioned about one's identity, being pressured to choose just one race, hearing things you might not hear if people thought you identified as you did (spying), or being thought of as exotic looking, there are specific issues and experiences related to racial combinations. For example, fewer persons of Black-White parentage are asked, "Where you are from?" compared to persons of Asian-White parentage. Even this question has changed in a generation. This was probably one of the two most frequently posed questions to persons of such heritage born through the 1960s. Few groups are as direct about asking the percentage of heritage, blood quantum, as in Native American interchanges. Persons of Latino descent are more frequently than any other group asked if they are bilingual. Persons of Asian descent particularly the 1.5 or second generation are also asked this question.

The Experiences of Mixed Race People

Below, I list 50 questions or comments that evolved from a questionnaire of experiences of multiracial people for a study on biracial siblings I conducted from 1996 to 1997. These questions and comments provide an introduction to the way in which race consciousness is brought up directly, sideways, and from all sides. These comments and questions, though not an exhaustive list, provide a window into how this country internalizes assumptions about race, belonging, and identity. They socialize the mixed race person to understand as well as question race, American style. It is a monoracial system, permitting one race per person. Not everyone experiences these questions or comments similarly. One person might enjoy being asked, "What are you?" whereas their sibling might dread and resent the question. This list provides a launching point for sharing, discussing, laughing, debriefing, and educating.

1. You have been told, "You have to choose; you can't be both."
2. Your ethnicity was mistakenly identified.
3. People assumed your race to be different by phone than in person.
4. You are accused of not acting or wanting to be Latino, Asian, Black, etc...
5. You have been told, "Mixed race people are so beautiful or handsome."
6. Strangers looked between you and your parent(s) to figure out if you were related.
7. You have been told, "You don't look Native, Black, Latino..."
8. You have been asked, "What are you?"
9. People say things they might not otherwise say if they knew how you identified racially.
10. You have been asked, "Where are you from?"
11. You have repeatedly been the recipient of stares or longer than passing glances from strangers.
12. You have been told, "You look exotic."
13. Your choice of friends has been interpreted as your "selling out" or not being authentic.
14. You have been accused of "acting or wanting to be White."
15. Judgments of your racial authenticity have been based upon your boyfriend's or girlfriend's (partner's) race.
16. Comments are made about your hair or hairstyle, skin color, eye

shape, etc.

17. You have been subjected to jokes about mixed race people.
18. You have been told, "You think you're too good for your own kind."
19. Grandparent(s) or relatives don't accept you because of your parents' interracial relationship.
20. Your parents or relatives compete to "claim" you for their own racial or ethnic group.
21. You have been told, "You have the best of both worlds."
22. You have been asked about your racial or ethnic heritage as an object of curiosity.
23. Upon meeting you, people seem confused by your last name. They do not think it "matches" you.
24. People assume you are confused about your racial identity or have had a hard time figuring it out.
25. People speak to you in foreign languages because of how they interpret your physical appearance.
26. You have been told, "Society doesn't recognize mixed race."
27. You have been told, "You aren't really Black, Latino, Asian..."
28. You have been mistaken for another person of mixed heritage who does not resemble you.
29. You have been told you must be full of self-loathing or hatred because of how you racially identify yourself.
30. You have been told, "You are a mistake."
31. Different people perceive your race differently based upon the company you keep.
32. The race people assign you varies in different parts of the U.S.A.
33. You have difficulty filling out forms asking for a single race.
34. You identify your race differently than others identify you.
35. You are told, "You aren't like other Indians, Asians, Latinos, etc..."
36. Your siblings identify their race differently than you do yours.
37. You have been called racial slurs of groups with which you do not share heritage.
38. Friends suggest that you date someone based upon the race or ethnicity with which they think you should identify.
39. Your parents identify your race differently than you identify.
40. You are told, "You aren't Black, Latino, Asian, etc...enough."

41. Your mother was assumed to be your nanny or babysitter.
42. A stranger assumes that your father is your "older boyfriend" or your mother is the "older woman."
43. You were treated differently by relatives or your parents than a sibling on the basis of racial features.
44. You were well liked by peers but were not asked for dates.
45. You wish you were darker and try to get as much sun as possible.
46. People assume your father was in the military.
47. You have enrolled in Spanish language classes in order to develop the ability to say affirmatively when asked the question, "Do you speak the language?" and remove one of the blocks to authenticity.
48. Your "friends" become more distant when they think associating with you will make their racial authenticity or popularity questionable.
49. When people see your mother or father, they change how they treat or think about you.
50. You have tried to hide one or both parents from view of people who know you but are not your closest friends.

Summary

Seldom is the racial discrimination that mixed race children and people experience discussed. Yes, mixed race people may get more than one experience. However, it is not always the best of both worlds. We are recipients of the old-fashioned type of racism directed towards each of the racial groups. We just get it sometimes for and from more than one group. We are also the recipients of the fear and prejudice that culminates in prejudice against race mixing and its result.

Thank goodness children are resilient to get through the verbal stone-throwing that thoughtless and fearful comments may represent. Their resiliency at the beginning of this new millenium are buoyed by knowing that there are many other children like them and much more information available for their parents and teachers. However, we must keep in mind that not all children are equally resilient. We must all share in educating ourselves so that our racial consciousness and work on anti-racism is deepened by understanding this aspect of the multiracial experience.

Binah
Filipina +
Caucasian

Jared
African American +
Caucasian

Avery
Black + Caucasian +
Native American

Michael
Filipino + Dutch

James
Black +
White +
Adopted

Elaine
Mexican + Irish +
Czech + Jewish

Kalani
Hawaiian + Filipino + Chinese +
Spanish + English + Irish +
Scottish + Portugese +
BlackFoot

Monique
African American +
Italian + Irish + Adopted

Janiva Cifuentes-Hiss
Age: 19
Racial/Ethnic Heritage: Colombian and Irish

My parents met in Colombia where my mother was a student and my father was in the Peace Corps. As a young child, I lived with my family in Bogotá, Colombia, which indelibly shaped my life experience and attitudes today. Both of my parents are bilingual and I was raised speaking Spanish as well as English. I experienced the culture shock of being in the first grade in the U.S. and, having spoken only Spanish, having to remember how to speak English again. I remember feeling frustrated that I couldn't communicate with my classmates and teachers.

I am thankful that my parents instilled pride and knowledge of our Irish and Colombian heritage from a young age. They bought me books about my Indigenous ancestors, and I became connected with my Irish heritage through the Irish music group where my father played.

My neighborhood and school were predominantly Caucasian. I was one of the few minorities in my school, and in some ways that shaped a heightened awareness and pride in my ethnicity. However, I experienced confusion about my multiethnic identity, and frustration when faced with the "Check Only One" box on application forms. I would check "Hispanic/Latino" because the box for White said "non-Hispanic." Generally, I was confused and perplexed that I felt dishonest no matter which box I checked. Growing up, there were few resources, TV shows, or teachers that explicitly dealt with mixed race issues, and I expressed my feelings of isolation in poetry detailing the paradox of tragedy and the blessing of "being on the outside" of two racialized worlds. I didn't question the system that forced people into boxes as

much as I felt angry for finding myself in a catch-22. Neither box could possibly capture the entirety of my identity. This, combined with the typical middle school angst, increased my feelings of being misunderstood by most of my peers and teachers.

In high school, I found pride and confidence in proclaiming my Latina identity. I became involved in the Hispanic Youth Network where I experienced support, inspiration, and leadership opportunities in the Latino community. Even so, I sometimes felt that, because of my appearance, I could never be Latina "enough." I hated the fact that my light complexion, blue eyes, and blonde hair seemed to betray my Colombian heritage. I resented that I could easily "pass" as White. I would do anything to be brown like my brother, sister, mother, and friends. I was frustrated by constantly feeling the pressure to "prove" my Latina ethnicity. In college, increasing awareness about the concept of *mestizaje*, the race mixing that is such a part of many Latin American societies, and racialized misconceptions about Latinos led me to gradually change my perceptions of being mixed.

Latinos come in all colors. Although I might not fit the stereotypical mold of the racialized "Latina" in the U.S., I have grown more confident in embracing everything that I am. I am aware of the implications of the White privilege I experience on a daily basis. However, I also recognize the unique experience and perspective that I have as a mixed race Latina. I will not deny my *Latinidad* simply because of the way I am perceived. I am proud to be a mixed race "*Colomgringa*."

Testimonial

Chapter 19

Children of Latino/Anglo Interethnic Families
Juanita M. Dimas, Ph.D.

People from the same ethnic and racial groups can have similar as well as very different experiences. Not only are there many different groups of Latinos/as (e.g., Mexican American, Puerto Rican, Cuban, etc.), there can be many different types of mixes. When thinking of multiracial issues, people often assume a mix of two races, forgetting about the possibility of there being more than two races. For example, Maria's experiences may be very different from Teresa's experiences even though both are of Latina/Anglo inter-ethnic families. Maria considers herself Mexican American of American Indian and Spanish ancestry on her father's side and Irish American on her mother's side. Teresa considers herself Puerto Rican, of Black/Chinese ancestry on her mother's side and White on her father's side. This chapter focuses on the Latino/Anglo mix, although it is more of an issue of culture and ethnicity than race. It is also useful to remember that the Latino/a experience by definition is multiracial, as the majority of Latinos/as are of mixed racial heritage (Latinos/as are a new world mix of native American and Spanish, along with many other influences, such as African, Chinese, etc.).

It is now generally accepted by biologists that race is not based in biology. Rather, race is defined by society, can change over time across different cultures, and is based on the political climate of the time and place. For example, someone considered White in Latin America quickly becomes non-White in the U.S.

	Maria	Miguel	Teresa	Mary
Calls self	1/2 and 1/2	Puerto Rican	Puerto Rican	Chicana
Father	Mexican American) (Native Am. & Spanish)	White	White	Mexican American (Native Am & Spanish)
Mother	Irish American	Puerto Rican (Black & Chinese)	Puerto Rican (Black & Chinese)	Irish American
Hair	dark brown	light brown	dark brown	blond
Eyes	dark brown	hazel	black	blue

Just as race is defined differently by different groups of people, so is mixed race defined differently. For example, Maria may not be considered mixed race by many of her relatives in Mexico, because they may identify as White, but they probably consider her to be of mixed ethnicity or culture, as Irish American is very different from Mexican or Mexican American—based more on culture than on color. But in the U.S., because of the definition of race and race relations, Maria is typically identified by the U.S. mainstream as non-White and treated accordingly. Remember, non-White in the U.S. mainstream is usually viewed and treated with less respect than White. U.S. Latinos/as typically are more interested in whether Maria acknowledges being Latina and if she speaks Spanish.

Being Latino/Anglo mix can be a very different experience than many other types of combinations with Anglo (e.g., Japanese/White). This difference is due in large part to two reasons: 1) Latino/a by itself is already a mix; and 2) Latino/Anglo mix is reflective of the historical origins of this country. The U.S. Census 2000 tried to recognize that Latinos/as can be of any race, but the creators of the census did not understand that Latinos/as do not typically identify with the common racial categories used in the U.S. For example, the Census 2000 was the first time people could mark more than one box for their ethnicity and race. The Hispanic/Latino/a origin question was asked before the race question. (Hispanics/Latinos can be of any race).

• Hispanic or Latino
• Not Hispanic or Latino

And then people could select all the categories that applied to them from the list of "Races:"

• White
• Black or African American
• American Indian and Alaska Native
• Asian
• Native Hawaiian and Other Pacific Islander
• Some other race

Almost all (97%) the people who marked "Some other race" were Latino/a! And almost half (43%) of all Latinos/as marked "Some other race"! Also, one in three of those who marked that they were mixed race said that they were Latino/a. It can get very confusing because one person's definition of race is not always the same as another person's definition. Latinos/as are often more focused on ethnicity or culture rather than race. Ethnicity is the cultural group that a person belongs to, referring to the customs, values, beliefs and behaviors that are passed on from one generation to the next. Race is defined differently by different societies, but is typically based on color and has only to do with the way one looks to other people and as a result how one is treated by other people. Typically, among Latinos/as, Puerto Ricans in New York, Cubans in Miami, and Mexicans in Los Angeles are considered different from the other ethnically, regardless of color. For example, it is most important to Teresa that she is Puerto Rican, not that she is Black, as others who do not know her tend to see her.

Given the great degree of racial mixing for centuries among Latinos/as, it is almost impossible to draw lines between "racial" groups. For example, within single-family units there is often a wide spectrum of color evidenced in the various family members: one child can appear very Black, another very White, another with strong Indian features, and the others all shades in between. No questions are asked, no impropriety presumed, and no consideration for implied ancestry focused upon. However, while Latinos/as do not fit neatly into the U.S. race categories, Latinos/as do have a value on colorism, where lighter is usually considered better than darker. The recognition of color exists among Latinos/as and there is more room to prove oneself, although admittedly it is more difficult the darker you are. For example, a full-blooded Indian, Benito Juarez, was elected President of Mexico; a Japanese Peruvian, Alberto Fujimori, was elected President of Perú; and a Black mestizo, Hugo Chavez, was elected President of Venezuela. These Latino ways still influence Latinos/as in the U.S., although the U.S. mainstream ways also influence U.S. Latinos, and U.S. Latinos/as gradually internalize the U.S. ways. When U.S. categories are imposed on Latinos/as, categorizations are made with very unclear boundaries, leading to much confusion.

While Latinos/as can often identify as "mixed White," U.S. social definitions have not included "mixed White" as a possibility, as White is only pure. In the U.S., Latinos/as have been treated as "non-White," and thus the White option among the provided racial categories is not a viable option for Latinos/as, as they are not allowed to identify with the dominant power group of the U.S. Latinos/as in the U.S. are treated by the dominant White European American group as a racial minority group and often treated with discrimination. Thus, U.S. Latinos/as experience the realities of racism. While Maria may on one hand identify as "White" and is able to mark that on the census, her experiences with U.S. society tell her that she is not "White." So she does not mark White on the census, and instead, marks "other" because none of the categories match with her experience. While traditionally Latinos/as have identified ethnically as Latino/a or with their specific nationality, rather than racially, there is a growing movement throughout the Americas to identify as "mestizo" or racially mixed. But the meaning of "mestizaje" or "mix" is different in Latin America than in the U.S. and it has been suggested that the Latin American meaning will influence how we think of race and mixed race in the U.S.

The second way the Latino/Anglo mix is different than other Anglo mixes is because the Latino/Anglo mix is reflective of the origins of this country. While either side, Latino or Anglo, may have recently immigrated to the U.S., it is most common that both sides have been in the U.S. for many generations. About half of third-generation Latinos/as marry non-Latinos/as, which gives them one of the highest rates of intermarriage. The term "American" can apply to both sides of the mix, even if the Latino/a recently immigrated, as there are three Americas, and all Latinos/as are thus "Americans." Mexican Americans are the largest Latino group in the U.S., many of who intermarry. Mexicans were on part of the land that is now called the U.S. (e.g., New Mexico, Texas, Arizona, California), even before the English arrived on Plymouth Rock. Mexicans historically are a mix of American Indian and Spanish. The current mix of Mexican American and Anglo can be a symbolic representation of the land that was once Indian territory, then French, then Mexican, and now U.S. The children of Latino/Anglo interethnic families are a microcosm of that history—sometimes peaceful, sometimes in conflict, sometimes accepted by one group, sometimes by the other group. This legacy gives a unique urgency to the questions "Who am I?" "How do others see me?" and "Where do I belong?"

All children ask these questions, but they are particularly important for mixed race and inter-ethnic children (see Identity Development Issues for Multiracial Multiethnic Youth 15 to 17 years old chapter in this book).

Identity and Adjustment Among Children of Latino/Anglo Interethnic Families

Some people believe that being mixed race causes problems of identity and adjustment, because the person does not belong to either group. Other people believe that it makes for stronger identity and better adjustment because the person has the best of both worlds. The little research that exists supports the idea of "the best of both worlds." The research also shows that family and society are very important in the process.

Although it is relatively uncommon for studies of inter-ethnic families to include Latino/a groups, one qualitative study examined "part" Japanese Americans in Hawai'i, as well as "part" Mexican Americans in New Mexico.[1] It was found that Latino/a identity was associated with physical appearance, percentage of fathers' Latino heritage, and identification with the Latino/a culture. Of interest was the common factor among the two sample groups that was associated with ethnic identity; the more the minority group (whether Mexican American or Japanese American) could be distinguished from other ethnic groups in the area, the more the interethnic individuals identified with the minority group. The salient distinguishing markers were different for Mexican Americans in New Mexico than for Japanese Americans in Hawai'i. In Hawai'i, the public identifier was Eastern religion (Shintoism and Buddhism), and in New Mexico, the public identifier was physical characteristics. For example, in New Mexico, Maria may identify more with Mexican American than Mary because her darker features allow others to identify her as Mexican American and not Anglo.

Another study of teenagers of Latino/a and European American inter-ethnic families in California also found that public identifiers were the last name and physical appearance. The more the teenager could be identified by others as Latino/a, through last name and physical appearance, the more the teen behaved and identified as Latino/a. In addition, the more the adolescent

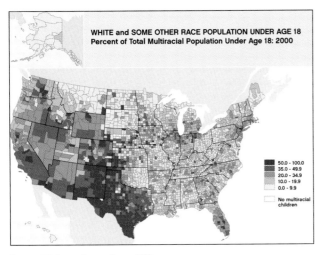

WHITE and SOME OTHER RACE POPULATION UNDER AGE 18
Percent of Total Multiracial Population Under Age 18: 2000

50.0 - 100.0
35.0 - 49.9
20.0 - 34.9
10.0 - 19.9
0.0 - 9.9

No multiracial
children

Source: U.S. Census Bureau, Census 2000.

This map shows a county-by-county look at the percent of multiracial children under age 18 who checked both "White" and "Some Other Race" in Census 2000. Many of the youth who did so had one Hispanic and one non-Hispanic White parent.

behaved and identified as Latino/a, the more psychological problems they reported.[2] It is probably not looking like a Latino/a that causes the problems, but rather being treated as a Latino/a in the U.S. There is no reason that name and physical appearance should be related to adjustment. Instead, it is the way that society's negative attitudes are targeted to certain individuals and the ways these individuals would then need to cope with the effects of discrimination. For example, Maria, whose last name is Gonzalez and has dark brown eyes and hair, is treated very differently from her classmate of the same inter-ethnic background whose name is Mary Jones, who is blonde and blue-eyed. Maria is recognized by her classmates and teachers as Latina, whereas they do not see Mary as Latina even though Mary identifies just as much with her Latina side as does Maria. We see that identity is both how the person sees herself, as well as how others see her and treat her. But Maria's and Mary's views of themselves are very much impacted by how they are treated by others. Maria is more uncertain about her academic abilities than Mary, even though she has better grades, partly because many teachers have lower expectations for Maria than they do for Mary.

Although not addressing inter-ethnic heritage, studies show how U.S.-born adolescents may internalize negative stereotypes attributed to their ethnic group.[3] Self-images held by *foreign-born* Mexican Americans included proud, religious, strong family ties, athletic, gregarious, friendly, happy, field workers, racially tolerant, short, fat and dark, practical, and well adjusted. Self-images held by *U.S.-born* Mexican Americans included emotional, unscientific, authoritarian, materialistic, old-fashioned, poor and of a low social class, uneducated or poorly educated, short, fat and dark, little care for education, mistrusted, proud, lazy, indifferent, and unambitious. We see that U.S.-born Mexican Americans hold significantly more negative stereotypes of their group than do Mexican-born. What the above study of interethnic families suggests is how easily one can be publicly identified to be the target of negative stereotypes, which in turn may affect adjustment.

Public identifiers may define a person's "place" in society and influence an individual's ability to negotiate the accompanying stressors that can influence his or her psychological adjustment. As this is suggestive of society's role in influencing individuals' psychosocial adjustment, there are immediate implications for families, schools and clinicians. This is supported by research indicating that children's positive adjustment is facilitated when parents recognize the existence of prejudice in the larger society, teach their children that racism is a reality, and the family communicates about race and racism. Maria and Mary have very different experiences and identity of being Mexican American and Irish mix, partly because of their different "places" in society. And Teresa's place is also very different, because she is also identified by others as something that she does not identify with. Because Teresa can appear Black, many times people who do not know her classify her as African American when Teresa does not identify with that cultural group. While she is quite sure of herself, she does constantly need to define who she is to others, whereas other people do not need to take the same time and energy to focus on that issue. However, people have a harder time in classifying her brother, Miguel, by looks. While Miguel does not have to correct the misperceptions, he does more often have to answer the question "What are you?" Teresa and Maria, who have dark features, often find themselves in the awkward presence of other Latinas speaking derogatorily of Anglos in their presence. They must choose whether to speak up and identify themselves as also belonging to that group or remain silent. Mary, who has light features, has the opposite experience: when Whites may speak derogatorily of Latinas in her presence she must decide whether and how to identify herself to them. Miguel is unique among the three because his physical looks could go either way. As a result, he can find himself in both awkward situations. While to be accepted by other Anglos, physical appearance is often the most important aspect, to be accepted as Latino/a by other Latinos/as, identity and behavior are usually most important. For example, although Mary has light features, she identifies as Chicana and speaks Spanish, and thus she is readily accepted as Latina by other Latinos/as.

The study with children from Latino/Anglo interethnic families in California also showed that cultural behavior and ethnic identity, of the parents as well as of the teenagers, are related to teen adjustment. The more parents *identify* as Latino/a, the more their children also *identify* as Latino/a. Latino/a *behavior* of the teenager is *not* related to their Latino/a parent's Latino/a *behavior*, but European American parents do impact how much their teenager engages in Latino/a customs. The more a European American (Anglo) parent follows Latino/a customs and embraces a Latino/a identity, the more adolescents also follow Latino/a customs. But, in this study, there were more Latino fathers and Anglo mothers. So it might not be so much whether the *Anglo* parent identifies and follows Latino/a behavior, as much as whether it is the *mother* that does. We all develop many different identities: gender, ethnic, sexual orientation, professional, and so on. Our parents are very important in exposing us to some of our options. Maria's, Teresa's, and Mary's mothers are important to each of them in many ways, including teaching what it is like to be a girl and a woman. Teresa can learn from her mother what it means to be a Latina, and a woman of color in our society, but Maria's mom is White. While Maria's mom cannot be a model of a woman of color, Maria's mom can learn and participate in Latino/a customs and show by example that Latino/a culture is an important and valuable aspect of Maria's life.

In summary, the majority of Latinos/as are of mixed racial heritage, which has different socio-political meaning to different groups of people. The different definition and importance placed on "race" and "ethnicity" come into conflict when the U.S. mainstream concepts of racial categories are imposed on Latinos/as in the U.S. Latinos/as are becoming the largest minority group in the U.S. with a large number of children and high rates of intermarriage. What is the implication in the Latino/a communities and in U.S. mainstream society when children of Latino/Anglo interethnic families become the largest multiracial population in future generations? Latino/a conceptualization of race and mixed race will influence U.S. discussions. We do know that in the U.S. it is important for both the Latino/a and European American parent to teach their interethnic children Latino/a culture so that the children can have positive images and identity to buffer against dominant society's negative images and stereotypes. Race and mixed race are social ideas that will be influenced and challenged by the Latino/a experiences.

Did you know?

Here are some well-known multiracial people of both Latino/a and Caucasian heritage:

Christina Aguilera (Singer)
Joan Baez (Singer)
Benjamin Bratt (Actor)
Zach De La Rocha (Singer, Political Activist)
Cameron Diaz (Actor)
Soledad O'Brien (Journalist)
Anthony Quinn (Actor)
Bill Richardson (Politician)
Geraldo Rivera (Journalist)
Christy Turlington (Model)

Notes

1 C. W. Stephan, "Intergroup Anxiety and Intergroup Interaction, 'Prejudice, Polemic or Progress,'" in *Cultural Diversity and the Schools,* eds. J. Lynch, C. Modgil and S. Modgil (London: The Falmer Press, 1992).

2 R. Buriel, "Integration with Traditional Mexican-American Culture and Sociocultural Adjustment," in *Chicano Psychology*, 2nd Ed., ed. Martinez (Littleton, CO: Academic Press, Inc., 1984).

3 J. M. Dimas, "Cultural Behavior in Children of Interethnic Families: A Structural Family Model," (in press).

Alice
Peruvian + Japanese + Quechuan

Fumie
Peruvian + Japanese + Quechuan

Anthony Brave

Age: 22

Racial/Ethnic Heritage: Pembina Band of Chippewa-Cree and Caucasian

My name is Anthony Brave. Honestly, I don't think I am a good advocate to write about being American Indian and White because I cannot advocate the idea of race in any way. It's just because self-identification is such a hard topic for me to clearly express my opinion. I am half American Indian and half White. Although I have grown up with both of these families, I also have an African American family, through my step dad.

So, I had a pretty diverse childhood, and I have been pretty hurt by people's stereotypes about me and my family. I don't choose to accept those stereotypes and I also do not choose to put myself in any sort of category. I haven't been Indian "enough" for Indians but not White "enough" for this society. I'm certainly not Black "enough" for Black people. As I get older I don't seem American "enough", or enough anything for people.

I noticed many things growing up pertaining to race as well as class. The White side of the family was pretty well off. The African Americans were not so well off. The American Indian side was kind of in the middle. They never intermingled and I didn't understand it.

Mostly what I couldn't understand was my own pain. My mother divorced my father when I was three years old, because he became an alcoholic. She later remarried another man, my stepfather, who unfortunately went to jail for life. Basically, our mom raised both my little brother and me. Both of my fatherly figures couldn't be with me, which broke my heart twice. I was also molested as a child. All the kids around me had parents and houses and confidence. I could hardly spend time with my own mom because she was working so much.

There were so many questions that I couldn't answer. As I grew older, adolescence plus great confusion did not make for a good combination. It blew up like a bomb. I was into drugs, stealing, drinking, smoking, and I dropped out of high school. When this started, it only increased my problems. I lost all hope for life and began spiraling towards suicide. I guess you could say that through the power of love, I was able to turn my life around.

When I was 17 years old I met a very sweet girl who became my girlfriend for almost three years. She was undergoing similar problems. For that time that we were together, we protected each other, no matter what, and slowly we learned about unconditional love. With that love we found, we used it as our strength to be the people that we wanted to be.

Notice, I used the word unconditional when describing the type of love that changed my life. That word transcends race, religion, class, gender, nationality: it transcends everything. Unconditional love comes from caring, understanding, and empathy. The gulfs between people, race or whatever else they may be, are purely illusions and can cause little more than a lifetime of pain. My girlfriend has supported my decision to not identify as anything but myself, regardless of what is in other people's minds. I hope everybody can experience unconditional love.

Testimonial

Chapter 20

But, You Don't Look Like an Indian...Children of Native American and Caucasian Heritage

Robin A. LaDue, Ph.D.

One of my relations was Chief Sealth, you know, the chief Seattle was named after. Well, this past week, the Secretary of the Interior decided my people were "extinct." So, does this mean I do not exist?

-Comments of a 16-year-old Duwamish youth upon hearing that the Secretary of the Interior, Gale Norton, declared the Duwamish people extinct.

How do you explain to your non-Native friends that the government has just declared you nonexistent? You are 16 years old. Your non-Native friends do not understand the implications of not being part of an ancient people. Your Native friends come from tribes that may have land, their own languages, and today, perhaps, casino monies that will fund them through school. How do you reconcile an inner sense of spirit and self with the seemingly capricious and possibly racist decisions of a White woman who makes a political decision to override the policy of her boss's predecessor? How do you explain your father crying when he heard the news?

These questions are not simply those being asked by people of the Duwamish tribe. Indeed, the issue of identity, quantum, enrollment, history, and a sense of self are concerns and issues that have been faced by Native people since the first day of contact with Europeans. What are the social and mental health implications for today's Native youth and those of mixed Native descent? How can professionals help in the journey of self-discovery and acceptance for Native youth? This chapter is intended to help answer some of these questions, but an understanding of the history and politics that affect life for Native youth and their families on a daily basis comes first.

But, you don't look like an Indian!
What part Indian are you?
How much Indian are you?

Being a young person of mixed Native American descent is an interesting proposition in the United States at the turn of a new millennium. Above is a small sample of the many comments and questions often endured by those of mixed Native descent, particularly those who do not fit the stereotypical picture of the dark eyes, long flowing dark tresses, Pocahantas/noble savage illusion. These comments are commonly the first reaction of both people from the United States and those from other countries around the world.

Given the decimation of many tribal groups by disease, cultural trauma, alcoholism, warfare, and simple grief, often the only chance a tribal group had to survive into the twenty-first century was to marry outside their kinship group with settlers or, in the 19th century South, with the slaves brought in to work the plantations. In reality, this small population (approximately four million people, according to Census 2000) of Native Americans and Alaska Natives are a remarkably diverse group with a rich past, present culture, and strength of courage and perseverance.

What tribe are you from?
Where is your land?
Are you enrolled?
What is your quantum?

These questions often come from other Native people, both those of mixed descent and "full-bloods." These questions are intended to establish authenticity and extended relationships. In fact, given the history of trappers coming across the country with the Hudson Bay Company and French fur traders, many people have blood connections, albeit separated by many degrees.

The other part of establishing authenticity among Native Americans has to do with the significant number of people who claim Native blood with no knowledge of, connection to, or participation in any traditional activities. One common response that will actually trigger a snicker or outright laugh is: "My grandmother was a Cherokee princess." If all people who claimed such descent were telling the truth, the Cherokee people would number in the many millions! What is being asked in these questions can be as simple as, "Who are you and do you know who you are and who your people are?"

The number of people claiming Native American blood, most of them being of mixed descent, rose from 2 million in 1990 to 4.1 million in 2000. There is an endless variety of combinations. Census 2000 identified 1,082,683 people who checked both Native American and European Caucasian, by far the largest number of the mixed descent Native Americans. But 182,494 people checked both Native American and African American; 52,429 marked both Native American and Asian; and 7,328 checked off boxes for both Native American and Hawaiian.[1] In actuality, Native American people have intermarried and had children with

the vast majority of other ethnic and cultural groups in the contiguous United States, and Alaska and Hawai'i.

There are Native Americans in every state with the largest populations in Oklahoma, Arizona, and California. Over half now reside in urban areas. While these basic facts give lie, in themselves, to the stereotypes often used to "determine if someone is Native," it is important to know some of the history that has led to the issues facing people of mixed Native American descent today.

Many older Native Americans, particularly those impacted by the boarding schools, still fight to overcome the trauma of all the damage such schools engendered. This was created by the deliberately drawn mandate of these institutions to "remove the Indian from the child." At this they often failed, but they did succeed in causing damage from emotional, physical, sexual abuse, loss of family and culture, and cultivation of shame over being Native or of mixed Native descent. The shame caused by being forced into such school placements has been passed on to their children. While some children, now adults, have struggled and succeeded in overcoming the denial of Nativeness and self-loathing this shame cultivates, it is not necessarily true for all members of any given family and/or kinship group.

The legacy of traumatized and shamed parents often makes it difficult for youths of mixed Native descent to find a balance in their self-identity. Although there has been a large movement in Canada against the boarding school and the horrendous psychological damage inflicted by these schools, there has not been a corresponding groundswell in the United States. Too often, the damage from the boarding schools is expressed in an ambivalence many Native parents feel towards their tribe, culture, and spiritual beliefs. While there is clearly more support for such practices today, many youth may not have spiritual resources within their own families or tribes but, instead, adopt a pan-Native view of the world.

I know that many Whites in [my town] are mad about the casino. Now, a lot of my friends at school are angry because everyone in my tribe gets casino money every month. I feel like I should apologize, but my dad says it is a small price for losing our land. I just don't know how to explain it to my friends. Their parents think we are just going to drink up every penny. My parents don't even drink.

–A 14-year-old Native girl's reflections on hearing the news that her tribe is going to start paying each tribal member from casino revenue.

Cultural and racial identification are not struggles that have ended for Native youth. Indeed, in many ways these struggles have increased in recent years. As casinos have sprung up around the country in many Native communities, tribes have begun a push for their young members to become educated, often paying tuition, books, fees, and a living stipend. While casino money has been a boon to many Native communities, it has also fostered anger, resentment, and an increase in the openness of racism in many communities. For many Native youth, it feels as if this is a "lose-lose" situation: get educated and lose your cultural identity; have resources and lose your friends.

The issue of being of mixed blood is no small one among Native people. Today, the questions of quantum may mean a free education or no education. It may mean housing, health care, and resources or being denied access to even the most basic aspects of life. It may mean watching your older sibling have access to the benefits of enrollment while you yourself are denied.

What of those youths who have one Native parent and one non-Native parent? The same issues of identification, belonging, and deciding what culture one sees as paramount exist. In the past if a woman married outside her tribe, her children were not allowed to be enrolled; but this is no longer the case. The issues become more internal to the family in terms of the family's comfort with mixed race and culture. It also raises issues of the extended family's support of the other side of the family. For example, if there is a strong anti-Native sentiment or a strong anti-Caucasian sentiment among extended family members, this can cause conflict within the immediate family and make positive self-identity more difficult.

The issues discussed in the previous paragraph are not unique to Native youth. What is different is that the issue of legal identification combines with the family issues—e.g., enrollment, quantum, and recognition—that other ethnic, racial, and cultural groups do not have. For Native youth, having one parent who is not Native may create problems with loyalty to that parent or group. If there is room in the family for multiple identifications, this may be less of a concern.

Crossbloods: Bone Courts, Bingo and Other Reports
Gerald Vizenor, University of Minnesota Press, 1990

(From the University of Minnesota Press) Gerald Vizenor is one of the few American Indian mixed-bloods who has had a significant career as a journalist. *Crossbloods* contains some of his best editorial articles, magazine stories, and several essays that were published in *American Indian Quarterly*. This collection includes essays on reservation treaties, bingo as a cash crop, and bone courts to protect tribal remains; Thomas White Hawk, cultural schizophrenia, and capital punishment; an editorial series on the rise of the American Indian Movement; and articles on crossblood identities, education, hunting and fishing, paraeconomic survival, and alcoholism.

It is an ironic note that Native American people are the only native-born Americans who carry cards or have to prove they belong to their ancestral group. In a country where one drop of African American blood has defined membership in that group, it is a further irony that the first people of this land lose their membership if they carry a certain amount of Native blood. A third irony is the number of people who now claim to be Native. Is this the loss of shame or, as postulated, simply another period of romanticizing the "noble savage" stereotype?

The Fighting Illini
The Florida Seminole
The Atlanta Braves
The Cleveland Indians
The Washington Redskins

The use of Native images for mascots, particularly in high school and college, is one that has often been minimized or trivialized by the media. In actuality, the dehumanization of Native people through the use of such terms is a concern. For people who are "visibly" Native or who strongly identify with their Native culture, marginalizing Native and mixed Native youth through stereotypes can lead to increased alienation and frustration. In the Seattle area, in the recent past, many students have come forward and formally requested that their schools' mascots be changed specifically to end the dehumanizing consequences of using Native images and stereotypes.

So, what does all this mean for youth of mixed Native American descent? What does it mean if some family members embrace their Native heritage and others do not? What does it mean to live in a country that would never allow a sports team to be called the "Yellowskins" or the "Blackskins" or the "Whiteskins" but proclaims the "Redskins" to be America's team? How does a young person of mixed Native descent come to a positive internal congruency in a world that judges and assigns membership on the basis of facial features, cheekbone structure, eye color, hair color and length, and the odd concept of a certain amount of blood?

In Seattle, there has been a recent push to remove the use of Native images as mascots in certain high schools. It is interesting that the impetus for change has come from the students themselves. These requested changes have also come after several racially charged incidents against Native students and Native people in general, including the burning of a totem pole by high school students. The youth involved in attempts to change mascots describe such efforts as reclaiming their heritage and being seen as people, not caricatures.

As the boarding schools have closed, more and more Native people have returned to their traditions, lands, heritage, and spiritual practices, finally allowed after the passing of the Indian Religious Freedom Act in 1978. The census data would indicate that more and more are claiming their heritage. Despite family pressure, more young Native Americans and those well into middle age are proclaiming their right to define who they are.

So, what can professionals do to aid Native youth in reaching a sense of identity? Many Native youth are searching for traditional activities and a chance to participate in them. For urban Native youth, finding such activities may be difficult. For youth of mixed Native descent, there may be some anxiety about being accepted if they seek to participate in traditional practices. Professionals can facilitate finding mentors to teach and guide youth of mixed Native descent. They can provide methods of processing concerns related to family support or lack of such. They can ensure a safe forum in which youths can explore their racial, cultural, and ethnic identity. Most of all, professionals can help mixed Native youth in realizing their right to choose whatever identity leads to the most spiritual and emotional congruity.

With the passage of time comes the fulfillment of the legends of a return to pride, dignity, and traditions. Among the Sioux people, this return was to be the birth of the white buffalo calf. The white buffalo calf has been born. Several tribes have recently received long-awaited federal recognition. Native people are embracing sobriety and taking to the courts to ensure that their treaty rights are respected. People of mixed Native descent are defining who they are by their blood, their hearts, their souls, and their own beliefs. As we have moved into the twenty-first century, the answer to the comment "But, you don't look like an Indian..." is now a quiet "Yes, actually I do."

Notes

1 For additional discussion on multiracial reporting in Census 2000, please see: Jones, Nicholas A. and Amy Symens Smith. 2001. *The Two or More Races Population: 2000*. U.S. Census Bureau, Census 2000 Brief Series (C2KBR/01-6). Washington, D.C. www.census.gov/prod/2001pubs/c2kbr01-1.pdf.

Did you know?

Here are some well-known multiracial people of both Native American and Caucasian heritage:

Ben Nighthorse Campbell (Politician)
Johnny Cash (Singer)
Cher (Singer, Actress)
Sequoyah (Created Cherokee writing system)

Akira, Grace and Zahra Masaoka
Ages: 13, 9, 9
Racial/Ethnic Heritage: Japanese and Caucasian

There is, of course, a large element of fiction in this testimonial, because my three children are not yet able to speak about their racial identity at any length. Since I am not hapa, but Sansei (third-generation Japanese American), and grew up in a different situation, I have an entirely different set of experiences. So I have elaborated mostly my point of view. I cannot really answer to the reality of what they experience on a day-to-day basis. I do get a strong impression that their multiethnicity is not a point of tension.

My nine-year-old twin daughters Zahra and Grace identify as half Japanese, and sometimes call themselves hapa haole (generally means "half-White" in Hawaiʻian), but when they say hapa haole, it is almost in the manner of answering a test question. I'm not sure they really know what it means; in fact, when I first asked them what race they identify with, they answered "female." My son who's 13 claims to have always considered himself "Asian." He claims he has always thought of himself as Asian, in large part because he likes being "different," and he thinks Asian people look "cool."

All three of our children are emphatic about never feeling confused or uncomfortable about their heritage. They all claim to feel "proud" of the fact that they are half-Japanese (interestingly, they never frame it as being "half-White"). I feel there are two major reasons why they have not experienced much conflict: one, is that they do not have strong Asian features and perhaps their peers do not even notice the subtle differences they do have; secondly, we live in a middle-class neighborhood, with a good elementary school that makes a point of valuing racial diversity. My wife and I have not experienced any problems with being a mixed couple in our neighborhood, and perhaps that lack of tension has also contributed to our children's feelings of acceptance.

It is a complex issue, being multiracial. What does it mean? In our family it sort of means that we value the Japanese side, as if that's where the good stuff comes from. It is, as my wife complains, very unfair, especially since she is the only "Whitey" among us. It seems that to be multiracial is to choose one side over the other; what side one chooses is situational. In our particular neighborhood, that is vastly White, it is "cool" to be a little different. Does this play into the "exotic" element of racism? In another neighborhood, would my kids try to pass for White? It's hard to say what they might do outside of the circumstances in which they actually live. What does it mean to be multiracial when being so doesn't cause one any problems? Where does one go with it and why?

In a sense, exploring one's multiracial identity might mean to pursue the aspect of one's self that is most oppressed by the society in which one lives. In this manner, it is firmly in the tradition of the Civil Rights Movement. The politics of race are one of the most dynamic forces in our society. When multiethnic people locate their own place in American culture, a different place than they have been assigned by others, and expand on it so the old definitions disappear and new definitions, their definitions, emerge; the dialogue, at that point, will become very interesting.

Testimonial

Chapter 21

Don't Worry, Be Hapa: Children of Asian and Caucasian Heritage
Matt Kelley

Growing up both Asian and White challenged me to develop an identity that relied on being "unique." This was how I coped with constant "What are you?" questions from strangers and feelings of alienation from both White and Asian people. Without parents or teachers equipped to help me negotiate my life in the borderlands of race, I grew up feeling forced to find the path to uncovering my "race place" alone.

The irony was that my experience was fairly common. I grew up in Washington State, which boasts the mainland U.S.'s highest percentage of mixed race young children.[1] Among multiracial families, White G.I. fathers and first-generation Asian mothers, like mine, are often seen as a "typical" interracial couple. Root describes those of us born in the late 1970s as the tail end of the vanguard generation, the generation immediately preceding the first biracial baby boom.[2] I grew up with other mixed race kids in my neighborhood and classroom, yet I felt alone. Unlike children whose parents are of the same race, mixed race youth usually do not have parents who have first-hand experience of what it is like to be multiracial in a society that still expects people to fit into one racial group. Though it may no longer be unusual, being multiracial can be isolating for mixed race youth whose parents or teachers are not equipped to address their unique

needs. In this chapter, I present a snapshot of what it is like to grow up both Asian and Caucasian today, explore issues that are relevant to *some* children of both Asian and European heritages, and provide tools for the parents and professionals who work with them.

Both White Americans and Asian Americans are incredibly diverse populations. In the U.S., we refer to over half of the world's population as "Asian." It is difficult to draw generalizations about Asian Americans, since "Asian" encompasses people representing a diverse spectrum of languages, cultures, skin colors, and religion. For the purposes of this chapter, I use "Asian" as an inclusive umbrella over the entire continent (including the Indian subcontinent). Generally, I am not including Pacific Islanders because of cultural differences and since Census 2000 separated them from the Asian race.[3] Since some Filipinos identify as Pacific Islander, this chapter includes Filipino/White youth who identify being Filipino as Asian. Readers should also note that mixed race children whose Asian parent immigrated to this country will have a different experience from American-born parents of Asian heritage. Likewise, the U.S. mixed race experience differs dramatically from multiracial children who grow up in Asia and come to the U.S. for college or later in life. My chapter specifically addresses the experience of growing up Asian and White in the United States.

In the absence of knowing words as a kid that could describe my heritage cohesively, I grew up referring to my heritage as "half-Korean." This description reinforced my feelings of being divided and not-quite whole. As young mixed race Americans claim and create language to define us, our lexicon is growing. Among mixed race people, words like "hapa," "Blackanese," and "Mexipino" are empowering and validating terms. In the interest of promoting a cohesive and undivided identity, in this chapter, I will mostly employ terms like hapa[4] and Eurasian when referring to people of both Asian and Caucasian heritage.

Who We Are

People who indicated both Asian and Caucasian on Census 2000 represented one of the U.S.'s largest mixed race populations. Contrary to popular belief, Census 2000 showed that more Americans identify as Asian and White than Black and White.[5] Of the 6.8 million people who checked more than one race, 12.7 percent or 868,395 people checked both "Asian" *and* "White." This represented the third largest mixed race group, with only "White" plus "Some other race" and "White" plus "American Indian or Alaska Native" comprising a larger population.[6] The Asian/White population, however, is disproportionately younger than these two groups and lives predominantly on the West Coast in states like California, Washington and Hawai'i.[7] It is interesting that Eurasian youth represent one of the largest mixed race populations, given the small size of the Asian American population (only 4% nationally). This can be attributed in large part to high out-marriage rates of Asian Americans—mostly with Caucasians.

Race is only part of a complex intersection of myriad different factors that shape mixed race identity.[8] For this chapter, I have identified six intertwined factors that may contribute to a hapa youth's identity: 1) physical appearance, 2) immigration status of the Asian parent, 3) Asian language proficiency, 4) names, 5) geography and proximity to Asian American communities, and 6) discrimination against Eurasian people. Within each section, I also provide suggestions for parents and professionals that can contribute to the development of healthy racial identities for hapa youth. I conclude with a discussion of the growing prominence of

hapas in mainstream society.

Physical Appearance

Variations in physical characteristics like skin color, body proportion, hair color and eye shape and color will influence how Eurasian youth perceive themselves and how others perceive them. "Hapa" or "Eurasian" are not widely acknowledged racial identities on the U.S. Mainland. Since it is often assumed that people can only be one race, curious strangers looking to categorize hapas will often scrutinize our features in search of a monoracial White, Asian, Latino, American Indian or Black race. If a good fit is not found, "What are you?" questions often follow. These dehumanizing questions are inevitable, so hapa youth should be empowered to avoid feeling victimized. Help your child create a confident response like, "I'm Adam," "I'm multiracial" or encourage them to respond with a question of their own, such as, "What do you mean?" Through books, Web sites and Eurasian celebrities, parents and professionals can help hapa youth see that they are "normal" and that awkward questions expose *other people's* ignorance. This can help ease feelings of alienation or otherness.

Like all mixed heritage people, there is significant diversity of physical appearance among hapas. Whereas some Eurasians are perceived as looking "White," others may be described as looking "Asian." It is difficult to draw generalizations about how phenotype impacts the identity choices made by Eurasian people. In some instances, a "White" appearing hapa may choose to identify as White, whereas another person may respond to her fair complexion and European features by actively asserting her Asian heritage. Again, society's pervasive monoracial assumption will classify Eurasians with more European features as almost White, while more Asian featured hapas will be more readily described as Asian by the mainstream society and almost Asian by various Asian American communities. For many hapas whose features fall somewhere inbetween, people may assume they are Latino/a or Native American. The monoracial assumption is so pervasive that Eurasian people will often unintentionally pass as monoracial in casual settings and superficial relationships. Intentional passing is also a reality for some hapas; however, this is largely unrealistic in serious relationships.

Perhaps the most widespread experience of Eurasian people is being perceived as Latino/a. An informal survey of my hapa friends showed that many of them are often perceived to be Mexican, Brazilian or other Latino/a cultures. Interestingly, many of them identified closely with these cultures, suggesting that outside perception and assumed membership influenced how they saw themselves. Outside perception may make some Eurasians more comfortable identifying with communities outside of their parents' heritages, despite criticisms of "authenticity" or honesty. Rather than characterizing this as self-loathing, Eurasian youth may find rejecting origin-based racial classifications or race itself empowering because their personal experiences expose the irrational and arbitrary way race is assigned in the U.S. It is important to recognize and accept that Eurasian youth may identify as White, Asian, both or neither—and to embrace each identity as valid. Give Eurasian youth access to a wide range of different cultures as well as examples of mixed race societies like Hawai'i and Puerto Rico as societies where being racially mixed is the norm.

Dominant White beauty standards also apply to hapas. Since both Asian men and women are often perceived as having "feminine" attributes, Eurasian women are often seen as "exotic," feminine and attractive by both genders. Women and gay men may view Eurasian men who do not possess "masculine" (more typically Caucasian) physical traits as unattractive. Interestingly, many "masculine" hapa male celebrities are widely perceived as either White (Keanu Reeves) or Latino (Dean Cain), rather than Eurasian. There is, however, a gay scene where Asian and Eurasian men are fetishized by White "rice queens" who may see hapas as exotic, yet familiar. Like many gay Asian men, Eurasian gay men may feel restricted by hypo-masculine stereotypes. Eurasian men who look more stereotypically "masculine" may feel less pressure to conform to stereotypes of gay Asian men. It is important for hapa youth to feel empowered to reject racist or heterosexist stereotypes. Resources and role models that do not conform to dominant beauty standards are a good starting point. Exposure to large communities of Asian and hapa people who demonstrate the diversity of Asian and Eurasian body types and lifestyles is also important.

The Sum of Our Parts: Mixed Heritage Asian Americans
Teresa Williams-León and Cynthia L. Nakashima, Temple University Press, 2001

This unique collection of essays focuses on the identity construction among mixed race Asian Americans. In a society dominated by a Black-White dichotomy, mixed heritage Asian Americans are rarely included. *The Sum of Our Parts* disrupts the status quo by discussing people of mixed Asian ethnicities. In an effort to reflect voices often unheard within the hapa community, the essays pay particular attention to "minority-minority" hapas.

Asian Language Proficiency

In my family, I remember sitting on the floor of my *halmuhnee's* (my mother's mother) small apartment for hours with my Korean-born aunts and cousins. The room was full of women peeling apples, cutting melons, speaking Korean loudly and laughing. The meaning of their expressive, excited voices and harsh guttural consonants were indecipherable to my sister and me. Like many immigrants, my mother did not teach us Korean in her effort to raise us as "Americans." Although not speaking Korean distanced me from my Korean relatives growing up, the impact was felt keenest after my parents' divorce. After their divorce, I lived with my mother. There was a time when my mother, Korean grandmother, cousin and neighbor would gather regularly in our home and speak Korean almost exclusively. Frustrated by my feelings of being an outsider in my own home, one day I regrettably lamented to my mother that I felt like I lived in the "Joy Luck Club."

Many second and third generation Asian Americans do not speak Asian languages. In less established Asian American communities, the ability to speak the language distinguishes an "insider" from an "outsider." My mother's decision to not teach us Korean confirmed our status as outside the Korean American community. In some Asian communities, like the established Japanese American community, for instance, Asian language plays a less prominent role in community affairs, allowing individuals who are not proficient to participate fully in cultural events and in the community.

Asian language proficiency is an asset to a Eurasian child. The ability to understand cultural nuances unavailable to non-speakers will help incorporate hapa youth more easily into Asian communities, if that is a path they want to take. It is common for Asian grandparents to assist in child rearing. Many grandparents would enjoy teaching grandchildren an Asian language. For families without native speakers, consider Asian language school, a tutor or low-cost classes at a community center. Having options is critical for Eurasian youth. Asian language proficiency gives hapa youth greater access to embracing an Asian identity, and how that choice will be embraced.

Immigration Status of the Asian Parent

Although some Asian Americans can trace their heritage in the U.S. back five or more generations, immigration continues to shape virtually every Asian American community.

Race is perceived differently in the U.S. than in other countries. Nationals from Asia often bring different perspectives on race. Some Asian countries do not have sizable minority ethnic communities. Most Asian countries do not have complex histories of slavery, race conflict and cross-racial mixing. Unlike mixed race children of African descent, there is no "one-drop rule" in the Asian American community. If anything, there is the opposite "rule:" one drop of non-Asian blood defines you as being *outside* the community. This is similar to the mechanism that maintains the farce of White racial purity. Many first generation Asian Americans may base unintentional rejection or exclusion on an unrealistic assumption that hapa children will be fully accepted as "Americans." For Eurasian youth, however, repeated experiences questioning our origin and ancestry suggest that we are not perceived as full-fledged Americans. Even today, there is little expectation in most Asian American communities for mixed race Asian Americans to identify with, or participate in, the community. I remember asking my mother once what generation I was if she was first generation Korean American and my cousin was what is called 1.5 generation. She replied, "You're not Korean, you're American."

My mother's response was influenced by her experience as an immigrant and because Korea lacks a large non-Korean population. For many people in her generation, there's no such thing as "half-Korean"—you either are Korean or you are not. In her eyes, I am not. This is changing. Today, some communities are responding to outmarriage and international adoption by becoming more inclusive. For instance, according to Kitano, for every 100 couples between two Japanese Americans spouses, there are 139 couples with a Japanese and a non-Japanese partner.[9] Since mixed race Asian Americans already comprise 14 percent of the Asian American population, and Eurasians make up the bulk of the mixed race Asian population, it is critical to the future of the Asian American community that Asian parents and community members make concerted efforts to include Eurasian youth into their definition of community.[10] Review printed materials offered by organizations to see if Eurasians are included. Be vigilant by recognizing overt or subtle anti-hapa bias. Encourage nonprofit organizations and schools to carry magazines like *MAVIN* that feature mixed race young people in normalized ways.

Names

Even in the U.S., where centuries of mixing has made ethnic European surnames like O'Malley or Fioricci less "racialized" than for our grandparents' generation, Asian surnames are still widely recognizable. Even if someone has more typically "Caucasian" features, if their last name is "Kim," "Tanaka," or "Singh," their surname is a clue to Asian heritage. Spanish colonization of the Philippines resulted in many Filipinos bearing Spanish surnames like Batista and Aquino, which may further confuse outsiders since multiracial Filipinos may already be perceived by an outsider as Latino/a. For the majority of Asian/Caucasian biracial people who have Anglo sounding names, this "clue" to their Asian heritage is not available. I know many Eurasian hapas with White fathers who were given Asian middle names, or claimed them later in life. Some people may choose to add their mother's Asian surname and create a hyphenated last name later in life to reflect their biracial heritage. Reasons vary from a desire for their name to reflect their Asian heritage to wanting greater acceptance in professional Asian American campus organizations or professional circles.

I have often joked that my Anglo name effectively makes me "White" or "Black" on the phone. Although largely symbolic, an Asian name publicly identifies your child to his or her Asian heritage and creates an important connection to that community. It also provides a fun way for children to connect to their Asian heritage through their name's meaning, how it appears in an Asian language, and its origin.

Geography and Proximity to the Asian Community

Geography and one's proximity to an Asian American community are important factors that shape the experiences of Eurasian youth. Cities on the U.S. West Coast often have sizable Asian American communities. There are fewer Asian American

EurasianNation

EurasianNation.com

If you are looking for an online magazine and community for people of mixed European and Asian descent, EurasianNation is your destination. The Web site's aim is to provide quality content on Eurasian issues and to act as an online forum where Eurasians can meet each other and share ideas. In late 2000, then 14-year-old Iris Van Kerckhove started a community site for Eurasians because she felt that her needs as a person of mixed European and Asian descent were not being met by traditional Asian and Asian-American community sites. Whether you call yourself hapa, hafu, Amerasian, luk kreung, Anglo-Indian, mestiza, indo, or just biracial, EurasianNation may be the place for you.
Learn more:
www.eurasiannation.com

enclaves on the East Coast and in the Midwest. Hapas who grew up in Asia will have a completely different experience. Besides the value of simply being around other people that "look like mom" or "look like me," living in close proximity to an Asian American community also gives a family access to resources like other families, ethnic bookstores, restaurants, festivals and culturally competent social services.

Unlike some other mixed race populations, Eurasian youth have access to a contemporary hapa homeland. In addition to traveling to both Asian and European countries, it could also be a good experience for your family to choose vacation spots like Hawai'i, where hapas are the norm. In fact, the majority of newborns in the state are themselves mixed race, which is surely a harbinger of things to come on the Mainland.

Discrimination

Fortunately, a growing number of Eurasian youth report no memorable experiences of overt racism. Generally, Caucasians and Asians experience less pernicious forms of racism than people of African descent in the U.S. This could explain why there is a large cohort of hapas who do not identify as oppressed minorities or as "people of color." That said, Eurasian youth might still be the targets of discrimination, often in ways that are unique to them. In comments made at a meeting organized by former Census Bureau director Kenneth Prewitt in 2002, I described five kinds of discrimination faced by mixed race people that I have adapted to address Eurasians:[11] They are: 1) Assumed monoracial status, 2) racism against all non-White people, 3) discrimination by people opposed to racial mixing, 4) discrimination by non-mixed Asian Americans, and 5) misapplied discrimination.

Assumed monoracial status

Although there have always been mixed race people in the U.S., there is still a pervasive assumption that all people belong to only one race. This legacy of the "one drop rule" posited that anyone with even "one drop" of African heritage was Black. This "rule" effectively kept the White race pure and was applied to the border between White and all other racial groups. During WWII, for example, persons of 1/16 Japanese heritage were also

sent to the internment camps.[12] Prior to Census 2000, Eurasians and all mixed race people were required to check only one race on virtually all forms requesting racial data, such as test forms, employment applications and health questionnaires. Assumed monoracial status can have alarming health consequences. For example, some diseases are more prevalent among specific races. Failure of doctors to know a patient's complete heritage can result in misdiagnosis and treatment. Additionally, the absence of a National Marrow Donor Program (NMDP) recruitment group to recruit multiracial bone marrow donors has made finding a bone marrow match exceptionally difficult for many mixed race leukemia patients.

Discrimination against non-Whites

Many Eurasians who show outward identifiers of Asian heritage and culture will experience discrimination targeted against non-mixed Asian Americans, i.e. "model minority" or "kung fu master" stereotypes, "Ching Chong" playground taunts, "Where are you from?" questions and "compliments" on their fluent English. Although racial discrimination is a painful reality for many Eurasians, there is generally less blatant or life-threatening discrimination than against people of visible African origins. This contributes to some mixed race people considering the Eurasian experience as somehow less oppressed as other mixes. Unfortunately, this perception may also discourage parents of hapa children from seeking resources or social networks to support their children. It is critical that parents and professionals acknowledge that their child may be the target of discrimination.

Anti-miscegenation

Although interracial marriage is increasingly common, White supremacist groups and organizations like the Nation of Islam remain opposed to interracial marriage. Among Asian communities, it is important to understand the historic rejection of mixed race youth in Asia. It is estimated that U.S. troops fathered millions of mixed race youth in Asia. Many of these children were abandoned by their American fathers and became the targets of vicious racism.[13] It is important for parents and people in the community to be cognizant of stereotypes against mixed race people that exist in Asia, as well as in the U.S., so that stigmas against mixed race Asians in some Asian countries are not perpetuated in Asian American communities.

Discrimination by non-mixed Asian Americans

Hapas can also be the target of racism by non-mixed Asian Americans. This may range from individual acts of bigotry, to institutionalized policies that prohibit Eurasians from leadership positions in Asian American organizations. Recent history has included authenticity tests and informal as well as formal blood quantum requirements in Japanese American cherry blossom courts and basketball leagues that excluded hapas.[14] Among Asian American youth, there may also be resentment against hapa peers because of a perceived greater access to White privilege and White beauty standards. This demonstrates a curious contradiction where hapas are seen as both inferior to full-blooded Asians, but also as a threat. This is an example of internalized racism and is a consequence of White racism. Since a stereotype of Eurasian people is that they are not "real" Asians, being connected to Asian culture and language will make it more difficult—though not impossible—for their "legitimacy" to be challenged.

Misapplied discrimination

A familiar experience for many Eurasians is being perceived as a member of a race or ethnicity that is different than either of our parents. This can result in hapas experiencing racism and discrimination intended for other groups. For instance, a Eurasian man I talked to recalled being labeled a "spic" by someone who thought that he was Latino. These experiences can help hapa youth notice the stupidity of race-based bigotry. It can also be an important way for them to empathize with other oppressed groups and build networks among communities of color.

Finding a Voice

Today, hapa youth can see Eurasian faces without looking very hard. Olympic gold medalist speed skater Apolo Anton Ohno and *Smallville* star Kristin Kreuk are both prominent Eurasians that appeal to a wide range of young people. One pioneering role

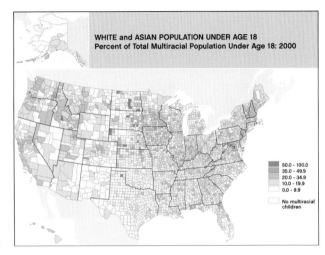

WHITE and ASIAN POPULATION UNDER AGE 18
Percent of Total Multiracial Population Under Age 18: 2000

50.0 - 100.0
35.0 - 49.9
20.0 - 34.9
10.0 - 19.9
0.0 - 9.9
No multiracial children

Source: U.S. Census Bureau, Census 2000.

This map shows a county-by-county look at the percent of multiracial children under age 18 who checked both "Asian" and "White" in Census 2000.

model is the *Today* show's news anchor, Ann Curry, who is both Japanese and Caucasian. Sandra Tsing Loh, Amy Hill and Kip Fulbeck are popular Eurasian performance artists whose work explores their mixed race heritage.

Hapas also play prominent roles in the multiracial movement. Maria P. P. Root (Filipina and White) is a trailblazing scholar who has published two landmark anthologies on the mixed race experience as well as a widely-distributed "Bill of Rights for Racially Mixed People." Greg Mayeda (Japanese and White) is a co-founder of Hapa Issues Forum (HIF), a California-based nonprofit organization serving people of mixed Asian/Pacific Islander heritage. Wei Ming Dariotis (Greek and Chinese) is the San Francisco chapter chair of HIF. Jen Chau (Chinese and Jewish-European) is the founder and executive director of Swirl, Inc., a multiracial/multiethnic/interfaith nonprofit based out of New York with several chapters across the country. Matt Kelley (Korean and White) is the founder and president of *MAVIN* magazine and MAVIN Foundation, a national magazine and nonprofit at the forefront of mixed race issues. Eurasians also continue to hold leadership positions in many campus mixed race student organizations.

With the rise of the Internet has come hundreds of Web sites dedicated to exploring the mixed race experience. Online destinations like EurasianNation.com, HalfKorean.com, and Hapas.com were created by young hapas eager to create affirming places to share their experiences and to shape what it means to be hapa. Young Eurasian men and women are affirming their experiences and growing community. A couple of years ago, we jokingly coined the word "quapa" at the MAVIN office to describe children who have one hapa parent and one White parent. Undoubtedly, creating a sense of community through shared experience is as important to hapa youth as it is for other people of color.

Hapa authors are creating a body of literature to capture the Eurasian experience and to provide a window into our lives. Kien Nguyen's *The Unwanted* and Kip Fulbeck's fictional autobiography, *Paper Bullets* are just two examples of this growing genre of mixed race memoirs. The ubiquity of hapa celebrities and resources is a positive development for Eurasian youth to help them develop positive identities. Despite their growing prominence, many of these resources are not widely distributed. Parents and teachers must deliberately seek out these role models and resources for their child so their child will have the opportunity to access and identify with them.

Conclusion

For me, growing up hapa has meant that I have felt both excluded by White and Asian communities and included into Black and Latino/a ones. This can be a confusing contradiction for a young person to negotiate. But instead of growing up thinking that our experiences outside conventional monoracial terms are wrong or weird, parents and professionals can help hapa youth recognize the liberation of blurring racial boundaries. After 24 years, I am finally at that place. Undoubtedly, the process would have been easier with Eurasian Web sites, movie stars and campus clubs, but I must admit that today I enjoy blending in at tribal gatherings and Mariachi shows.

The reality is that the upcoming generation of hapa kids can grow up seeing people who look like them on television, in movies, as role models and mentors. But parents and professionals must be vigilant. The pervasive monoracial assumption in the U.S. still tells hapa children to deny their heritage by checking "only one race" and incites awkward, dehumanizing questions like, "What are you?" Discrimination and racism against Eurasian people is real. Fortunately, there are resources available today to assist teachers and professionals to actively create environments that nurture healthy identities for multiracial young people. If we are successful, the outcome will be hapa children and youth who do not feel confused or isolated because of the wonderful opportunity of being mixed race.

Did you know?

Here are some well-known multiracial people of both Asian and Caucasian heritage:

Devon Aoki (Model)
Rae Dawn Chong (Actor)
Ann Curry (Journalist)
Kristin Kreuk (Actor)
Norah Jones (Musician)
Bruce Lee (Martial Artist)
Sean Lennon (Musician)
Susan Molinari (Politician)
Apolo Anton Ohno (Speed Skater, Olympic gold medalist)
Rob Schneider (Actor)
Tiger Woods (Golfer)

Notes

1 According to Census 2000, among children under five years old, Washington State boasts the third highest percentage of children identified as belonging to more than one race (8.6 percent). Only Hawai'i (39.7 percent) and Alaska (18.2 percent) reported higher percentages.

2 See M. P. P. Root in *Biracial Women in Therapy: Between the Rock of Gender and the Hard Place of Race*, ed. Angela R. Gillem and Cathy A. Thompson (Binghamton, NY: Haworth Press, 2003).

3 To read an excellent discussion on mixed heritage Pacific Islanders, please see Suni Tolton's chapter in this book titled, "Multiracial Pacific Islander Youth."

4 Hapa haole is originally a Hawaiian term meaning "half-foreigner" and later "half-White." Although today "hapa" is used more generally to refer to any mixed heritage person of Asian or Pacific Islander descent, I am using it specifically to describe people of both Asian and White heritage.

5 For more information, see N. Jones and A. Symens Smith, "The Two or More Races Population: 2000," *U.S. Census Bureau, Census 2000 Brief Series* (C2KBR/01-6, 2001). Please also see Nicholas Jones and Amy Symens Smith's chapter in this book titled, "A Statistical Portrait of Multiple Race Children in Census 2000."

6 According to Census 2000, three Western states reported the largest populations of people under age 18 who checked both "Asian" and "White": California (132,410), Washington (26,080) and Hawai'i (25,824). The Eurasian population is also young. Whereas only 25% of the total U.S. population who reported only one race is under age 18, 42 percent of people who checked more than one race were under 18, and 51 percent of people who checked Asian and White were under 18.

7 According to Census 2000, 868,395 people reported both "Asian" and "White." The number of people who indicated both "Black or African American" and "White" was 784,764.

8 For more information, see M. P. P. Root's chapter in this book titled, "Racial Identity Development and Persons of Mixed Race Heritage."

9 See H. L. L. Kitano, D. C. Fujino, and J.T. Sato, "Interracial marriages: Where are the Asian Americans and where are they going?" in *Handbook of Asian American Psychology*, ed. N. Zane and L. Lee (Newbury Park, CA: Sage Publications, 1998).

10 According to Census 2000, 10,242,998 people reported "Asian" alone. 1,655,830 people reported "Asian" in combination with one or more other races. Mixed race Asian Americans account for 13.9% of the total Asian alone and in combination with other races population.

11 Adapted from comments made by Matt Kelley at the November 11, 2002 meeting of former U.S. Census director, Kenneth Prewitt at the New School University in New York City.

12 See P. R. Spickard, *Intermarriage and Ethnic Identity in Twentieth-Century America* (Madison, WI: University of Wisconsin Press, 1989).

13 For a poignant memoir on growing up mixed race in Vietnam, see K. Nguyen, *The Unwanted* (London: Little, Brown and Company, 2000). Also see Kieu Linh Caroline Valverde, "From Dust to Gold: The Vietnamese Amerasian Experience," in *Racially Mixed People in America*, ed. M. P. P. Root (Thousand Oaks, CA: Sage Publications, 1992).

14 See R. C. King and K. M. DaCosta, "Changing Face, Changing Race: The Remaking of Race in the Japanese American and African American Communities," in *The Multiracial Experience: Racial Borders as the New Frontier*, ed M. P. P. Root (Thousand Oaks, CA: Sage Publications, 1996).

Jared Medina Bigelow
Age: 19
Racial/Ethnic Heritage: African American and Caucasian

My life has always been supersaturated with the values and expectations of White America. From my youth, both my parents and the media subconsciously molded me to conform to the habits of my White peers. My peers accepted me to an extent, but somehow I was never "White enough" to be one of them. I was "pretty cool for a Black kid," and I was always the one that stood out in a crowd, with my nappy head, caramel-colored skin and thick lips. My mother, who is White, always tried to make me see that it didn't matter whether or not I was Black or White because I was "special," I was both. Not a single one of my White friends could ever know what it was like to be me, and I could never fully know what it was like to be White. So my "specialness" rested on me being in a state of racial limbo that was impossible to describe to any member of either of my constituent races; an interesting place to be. Despite my mother's best efforts to comfort me, something still didn't feel right about my identity, and the other side of the spectrum would prove to be no less cold.

From my initial "White phase" I progressed to being "Black as can be" at age 15 or so. "White" became a four-letter word for me, and I'd have nothing to do with it for another three years. My household never fostered such feelings, so it follows that once I recognized my "Blackness" as an irreconcilable difference separating me from "them," I focused on it and nurtured it, making it my defining characteristic. With my newfound and angry identity leading the way, I sought out the comfort of Black America, assuming that we shared an awareness of discrimination and imposed inferiority that would unite us. To my surprise, Black America saw me as a "White boy" or something worse, a "half-breed." As they explained to me, I could never know what they had endured in the past and I would never be "Black enough" to be accepted into their inner circles. Also to my surprise, many Blacks expressed an even greater contempt for "half-breeds" than for Whites, something that threatened to hurt my very soul. I was seen as the enemy infiltrating the sanctity of Black culture, and I hated myself for it.

When I was 18 or so, I looked at my Black "friends" that saw me as "not quite Black" and my White "friends" that saw me as "not quite White." I realized that I couldn't define myself by other's views, but through my own integrity and achievement. Black, White, or "other," I was determined to make myself stand out in the crowd in ways that didn't have anything to do with my hue. I excelled in school and won a four-year academic scholarship to Seattle University. It was there that I heard about multiracial advocacy organizations like MAVIN. Soon after, I co-founded a multiracial student organization called "hi'brid" in an attempt to give multiracial students on campus a voice and a forum in which to discuss their frustrations and triumphs. After years of searching and frustration, I know that I'm not Black or White. I'm something else, and I'm proud to be multiracial.

Testimonial

Chapter 22

Relationships and Black/White Multiracial People
Charmaine L. Wijeyesinghe, Ed.D.

This chapter explores Black/White multiracial people and their relationships with other multiracial populations, as well as with Blacks and Whites. It also examines dynamics within the multiracial Black/White community and interactions between these multiracial people and parents, teachers and helping agents. Strategies for building greater understanding and stronger coalitions within all of these relationships are presented in the final section.

The scope and length of this chapter prevents a full overview of historic and social dynamics related to race. However, historical perspective is included in some sections to underscore the long-standing roles that racism and relationships between Blacks and Whites play in current discussions of Black/White multiracial identity. It is within this context that Black/White multiracial people develop their identity, form relationships with other racial groups, and are understood or misunderstood by other racial communities.

For example, race in America has historically been framed primarily in terms of Black and White. Although centuries old, this legacy permeates modern visions, thoughts, and feelings about multiracial people in general, and people with Black/White ancestry in particular. Currently, the widespread image of the "typical" multiracial person in America is someone whose racial ancestry is African American and European American. The majority of books and research studies on multiracial issues reflect aspects of the Black/White multiracial experience. Media coverage of multiracial identity focuses mainly on Black/White people. Contrary to the findings of the 2000 Census, being multiracial means being Black and White in the eyes of the American public.[1]

Black/White Multiracial People and Relationships with Other Multiracial Populations

Given the restrictive imagery of multiracial people portrayed in society, a multiracial Black/White person may consciously or unconsciously adopt the dominant social belief that they represent the most prevalent or "truest" multiracial group. Such assumptions can foster a sense of hierarchy of multiracial experience with various groups assigned to levels based on factors such as appearance, perceived weight of historical oppression, and level of public acknowledgement. This dynamic is already played out in interactions between "monoracial" communities of color, for example, underlying some of the tensions between African Americans and Asian Americans. Believing that Black/White ancestry is the most common or significant racial combination can create barriers to communication and coalition building

Black, White, Other: Biracial Americans Talk About Race and Identity

Lise Funderburg, Quill, 1994

In this groundbreaking book, Lise Funderburg presents the lives of 46 adults of Black-White marriages. Topics include love, marriage, workplace racism and raising mixed race children in a racially divided world. *Black, White, Other* is the first book to explore the lives of adult children of Black-White couples. This is an excellent book for individuals who are interested in personal narratives on the mixed race experience.

with other multiracial groups.

The task of defining who is multiracial is a work in progress. In my work, I distinguish between multiracial ancestry (those people whose family of origin represents two or more socially defined racial groups) and multiracial identity (the choice of a racial identity that reflects more than one socially defined racial group). Several other definitions are evident in the literature, with varying degrees of breadth and controversy. In one article on Black/White identity that I was asked to review for publication, multiracial people were described as individuals whose appearance led others to believe they had multiracial ancestry. However, this would include "monoracial" Black people since African Americans represent a spectrum of skin color from very dark to white. The existence of competing definitions and the image that multiracial people with at least some Black ancestry are the best representatives of the multiracial experience fuel tension between multiracial groups. For example, on a college campus, the leaders of an emerging multiracial student group (who were Black and White) could not agree on who should be allowed into the organization. The ensuing debate and misunderstanding made the group unattractive to prospective members, who were unclear about whom the group represented.

Black/White Multiracial People and Relationships with Blacks and Whites

Many of the challenges that Black/White multiracial people receive from African Americans are rooted in historical relationships between Blacks and Whites. In all but the last decade or so, choosing a multiracial identity was not an option under the "one-drop rule." Some monoracial and multiracial Black people could and did "pass" as White in the past. Some identify as White today. Denying one's Blackness in order to gain acceptance, social status, or tangible benefits caused pain, conflict, and resentment for individuals, families, and the larger Black community. The continued strength of these feelings is evident in criticism that individuals who now embrace a multiracial identity are attempting to distance themselves from Blacks, or to be "anything but Black."[2] In the context of the modern multiracial rights movement, Black/White multiracial people who identify with all of their racial heritages acknowledge their White ancestry for different reasons than those individuals who passed as White before.

Discussion and debate preceded the change in the 2000 Census that allowed people to check more than one box to indicate race. One major concern was that a multiracial category or option would have a major, negative impact on African American social and political power, since the number of Blacks reported would decline if some people were recorded as multiracial.

Institutionalizing multiracial identity was seen as a threat to hard won victories of only a few decades ago and continuing struggles for racial equality.[3] [4] Many of the multiracial children who, along with their parents, were at the forefront of the multiracial rights movement, were born after the Civil Rights and Black Power Movements. To some Blacks and Whites active during these social struggles, such multiracial youth seemed uninterested or uninformed of the significance of this history.

Tensions are also played out between younger peers. For example, groups for multiracial students have formed on increasing numbers of college and university campuses. Some of these groups encounter rejection or resistance when forming relationships with monoracial groups, such as organizations for Black or Latino students. These relationships can be understood, in part, through Black identity models that emerged from the Civil Rights Movement.[5] [6] [7] Black students involved in groups like Black student unions and Black Greek organizations often possess behaviors and attitudes described in the middle stages of the Cross and Jackson models. Some of the goals of individuals in these stages include rejecting dominant social images of Blackness; immersing oneself in Black history, culture, and values; actively rejecting and confronting Whites and White racism; and challenging African Americans who do not share similar perspectives. Individuals pursuing these goals are unlikely to support multiracial Black/White people who want to embrace all of their racial heritages. In a sense, multiracial students in this scenario are "looking for love in the wrong places." However, African Americans who represent later stages of the Cross and Jackson models are in a better position to support and mentor multiracial Black/White people.

Little attention has been paid to the relationship between Black/White multiracial people and Whites. Some of the same arguments against claiming a multiracial identity raised in the Black community resonate with some Whites. For example, many Whites subscribe to the "one drop" standard for racial classification and racial identity for people with any African ancestry. The various responses by Whites to multiracial identity can be informed by Hardiman's White identity model.[8] [9] Using this model, Whites can be seen as supporting multiracial identity without knowledge of historical issues and dynamics (early stage); rejecting multiracial identity (middle stages) based on similar concerns described in the previous college group example; and supporting multiracial people within an understanding of complex racial history (later stages).

Black/White Multiracial People and Relationships with Each Other

A key question raised by the discussion of multiracial people is whether racial identity is a choice made by an individual versus a label assigned by social or legal institutions. Black/White multiracial people choose a variety of racial identities, including Black, White, and multiracial.[10] [11] Increasing awareness of these choices and of multiracial identity in general leads to further questions, and at times, confusion and disagreement. In a recent conversation, for example, a White neighbor asked me how Halle Berry could be Black when her mother was White. My response was that Ms. Berry chose to identify as Black, and that choice of identity was accepted and affirmed by others.

Black/White multiracial people have opinions and feelings about the racial identities chosen by people within their own community. Individuals developing their racial identity during the current multiracial rights movement may believe that everyone with Black and White ancestry should identify as multiracial. Other Black/White people feel that a Black identity is more appropriate to avoid creating splits in racial communities still fighting for racial justice. The choice of a White identity draws the most criticism, even if this reflects how the Black/White person is seen and treated in day-to-day life.

Relationships with Parents, Counselors, and Other Helping Agents

Parents, counselors, and teachers often focus on issues facing the multiracial people in their lives. This is understandable given the long standing societal concern: "what about the children" posed to many interracial couples in the 1970s and 1980s. Less

More Than Black? Multiracial Identity and the New Racial Order
G. Reginald Daniel, Temple University Press, 2001

For centuries, the protection of White racial purity and social privilege in the U.S. classified anyone with even a trace of African American ancestry as Black. By the 1990s, however, the dramatic rise in interracial marriages and multiracial offspring began to threaten the exclusive racial categories of both White and Black America. The political organizing of mixed race Americans in the late 20th century resulted in institutional changes, like Census 2000, which allowed Americans to check more than one race for the first time. In *More Than Black?: Multiracial Identity and the New Racial Order*, G. Reginald Daniel argues that our society is at a crossroads, with members of a new multiracial movement leading the way toward a multiracial society.

attention is paid to the assumptions about race, racial identity, and multiracial people held by parents or helping agents. For example, when leading a discussion for a group of parents of multiracial, primarily Black/White children, I asked individuals to reflect on their assumptions and expectations of their child's racial identity, and what role *they* expected to have in shaping that identity. Initially, the participants were surprised that the questions focused on their experiences and beliefs. Over the last several years that their group had been together, they always discussed the needs of their children and had yet to talk about themselves.

Monoracial parents may struggle with the idea that they cannot fully understand the experiences of their Black/White multiracial children. In some cases, White parents play down the impact of race on their children's life or identity formation. In contrast, Black parents may feel that race is a significant part of their lives and the lives of their children. This might be especially true if that child can be considered Black or a person of color based on his or her appearance. In this case, White parents may be concerned that they are unable to empathize and therefore participate in their child's racial identity development. Other White parents fear being rejected by their child during some phases of this process.

Counselors working with multiracial clients may be influenced by the biases that appear in their professional literature related to Black/White identity issues. Several early studies of multiracial people in clinical settings described extraordinary levels of identity confusion in Black/White multiracial people.[12][13][14][15] In the social context where race is defined in shades of black and white, choosing to identify as multiracial requires a person to embrace the ultimate oppressor (Whites) and the ultimate oppressed (Blacks). To many, this kind of blending is impossible, or can only result in trauma and confusion for the multiracial person. In addition, counselors may not reflect on their own beliefs about multiracial identity, and their assumptions about the different choices of identity made by multiracial people.

Strategies for Building Relationships

This section identifies specific strategies for building stronger relationships between Black/White multiracial people and each of the groups discussed in previous sections. Strategies move from lower to higher degrees of emotional and interpersonal investment, as well as level of training required for people implementing the strategies.

Building Relationships with Other Multiracial Groups/Populations
- Develop projects or programs that bring together a range of multiracial people. The communication and cooperation generated over the life of a project can be used later in deeper discussions and dialogues.
- Present educational programs on the historical contributions of various multiracial groups. These sessions could combine historical records, personal narratives, and guest speakers to highlight the experience of multiracial people of various ancestries over time, and identify commonalties and differences between diverse multiracial groups.
- Offer facilitated dialogues between Black/White multiracial people and people with other multiracial ancestries. These programs can range from one meeting to regular gatherings over an extended period. They take participants to a deeper intellectual and emotional level to uncover barriers to coalition building, lingering stereotypes and negative responses, and historical tensions between racial groups.[16]

Building Relationships with Blacks and Whites
- Form study groups to review key aspects of American history related to relations between Blacks and Whites, as well as the treatment of multiracial people. Through analysis of a variety of sources, identify issues that contribute to tension as well as coalition building between African Americans, Whites, and multiracial Black/White people.
- Develop programs aimed at assisting multiracial Black/White people to identify assumptions and beliefs about their personal relationships with Blacks and Whites. Through group discussion, identify strategies for responding to criticism or challenges about their own choice of racial identity. Help individuals to develop and practice listening and communication skills to use in conflict situations.
- Create facilitated dialogue groups including Black/White multiracial people, Blacks, and Whites. See description from

preceding list of strategies.

Building Relationships with Each Other
- Have Black/White multiracial people review books and other written material, and video resources that represent the range of experiences of multiracial Black/White people. Facilitate discussion as to how the material compares with their process of identity development.
- Encourage individuals to reflect on how they came to their current sense of racial identity and the factors they use to determine their racial identity (i.e., appearance, early socialization, ancestry, etc.). Where appropriate, share theories of identity development in multiracial people and discuss how the models fit and do not fit the individual's experiences.
- Develop programs that allow Black/White individuals to explore the impact of other social identities (e.g., gender, socio-economic class, and sexual orientation) on their experiences of being multiracial. Goals include identifying similarities and differences in their experiences and building awareness of

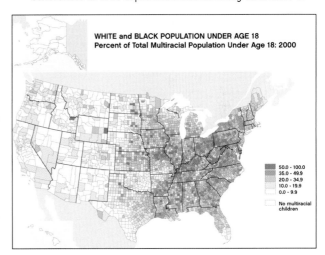

WHITE and BLACK POPULATION UNDER AGE 18
Percent of Total Multiracial Population Under Age 18: 2000

50.0 - 100.0
35.0 - 49.9
20.0 - 34.9
10.0 - 19.9
0.0 - 9.9

No multiracial children

Source: U.S. Census Bureau, Census 2000.

This map shows a county-by-county look at the percent of multiracial children under age 18 who checked both "Black or African American" and "White" in Census 2000.

other forms of oppression (such as sexism and heterosexism) within society.

Strategies of Parents, Counselors, and Helping Agents

- Develop training sessions that allow individuals to examine their own assumptions about what constitutes race and racial identity, as well as expectations they may have about the racial identity of Black/White multiracial people. Have people identify beliefs that might block communication and sincere relationships with Black/White multiracial people.

- Encourage monoracial parents of Black/White children to consider ways in which their experiences will be similar and different from those of other children. Assist parents in developing strategies for supporting their child's choice of racial identity, especially if this choice does not reflect a particular parent's racial ancestry, or is inconsistent with the parent's preferred identity for his/her children.

- Include discussion of Black, White, and multiracial identity development models in counselor pre- and in-service training programs. Provide opportunities for counselors, teachers, and other helping agents to identify and discuss their beliefs and assumptions about multiracial identity and how these may influence their interaction with multiracial clients and students.

Did you know?

Here are some well-known multiracial people of both Black and Caucasian heritage:

John James Audubon (Orinthologist)
Halle Berry (Actor)
Craig David (Singer)
Frederick Douglass (Abolitionist)
Alexandre Dumas (Writer)
Lani Guinier (Civil Rights Advocate, Legal Scholar)
Derek Jeter (Baseball Player)
Alicia Keys (Singer)
Lenny Kravitz (Musician)
Bob Marley (Musician)
Samantha Mumba (Singer, Actor)
Booker T. Washington (Educator)

Notes

1 Of the nearly 7 million people who checked more than one racial category, only 16% checked at least Black and White in their response. U.S. Census Bureau, Census 2000 Redistricting Data, Public Law 94-171 Summary File.

2 An example of this dynamic is evident in the article entitled "Who's Black and Who's Not" where celebrities such as Jennifer Beals, Prince, and Lenny Kravitz are criticized for describing themselves as something other than, or in addition to, Black upon achieving commercial success. See: L. Normant, "Who's Black and Who's Not?: New Ethnicity Raises Provocative Questions About Racial Identity," *Ebony* 45(5) (1990).

3 R. S. Jones, "The End of Africanity?: The Bi-racial Assault on Blackness," *The Western Journal of Black Studies* 18(4) (1994), 201-210. This essay presents one perspective on the diverse aspects of multiracial identity.

4 M. K. Frisby, "Black, White, Other," *Emerge* 7(3) (1996): 48-57. In this article, the author discusses a number of issues related to the multiracial category in the 2000 Census, including resistance to the change based on concerns involving social and political power.

5 W. E. Cross, "Discovering the Black Referent: The Psychology of Black Liberation," *Beyond Black and White: An Alternative America*, eds. V. J. Dixon and B. G. Foster (Boston: Little Brown, 1971), 96-110.

6 B. W. Jackson, *The Function of a Theory of Black Identity Development in Achieving Relevance in Education for Black Students*, Dissertation. Amherst, University of Massachusetts (1976).

7 R. Hardiman and B. W. Jackson, "Racial Identity Development: Understanding Racial Dynamics in College Classrooms and on Campus," in *Promoting Diversity in College Classrooms: Innovative Responses for the Curriculum, Faculty, and Institutions*, ed. M. Adams (San Francisco: Jossey-Bass, 1992).

8 R. W. Hardiman, *Identity Development: A Process Oriented Model for Describing the Racial Consciousness of White Americans*, Dissertation. Amherst, University of Massachusetts (1982).

9 R. Hardiman and B. W. Jackson, *Promoting Diversity in College Classrooms* (1997).

10 C. Wijeyesinghe, *Towards an Understanding of the Racial Identity of Biracial People: The Experience of Racial Self-identification of African-American/Euro-American Adults and the Factors Affecting their Choices of Racial Identity*, Dissertation. Amherst, University of Massachusetts (1992).

11 C. Wijeyesinghe, "Racial Identity in Multiracial People: An Alternative Paradigm," in *New Perspectives on Racial Identity Development: A Theoretical and Practical Anthology*, eds. C. L. Wijeyesinghe and B. W. Jackson (New York: New York University Press, 2001).

12 M. R. Lyles, et. al., "Racial Identity and Self-Esteem: Problems Peculiar to Biracial Children," *Journal of the American Academy of Child Psychiatry* 24(2) (1985), 150-153.

13 J. T. Gibb, "Identity and Marginality: Issues in the Treatment of Biracial Adolescents," *American Orthopsychiatric Association* 57(2) (1987), 265-278.

14 J. B. Brandell, "Treatment of the Biracial Child: Theoretical and Clinical Issues," *Journal of Multicultural Counseling and Development* 16(4) (1988), 176-187.

15 P. M. Brown, "Biracial Identity and Social Marginality," *Child and Social Work Journal* 7(4) (1990), 319-337.

16 Individuals planning and facilitating dialogues should have significant training in human relations skills and group dynamics. In addition, they need to engage in substantial personal reflection on issues of race, racial identity, and multiracial issues.

Meraiya L. Turner

Age: 5
Racial/Ethnic Heritage: African American, Puerto Rican, and Native American

My five-year-old daughter Meraiya is multiracial. I am Puerto Rican, and her father is African American with Native American ancestry. I was not aware that both of Meraiya's ethnicities could be recognized because the forms I filled out always called for choosing only one. It made me feel like the forms were inaccurate, incomplete, and untruthful because it did not provide all of her information. I felt like whichever one I was picking forced me to "sell out" on the other. Also, because both her father and I belong to minority groups, we ended up feeling that Meraiya was Black by default. But, ethnically and culturally she was also Latina, and it bothered me that this was not being recognized.

Recently, Meraiya started kindergarten, where another kindergartener asked if she had the same skin color as her mother or father. She answered no, and the little girl told Meraiya she did not belong with either family because she did not have the same skin color as either. After this incident, Meraiya became extremely self-conscious and sad about the fact that she was different from both of her parents. She constantly asked me if she could change her skin color so that it would "match" one of her parents. She would say that her daddy was "chocolate brown" and that her mommy was "peachy White", and that she wanted to "match", too. While Meraiya and I drafted our annual "Dear Santa" letter, she wanted me to write to Santa and ask him if he could change her skin color. Obviously, my heart ached for the anguish of my daughter, and I could no longer just let this phase pass.

Before kindergarten, I think Meraiya was either comfortable or oblivious with her dual ethnicity. It was not until she entered kindergarten that she started to associate being different with somehow being wrong or bad. Her father and I didn't think of explaining her unique ethnicity to her. The confrontation with the other kindergartener may have been a blessing in disguise because it helped us face the fact that she does have two ethnicities. That experience has taught us to understand Meraiya better.

Some of Meraiya's feedback suggests that we should have done more to educate her about her multiracial background. By being unaware of the possibility of issues that she could face, we were, in a way, dismissing her as a person. Her multiethnicity is not just about the issues she faces but also about the blessings that make her unique.

Though in Meraiya's classes her teachers have done a great job recognizing different cultures and traditions, there is still room for improvement. There needs to be trainings on multiracial and multiethnic issues in our schools. Without this training, we cannot blame educators for a lack of sensitivity in these areas.

Meraiya has a beautiful history that makes her so fascinating. In this day and age, we are all so quick to put labels on each other, but this is so much more than that. This is about understanding who you are and being proud of it. This understanding comes from knowledge of your past and genuine acceptance of it as part of the fabric that makes up each individual. In this manner, our children accept themselves in the same way we always have—with love and pride.

Testimonial

Chapter 23

LatiNegros: Afro Latinos' Quest for Identity

Lillian Comas-Díaz, Ph.D.

Latinos with visible African roots face unique circumstances as a mixed race group in the United States. In this chapter I present their sociocultural context, explaining how they cope and adapt in relation to the dominant society. Additionally, I offer psychological and educational techniques for parents, educators, and other providers to use to address the needs of this special population.

Afro Latinos, Black Latinos or LatiNegros

Josefina, a 14-year-old Colombian student, refuses to learn English. A Costa Rican accountant, Carlos, speaks English with a non-standard Black accent. Cheryl, a 40-year-old engineer, identifies herself as African American, forgetting that her parents were Panamanian. On the other hand, Arturo, a 25-year-old Puerto Rican law student, has established Blatinos.com, "a vehicle for affirming Latinos' African roots." Denise, a 40-year-old Black author explores her maternal Cuban ancestry through Santería (an Afro Latino religion). Juan, a 50-year-old Cuban college professor, teaches a course on Afro Latinos.

The above mentioned individuals are Hispanics who "don't look Latino." The question "Are you Latino?" followed by the reply "You don't look it," is a constant reminder that mass culture denies a significant portion of Afro Latinos' culture and ethnicity.

Consider David, a 10-year-old Dominican student, who comes home from school crying because his classmates tell him that he is Black and not Latino. Conversely, 12-year-old Ana (now Ann) calls herself Black and refuses to visit her Dominican grandparents. Many Latinos with visible African roots have difficulty establishing their ethnic identity. While Josefina, Carlos, and Cheryl deny their Blackness, Arturo, Denise, and Juan affirm it. As David struggles to keep his Afro Latino ethnicity, Ann chooses the African American identity.

Afro Latinos like Cheryl and Ann assimilate in the dominant society as African Americans. Some, like Carlos, change their accent, adopting a non-standard Black English.[1][2] Many are absorbed into the African American community, losing their Latino identity.[3] Afro Latinos differ from other mixed race individuals in that there is no curiosity regarding their racial identity. They have unambiguous racial features—they are perceived as Black. However, like other biracial individuals, Black Latinos need to accept both sides of their racial heritage and exercise the right to declare how they wish to identify racially—even if this identity is discrepant with how they look. Like 10-year-old David, whose classmates do not allow him to identify as Latino, many Afro Latinos are denied the ability to choose their racial identities.

Latinos have a complex relationship with Blackness. Historically, Spaniards intermixed with people of African descent on a number of occasions, including when the North African Moors conquered and occupied Spain for nearly 800 years,[4] and when Black slaves were brought to Latin America. This legacy resulted in an unconscious perception of Black people as both conquerors and oppressed. As part of the Latino self, Blackness often produces intense ambivalence. Mixed race Latinos struggle with their darkness at an emotional level, where Blackness is both loved and hated. The Latino reaction to dark Latinos frequently involves a confrontation of their own Blackness. Indeed, most of the terms used to designate people with visible African roots are both endearing and insulting. *Negro*, or its feminine *negra*, for instance, is used both in a derogatory way and as an expression of affection.

I prefer the term *LatiNegro*[5] over Afro Latino. LatiNegro resists the society's systematic negation of African Latinos' Latinness.[6] This term also affirms both the Latino and African components of a person's multiracial identity.

La Raza: Historical and Sociopolitical Influences

La Raza is used to designate Latinos in the United States. In 1925 José Vasconcelos coined the term, arguing that the future of humankind was *mestizaje*, or the union of Indian, White, "Mongol," and African races. He identified *La Raza Cósmica* (the cosmic race) as the result of the synthesis of the Spanish Empire in Europe, the Americas, the Philippines, and Africa. The African presence varies in Latin America. For instance, Brazil, Colombia, Cuba, the Dominican Republic, Panama, Puerto Rico, Venezuela, and Veracruz (in Mexico) have significant Black African populations. In many ways, Brazil, Venezuela, Colombia, and Panama have more in common racially with Puerto Rico, Cuba, and the Dominican Republic than they do with the rest of South America. Indeed, due to racial cleansing, Uruguay, Chile, and particularly Argentina have virtually no Blacks.

The Catholic religion was partly responsible for the historical recognition of Latin America's mixed racial composition. Although the Church officially discouraged intermarriage, its condemnation of sexual cohabitation as living in sin facilitated the legalization

of interracial unions. As a result, children of such liasions were officially recognized. During the Spanish colonization, a wide vocabulary of race, including words like *jarocho*—the offspring of a Black and Indian union[7]—was used to describe the many racial permutations found in South America. Contrary to the North American dictum that one drop of African blood makes you Black, in Latin America, one drop of White blood makes you not Black.[8] In the racial glossary, differences are expressed according to gradations of color and racial features. As an illustration, *mestizo/a*, literally means a person with mixed blood; *mulato/a* is the equivalent of mulatto; *cuarteron/a* (similar to quadroon) indicates that one out of four immediate ancestors is Black; *jabao/a* (equivalent to the African American yellow) is the light-skinned individual with African features; *grifo/a* has European features with frizzled or coarse hair; *trigueño/a* is olive skinned; *indio/a* has Indian characteristics; and *negro/a* or *prieto/a* is African Black.[9] [10] [11] Although the term *moreno/a* means dark, many Latinos call African Americans *morenos* in public, while referring to them as *negros* in private.

Historical, political, social, and economic factors mediate relationships between individuals with different racial appellations. The legacy of North American slavery, where lighter complexioned Blacks (progeny of White plantation owners) were preferred over darker complexioned slaves as house servants, affected the relationships between lighter and darker slaves, and created jealousies and resentments.[12] This legacy was also present in Latin America. The preferential treatment based on skin color resulted in distorted feelings about race for many Black and non-Black Latinos.

Many Latinos in the United States are both ethnic and racial minorities. The United States' individual and institutionalized racism encourages polarized racial identification, either Black or White. The dominant society often forces Latinos with visible African heritage into defining themselves as Black.

Racismo: Color and Class Interaction

In order to understand LatiNegros we need to be familiar with Latino racism. *Racismo* operates differently from its North American sibling. After slavery was abolished, Latin America treated its slaves and their descendants very differently from the way the United States treated its slaves.[13] As a result, Latin America today is far more racially integrated than the United States. Partially due to this, many Latinos pride themselves on being non-racist—an assertion which is at best a distortion and/or denial, and at worst, racism.

Although *racismo* permeates all spheres of the Latino society, it is not as institutionalized as its North American counterpart. *Racismo* is covert, contextual, and subjective. Race and *racismo* are related to socioeconomic class. In other words, color is class in Latin America. The higher the person's social class, the whiter the person is perceived to be. As an illustration, a mulatto from a high social class is perceived as non-Black and subjected to less racism than a mulatto from a lower social class. Fame and money whiten Latinos. LatiNegros like baseball stars Roberto Clemente and Sammy Sosa, freedom fighters Pedro Albizu Campos and Ramon Emeterio Betances, actor Juano Hernandez, and musicians Celia Cruz, Susana Baca, Rafael Hernández, and the Buena Vista Social Club artists create a color dissonance among *norteamericanos*, challenging what "Latinos look like."

Although some Latinos acknowledge their African ancestry, many others have agreed to ignore it. The fluidity of race allows Latinos to be selective in their racial perception. For example, among Puerto Ricans, racial perception is associated with individuals' racial self-identification: the race of a dark-complexioned Puerto Rican may be perceived differently by two persons according to their own racial identification.[14] In other words, one person can be assigned to different racial categories depending on the color of the observer. The relationship between racial perception and racial self-identification persists among Puerto Ricans in the continental United States.[15] This subjective perception engenders a racial projection, since many Latinos are racially closeted. Some accuse each other of being Black and/or having a *rajita* (a racial characteristic denoting African ancestry).[16][17]

Many Latinos internalize *racismo* and its dynamics. Latin American broadcasting media are notorious for perpetuating *racismo* by placing White-looking Latinos in the role of good guys, as opposed to darker actors who act as criminals, deviants, or servants.[18][19] Univision, the Spanish language cable TV channel

based in the United States, has been accused of not depicting Afro Latinos in its programming.[20] The denial of Blackness can be interpreted as an attempt at passing, or Latinos' active efforts to appear White, or at least, non-Black. African Americans have used "passing" as an adaptive survival mechanism. Some LatiNegros wish to pass as non-Black because they don't want to identify with African Americans, seen as the group of lowest racial and socioeconomic status. Passing is common among other dark-complexioned ethnic groups such as Asian Indians, who prefer to be mistaken for Latinos instead of Blacks.[21] However, when passing is related to the belief that being Black is a sign of inferiority, it is an expression of internalized racism.[22]

Latino beauty standards show the obsessive importance placed on the ability to pass. Although Blackness (dark skin, African features, coarse hair, and body shape) does not necessarily imply racial inferiority, individuals with light skin and White features are considered more attractive than dark-skinned Latinos.[23] Many LatiNegros attempt to whiten (*blanquear*) themselves—torturing their hair and scalp by chemically straightening their hair; using bleaching creams, and generally trying to look less Black.[24] Regardless of skin color, many Latinas dye their hair blonde in order to appear less dark.

Latinos in the United States contend with both racism and *racismo*. Although there are differences between LatiNegros in the United States and those in Latin America, the racial exclusions faced by most of them are similar. Both communities deny their Blackness, creating identity conflicts among LatiNegros.

La Familia and the Community

The major source of transmitting values, mores, beliefs, and behaviors, the family is expected to socialize LatiNegros. Unlike African Americans, *la familia* does not have the socialization skills necessary in an overtly racist environment. African American families socialize their children to cope with racial problems in the context of love and support.[25][26] Conversely, Latino families reject their children's Blackness, obstructing their self-acceptance as Black Latinos. Most *familias* do not racially socialize their LatiNegro children. Although they may be able to effectively teach LatiNegros how to cope as Latinos, they cannot

**Half and Half: Writers on Growing
Up Biracial and Bicultural**
Claudine Chiawei O'Hearn,
Pantheon Books, 1998

Claudine Chiawei O'Hearn's edited
collection is a delightful collection of
literary-quality creative nonfiction
essays by biracial and bicultural
people who are immigrants, children
of immigrants and often themselves
the parents of biracial children. Each
of the book's pieces are thoughtful
and well crafted and the reader can
easily seek out other books by
these writers. Furthermore, a diversity
of male and female perspectives
and racial/ethnic backgrounds is
represented, instead of the more
usual Black/White or Asian/White
examples of biraciality.

teach emotional defenses and skills as Black Latinos. Many non-Black Latinos do not experience racial stress and, thus, cannot minimize its effects on their LatiNegro children, nor teach them coping mechanisms to deal with racial stress, prejudice, and discrimination.

The lack of racial socialization is heightened when *la familia* has recently immigrated and is learning a new culture, language, and racial dynamics. When mixed race Latinos arrive to the United States, they are shocked to be perceived as Black, especially if they saw themselves as non-Blacks in Latin America.[27] Many encounter racial shock due to being perceived in a racially dichotomous manner, being the subject of racial discrimination, suffering overt individual and institutionalized racism, and being considered inferior due to their race.

The racial shock may persist for generations after immigration. Feelings about self and others become entangled with color differences. Non-White Latinos such as *trigueños, jabaos, mulatos,* and *grifos*, can experience identity confusion. Considered non-Black among Latinos, they are perceived as non-White in American terms. Consequently, LatiNegros become a painful reminder of non-White Latinos' Blackness, creating resentment which can lead to destructive and unhealthy relationships between members of the Latino community.[28] [29]

The dominant society often forces Latinos with visible African heritage into defining themselves as Black. Due to the racism prevalent in the White and Latino community, LatiNegros frequently develop solidarity with African Americans. LatiNegros and African Americans share the common denominator of being Black in an openly racist society. LatiNegro adolescents turn to their African American friends for peer socialization. These bonds ignite conflict between LatiNegros and their *familias*, facilitating their assimilation into the African American diaspora. Some deny sharing a collective experience with other individuals of African descent, instead asserting their individuality.

Nonetheless, when color supersedes ethnicity and culture as the source of identity for non-White Latinos, many internalize the racial antagonism that surrounds them,[30] excluding Latinness or Africanness from their identity. Renouncing one aspect of identity implies denial of the self, disruption in ethnic continuity, and loss of a cultural holding environment. One result is that lighter Latinos may frequently marry White Americans, Latinos or other non-Black individuals, while darker Latinos often marry African Americans or other Blacks. The LatiNegra who marries an African American man often gives birth to children who are perceived as non-Latinos in the Latino community.

Color, Gender and Culture

La familia's lack of racial socialization affects LatiNegras differently than LatiNegros. The vast differences between the Latina mother's racial experiences and those of her LatiNegra daughter impede racial and gender socialization. In other words, mothers do not prepare LatiNegras to become Black women. Latina mothers do not communicate the racial and sexual problems that Black females confront, or how to cope with them. Neither do they teach LatiNegras how to cope with being a stereotyped sexual being[31] who conjures exoticism, evil, dark power, sensuality, and strong sexuality.

Many Latinas are socialized to assume primary responsibility for family relationships and to subordinate individual needs to those of the group. Endorsing collectivism, they derive self-esteem from significant others' approval. Unfortunately, *la familia* targets LatiNegras for racial exclusion due to their race and gender. Although there is a color-based glass ceiling for LatiNegros, the glass ceiling is double-paned for females.[32] A combination of racism, sexism, and elitism contributes to their rejection. From infancy, LatiNegras hear family and community making racist-sexist remarks towards other Afro Latinas. Their individual characteristics are viewed through the lens of ugly female Blackness. Racial rejection from significant others can be devastating for LatiNegras, resulting in diminished self-esteem.[33]

Although Latinos do not object to socializing with LatiNegros, they profoundly object to their offspring marrying them. A LatiNegra daughter-in-law—more than a LatiNegro son-in-law—is perceived as a sign of a decline in the family's status due to female centrality in the family. It is usually more acceptable for a Latina to "marry down" by marrying a LatiNegro, than for a Latino to marry a LatiNegra. Marrying a LatiNegra is anathema to the Latino dictum of *adelantar o mejorar la raza* (to improve the

race)—going through a whitening process by marrying someone light-complexioned or White.[34] Therefore, LatiNegras are not desirable spouses because they do not *improve the race*; instead, they *damage the race*.[35] This process is compounded by the fear of *requintar* (from the word fifth): the inheritance of African traits not manifested in the parents nor grandparents but present in an ancestor five generations back (great-grandparent). Thus, non-Black Latinos fear their African ancestry has greater probability of *requintar* in their descendents if they marry LatiNegros or non-White Latinos.

The fact that the mother typically takes the primary role in socializing Latinos also contributes to the rejection of LatiNegras as potential wives. LatiNegras are considered more threatening to the family racial perception than LatiNegro fathers because they are expected to be physically and emotionally present in the lives of their children, while such an expectation does not apply to fathers. Consequently, LatiNegro fathers are less visible than LatiNegra mothers who are harder to hide in the family racial closet than LatiNegros. A visible LatiNegra mother is a clear sign of her children's mixed racial ancestry, increasing the fear of *requintar*, and reducing their opportunities to improve the race.

Racismo and racism have gendered effects on LatiNegros, who tend to fare worse than their Latino brothers. The darkest male in Latino families is usually the least successful child. This also holds true at the national level. LatiNegros and/or dark-complexioned Latinos are overrepresented in the criminal system.[36] Gay LatiNegros and lesbian LatiNegras are more severely affected within their needs of acceptance and belonging. Besides the dominant society's racism, sexism, and homophobia, many gay and lesbians of color face the additional stress of coping with the White gay and lesbian community's racism, in addition to the homophobia and internalized racism of their own ethnic community.[37][38] This situation creates profound conflicts around identity and ethnic loyalty among LatiNegro adolescent gays and lesbians, making them a high-risk population for self-destructive behaviors.

Latinos Growing up Black in the United States

"Why don't you admit we're Black?" 13-year-old Cristina asked her Cuban mother.

"Because we're not," replied her mother.

Latinos need to rescue their Blackness. If they do not, younger generations will embrace Blackness with the same fervor that many Latinos currently deny it. In the 1960s and 1970s, the Brown Pride movement encouraged Latinos to reclaim their indigenous heritage; today, the "Viva Mama Africa" movement[39] is rescuing Latino African roots. Mixed race Latinos such as pop music diva Mariah Carey, who acknowledged that her father was Black Venezuelan and her mother Irish American, are emblematic of this trend. Since many Latinos have ignored, repressed, and dismissed their African heritage, parents, educators, and other providers can facilitate Latinos' reconciliation with their African ancestry.

Color Consciousness

Color consciousness is the process whereby Latinos learn to identify and accept their Blackness. By increasing awareness, color consciousness helps Latinos recognize and preserve their African legacy. Following a "reclaiming identity and restoring dignity" approach helps LatiNegros integrate their mixed racial identity. Accepting the African legacy in everyday life through music, spirituality, and cultural practices increases Latinos' understanding of their African ancestry.[40] [41] As an illustration, Latinos can take pride in music such as salsa, Latin jazz, merengue, and mambo, as well as the Moorish flamenco and *cante hondo*, as African-derived rhythms.[42] [43] Literature such as Nuyorican poetry can also help recognize Latinos' debt to Africa.[44] In the same vein, memoirs dealing with racial issues such as *When I was Puerto Rican, Family installments: Memories of Growing Up Hispanic,* or *Growing Up Latino: Memoirs and Stories*, can be used as color awareness tools.[45] [46] Non-fiction books and media can be excellent avenues for increasing color consciousness. Watching films and documentaries *en familia* helps to promote color awareness and combat negative images promulgated by the media. This psychoeducation is crucial for LatiNegro youth.

Educators can play a central role in increasing LatiNegros'

color consciousness by helping them to recall their collective memory. Teachers can become archeologists and help excavate the historical contributions of Latinos and Hispanics of African descent. Some of these figures include Pedro Alonso Niño, the African explorer who navigated one of Christopher Columbus' ships; Vicente Guerrero, known as the Black Warrior, who fought in Mexico's war of independence, became Mexico's second president, and abolished slavery in 1829, and many others.[47] This cultural unearthing can help LatiNegros who have assimilated into African American society reclaim their lost Latinness. For instance, painter Jean Baptiste Basquiat, the son of a Black Puerto Rican mother and a Haitian father, created a new style of painting during the 1980s. Furthermore, educators can follow a cultural awareness program to restore ethnic and racial pride among Latinos with visible African roots.[48] As a concrete step, they can start by acknowledging Afro Latino presence during the Black History Month celebration.

Arpillera: A Racial Healing Tapestry

Families should trace their racial and ethnic history. Genealogy is useful to explore racial and cultural legacies in a multigenerational basis. As a psychologist, I utilize a genogram—a family tree tool highlighting family relations and dynamics.[49] In addition, I use folklore, photographs, art, literature, and music to diagram clients' and families' racial journey in the cultural transitional map.[50] I emphasize using photographs to help individuals visualize racial characteristics.[51] When photos are not available, I encourage my clients to draw their ancestors from "memory" or to provide a picture of another person that could resemble the ancestor. After gathering all the data, we collaborate in constructing an *arpillera*. I borrowed the *arpillera* from Latin Americans who express their stories of oppression, resistance, and liberation in an artistic weaving.[52] *Arpilleras* are healing tapestries where Latinos weave in their personal, familiar, cultural, and racial history.

Color consciousness, cultural awareness programs, and *arpilleras* are tools that can help with racial reconciliation. As many Latinos and African Americans use spirituality and religion for coping with problems, spiritual reconciliation is an aspiration.[53] [54] Endorsing a people of color's spiritual framework, Abadio-Clottey and Clottey developed a 12-step program for racial healing.[55] Among other beliefs, their 12 principles include "healing is conquering fear;" "developing forgiveness;" and "viewing life as a learning experience."

Many Latinos value darkness within their spiritual orientation. Some Latinos invoke our Lady of Guadalupe, *La Morenita* (the Little Darkling) who is the patron saint and Goddess of the Americas. Guadalupe appeared to the Aztec convert Juan Diego in the place of worship of the Mexica goddess Tonantzin, blending indigenous with Spanish beliefs. Transcending the Catholic religion, Guadalupe is a Black Madonna that affirms darkness, imparts dignity to Latinos, and helps them to preserve their ancestral identity.[56] [57] Oppressed people all over the world favor the Black Madonna, a symbol of struggle, resistance, and liberation.[58] [59] Another Black Madonna, Our Lady of Montserrat also known as La Morenita, is worshiped in many Latin American countries with African ancestry.[60] Montserrat's fights oppression and promotes rebirth and empowerment.[61]

African beliefs infuse Latino spirituality. Some Latinos carry the Orisha beads of Santería under their business suits, indicating belief in Yoruba-based traditions.[62] Some Latinos in the United States practice religions that syncretize African, Indigenous, and Christian beliefs such as Santería, Candomble and Umbanda.[63] [64] Some are transforming Santería and Spiritualism into Santerísmo, blending the African and European traditions.[65] As the practice of these beliefs helps Latinos affirm identity, LatiNegros assert their Blackness.

From Invisibility to Prominence: LatiNegro Identity Reformulation

Latinos and Hispanics of mixed race African descent struggle against internalized oppression. Self-designation signals the beginning of liberation, and today LatiNegros are turning denial into pride.[66] They are reformulating their identity, naming themselves Latino, Hispanic, Afro Latino, Blatino, LatiNegro, Americano, or any other denomination they wish to adopt. As their identity re-emerges, LatiNegros' presence will no longer remain invisible.

Did you know?

Here are some well-known multiracial people of both Latino/a and Black heritage:

Mariah Carey (Singer)
Roberto Clemente (Athlete)
Gina Ravera (Actor)
Sammy Sosa (Athlete)

Notes

1 Del Valle, Personal Interview, 1993.

2 E. Seda Bonilla, *Requiem por una Cultura* (Requiem For a Culture) (Río Piedras, Puerto Rico: Editorial Edil, 1970).

3 L. Comas-Díaz, M. B. Lykes and R. Alarcón, "Ethnic Conflict and Psychology of Liberation in Guatemala, Perú and Puerto Rico," *American Psychologist* 53(7), 778-792.

4 A. Castillo, *Massacre of the Dreamers: Essays on Xicanisma* (New York: Penguin, 1995).

5 L. Comas-Díaz, "LatiNegra: Mental Health Needs of African Latinas," *Journal of Feminist Family Therapy* 5 (1994), 35-74.

6 I. Zenón Cruz, *Narciso Descubre Su Trasero* (Narcissus Discovers His Buttocks) (Humacao, Puerto Rico: Editorial Furidi, 1975).

7 N. Leon, "Las Castas de Mexico Colonial o Nueva España (The Castes from Colonial Mexico or New Spain)," Mexico City: Departamento de Antropología Anatómica. Talleres Gráficos del Museo Nacional de Arqueología, Historia y Etnografía. (1924).

8 J. F. Longres, "Racism and its Effects on Puerto Rican Continentals," *Social Casework* 55 (1974), 67-75.

9 L. Comas-Díaz, "Puerto Rican Women's Cross Cultural Transitions: Developmental and Clinical Implications," in *The Psychosocial Development of Puerto Rican Women*, eds. C. Garcia Coll and M. L. Mattei (New York: Praeger, 1989), 166-199.

10 A. Jorge, "The Black Puerto Rican Woman in Contemporary American Society," in *The Puerto Rican Woman*, ed. E. Acosta-Belén (New York: Praeger, 1979), 134-141.

11 J. F. Longres, *Social Casework* (1974).

12 B. Greene, "Still Here: A Perspective on Psychotherapy with African American Women," in *New Directions in Feminist Psychology: Practice, Theory and Research*, eds. J. Chrisler and D. Howard (New York: Springer, 1992), 13-25.

13 A. M. Borrero, "Honor our African Roots," The Hispanic Magazine Online (April 2000)

14 A. B. Ginorio, *A Study of Racial Perception in Puerto Rico*, Unpublished Master's Thesis. Rio Piedras, Puerto Rico, University of Puerto Rico (1971).

15 M. Del Valle, *Acculturation, Sex Roles and Racial Definitions of Puerto Rican College Students in Puerto Rico and the United States*, Dissertation. Amherst, University of Massachusetts (1989).

16 L. Comas-Díaz, *Journal of Feminist Family Therapy* (1994).

17 I. Zenón Cruz, *Narciso Descubre Su Trasero* (1975).

18 L. Comas-Díaz, *Journal of Feminist Family Therapy* (1994).

19 V. Perez, "The Color Issue: The Apparent Favoritism of Lighter Skin Reverberates within the Latino Community," Hispanic Magazine Online (26 June 2000).

20 Ibid.

21 Almeida, Personal Interview, 1993

22 B. Greene, *New Directions in Feminist Psychology: Practice, Theory, and Research* (1992).

23 J. F. Longres, *Social Casework* (1974).

24 J. Rodriguez, "Guadalupe: The Feminine Face of God," in *Goddess of the Americas/La Diosa de las Américas: Writings on the Virgin of Guadalupe*, ed. A. Castillo (New York: Riverhead Books, 1997).

25 A. J. Franklin and N. Boyd-Franklin, "A Psychoeducational Perspective on Black Parenting," in *Black Children*, eds. H. McAdoo and J. McAdoo (Beverly Hills: Sage, 1985).

26 B. Greene, "What Has Gone Before: The Legacy of Racism and Sexism in the Lives of Black Mothers and Daughters," *Women & Therapy* 9 (1990), 207-230.

27 D. Fears, "People of Color who Never felt they were Black: Racial Label Surprises Many Latino Immigrants," *The Washington Post* (26 December 2002), A01.

28 E. Rivera, *Family Installments: Memories of Growing up Hispanic* (New York: William Morrow & Co., 1982).

29 P. Thomas, *Down these Mean Streets* (New York: New American Library, 1967).

30 J. F. Longres, *Social Casework* (1974).

31 C. Nakashima, "An Invisible Monster: The Creation and Denial of Mixed Race People in America," in *Racially Mixed People in America*, ed. M. P. P. Root (Thousand Oaks, CA: Sage, 1992).

32 M. Ramos Rosado, "La Mujer Puertorriqueña Negra, "La Otra Cara de la Historia" (The Black Puerto Rican Woman, "The Other Face of History")," *Homines* 10(2) (1986), 491-497.

33 A. Jorge, *The Puerto Rican Woman* (1979).

34 Ibid.

35 I. Zenón Cruz, *Narciso Descubre Su Trasero* (1975).

36 P. Thomas, *Down these Mean Streets*, 1967).

37 B. Greene, "Human Diversity in Clinical Psychology: Lesbians and Gay Sexual Orientations," *The Clinical Psychologist* 46 (1993), 74-82.

38 V. Kanuha, "Compounding the Triple Jeopardy: Battering in Lesbian of Color Relationships," *Therapy & Women* 9 (1990), 169-184.

39 A. M. Borrero, "Honor our African Roots" (2000).

40 Ibid.

41 V. Perez, "The Color Issue" (2000).

42 A. M. Borrero, "Honor our African Roots" (2000).

43 J. J. Klor de Alva, "The Invention of Ethnic Origins and the Negotiation of Latino Identity, 1969-1981," in *Challenging Fronteras: Structuring Latina and Latino Lives in the U.S.* eds. M. Romero, P. Hondagneu-Sotelo, and V. Ortiz (New York: Routledge, 1997), 55-74.

44 M. Algarín and Piñero, eds., *Nuyorican Poetry: An Anthology of Puerto Rican Words and Feelings* (New York: William Morrow & Co., 1975).

45 E. Rivera, *Family Installments: Memories of Growing up Hispanic* (New York: William Morrow & Co., 1982).

46 H. Augenbraum and I. Stavans, *Growing up Latino: Memoirs and Stories* (New York: Houghton Mifflin Company, 1993)

47 A. M. Borrero, "Honor our African Roots" (2000).

48 L. Comas-Díaz, A. Arroyo, and J. C. Lovelace, "Enriching Self-Concept Through a Puerto Rican Cultural Awareness Program," *Personnel and Guidance Journal* 60(5) (1982), 306-308.

49 M. McGoldrick and R. Gerson, *Genograms in Family Assessment* (New York: Norton, 1985).

50 Ho, "In Search of a Female Self: Toni Morrison's *The Bluest Eyes* and Maxine Hong's *The Woman Warrior*," *American Studies* 17(3) (Sept. 1987), 1-44.

51 L. Comas-Díaz, "The Black Madonna: The Psychospiritual Feminism of Guadalupe, Kali and Monserrat," in *Feminist Family: Empowerment and Social Location*, eds. L. Silverstein and T. J. Goodrich (Washington, DC: American Psychological Association, in press).

52 L. Comas-Díaz and M. A. Jansen, "Global Conflict and Violence Against Women," *Peace and Conflict: Journal of Peace Psychology* 1 (1995), 315-331.

53 A. J. Franklin and N. Boyd-Franklin, *Black Children* (1985).

54 C. Martinez, "Mexican Americans," in *Clinical Guidelines in Cross Cultural Mental Health*, eds. L. Comas-Diaz and E. H. Griffith (New York: Wiley, 1988).

55 A. Abadio-Clottey and K. Clottey, *Beyond Fear: Twelve Spiritual Keys to Racial Healing* (Tiburon, CA: H. J. Kramer, 1998).

56 A. Castillo, ed. *Goddess of the Americas/La Diosa de las Américas: Writings on the Virgin of Guadalupe* (New York: Riverhead Books, 1996).

57 J. Rodriguez, "Guadalupe: The Feminine Face of God," in *Goddess of the Americas/La Diosa de las Américas: Writings on the Virgin of Guadalupe*, ed. A. Castillo (New York: Riverhead Books, 1996).

58 E. Begg, *The Cult of the Black Virgin* (London: Arkana/Penguin Books, 1985).

59 C. Galland, *Longing for Darkness: Tara and the Black Madonna* (New York: Compas/Penguin Press, 1990).

60 L. Comas-Díaz, *Feminist Family: Empowerment and Social Location* (in press).

61 E. Begg, *The Cult of the Black Virgin* (1985).

62 A. M. Borrero, "Honor our African Roots" (2000).

63 M. Gonzalez-Wippler, *Santería: The Religion* (New York: Harmony Books, 1989).

64 M. C. Zea, M. Mason, and A. Murguia, "Psychotherapy with Members of Latino/Latina Religions and Spiritual Traditions," in *Handbook of Psychotherapy and Religious Diversity*, eds. P. S. Richards and A. E. Bergin (Washington, D.C.: American Psychological Association, 2000), 397-419.

65 A. Perez y Mena, *Speaking with the Dead: Development of Afro-Latin Religion Among Puerto Ricans in the United States* (New York: AMS Press, 1991).

66 A. Castillo, *Massacre of the Dreamers: Essays on Xicanisma* (1994).

David and Alena Prendez

Age: 6 and 4

Racial/Ethnic Heritage: Mexican, Filipino, Spanish, Italian, and Native American

My name is Jacobo Prendez. I am writing for my two children, David Miguel Madayag Prendez, age six, and four-year-old Alena Jade Madayag Prendez. David and Alena are a beautiful mixture of Mexican, Filipino, Italian, American Indian (Choctaw and Chicasaw), Spanish, and other European heritages. I jokingly call my childrens' race "Mexipino." They get their Mexican, Italian, American Indian, and European mixture from me, and their Filipino and Spanish blood from their mother.

I met their mother many moons ago at Maywood Hills Elementary school in Bothell, Washington, a suburb on the outskirts of Seattle. David and Alena's mother and I did not formally get to know each other until high school even though we attended the same schools throughout the years. We quickly became high school sweethearts and married a few years after graduation.

Since I am multiracial myself, I wanted my kids to know and embrace the mixed race experience and enjoy the beauty of their entire cultural backgrounds. I would love for my children to celebrate *Fiestas Patrias*, *Dia de los Muertos*, *Quinceneras*, Debuts, *Pistasanayan*, and Indigenous Peoples' Day, and protest Columbus Day. I know from my own experiences that my children will, at a time in their lives, struggle to understand their identity as I did. I remember trying to choose just one side and trying to be Chicano to the extreme. I remember feeling forced to be one thing and pushed into a corner of homogeneity. I remember elementary school teachers telling me "I couldn't be all of those things" when I gave my response on my race. I remember seeing on my high school transcript my racial category as "White" and my best friend who was also half-

Mexican marked as Hispanic. I remember hearing racial slurs from my high school teachers in my mostly White high school and feeling alienated from the other students. I felt helpless, angry, and alone in the classroom. I now fear my children will have to endure many of the same experiences. I hope that issues of multiracialism and biracialism will be addressed in their schools, and we as a nation have progressed since my days.

I truly owe a debt of gratitude to MAVIN Foundation because of their work with multiracial issues for helping me come to a understanding of myself as a multiracial individual. It is a shame that through my 12 years of public education I did not learn as much about who I was as I did from my one year interaction with MAVIN Foundation. While today I strongly align myself with Chicano politics and I am currently working on my master's in Chicano studies at California State University at Northridge, I accept and embrace my multiracial experience, and continue to write and research issues of the mixed race experience.

I, like every father, have many hopes and dreams for my children. I want to shelter them from the world and at the same time release them into the great unknown to marvel at all they will accomplish. I feel that the growing recognition of multiracial and multiethnic people in the United States will prevent them from growing up feeling like a biological experiment gone wrong. Instead, they will see themselves as a wonderful amalgamation of races and cultures that will one day be the exquisite norm.

Testimonial

Chapter 24

Raising Asian-Latinos
Sheila R. Chung

Rarely in the public eye, *Asian-Latinos*—people of mixed Asian and Latino heritage—represent a distinct population that has been growing in the United States since the 1940s. In those days, interracial marriages between immigrant Punjabi bachelors and Mexican women in the farming towns of Arizona, California, Texas, New Mexico, and Utah gave birth to one of the country's first Asian Latino populations.[1][2] Today, the United States is home to over 200,000 Asian-Latinos, the bulk of whom reside in California.[3]

The appearance of this group of people can be explained by several trends, including steady migrations from Asian and Latin American countries; the physical proximity and increased interaction of ethnic groups in large cities and farming communities; and the progressive rates at which multi-generational Asians and Latinos marry across racial lines. Today, California is a culturally pluralistic state where interracial marriages have become commonplace, if not nominally accepted. Indeed, one quarter of the United States' interracially married couples live in California.[4]

The Golden State, however, has not always been a safe-haven for interracial unions. Less than six decades ago, state laws prevented people of color from marrying Whites. Latinos, racially classified as White or brown depending on skin tone or arbitrary allocation, were also subject to these discriminatory laws. It was not until 1948 that *Perez* v. *Sharp* rescinded California's anti-miscegenation laws, stating that they were "by their very nature, odious to a free people."[5]

Both *Perez* v. *Sharp* and *Loving* v. *Virginia*—the 1967 U.S. Supreme Court case that ruled remaining anti-miscegenation laws unconstitutional—heralded a new era of interracial unions and mixed heritage births across the nation. By the 1970s, a biracial baby boom was well under way.[6]

Born in 1976, I am part of the boom generation that has come of age to articulate its needs, forge new identities and community visions, and tell its personal stories. My own story is rich and complex. Prior to the Vietnam War, my father emigrated from Korea to Argentina where he worked in the textile industry of Buenos Aires. He fell in love with my mother, an Argentinean of Italian and Spanish descent who was studying in college. My parents married in Canada and later settled in Los Angeles where they hoped to make their fortune and raise a family. Charles, my younger brother, and I were born in East Los Angeles and four years later, my parents divorced. My mother's second marriage was to an immigrant doctor from Monterey, Mexico. She and my stepfather gave birth to my two youngest brothers—David and Anthony.

I recall my childhood being filled with Argentinean School on Saturdays, World Cup soccer games, Filipino American teenagers driving lowered Hondas, mouth-watering *asados* on the grill, and Catholic schools filled with people of color. I also remember learning the art of *empanada*-making from my grandma, stepping onto Argentine soil for the first time, meeting my Korean grandparents and extended family in Toronto, Canada, and listening to my mother's constant observations on race. These collective experiences had profound impacts on my identity formation. They have made me into the person I am today.

In this chapter, I draw upon my personal experiences and those of eight Asian-Latinos to share with parents and educators 1) the distinct qualities of being of Asian *and* Latino descent, and 2) practical steps that families and teachers can take in raising mixed heritage Asian-Latino children.

The Asian-Latino Experience

What is particular about being Asian *and* Latino? While mixed heritage young people share common experiences like having strangers ask them the infamous "What are you?" question, and accepting racial identity changes over time, Asian-Latinos have particular experiences that distinguish them from others in the mixed heritage community. They include identifying as minorities, being forced to choose between people of color communities, being asked to serve as bridge-builders between those groups, and maintaining a low level of visibility amongst other mixed heritage Asians.

Are Asian-Latinos Different from Other Mixed Heritage Asians?

Unlike mixed heritage people of Caucasian and Asian descent who are often forced to choose between a U.S. majority and minority group (oppressor or the oppressed, privileged or under-privileged), the Asian-Latinos I interviewed readily identified as people of color.[7] They never questioned their status because, in essence, it had already been decided for them. Although some of the interviewees recognized that their Asian and Latino communities may have differing access to education, employment, and financial resources, they also acknowledged that both groups shared a common history of oppression as people of color in a White-dominated society. On a big picture level, this connects them. Chris Durazo, a third-generation Chicana and fourth-generation Japanese American, draws parallels between her two communities of color:

> I'm a woman of color and since I come from two different people of color groups, I feel very strong in that. My families were both poor families that came from migrant worker and sharecropping backgrounds. They both had difficult racist experiences. They both went through different responses to overcome those, but they are very similar in many ways. Both my parents and their generation were the first to go to college. I feel like I'm the culmination of very different, but parallel efforts on both sides. My father's family went through boycotts, marches, and Cesar Chavez. The Japanese side went through reparations. It's kind of amazing.[8]

The experience of Asian-Latinos is often compared to that of Asian-Blacks because they, too, share a minority-minority background and an identity as people of color. Yet, Asian-Blacks, unlike Asian-Latinos, must contend with the "one-drop rule." Under this race notion, a child that has one drop of "Black blood" is seen and generally accepted as Black by the African American community.

Within Asian and Latino communities, however, acceptance of a mixed heritage child depends on his or her possession of the "right" cultural tools, which might include physical appearance, language, knowledge of culture, mannerisms, and so on. For example, East Asians (Chinese, Japanese, and Koreans) might embrace an Asian-Latina if she has light skin, but reject her darker complexioned sister, since fair skin is often prized in Asia. There is no static formula for acceptance. It varies by group, geography, and multiple other factors, but it is clear that acceptance in Asian and Latino communities stands in stark contrast to the blanket "blackening" of Asian-Blacks under the "one-drop rule."

Whose side are you on?

While Asian-Latinos may find comfort in their identity as people of color, they are not exempt from questions of group allegiance imposed by one or more ethnic communities. The young people I talked to noted that, particularly in high schools and colleges prone to racial separatism, they were often forced to choose sides. Paul Salazar Ota talks about the division of student groups at his university:

> As soon as you walk on campus, a bunch of student groups try to get you to join their clubs. But they're all sectioned off into separate camps — Hong Kong Student Association, Jewish Student Union, MEChA, Hermanos Unidos. What ethnicity group you identify with becomes important. It impacts who you associate with on campus and even what classes you take.[9]

Paul's experience reminds us that communities naturally form around race and ethnicity, and that Asian-Latinos are often faced with difficult group choices. Children may encounter the pressure to choose sides when asked by curious acquaintances "Which side do you identify with more—your mom's or your dad's?" and "What group do you hang out with at school?" Rarely is the notion of being part of all groups an option. So how do we prepare our children to respond to such questions? The short answer is to develop in the child a strong foundation in her history and to make room for an identity that invites complexity and change. At the end of this chapter, the young people I interviewed offer practical suggestions for equipping your child with the tools to make the right personal choice.

Will You be Our Bridge-Builder?

Although Asian-Latino youth are commonly forced to decide on one group, they are occasionally asked to play a very different role—that of bridge-builder. My younger brother Charles, who attended a school with a predominantly Filipino American and Mexican American student population, describes his experience:

> In high school, it's such a popularity contest. It was advantageous for both the Asians and Hispanics to accept me into their groups. I gave them another network of people. They could say, 'I was hanging out with Charles who is part of that group.' It gave them a way to connect.[10]

In a country where Latinos are moving in droves to the South and enrolling their children in traditionally Black schools; where Peruvians, Mexicans, Taiwanese, Vietnamese, Filipinos, and Koreans are changing the face of Southeast Los Angeles; and where Asian American organizations in New York are providing social services to non-Asian populations in their boroughs, we find ourselves searching for young people who can translate the nuances of 21st century race relations. We also find ourselves seeking individuals who can build tolerance and understanding amongst polarized groups.

With perceived "built-in links" to their ethnic origin groups, Asian-Latinos are seen as the "children of the future"—children who can save us all from racial conflict and build a harmonious society, particularly amongst people of color. But we need to be cautious. Just because a child is of Asian and Latino descent does not mean that he or she has the capacity to resolve heated tensions between kids of those backgrounds at school. As with all responsibilities, assuming the role of bridge-builder depends on the interest, level of comfort, and experience of the child. Parents and teachers can offer such a leadership role as an option, but by no means, should they make it a requirement.

Can We Move Beyond Black and White? Can We Move Beyond Asian and White?

Moving beyond the individual child's experience, we can take a look at how shifting conversations around multiraciality have impacted Asian-Latinos. In the 1980s, when the mixed heritage writings of scholars, journalists, and psychologists blossomed, most discussions focused on people of African American and Caucasian descent. Given the U.S.'s history with slavery, the "one-drop rule", and the Civil Rights Movement, this limited focus came as no surprise. But rarely did these discussions break away from the

hapas.com

Hapas.com

Hapas.com was created by Alvin Soltis as an online forum and community all about the mixed race Asian experience. The Web site provides a variety of information, articles, as well as photos of the different people of various mixed race heritages that all fall under the inclusive term, "hapa." According to Soltis, hapas.com is a resource that provides a place to discuss the cultural and psychological experiences associated with being hapa and a place for people that defy racial categorization.

Learn more:

www.hapas.com

"Black-White dichotomy" to talk about the rapidly growing mixed heritage Asian population.

With the advent of student and nonprofit organizations addressing pan-ethnic issues, the dialogue widened to include Asians, Arabs, Latinos, and American Indians. But an interesting phenomenon took place, particularly in mixed heritage Asian organizations. Asian-Caucasians, who represent the largest group of mixed heritage Asians, effectively shifted race discussions away from the traditionally Black-White dichotomy toward an Asian-White one (at least in areas with large Asian populations). The appearance of Asian-Caucasians in Hollywood, the arts, academia, and leadership positions within the mixed race movement also proliferated this new focus.

So what did this mean for young Asian-Latinos? It meant broadened discussions on multiraciality, but discussions that still remained too shallow to give voice to their experiences. Teachers, parents, and the mixed heritage community have an opportunity now to spotlight the Asian-Latino experience, along with other groups that have traditionally been less visible. The suggestions that follow will be particularly useful in giving space to Asian-Latinos to explore and celebrate their identities.

Aladdin's Lamp

Having outlined some of the challenges facing Asian-Latino youth, I thought it would be useful for parents and educators to read practical tips on raising children from the young people I interviewed. Using the premise of Aladdin's magical lamp, I asked, "If you could have any wish granted, what would you have wanted to help you develop your Asian-Latino identity?"[II] Below are their responses:

Wish 1—I wish I knew more about my family history.

I didn't find out about my history until college when a professor had us do an immigration story on our families. I talked to my aunt, my dad's sister. She showed me old photos of my grandmother who died when I was a baby. She also told me my grandma was religious and that she carried around a statue of the Virgin Mary with a rosary wrapped around it. It was weird because I've always had a Virgin Mary statue with a rosary around it. It totally made me identify with my grandmother...I wanted to find out more.[12]

Chrissy's experience highlights the connections that can be made by unearthing family stories. Educators might consider assigning their students genealogical or family history projects. Parents and extended family members can share family folklore, memorabilia, videos, photographs, and other significant memories. Children should also be encouraged to ask questions and continue the storytelling, perhaps by sharing with younger siblings.

Wish 2—I wish I could speak [fill in language].

Although raised in San Jose, California—home to numerous Latinos and Asians—Stephan Garcia was taught to speak only English at home. His parents did not see a need for him to learn Spanish or Japanese. Stephan came to think otherwise:

When I go to Miami, I spend time with my family, but I don't learn about Cuban culture because I don't speak Spanish. Not knowing Japanese also isolates me from my mother's side of the family. While my father's side speaks English to some extent, my mother's doesn't and it completely shuts the door on knowing those relatives. I'm not too stressed about not speaking those languages because I don't know what I've missed. I just wonder where those paths could have led.[13]

Teaching children to speak multiple languages, whether through home conversations, language schools, or relatives, equips them with tools to communicate and explore culture. Languages open up conversations between children and their monolingual, non-English speaking relatives. They facilitate research that mixed heritage Asian-Latinos may conduct when seeking out their histories.

While a second or third language may not be spoken in the home, it is still worth introducing the child to another "heritage language." As adolescents, my siblings and I attended *La Escuela Argentina de Los Angeles* (LEALA) on Saturdays to cultivate our Spanish skills and learn about Argentina. Yes, it was painful missing Saturday morning cartoons every week. But the language skills we learned at LEALA became invaluable. They permitted us to travel to Latin American countries with ease, to secure jobs requiring bilingual skills, and to cultivate deep relationships with our monolingual grandparents.

Wish 3—I wish I had connected with my communities at a younger age.

Romy Chavez de Ropp was often the only person of Japanese descent in her classrooms. It was not until a friend invited her to volunteer as a *Nikkei* (meaning of Japanese descent) summer camp counselor that Romy felt connected to the Japanese Peruvian community of Lima. She says, "I would like to have become more active in the community at a younger age." Romy was 10 when she started playing sports in the *Nikkei* community, and 15 when she started volunteering in youth programs.[14]

Exposing children to ethnic community activities at an early age provides them with a context to later engage as adults. Working in San Francisco's Japantown, I have repeatedly been impressed by young people who take on community leadership roles. I find that they tend to be youth whose parents encouraged them to become active contributors to the community at an early age. They played *taiko*, competed in *Nikkei* basketball leagues, and volunteered at street festivals.

Other ways that parents and educators can expose mixed heritage children to their communities are by organizing school field trips to ethnic-specific museums and nonprofit organizations, attending church, engaging in community service activities, and becoming supporters of cultural arts.

Wish 4—I wish we had spent time with our extended family.

Family plays an important role in the development of a child's self-esteem and sense of self. Under the right circumstances, family can function as an automatic network of supporters—supporters that teach the child about culture experientially. This might entail following cultural traditions, preparing special foods, celebrating holidays, and sharing stories of struggle and triumph. Paul Salazar Ota and Chris Durazo describe the value of extended family:

> Growing up, I was always around my extended family. My mom's mom felt it was important to have the kids around, so every weekend she made dinner and the whole family got together. During religious holidays, we ate tamales and nopales. On New Year's, we would set up mochi offerings and decorate with dolls and paintings.[15]

> Both my parents came from big sibling families and those siblings have a lot of fun together — in very different ways. On the Mexican side they're louder. They dance and sing. On my mom's side, they tell old stories. I would want my kids to experience both joys. They're so different.[16]

Wish 5—I wish I had seen media images of people like me.

In recent years, the media has spotlighted mixed heritage celebrities such as news anchor Ann Curry, golf champion Tiger Woods, actress Tia Carrere, and speed skater Apollo Anton Ohno. But few, if any, of these high profile individuals are of Asian and Latino descent. For kids searching for Asian-Latino role models, the task can seem daunting. So what can parents and educators do to help?

They can point out celebrity role models in both Asian and Latino communities. These images prove especially vital during a child's identity formation because they effectively communicate, "You can be just like us—the Asian American singers, the Latina CEOs, the Asian American writers." Parents and educators can then connect the identity of the child with those of the celebrities— "You're Latina and you're Asian. You can grow up to be like any of these people."

On a local level, parents and educators can seek out older Asian-Latinos to serve as mentors. These might be high school or college students with similar ethnic backgrounds, or even relatives. Having someone close by who understands the child's experience can help him understand identity changes, work through issues at school, in the home and amongst friends, and see the myriad possibilities that lay ahead.

Conclusion

I am grateful to my family and teachers for the many gifts they shared with me as they nurtured and cared for me. They fulfilled many of my Aladdin-like wishes, and they did so by exposing me to family history and customs, encouraging me to be inquisitive, answering questions fully and without reservation, and giving me the freedom to be what I wanted. Perhaps the best advice I can leave you with comes from a mother I met on a flight to Los Angeles. "You can't force your kids to identify a particular way. The best thing you can do as a parent [or as a teacher] is to expose them to as much as possible, and give them the support they need to make their own choices." I hope you will do the same.

Did you know?

Here are some well-known multiracial people of both Latino/a and Asian heritage:

Franklin Chang-Diaz (Astronaut & Scientist)
Enrique Iglesias (Singer)

Notes

1 B. Lindelof, "In Yuba City, Traces Remain of Fading Mexican-Hindu Culture," *Sacramento Bee* (11 November 1991).

2 K. Leonard, "California's Punjabi Mexican Americans: Ethnic Choices Made by the Descendants of Punjabi Pioneers and their Mexican Wives," *The World & I* 4(5) (May 1989), 612-623.

3 U.S. Census Bureau, 2000.

4 "All Mixed Up." *Salon.com* (14 Feb 2000).

5 *Perez v. Sharp* (1 October 1948) 32 Cal.2d 711, 198 P.2d 17.

6 C. Jaret and D. C. Reitzes, "The Importance of Racial-Ethnic Identity and Social Setting for Blacks, Whites, and Multiracials," *Sociological Perspectives* 42(4) (1999), 711-737.

7 C. C. Iijima Hall and T. I. Cooke Turner, "The Diversity of Biracial Individuals: Asian-White and Asian-Minority Biracial Identity," in *The Sum of Our Parts: Mixed Heritage Asian Americans*, ed. T. Williams-Leon and C. L. Nakashima (Philadelphia: Temple Press, 2001), 81-83.

8 C. Durazo, Personal Interview, 13 May 2002.

9 P. S. Ota, Personal Interview, 5 May 2002.

10 C. Chung, Personal Interview, 23 May 2002.

11 *Aladdin* is a story in which a genie grants the son of a poor tailor every wish the boy commands. See: "The Story of 'Ala-ed-Din and the Wonderful Lamp,'" in C. W. Eliot, ed., *Stories from the Thousand and One Nights* vol. XVI, (New York: P.F. Collier & Son, 1909–14, 2001).

12 C. Flores, Personal Interview, 5 May 2002.

13 S. Garcia, Personal Interview, 13 May 2002.

14 R. C. de Ropp, Personal Interview, 12 May 2002.

15 P. S. Ota, Personal Interview, 5 May 2002.

16 C. Durazo, Personal Interview, 13 May 2002.

Damien Burt

Age: 19
Racial/Ethnic Heritage: African American and Cherokee

My identity has definitely changed from when I was younger. I identify racially as both African American and Cherokee Indian, but I don't know which percentage is higher. Until recently, I have always said that I was Black, because that's what I thought. But when I was about 15 years old I asked my mom about it, and she finally told me that I had both African American and Native American roots on my father's side. From then on, I identified with both.

I grew up in my mother's home, and have a younger brother who is Black and White, and a younger sister who is also mixed. Looking back, I wish that my mother had done more. She never talked to me about being multiracial, and so now it even feels like I don't "qualify" as multiracial. If she had let me know about my ethnicity before adolescence, it would have helped me to find myself earlier and to feel more whole. My mother made it seem like it wasn't a big deal. I think she feels that I have been shut out by a lot of other African Americans and that I feel rejected and so am trying to identify with being multiracial when (she thinks) I'm not. Now, however, she realizes how much the issue really affects me.

Growing up, I liked to study different cultures, and because of my lighter skin I had always wondered if I was mixed with something else. Even before I found out about my Native American roots, I felt a spiritual connection with Native Americans, but I didn't feel comfortable talking about it because people didn't accept it. At the same time, I also felt uncomfortable because people told me that I wasn't Black enough and acted too White. This made me question the characteristics of these stereotypes.

I came across the "check one" box all the time growing up. I saw it on employment applications, school forms, and registration and testing forms. My mom would just check "African American" for me, but I felt cheated by it; having to check only one box was like I was not able to represent all of myself. I didn't think that it was fair. I loved all of my teachers and felt like they were doing a good job. However, I don't remember talking about multiracial issues in school.

I wish that I would have become more comfortable with my racial background sooner, and that in my childhood I had known that I was multiracial, because then I would have wanted to explore it at a younger age. It would have been nice to have had role models I could have identified with growing up.

Now that I know more about my ethnic heritage, I am trying to get more involved with multicultural communities. I am the former president of Teens Against Prejudice, a group that encourages people to expose themselves to diverse cultural events. Through activities like this, I have found ways to relate to other people and cultures.

Testimonial

Chapter 25

Just Trees: Reflections on Ancestry Among Black Indians
Kevin Noble Maillard, Ph.D.

Where I am from, there is an old oak tree that sits by itself in the middle of a field. Its branches are low and wide, its roots thick and substantial. Its arms, legs, and torso spark the playfulness of children, who swing and jump on the boughs of history. This tree has seen the flow of generations of family, and it continues to witness more. I admire this tree because it sits alone, defiant yet proud of its surroundings—an understated announcement of decided existence. It has branches new and old, the younger supported by the older, with a massive, common trunk that connects them all. It houses a deciduous community that reflects the changes and developments from the passing of time. Broadly categorized from afar, yet closely scrutinized from within the tree is an impressionist composition of diversity and order.

Strange things happen when people address my racial identity. A college friend had assumed for years that one of my parents was White (which is not true). Another acquaintance insisted that my father was French (although they had never met). In other situations, I often get chatted up by cab drivers who are curious to know "where I am from" (guessing India). Depending on who I am with, what I am wearing, and whether I open my mouth, it seems that other people want to have a stake in defining my ethnic allegiances. My body exists as a palette for others to paint their expectations of race on unfamiliar territory. My speech, my hair, my cheekbones, my skin—each tells different stories about a racial history. Each one pulls in a different way to tell a story about origins and influences. The truth is, I cannot always be sure what I look like to other people.

To myself, I look like any Black person on the street, with a serious shade of red belying my "true" racial identity. To others however, it is enough to spark a prying conversation about mixed people or interracial marriage. I am a member of the Seminole Nation in Wewoka, Oklahoma, where my mother's family has lived for generations. I shy from romanticizing home, as I was always eager to move East. But Oklahoma is a place where people generally understand what it means to be a contemporary Indian. California aside, more American Indians live in Oklahoma than any other state. It may be safe to say that a substantial portion of Oklahomans have some degree of "Indian blood," although many of these individuals assert Native ancestry in curious opposition to an established identity as White.

As Vine Deloria, Jr. points out, the "Indian Princess Grandmother" stands as a popular trope: "Ah, there was royalty for the taking. Somehow the White was linked with the noble house of gentility and culture if his grandmother was an Indian princess who ran away with an intrepid pioneer." I cannot count the number of times that a perceptibly White person has eagerly told me of their Native ancestry. Usually, the person cannot identify a specific tribe, and if they can, they say, "Cherokee." These assertions of race are curious, perhaps because the primary identity as White is not disturbed by a remote non-White variable. Or, the willingness to share their fall from White racial purity adds to the sincerity of the story. Either way, the admittance of the Indian grandmother does little to augment the racial identity of the White person.

When Black people claim Indian ancestry, the case is remarkably different. In what is seen for Whites as a proud declaration of distinct, if not exotic origin, for Blacks the same assertion faces criticisms of disbelief or derision. Being Black, as it stands, already asserts a distinct racial presence, and other racial variables are not strong enough to disturb its primary claim on a person's identity. In the American racial system, Black ancestry supplants the existence of others, even when these "others" are also minority groups. Thus, a person is already "Black," and seeing this same person as "Indian" becomes a difficult task. The assertions of Native American ancestry may be interpreted by some (namely Blacks) as attempts to evade a Black identity. Thus, mixed race persons are seen as either avoiding Blackness or boasting difference. From both angles, the case for multiracial identity finds obstacles in the immovable specter of Black blood.

Within tribes themselves, it is my opinion that accepting and recognizing Black Indians as members potentially threatens a protected sense of identity. It is not enough to say that Indians wish to be treated as *Indians*, but that the goal of maintaining a unique community be unfettered by competing interests. The actual number of people eligible for tribal membership is quite small, considering the population at large. For the few people who can meet the criteria, it is hoped that they would enter the Indian community with a strong and concerted identity as citizens who will bolster, not enervate the existing population. Thus, biracial or multiracial identity poses a threat to a singular, albeit diversified, identity as Native. But this is not to be identified as a sort of xenophobia or exclusion; rather, it is an emphatic inclusion of

all Indians, multiracial or not, to cast their lot with the tribe.

Generally, I do not believe that a prejudice exists on behalf of non-Black Indians toward Black Indians. Physical appearances may generate assumptions that the Black Indian cannot be Indian, and this ancestral combination even sparks disbelief that that the person could really be Indian. In recent history, the Navajo tribe selected Radmilla Cody as Miss Navajo Nation, leading her to justify her Native identity: "My grandmother raised me herding sheep, weaving rugs, and speaking the Navajo language being that was our source of communication." I cannot help but think whether such emphasis would carry the same meaning for someone else. Not only must Black Indians announce their identity by proving ancestry, they must qualify it by exhibiting Indian characteristics and traditions. It is not enough, then, in the eyes of other tribal members, to have "Indian blood", but to "be Indian" as well. This is a common trope, specter, or issue for most Indians, but for Black Indians, the question posed is a familiar hurdle: Aside from blood, why are you Indian?

The idea of being a member of two minority groups brings concerns of allegiance, and an allocation of moral energies. We can guess that it is never "easy" being Black/White or Asian/White, or Native/White. Surely, such mixtures are about integrating minority and majority cultures. So being part White involves a possibility of assimilation or accommodation with majority culture; non-White heritage distinctly contrasts with the majority group. Particularly in America, where "White" seems to mean the lack of race, or better conceived, a normalcy of race, the inclusion of a non-White identity generates distinctly different issues than do minority-minority mixes. In these cases, such as Black/Indian, Latino/Asian, Arab/Black, the pull for inclusion comes from both sides. In fact, it is a dual call to represent different minority groups, each with a distinct minority culture. It is a competition, a dynamism, even a tug-of-war, to satisfy the calls for cultural allegiance.

In Native American culture and in African American culture, the extended family has always played a large role in the construction of a community. Anyone is a cousin or an aunt if you know them long enough (and in real cases, some "real cousins" that you just met are just family in the formal sense). Grandparents may serve as primary parents, while aunts and uncles may step in as elder figures, whether they are related to you or not. I have never had actual grandparents during my lifetime, but I have their siblings and friends as irreplaceable substitutes. My nephew was raised by his grandmother the first five years of his life, and another cousin was raised by her grandmother while her biological mother lived next door. The absence of a rigid family structure gives way to a fluid notion of function, which encourages improvisation and accommodation.

Nowhere does this nexus between two cultures run more strongly than the tie to the land. For Indians, the connection is spiritual and historical: the idea of the ancestral home and sharing this in common is what defines and distinguishes one community from another. American, Western, or even "White" ideas of property are different: land must be improved, divided, and fenced. Separation is integral to maintain your possessions from others. But for Indians, land is a place to come together, cohabitate, and share with others. Political movements such as the Allotment Acts worked to destroy the establishment of land held in common; they took the ancestral land away and divided unknown, unseen plots for individual families. This was not a welcome move, yet the love of land was rechanneled in a different way to reflect a private approach to public issues that distinguished Indian land from others. These plots, farms, acreages, with their attendant hills, lakes, cabins, and dirt, come together, one by one, to form Indian Country. African American culture reflects a unique connection to land as well, in the ancestral home of the South. The history that exists behind its origin and exodus is rife with memory, painful and joyous, practical and romantic. But, like for Indians, there is a realization of a place called home, whether this reflection is cajoled or sought, that mixes one's practical, historical, and spiritual experience as a person of color with the physical independence of the soil.

Talk of family and land brings about ideas of inheritance, of the genealogical sort. A notable difference in Black/Indian identity from others is the predominance of multigenerational intermixture. It may not be entirely correct to classify most Black Indians as "biracial," if that term is to signify persons of mixed racial descent with racially distinct parents. In most cases, people with

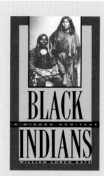

Black Indians
William Loren Katz, Pocket Books, 1997

This illustrated young adult book explores the often overlooked story of Black Indians—people of both African and American Indian heritage or African Americans who lived primarily with Native Americans. Using intriguing biographies and research, the author documents how this community was created during the settlement of the American West.

dual Red and Black heritages do not simply have one Black parent and one Indian parent. Rather, it is more likely that one or both parents are of partial Indian ancestry, thus complicating a simple declaration of "half and half." Similar to Louisiana Creoles, racial intermixture develops over time, with racially "pure" individuals existing far back in one's genealogy. Many tribes, such as the Seminoles, Creeks, and Mashpee, have long histories of intermarriage between Blacks and Indians, and this results in a population of tribal members with variegated racial histories. Because most people of Black/Indian ancestry are not directly connected to a living full-blooded Indian, claims to this Indian identity are met with suspicion.

Yet, the ability to identify a full-blooded Indian as an ancestor is necessary for membership in a tribe. For those Black Indians who are enrolled as tribal members, they were able to provide documentation of their ancestry, which goes beyond hearsay and oral histories. Most tribes have a historical membership roll, and applicants must identify a pre-existing tribal member as an ancestor in order to be enrolled. From this list, one's blood quantum is calculated, and tribes vary in their minimum blood levels. Many tribes hover around the one-quarter requirement, while others require no minimum at all. Nevertheless, tribal membership, as an official recognition of one's status and identity as Native American, solely depends upon an accepted demonstration of genealogical ties to Indian people.

These requirements are not entirely unassailable, however. A number of tribes in Oklahoma, including my own, base their membership upon rolls drawn according to nineteenth-century separatist conceptions of race. In this Jim Crow scheme, Blacks with mixed racial ancestry were included in tribal membership, but were placed on separate rolls apart from the rest of the membership. In the Five Tribes (Cherokee, Chickasaw, Creek, Choctaw, and Seminole), agents of the federal government segregated tribes into "Blood Indians" and "Freedmen," the latter signifying those of Black ancestry who had been adopted, who intermarried, or who were born into the various tribes. The government refused to recognize Freedmen as tribal members related by blood, despite the fact that people of White-Indian ancestry with less "Indian blood" were classified as Blood Indians. As a

result, no blood quantums were indicated for Black Indians—a historical practice that influences current membership policies. No blood, no membership.

There is no uniformity of a Black/Indian identity. The gamut ranges from the descendant of the Cherokee princess to the active member in tribal culture and politics. In rural areas, where tribal politics and culture thrive, Black Indians have greater affiliations with native life. In reality, however, the majority of Indian people live in urban areas. Maintaining a connection to this culture, by subscribing to the tribal paper or newsletter, voting in tribal elections, and visiting home all keep Indian culture alive. Such concerted efforts prevent tribal members and affiliates from losing a distinct identity as Black Indians.

Did you know?

Here are some well-known multiracial people of both Native American and Black heritage:

Jimi Hendrix (Musician)
Mildred Loving (Civil Rights Activist)
Tina Turner (Singer)

Notes

1 M. A. Jaimes, "Some Kind of Indian," in *American Mixed Race*, ed. N. Zack (Lanham, MD: Rowman and Littlefield Publishers, 1995), 139.

2 V. Deloria, Jr., *Custer Died for Your Sins* (Norman, OK: University of Oklahoma Press, 1988), 11.

3 Radmilla Cody, Miss Navajo Nation 1997-1998. Quote found on Navajoland Online, 7 March 2003.

4 C. Harris, "Whiteness as Property," in *Critical Race Theory*, eds. K. Crenshaw, et. al. (New York: New Press, 1995), 281.

5 For a general discussion of the Alloment Acts, the motives and the effects on Native Americans, see: F. P. Prucha, *The Great Father, The United States Government and the American Indians* (Lincoln, NE: University of Nebraska Press, 1986).

6 Two books readily come to mind that address the unique character of multi-generational intermixture. See: W. L. Katz, *Black Indians: A Hidden Heritage* (New York: Atheneum, 1986). Also see: J. Brooks, ed. *Confounding the Color Line* (Lincoln, NE: University of Nebraska Press, 2002).

7 G. Torres and K. Milun, "Translating 'Yonnondio' by Precedent and Evidence: The Mashpee Indian Case," in *Critical Race Theory*, eds. K. Crenshaw, et. al. (New York: New Press, 1995), 181.

8 M. A. Jaimes, *American Mixed Race* (1995), 137.

9 W. Glaberson, "Who is a Seminole, and Who Gets to Decide?" *New York Times* (29 January 2001).

Tuvaelagi C. Siufanua
Age: 16
Racial/Ethnic Heritage: Samoan and African American

My name is Tuvaelagi Siufanua and I am 16 years old. My father is African American and my mother is Samoan. I see myself as Samoan and Black, because my heart and soul are Africa, but my spirit is truly Samoa. I am the youngest of three strong, beautiful, proud Samoan and Black children.

While growing up, my mother told me I was a Samoan girl. Even though she would always say "Tuvaelagi, you are Samoa", my parents always made it a point to instill African American awareness and pride of culture in me. I think that my mother repeatedly told me that I was Samoan because anyone could see by looking at me that I was Black. She wanted me to never forget who I was or where my roots were. My skin shouted out African American, but my insides were screaming Samoan.

I used to hate my name. I felt ashamed when the students and teacher at my school would mispronounce it. People often asked me if I was Ethiopian or Puerto Rican, and it hurt me. I only recently became comfortable with my name. When I found out what my name meant it gave me strength and power. The power to say, "I am not Ethiopian, I am Samoan!" The name Tuvaelagi in itself holds all of the beauty and majesty of Samoa. When I found out that Tuvaelagi meant to stand between the heavens, I never let people mispronounce it again.

My father has always supported my mother in raising my brother, sister and me *fa' Samoa*, (in the Samoan way). In the Samoan culture children show love for their parents by doing things for them. Your parents take care of you so that one day, God willing, you will be able to take care of them. For example, when my grandfather became ill, before he passed I took a semester off from school to take care of him. It was an honor and a privilege to be chosen to care for a man as great as my grandfather. Through taking care of him I gained knowledge and countless blessings. I thank God every day for the time he gave me with my papa, Faulalo Ita Siufanua.

Sometimes I feel like the way things are done on my dad's side of the family are so different. I've seen so many generations of my father's family in one room that it is amazing. The Black culture is so rich and beautiful. Relatives I've never seen embrace me as if we were never apart. The sense of family unity and love is sometimes overwhelming. My love for people, my wonderful sense of family, and pride in myself—I owe all of this to my father. I am a strong beautiful Black woman.

When you are multiracial, it is hard to find yourself. There are no multiracial people in the media to look up to. When you're young trying to figure out why your skin is so dark or so light, just remember you are what God made you. Love yourself for who you are; you are beautiful. Today I know who I am and I love it. I am Samoan and Black. My heart and soul are Africa, but my spirit is truly Samoa.

Testimonial

Chapter 26

Multiracial Pacific Islander Youth
Suni Tolton, MSW

The goal of this chapter is to promote recognition of the diversity of Pacific Islanders and to contribute to the understanding of the unique experience of multiracial Pacific Islander youth. Many of the issues facing multiracial Pacific Islanders are comparable for multiracial youth of any background; however, it is important for Pacific Islander youth to be recognized for their distinct heritage and cultures. Unfortunately, there is very little research specific to Pacific Islanders, let alone focused research on multiracial Pacific Islander families and youth. In a periodical literature review by Fong and Mokuau, 22 out of 230 journal issues had articles on Asians and Pacific Islanders.[1] In these 22 issues, there were only 24 articles with content on Asians and Pacific Islanders. Of the 24 articles, only two were related to Pacific Islanders. One article mentioned Pacific/Asian Americans in regard to improving social work curricula and the other article focused on using a family centered approach with Native Hawaiians.[2] Parents, teachers, social workers, and other helping professionals need culturally specific resources to provide high quality services for multiracial Pacific Islander youth.

Introduction to The Pacific Islander Population

In order to begin the dialogue, it is important to become acquainted with the wide range of cultures and countries that the Pacific Islander population contains. The Pacific Islander Community Council (PICC) in Southern California requested information on how many Pacific Islanders were served at health centers and found that many organizations confused Pacific Islanders with Asian Americans. Jane Ka'ala Pang of PICC found that many health centers mistakenly came back with numbers for how many Pacific Rim Asians they served.[3] It is common to see Pacific Islanders grouped together with Asian Americans, thus contributing to the lack of appreciation for the broad diversity that this political category includes. Pacific Islanders have varied cultural backgrounds, countries of origin, and different historical and political relationships with the United States.[4] Pacific Islanders can be divided into three large categories: Polynesians, Micronesians, and Melanesians. Polynesians, which are the largest Pacific Islander group in the United States, include Native Hawaiians, Samoans, Tongans, Tahitians, Tokelauans, Maoris of New Zealand, and Niueans. Micronesia, the second largest group, is primarily made up of Guamanians or Chamorro. It also includes the Mariana Islanders, Saipanese, Palauan, Carolinian, Kosraean, Pohnpeian, Chuukese, Yapese, Marshallese, and Kiribati. Fijians are the largest of the Melanesian group, which also includes people of Papua New Guinea, Solomon Islands, and Vanuatu.[5] This overview is without the comprehensive analysis of past political issues, which impacts the present for multiracial Pacific Islander youth. Historical knowledge is an important component to understanding the experience and cultural influences for a group of people.

Demographics

In the 2000 Census, there were 399,000 people, or 0.1% of the total U.S. population who reported to be only Pacific Islander. The total population of Native Hawaiians and Other Pacific Islanders, including individuals checking other race categories, was counted at 874,000, or 0.3% of the U.S. population. Of the total 874,000, 58% live in Hawai'i (283,000) and California (221,000). On the whole, most Pacific Islanders live in the Western region of the U.S. In comparison, in each of the Midwest, Northeast, and Southern regions, less than 0.1% of all respondents reported to be Pacific Islander. Vermont has the smallest number of multiracial Pacific Islanders reported with 167.[6]

Of all the racial groups identified by the 2000 U.S. Census, Pacific Islanders had a much higher proportion of individuals checking more than one racial category. About 54%, or an additional 476,000 people, reported to be Pacific Islander in combination with another race group. The most common multiracial combination was Native Hawaiian and Other Pacific Islander *and* Asian at 29%, Native Hawaiian and Other Pacific Islander *and* White at 24%, and Native Hawaiian and Pacific Islander and White *and* Asian at 19%. The Pacific Islander population was also the only category in which the number of individuals reporting a single race was less than the number of individuals reporting two or more races.[7]

This census data provides information on the multiracial respondents across the different race categories of White, Black or African American, American Indian and Alaska Native, Asian, or Some Other Race. However, these figures do not give an accurate reflection of the number of multiracial individuals *within* the Pacific Islander grouping. Individuals who reported their race as being more than one Pacific Islander group, such as Tongan and Samoan, were counted as part of the Pacific Islander alone category because both groups are counted as part of the larger Native

Hawaiian and Other Pacific Islander race category.[8]

Factors Affecting Multiracial Hawaiians

In general, a youth's reaction to his/her multiracial background is affected by the racial diversity in his/her environment, the amount of contact he/she has with other multiracial individuals, and the equity present among different groups. An adolescent's acceptance or rejection of his/her racial heritage is influenced by the interactions he/she witnesses in his/her community.[9] It would stand to reason that the experience of multiracial Pacific Islanders who are living in largely multiracial communities would differ from the experience of multiracial Pacific Islanders who live in communities in which they are not largely represented. For example, considering the major differences in the geographical location of multiracial Pacific Islanders, it is important to take into account how the experience of multiracial Pacific Islanders in Hawai'i may compare to the Continental United States, or the "mainland," as it is commonly referred to in Hawai'i. In Hawai'i, there are many multiracial Hawaiians who are looked to as positive role models, including the United States Senator Daniel Akaka and former Governor John Waihee. There are also many events and activities available to celebrate one's Pacific Islander heritage. The resurgence of the Hawaiian language through the Department of Education and the Hawaiian sovereignty movement are examples of such opportunities. Hawaiians on the "mainland" do not often have the same opportunities to learn about and celebrate their Hawaiian traditions and may be less likely to identify themselves as Hawaiian.[10] This may also be a similar dynamic for other multiracial Pacific Islander groups.

In addition to the large percentage of multiracial Pacific Islanders in Hawai'i, the long history of interracial marriage also impacts the experience. Interracial marriages have been accepted in Hawai'i, and Hawaiian men and women of mixed ancestry have held important political and social positions for over two hundred years. Queen Emma, an attendant of Kamehameha IV, and Princess Kaiulani, heir of Queen Lili'uokalani were both multiracial: Hawaiian and White. The Hawaiians supported a sense of inclusiveness, and multiracial individuals remained well connected to the general community and embraced by families. This differs from the experience of many interracially married White Americans who were rejected by White communities.[11][12] Many in Hawai'i feel that ethnicity or the history of multiple racial groups is not a major barrier to acceptance by community members and social situations. In contrast, growing up in Hawai'i and being "local" or having the cultural norms widespread in Hawai'i, is much more important than one's ancestral background.[13][14]

It is remarkable that in the method of classifying race by Hawai'i's Department of Health, Hawaiian ethnicity supercedes Black heritage. An individual who is part-Black and part-Hawaiian will be classified as Hawaiian, even if the person is three-fourths or more Black. The "one-drop rule" was historically negatively used to keep Black people apart from White society and prevent them from bene-fiting from the privileges enjoyed by Whites. In contrast, the Hawaiian "one-drop rule" was positively used to give part-Hawaiians the same social status as full-blooded Hawaiians who were at that time the majority in society. More recently, the priority of Hawaiian ethnicity in identity allows for individuals to benefit from programs and privileges set up for Native Hawaiians.[15] The experience of a multiracial Pacific Islander youth in Hawai'i may be less stigmatizing due to the existence of historical and present-day multiracial role models, the large multiracial population, and the availability of events and activities to connect with Pacific Islander cultural her-itage. Further information is needed to understand better how mul-tiracial Pacific Islanders on the "mainland" handle challenges related to identity and what factors have the most significant impact for positive identity development.

Other Considerations for Multiracial Pacific Islanders

Discussion of multiracial Pacific Islanders is somewhat limited by the resources available, which are primarily about Native Hawaiians in Hawai'i, and that is a significantly different experience given the large percentage of multiracial populations in Hawai'i compared to the continental U.S. It would be interesting to learn how multiracial Pacific Islanders on the U.S. "mainland" identify and if they are more likely to identify with other racial groups when they do not have access or connection to their Pacific Islander community. For example, darker complexioned multiracial Pacific Islander youth, who have limited exposure to their Pacific Islander heritage, may find it easier to fit in with African American

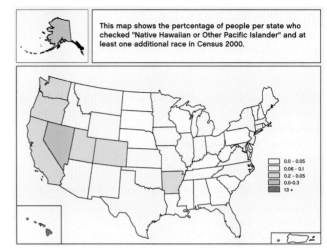

This map shows the pertcentage of people per state who checked "Native Hawaiian or Other Pacific Islander" and at least one additional race in Census 2000.

0.0 - 0.05
0.06 - 0.1
0.2 - 0.05
0.0 - 0.3
13 +

youth. Similarly, multiracial Pacific Islanders who look more Asian may find it easier to keep company with other Asians. Because Pacific Islanders are not often recognized for their unique cultures, youth on the U.S. "mainland" may find themselves under more pressure to try to fit whatever "box" the majority culture views them in. On the other hand, in communities where Pacific Islanders are not broadly recognized, with less ethnic diversity, there may be unfamiliar benefits for youth to identify as Pacific Islander.

Maintaining one's cultural heritage is an important value in Pacific Islander families and can have a significant effect on how an individual negotiates relationships with the majority society. Although only 13% of Pacific Islanders are foreign born, acculturation is still a relevant matter as multiracial Pacific Islander families experience conflict through the balancing and integration of traditional and mainstream cultures.[16] Higher stress levels were found to be associated with Samoan men of mixed ancestry or men who had close non-Samoan family members in Western and American Samoa, where they are in the minority when compared with men living in Hawai'i. The stress may be associated with their minority status, which limits individual and family mobility.[17] These effects of acculturation and racism on multiracial Pacific Islanders are major areas for further exploration.

Implications for Professionals Serving Youth

There are some general recommendations that may be applicable to multiracial Pacific Islander youth. In working with multiracial youth and families, professionals should be sensitive to the additional stress due to negative racial comments from other youth, adults, and in some cases, overcoming the loss of economic and emotional support from disapproving family members. Professionals need to learn more about the social taboos regarding interracial marriage in U.S. history and explore their own views about people who marry out of their ethnic group in order to recognize the normalcy of interracial families and youth. Wardle lists many recommendations for professionals on a micro level that may be taken with multiracial Pacific Islanders.[18]

Suggestions Include:

- Among youth with one White biological parent, do not assume that the youth has the identity of the parent of color. Most importantly, let the parents and adolescents know that they can choose a multiracial identity.
- Both parents of multiracial Pacific Islanders may be people of color. Youths may be encouraged to identify with their Pacific Islander heritage and deny their other half. For example, a Samoan mother of a Samoan Chinese son told me that everyone always "mistakes" her son for a Chinese person. This type of statement denies the Chinese side and sends the message that Chinese is not an acceptable part of his identity.
- Support and encourage families in connecting to their heritage through books, art, music, and drama.
- Connecting to the Pacific Islander heritage can be more difficult in the continental U.S. than in Hawai'i, which may make these actions even more significant to youth who live in more homogenous places. A youth who is disconnected from his or her Pacific Islander heritage may not know very much about customs and traditions. The smallest gesture, such as having a book or poster from a youth's Pacific Islander background can make a youth feel supported in a community where his/her Pacific Islander heritage is not commonly recognized.
- Facilitate open discussion regarding all aspects of multiracial heritage, including skin and eye color, language, and other difficulties that stem from prejudice.

- Multiracial Pacific Islanders can have external pressures on hair and body image that are based on racism. Messages from Pacific Islander adults commonly praise the looks of half-White youth.
- Gain awareness of the vast individual differences within racial and ethnic groups, including class, culture, religion, political affiliation, and education.
- Become familiar with the different histories of Pacific Islanders to understand the political relationships that influence their lives today. Many youth are met with blank looks, when they say where they are from and then asked the question, "Where is that?" I have heard an adult confuse Rarotonga, an island of the Cook Islands with the country of Tonga. The youth did not feel comfortable correcting the adult, as Pacific Islander youth are taught to respect their elders, but was left with the feeling that her Pacific Islander heritage was not recognized. It is important to be sensitive to conflicts within Pacific Islander groups. Some may not know the stress a Tongan and Samoan youth may bear without understanding the differences of the islands and history.
- Among youth with one White biological parent, avoid labeling a multiracial youth with the stereotypes of the parent of color—such as assuming interest in certain activities or events.
- Some multiracial Pacific Islander youth, especially on the U.S. "mainland", may have never been exposed to the events or activities that others connect to their culture. Popular media often misrepresents the cultural customs and traditional dress of the various Pacific Islands, showing the grass skirt, fast hip-shaking dancing on every show taking place on a Pacific Island. I remember a young Tongan woman state specifically in an interview that she did not hula, which is the traditional dance of Native Hawaiians, as though she was preempting the inevitable question.

Professionals working with youths need to educate themselves by reading books, joining multiracial groups, talking to colleagues, and becoming aware of their own perceptions and values regarding multiracial Pacific Islander youth. Individuals can request workshops regarding multiracial sensitivity, provide written resources, and work with agency administrators in creating appropriate ways to enhance cultural enrichment. Youth can be supported in exploring their choice between a multiracial identity and other aspects of their identity.[19] Above all, youth-serving professionals need to stand up against racism everyday, in macro and micro levels on intervention. This includes awareness in individual practice, educating staff in the workplace, and working for policies that promote acceptance of diversity in communities.

Did you know?

Here are some well-known multiracial Pacific Islanders:

Dwayne Johnson a.k.a. "The Rock" (Professional Wrestler)
Greg Louganis (Diver, Olympic gold medalist)
Keanu Reeves (Actor)

Notes

1 R. Fong and N. Mokuau, "Not Simply 'Asian Americans': Periodical Literature Review on Asians and Pacific Islanders," *Social Work* 39 (1994), 298-305.

2 Ibid.

3 H. Ross, "Serving Pacific Islanders in Southern California," *Closing the Gap* (June/July 2000), 14.

4 D. T. Takeuchi, N. Mokuau and C. Chun, "Mental Health Services for Asian Americans and Pacific Islanders," *Journal of Mental Health Administration* 19(3) (1992), 237-245.

5 U.S. Census Bureau: "The Native Hawaiian and Other Pacific Islander Population: 2000 (Table) 4" 2001.

6 Ibid.

7 Ibid.

8 Ibid.

9 M. P. P. Root, "Resolving the 'Other' Status: Identity Development of Biracial Individuals," *Women & Therapy* 9(1-2) (1990), 185-205.

10 S. Jaworowski, "Hawaiian Demographic Data: 'Ehia Kanaka Maoli?" *Legislative Reference Bureau Report* (1998).

11 Ibid.

12 R. C. Johnson, "Offspring of Cross-Race and Cross-Ethnic Marriages in Hawai'i," in *Racially Mixed People in America*, ed. M. P. P. Root (Thousand Oaks, CA: Sage, 1992), 239-249.

13 Ibid.

14 "Leadership Challenges and Opportunities: Asian American and Pacific Islander Woman's Lens," Online: Asian Pacific American Women's Leadership Institute (2003).

15 S. Jaworowski, "Hawaiian Demographic Data: 'Ehia Kanaka Maoli?" (1998).

16 E. Lee and N. Mokuau, "Meeting the Mental Health Needs of Asian and Pacific Islander Americans," *Cultural Diversity* (2002).

17 J. M. Hanna, "Migration and Acculturation Among Samoans: Some Sources of Stress and Support," *Social Science Medicine* 46(10) (1998), 1325-1336.

18 F. Wardle, "Children of Mixed Parentage: How Can Professionals Respond?" *Children Today* 18(4) (1989), 10-13.

19 F. Wardle, "Interracial Children and Their Families: How School Social Workers Should Respond," *Social Work in Education* 13(4) (1991), 215-223.

Zack
Libyan +
Chinese +
Irish

Juleah
Guamanian +
Filipina +
Swedish +
European

Liz
Japanese +
Puerto Rican

Fred McHenry Rabb
Age: 18 years old
Racial/Ethnic Heritage: Japanese and African American

My name is Fred Rabb, and I am 18 years old. My mother is Japanese American, born in Spokane and raised in Priest River, Idaho. When she went to college, she came to Seattle to study law. My dad, who is African American, was born in Louisiana and was brought up north by his parents when he was just three years old. Just out of college, my dad landed a job working in a budget office and met my mother. A few years later they got married. They had two children, my older brother, James, and me. He is two years older than me. We have always had a good relationship with each other and since he has gone to college, we have begun to realize the special bond that only two brothers can have.

I grew up in Seattle's Central District. From preschool to high school, my neighborhood was comprised mainly of African Americans, some Mexicans, and one Caucasian neighbor. One of the factors that shaped my identity was my playing outside with other neighborhood kids on the basketball courts. Since there were no other Japanese Americans in our neighborhood, I identified myself more as an African American.

As a kid, my parents would talk to my brother and me about being multiracial and the benefits that come with it. They did this by talking to me almost every day about social issues pertaining to race. When I was in grade school, I began to go to Japanese language school so that I could learn to speak Japanese. Most of the kids there had at least one parent who could speak Japanese, so I was an exception.

When I was having a hard time learning the language, I began to rebel against it by not doing my homework. My rebellion also led me to view myself more closely with my African American side. I probably didn't welcome the Japanese side of my culture because I was being forced to go to school on Saturday mornings from 8:30 to 12. During this time I would miss all of the X-men cartoons. The only reason why I remotely accepted my Japanese heritage was because my family would celebrate some Japanese traditions where we got to eat a lot of traditional food. One of the celebrations we practiced was the New Year's festival, *Oshogatsu.* During grade school, my best friend was African American and Chinese. Together, we were our own two-person clique because we were both mixed and proud of it.

When I began high school, I started to realize that it was important to embrace both of my cultures. I felt that I had a responsibility to represent both of my parents equally by acknowledging their different ethnicities. On the entrance exam to high school, there was a survey about race that stated that a student could only check one box for their ethnicity and I chose to check "other" because of my mixed heritage. At a predominately White school I was seen as "Black" by almost all of the White students and teachers. When people inquired about where I was from, I would tell them that I was mixed. Most of them were surprised. Today, I value both sides of my heritage equally and try to participate in organizations that support multiracial people.

Testimonial

Chapter 27

Rice and Beans: Asian/African Americans in the United States
Christine C. Iijima Hall, Ph.D.

Asian (and Asian American) and Black (or African American) biracial individuals represent a small portion of the 2.4% of the U.S. population of mixed raced individuals. Many of these Asian/Blacks are the result of war era unions, such as World War II, the Korean War, and the Vietnam War. The more recent relationships primarily stem from integrated communities (such as Gardena, California and the Crenshaw area in Los Angeles), schools, and work. The more common mixture is an African American male and an Asian female. The majority of African American/Asians live psychologically healthy lives. With the increasing number of mixed race people in the United States, there is more acceptance and understanding of mixed race individuals, thus less problems for multiracial individuals.

Identity

The African American/Asian individual encounters similar ethnic identity phases of development, as do other monoracial and mixed race individuals. He or she may experience a time when he or she chooses one group over another or becomes confused and experiences problems. For example, many years ago, this author was called by the mother of a five-year-old Black/Asian girl who was having self-esteem problems in an all-Asian school. She was concerned as to why she had "meatball" hair while the other girls had "spaghetti" (straight) hair. After her mother enrolled her in a more ethnically diverse school, her self-consciousness disappeared. Many confusing and problematic periods are part of the developmental process of any individual, regardless of race. Some are normal while some need to be addressed professionally.

Most biracial people may experience a time when they feel they need to choose between groups because the norm in the United States is to choose a single ethnic/racial identity. However, within the past several years, biracial people are choosing biracial identities. Biracial identity feels natural for many because they identify with both groups and have knowledge of both cultures either through parental involvement or through external resources such as friends or school. Most Black/Asian individuals express comfort with both cultures and have expressed the ability to move in and out of their respective cultures as needed (situational identity).

Situational identity is a common characteristic of mixed race people. The Asian/Black individual can interact in Black groups and Asian groups and know the "rules" of behavior for both. They have also expressed the ability and ease to move in other ethnic circles—the true metropolitan person.

Hapa Issues Forum (HIF)

Hapa Issues Forum is a national nonprofit organization that provides diversity training to community organizations and leadership development to youth and young adults. HIF is dedicated to enriching the lives of Asian Pacific Islanders of mixed heritage and developing communities that value diversity. Based in San Francisco, HIF has seven chapters across the state of California, which include: two community chapters in San Francisco and Los Angeles, and five student chapters at Stanford University, UC Berkeley, UC Irvine, UC Los Angeles, and UC San Diego.

Learn more:
www.hapaissuesforum.org

Acceptance

Over the past 20 years, research has shown the majority of mixed race people live mentally healthy lives and experience similar stresses as do other people of color. The additional stress of being mixed race can differ depending on the ethnic mixture. That is, biracial African American/Asians are different from their Asian/White or Black/White brothers and sisters. Biracial White individuals may be identified as being either White or minority while the Asian/Black individual is definitely a minority. This minority identification may involve less trauma than living in-between the minority-majority world. That is to say, minorities in the United States are treated a particular way while Whites are treated another. The minority/White individual may be treated as White sometimes and minority at others. A minority/minority will always be treated as a minority. In addition, the minority/White individual may have White relatives and acquaintances who may say something negative about minorities. This puts the minority/White individual in an awkward and painful position. However, it should not be forgotten that a similar situation may occur with minority/minority individuals. That is, there is also difficulty in navigating acceptance and identity in a minority world.

Thus, acceptance and identity can be problematic when the two minority worlds are in conflict. Historically, in the United States, the African American and Asian American communities have been at odds. Examples of this are Koreans and Blacks in Los Angeles, and Chinese and Blacks in New York. Thus, biracial Asian/Blacks may not be accepted by Asians because they are Black and not accepted by African Americans because they are Asian.

Additionally, the Asian/African American may also receive discrimination from the Asian American community for not being "all Asian" and the Black community because they are "not all Black." The Black/Asian individual may have mannerisms or language patterns different from other Blacks or Asians. This may be the result of geographic location, socioeconomic level and what group she or he interacted with during his or her formative years. These biracial Black/Asians may not be trusted and totally accepted by African American or Asian groups. This author has heard numerous stories such as individuals not being allowed

Two Mrs. Gibsons
Toyomi Igus, Children's Book Press, 1991

In alternating passages, a young multiracial girl lovingly remembers the two different Mrs. Gibsons in her life. One is an elderly African American woman while the other is a younger Japanese woman. It is not until the end of the book that the reader learns that the first Mrs. Gibson is her grandmother and the second is her mother. Both women encourage the young Toyomi to explore her rich heritage; her African American grandmother enjoys southern cooking and has a large collection of church hats. In contrast, her mother cooks traditional Japanese dinners and lets Toyomi play with kimonos tied with obi sashes. An author's note tells readers that this is Igus' personal story. Great for ages 5-8.

to vote in ethnic student organizations or individuals not being perceived as Black or Asian enough politically or in physical appearance. Discrimination from one's own ethnic group can be especially disconcerting and painful. Most Asian/African Americans survive this period and find Asian, Black, or other individuals/groups with which they are accepted and feel comfortable.

Physical Appearance

Physically, mixed African American/Asians may not appear fully African American or fully Asian. However, some individuals may look very Black or Asian since there is diversity in physical appearance within the group (there are Asian-looking Blacks and darker-complected Asians with curly hair!). Generally, most Asian/Blacks resemble Polynesians or Filipinos. Many possess the classic mixed race "ambiguous" or "ubiquitous" look, as they resemble no particular race or look like all races, respectively. They have an exotic look and are frequently asked "What are you?" or "I thought you were _____" on a regular basis.

Regardless of what race others perceive them to be, research has shown that most biracial people are pleased with their physical appearance and have a positive body image. They feel they have received the best physical attributes of both groups. While physical appearance would seem to be a factor in one's ethnic identity choice, research has shown that mixed race people may even identify with the group they resemble least.

Stereotypes

Another stressful issue encountered by Black/Asians is opposing racist stereotypes. For example, Asians are stereotyped as industrious and studious while African Americans are stereotyped as lazy and unintelligent. When this author received her Ph.D., many people commented that it was due to her Japanese mother promoting education. This was an insult to her African American father who had always stressed education being the key to independence, freedom, and a positive future. Stereotypes cause mixed race individuals stress, as they do other groups, because they rob people of their individuality.

Summary

The title of this chapter, "Rice and Beans," comes from a cultural

faux pas made by this author over 20 years ago. She was invited
to a Black dinner function where, among other foods, a pot of rice
and a pot of beans were served. As many Asians would do, she put
the rice and beans separately on her plate. Many of the guests
laughed at her lack of knowledge that in the Black culture, rice
and beans are to be mixed together. This author survived this
embarrassing etiquette error. She now serves rice separately at
Japanese functions and triumphantly mixes them together at
African American functions. She is truly multicultural...until the next
faux pas.

Did you know?

**Here are some well-known multiracial people of
both Asian and Black heritage:**

Foxy Brown (Singer)
Ananda Lewis (Talk Show Host)
Rozonda Thomas a.k.a. "Chilli" from TLC (Singer)

Toni
Black +
Indonesian +
Native
American

Priscilla
Filipina + Mexican

Kota
Japanese + German + Irish + Austrian

Samar Al-Bulushi
Age: 24
Racial/Ethnic Heritage: Omani, Tanzanian, and European

As a 12-year-old middle school student on suburban Bainbridge Island, I remember learning about the forced internment of Japanese Americans during World War II. Following the bombing of Pearl Harbor, Japanese Americans were unjustly branded as spies and traitors, therefore unworthy of the constitutional protections afforded their fellow Americans. This dark period in our nation's history was of particular significance to Bainbridge residents, where members of our community spoke out defiantly against the unfair treatment of their neighbors. While on the one hand I was disturbed by our government's actions, I was reassured by the unwillingness of many Bainbridge Islanders to be silent in the face of injustice. Little did I know that just a few decades later, another group of Americans would become the target of fear, ignorance, and hate. This time, I am a member of the targeted group, and this time, few appear willing to speak out in our defense.

My heritage includes European, Tanzanian, and Omani roots. I was born in the Persian Gulf state of Bahrain and generally identify as an Arab American woman. In high school, I blended in easily and my ethnic background was generally not an issue. In college, however, I met and got to know many other Arab American students and naturally identified with them and their culture. Because we were a small population, we developed a tight-knit community and became active politically on issues related to the Arab world. Before September 11, I was already familiar with American ignorance of the Arab and Muslim world. I was not, however, familiar with the level of intolerance that would emerge afterwards. As I watched the Twin Towers crumble from the roof of my Manhattan apartment, I immediately began to fear for the safety of my family and friends. Whether or not those responsible for this horrific crime against humanity had any connection to the Arab world, I knew we would be the first to blame. In the lounge of the Columbia University student center, I watched as newscasters blurted out the names of one Arab group after another as the likely guilty party. I began to slouch further and further into my chair, conscious not only of my Arab heritage, but also of my political activism on campus.

In the days following the attack, I mentally prepared myself for the kind of looks or comments I might receive. Indeed, many Americans have convinced themselves that any and all Arabs/Muslims are somehow connected and therefore responsible for this tragedy. The first signs of intolerance were based on physical appearance. Anyone who looked Arab or Muslim—even if they were not—quickly became the target of verbal and physical abuse, sometimes resulting in death.

In a world of increasingly fluid boundaries, our actions and decisions have a daily effect on the lives of others across the globe, just as their actions affect us. Ultimately, for all humans, security translates into the ability to live one's life in the absence of fear or want. We are all, naturally, in search of security.

Should we choose instead to go about living our lives without a care for the lives of others, it is worth recalling the words of Dr. Martin Luther King, Jr.: "Injustice anywhere is a threat to justice everywhere."

Testimonial

Chapter 28

Multiracial Arab Americans
Devon Alisa Abdallah, Ph.D.

Multiracial Arab Americans will be discussed in this chapter, focusing on their personal experiences. With Arab culture and bias against Arabs and Arab Americans tending to be stronger factors for multiracial Arab Americans than being racially mixed specifically, it is important to understand Arab culture and the struggles of Arab and Arab Americans in the United States. To facilitate understanding of Arab culture, this chapter will begin by describing Arabs and Arab Americans. With religion playing an important role in Arab American culture, religion will be discussed briefly in the next section. Next, the aspects known as the "invisible community" will be examined. Following, stereotypes of Arab Americans will be discussed briefly. Finally, multiracial Arab Americans and their experiences will be explored including personal stories.

Who are we?

Arab Americans are not a racial group but a cultural group. Arabs are bound by similar cultures and a common language —Arabic. In the United States, all Arab Americans may not speak Arabic, particularly second, third, or fourth-generation Arab Americans, but are still connected by ancestral and cultural roots.

Arab Americans originally came from a variety of countries within the Arab world, which is comprised of 22 countries.[1] The countries span from Morocco in the west to Oman in the east and from Iraq in the north to Somalia in the south. Unbeknownst to most people, Iran and Turkey are not Arab countries.

While culture and language are common amongst the Arab countries, physical differences amongst the persons of these countries exist. While the majority of the Arab people may hold the more stereotypical features of olive colored skin, black hair, and brown eyes, it is not uncommon to find blue-eyed, blonde-haired, fair-skinned people in Lebanon with the people of Somalia tending to have darker skin and more African features. While the majority of persons in the Arab countries follow the religion of Islam, the majority of Arab Americans are Christian. Similarly, dispelling popular stereotypes, the vast majority of Arab Americans are born in the United States with roughly 80% of Arab Americans being U.S. citizens.[2] Over 50% of Arab Americans can trace their ancestral roots to Lebanon, with Syria, Egypt, Palestine, and Jordan as the next four largest national groups.

Culturally, family plays a significant role with family considered more important than the individual and even nationality. Similarly, Arab Americans tend to place a large emphasis on education.

Amongst Arab Americans, a higher than average percentage (36%) than the average American holds bachelor's degrees.[3]

Religion

As mentioned earlier, the majority of Arab Americans are Christian, with Christians constituting 63% of persons of Arab descent in the United States.[4] Muslims are the next largest majority, with Judaism and other religions existing amongst Arab Americans. Many Arab Americans define themselves by their country of origin and their religion—Lebanese Catholic or Palestinian Muslim—since there are differences between the religions that contribute to defining a person's experiences and culture.

The first wave of Arab immigrants in the 19th century were Christian and had an easier time assimilating in the Christian dominated society of the United States.[5] Since the 1950s, Arab Muslims have constituted the fastest growing sector of Arab Americans. In the United States, Muslim Americans are more visible than Christian Arabs due to religious practices that direct personal behavior, such as women wearing *hijabs* (or headcovers), beards for men, praying five times a day, and fasting at Ramadan for one month. Also, daily prayer requires accommodations at work and school. With customs and personal practices often different than mainstream society, Muslim Americans are frequently the victims of prejudice and bigotry. As a result of American discrimination and in order to teach Arabic to U.S.-born children—a requirement in reading the Koran—private Islamic schools have opened throughout the United States.

The Invisible Community

Arab Americans have been described as the invisible minority, since they are not recognized as a community of color by most people, including the United States Government. The U.S. Census classifies Arab Americans as White along with the dominant European American majority. As a result, little statistical facts are known about persons of Arab descent in the United States, including how many persons of Arab descent live in the United States. It has been estimated that over three million Arab Americans live in this country, but with the U.S. Census denying Arab Americans their own classification, this number has been established by the U.S. Census estimating from the longer version of the census, which was sent out to one in six households, and other sources.[6]

Moreover, federal money is not distributed for federal, state, and municipal programs serving Arab American communities or for the funding of research on and for Arab Americans. The federal government also does not distribute funds to serve the mixed race community. Similarly, neither Arab Americans nor multiracial Arab American youth are eligible for minority scholarships. At the same time, the majority of Arab Americans do feel that they neither hold the same privileges as White people nor are accepted by the dominant White society either. These feelings of isolation and invisibility are experienced even deeper by multiracial Arab Americans who may not feel entirely accepted by the Arab American community as "true" Arabs, but are not accepted by the White community or other communities of color either.

Many Arab Americans are asking for minority group classification from the government, so that they may have protection from the same issues that affect other communities of color, such as racial profiling, stereotyping, and exclusion from housing and employment. Moreover, it is a sense of pride for many to be acknowledged for their cultural and ancestral roots instead of as White.

Similarly, the majority of persons in the United States, including other communities of color, have not recognized Arab Americans as people of color either. After September 11, 2001, this perception has begun to change. People have begun to recognize the struggles, biases, and prejudices with which Arab Americans have had to contend. While many believe that these discriminations began shortly after the September 11 tragedies, they have existed for years.

Stereotypes

Many stereotypes of Arabs and Arab Americans have existed, none of which have been positive. While these negative stereotypes may be attributed to Arabs and Arab Americans, multiracial Arab Americans feel the shame, anger, and hurt as well. Often multiracial Arab Americans, particularly those with lighter complexions, are witness to racial jokes and slurs by individuals who are ignorant of their being of Arab descent.

Originally in the United States, Arabs and Arab Americans were often associated with sheiks, belly dancers, deserts, harems, and camels. During the early 1970s, the nefarious oil sheik attempting to swindle Americans out of their money became a popular stereotype. The stereotype digressed to Arabs as terrorists shortly thereafter. After September 11, 2001, the terrorist stereotype has been inscribed in stone. This stereotype has been further perpetuated by television, movies, and advertising.

As with any group of immigrants, the first immigrants from Arab countries faced discrimination, ignorance, and anti-foreign sentiment in the United States. The anti-Arab sentiment has increased drastically since the 1970s with a change in U.S. governmental policy. At this point, the United States became a strategic player in the Middle East and a strong supporter of the state of Israel. As a result, more negative stereotypes of Arabs and Arab Americans have incurred. At the same time, public policy began to become anti-Arab. Several government investigations, executive orders, and legislative provisions aimed at combating terrorism had a negative impact on Arab American activism and violated the rights of some Arab Americans. After the tragedy of September 11, further governmental policies, including the U.S.A. P.A.T.R.I.O.T. Act, have adversely affected Arabs living in the United States and Arab Americans with numerous civil and constitutional rights being violated. Thousands of persons of Arab descent have been held for questioning. Arab Americans have undergone massive racial profiling by the government, the media, and the American public. Numerous persons have lost their jobs, have been discriminated against by the airlines when flying, have been deported by the Immigration and Naturalization Service (INS), and have become victims of hate crimes and hate incidents.

In Hollywood, the Arab is a favorite villain with numerous movies portraying Arabs as terrorists and inhuman killing machines. Very few movies produced in Hollywood actually portray either Arabs or Arab Americans in a favorable or humane light. Similarly, the media has further exasperated the stereotype with often biased reporting of the news, particularly the Arab-Israeli conflict, showing Arabs as angry, unreasonable individuals or terrorists.

Like many communities of color, Arab Americans feel like perpetual foreigners in the United States. They are often asked "Where are you from?," told that they "speak excellent English," or worse told to "go back to where they came from." Even third, and

Arab American Institute

(From www.aaiusa.org) Founded in 1985, the Arab American Institute (AAI) is a nonprofit organization committed to the civic and political empowerment of Americans of Arab descent. AAI provides policy, research, and public affairs services to support a broad range of community activities. The institute serves as a clearinghouse for Arab American participation in national, state, and local politics and government; research on the Arab American constituency; and a forum for consensus positions on pressing domestic and foreign policy matters. Through its board and staff, AAI acts as a resource to U.S. opinion and policy makers on a range of Arab American policy concerns, including U.S. Middle East policy and political trends in the Arab world.

Learn more:
www.aaiusa.org

fourth-generation Arab Americans often do not feel totally accepted by society.

Similarly, ignorance of Arab cultures and Arab Americans has led to frustration for many Arab Americans. With a common stereotype of all Arabs as Muslims, many Arab Christians are tired of explaining that they did not convert to Christianity upon arriving in the United States but come from a long history of Christianity.

Multiracial Arab Americans

The level of marriages of Arab Americans outside the Arab community may be higher than average due to several factors. For one, assimilation into mainstream American society may have perpetuated marriages to "real Americans." Also, many Arab Americans tend to marry persons from similar religious backgrounds. As a result, numerous multiracial children of Arab descent exist.

Since Arabs and Arab Americans differ vastly in physical appearance, many Arab Americans and multiracial Arab Americans are not easily recognizable as Arab. Some can pass as White, particularly Greek or Italian, other Arab Americans may appear more Latino. For many Arab Americans, especially multiracial Arab Americans, they can easily blend into mainstream society. Of course, women who wear the hijab are more physically distinctive and fall victim to more bias.

Blending in physically with the dominant society can be a double-edged sword. While some Arab Americans, particularly lighter-skinned multiracial Arab Americans, may wear the "White privilege," they have endured racial slurs of Arabs and Arab Americans often in their presence. As one multiracial Arab American has said "I'm tired of people making racial slurs about Arabs in front of me. I get to hear people's real feelings about us. All I can say is 'ignorance is bliss'."

Moreover, people often tend to discredit many multiracial Arab Americans' feelings of discrimination since they have lighter skin. Similarly, many lighter complexioned Arab Americans, in particular multiracial Arab Americans, feel that numerous persons deny them their heritage and culture. One woman's story portrays this.

This may sound silly, but I didn't even know anyone thought of me as White until I was 27 when an African American guy made a comment about me being White. I was shocked. Growing up I had always been told that I was part Lebanese and that's how I saw myself. Obviously, I knew I had light skin, but it was so ingrained in me that I was Lebanese I just thought everyone knew, besides the fact that I have a very Arab last name. I guess it really hurt when I realized that people didn't see me for what I saw myself.

Names also play an important role in blending into dominant American society. Individuals with more "ethnic" names, including family names, such as Mohammad or Abdullah, are more likely to be identified as Arab. For many Arab Americans and multiracial Arab Americans, identifying as Arab American is a choice that they proudly make.

Many multiracial Arab Americans feel that being only part Arab is not nearly as difficult as being of Arab descent. As one man of Egyptian and European heritage said, "The 'half thing' has never been an issue" and that he feels accepted by the Arab community. He went on to say that he has had to deal with racial slurs and some teasing as a child.

Another woman of mixed Arab descent has had different experiences and is quoted as saying,

It's been a constant struggle for me. I don't feel completely accepted by White people, but I don't feel that other Arab Americans fully accept me either. Even other people of color don't acknowledge me as a person of color or believe that I have had to struggle with prejudice. I guess I'm lucky in some ways since I have such White skin, but I don't feel entirely comfortable around White people either. I tend to hide my Arab side from them. It can be exhausting. It's not that I'm ashamed of being part Arab, it's just that they [White people] don't seem to get it, especially the whole value of family and the concept of duty to one's family.

She agreed with the previous man that being Arab American was more difficult than only being part Arab.

Overall, the Arab community seems to be accepting of multiracial Arab Americans, with many multiracial Arab Americans feeling accepted by the broader community. The larger cultural dividers between many Arab Americans are likely generational gaps, language, and religion.

The majority of Arab Americans, whether of mixed Arab heritage or not, agree that people's ignorance, misconceptions, prejudices, and biases are extremely frustrating and damaging. Also, that people's prejudices can be especially damaging when applying for jobs and housing. The recent upsurge, post-September 11, 2001, in racial profiling of Arabs and Arab Americans has negatively affected many Arab Americans, particularly Arab males and immigrants.

Moreover, many Arab Americans are particularly frustrated with not having a race category for themselves and are tired of checking "Other" or "White." One multiracial Arab American's story explains this. After being accepted to graduate school, he was filling out the paperwork and when he reached the race section, there was no box to describe himself so he wrote in "Arab American." The school sent him a letter stating that he needed to select a designated racial category. He replied by writing back "I'm Arab American. Put me in any box you want."

Conclusion

In summary, Arab Americans and multiracial Arab Americans are proud of their heritage and culture. In working with multiracial Arab Americans, one should be sensitive to how the person identifies him or herself. While the person may or may not look stereotypically Arab, he/she may identify him/herself as Arab American. Nobody likes to be denied his/her heritage and experiences.

Did you know?

Here are some well-known multiracial people of Arab heritage:

Paula Abdul (Singer, Choreographer)
Salma Hayek (Actress)
Abdullah Bin al-Hussein (King of Jordan)
Queen Noor (Queen of Jordan)
Karim Rashid (Designer)
Shakira (Singer)

Notes

1 League of Arab States. The 22 Arab countries are Algeria, Bahrain, Comoros, Djibouti, Egypt, Iraq, Jordan, Kuwait, Lebanon, Libya, Mauritania, Morocco, Oman, Palestine, Qatar, Saudi Arabia, Somalia, Sudan, Syria, Tunisia, United Arab Emirates and Yemen.

2 H. H. Samhan, "Who Are Arab Americans?" *Groliers Multimedia Encyclopedia*, CD-ROM (New York: Grolier Electronic Publishing, 2001).

3 Arab American Institute Website, Arab American Institute (2002).

4 Arab American Institute (2002).

5 H. H. Samhan, *Groliers Multimedia Encyclopedia* (2001).

6 Arab American Institute (2002).

Philipp
Black + German + Irish + Cherokee + Indian

Cindy
Korean + Black

Jennifer Mariko Pang
Age: 22
Racial/Ethnic Heritage: Japanese American and Chinese American

I am an Asian American in every sense of the word. I am a fourth-generation Japanese-Chinese American. Even my name reflects my heritage. Like so many women of my generation, my first name is Jennifer, then comes my Japanese middle name, which came from a strong female role model, and lastly a Chinese surname. So much can be inferred from my name.

Sometimes I'm not even aware of my own Asianness. I go along and talk to my friends in the blinding cement quad of my college or I go for a burger at In-n-Out. And then I read the *Joy Luck Club*, a novel that acknowledged the "Asian American" female experience, and I'm surprised when I identify with several characters. I recently read Kip Fulbeck's *Paper Bullets*, which is a "fictional autobiography" of a "hapa" (half-Asian—in this case Chinese/half White) surfer/artist who grew up in Southern California. And though I mostly grew up "Japanese Americans," I recognized myself in this conversational piece, the half-Chinese kid growing up in Southern California.

My life is filled with many things: Oversized cotton shirts from the Gap, prose of Jane Austen and J.K. Rowling, four creepy seasons of the X-Files on DVD, biochemistry books, chopsticks and hum bow- a bun filled with the treasure of barbeque pork, silver star necklaces, REM CDs, *mochi*- a sweet Japanese dessert, and rubber stamps. These things that make up parts of my life do not conflict. My two Asian cultures very rarely conflict in my eyes, but sometimes others are confused about who I am.

I was the first grader who was embarrassed when the other kids pulled back the sides of their eyes, slanting their eyes upwards, downwards, pretending to be either Chinese or Japanese, respectively. And then they would slant one eye up and the other down, and "pretend" they were both Chinese *AND* Japanese, showing how messed up a child of such descent would look. But they were talking about me. I was that Chinese-Japanese kid. And even though my six-year-old eyes looked similar to my White friends', not slanted in any way, I never knew what to say or do when the other kids chanted that rhyme on the playground. I don't even think they even understood what they were doing, or that it even had an effect on me. I would swing on monkey bars or hang upside down with the same kids. They included me in their jokes and we would play He-Man in the trees with roots that came out of the ground. I don't think my classmates thought they were making fun of me. It probably never occurred to them that they were acting in an offensive way, and the fact that I didn't stand up for myself never occurred to me either.

I am a fourth-generation Japanese-Chinese American woman. I am also a singer and a writer and a scientist. I will never speak Cantonese flawlessly, but I will sing an Ave Maria. I will continue to eat *udon* and *dim sum*, as well as enchiladas and spaghetti. I will shop at Trader Joe's and go to Pike Place when the weather is warm. I will eat taquitos with chopsticks and read about lymphocytes and listen to Lisa Loeb in the same sitting because that's who I am.

Testimonial

Chapter 29

"What Are You?" Multiethnic Asian Americans

Valerie Ooka Pang, Ph.D., Jennifer Mariko Pang and Matthew Akio Pang

It is a perennial question: "What are you?" This question usually refers to one's so-called "race" or ethnicity.[1] For some Asian Americans this can be an uncomfortable question because individuals often assume that a person is of one ethnic group. The individual may say, "You must be Filipino." Very rarely will someone ask, "Are you Vietnamese *and* Chinese?" People usually assume that Asian Americans have roots in only one ethnic community. Multiethnic Asian Americans are often regarded as monocultural; multiethnic people are rarely acknowledged.

Multiethnic Asian Americans and multiracial Asian Americans face similar issues. For example, both may be confronted with racial and ethnic prejudice, cultural ambiguity, identity confusion, acculturative stress, parental pressure for academic achievement, and dating issues.[2][3] However, their experiences also differ. For multiethnic Asian Americans, ethnic identity development can be conflicting because they must navigate between two or more ethnic communities that they may see as different, but others perceive as being the same. In addition, individuals are developing a sense of national identity along with their ethnic identities. For example, mainstream society often pushes Asian Americans to disregard or disengage themselves from ethnic affiliations.

Census Information

Many people may not know that the U.S. Census 2000 identified numerous distinct Asian American communities in their total count of 11,898,828 Asian alone, or Asian in combination with one or more races.[4][5] The list included large, well-known groups like the Chinese (2,314,537), to smaller groups like the Nepalese (7,858).[6] As our country becomes more diverse, the birth of multiethnic children will continue to grow. Of the nearly twelve million Asian Americans, 232,816 reported being members of two or more Asian Pacific American groups. This is only one-eighth the population of multiracial Asian Americans (1,655,830), which may further isolate multiethnic Asian Americans.[7]

Key Issues

Multiethnic Asian Americans mature and develop within the complex cultural and social context of a mainstream society in which Asian Pacific Americans are often seen as "whiz kids," "model minorities," "nerds," "techies," "martial artists," and/or dangerous gang members. Unfortunately, U.S. corporations also play a part in perpetuating offensive stereotypes. A 2002 sales campaign from clothing company Abercrombie & Fitch marketed t-shirts in their online catalogue with the following phrases: "Wong Brothers: Two Wongs Can Make It White"; "Pizza Dojo: Eat

In or Wok Out"; and "Buddha Bash: Get Your Buddha On the Floor." This company was selling racist messages and reinforcing racism.

Cultural stereotypes and the push towards assimilation are powerful forces in American society. Many teachers and service providers may not understand that they have internalized these values and expect Asian American youth to be well-adjusted, high-achieving, almost "super-American" students.[8] These messages are tied in with the underlying belief that an Asian American, whether an immigrant or fifth-generation native-born, is still a foreigner and not an "American" because he or she does not look White. So no matter if one is Chinese, Japanese, Korean, Vietnamese, or Filipino, or a combination of Asian ethnicities, one is still seen as a foreigner and not a full-fledged "American." Multiethnic Asian Americans must continue to deal with these underlying beliefs that others hold. Within this context, many multiethnic Asian Americans may not want to view themselves as members of several ethnic groups, but may identify as "just Americans."

Ethnic identity formation in the United States is a complex process, made more so because Asian stereotypes are so common in society and people of Asian ethnicity are often seen as foreigners. Multiethnic Asian Americans must cope with a variety of messages that they may receive about their multiple identities. Take a fifth grader, Amy, who is both Chinese and Japanese. Since the fifth-grade social studies curriculum covers U.S. history, a perennial event discussed in schools is the bombing of Pearl Harbor by the Japanese. Though Amy did not participate in the event, she feels "guilty" by ethnic association. Some of her classmates stare at her. Amy looks like the enemy of the past and she is Japanese; some students hold an almost unconscious understanding that Amy is not really an American and as a person of Japanese ancestry she is somewhat responsible for events like Pearl Harbor. Later that day, Amy goes out on the playground and her peers taunt her with "Ching, Chong Chinaman." Amy must sort through these messages as both a Chinese American and a Japanese American. Teachers may not understand how these negative messages can create confusion in her identity development. Amy's classmates may hold questionable beliefs about both Amy's Japanese and Chinese identities. Amy is not fully accepted by her peers, even

though she was born in Dubuque, Iowa and is a fourth-generation American. This is less likely to happen to someone who is White. Take an adult like Ted Koppel as an example of how one's physical appearance can impact what others think. Ted Koppel is seen as a "true" American who holds an important position as news anchor for a major television network. Few people may know that Koppel is an immigrant from the United Kingdom. His allegiance is rarely questioned like some Asian Americans, native or immigrants, because he is physically White.

Multiethnic Asian Americans must not only deal with common stereotypes about Asian Americans in society, but the belief that all Asian Americans are the same. Today there is a proliferation of businesses that mix Asian ethnic traditions and so reinforce the idea that Asians are all alike. For example, there are Asian restaurants that may be called The Thai Plaza or Vietnamese Noodles and they serve a whole menu of dishes like chicken *katsu* (Japanese), *pad thai* (Thai), *chow mein* (Chinese), and *phó* (Vietnamese). This can lead to further confusion on the part of those who have little knowledge of Asia, and blur the distinctions between these nations and ethnicities.

So how can teachers and counselors assist multiethnic Asian Americans in developing a healthy and balanced ethnic identity? First, as Williams-Leon and Nakashima recommend, do not push students towards cultural assimilation.[9] Our country is a diverse one and diversity is one of the most important themes of this land. We are a nation of many peoples, immigrant and native born. In fact, when Columbus and other explorers landed on what is now known as the continental United States, there were over 500 Native American tribes living on the land.

Second, do not force young people to choose one Asian cultural identity over another. Young people may feel confusion or conflicting feelings regarding the place each cultural group plays in their lives. The belief systems of Asians, though often similar, have major differences. For example, individuals from the Japanese American community may not celebrate as many old country customs as members of the Chinese American group. Japanese Americans have demonstrated a faster rate of assimilation than other Asian groups, partially in response to their experiences during the forced internment of Japanese Americans on the West Coast during World War II. A child who grows up within a family context that integrates two Asian cultures may be uncertain about how to mediate and integrate the different cultures, and feel he or she must choose one cultures group over another.

Multiethnic Asian Americans must choose for themselves how they will navigate between diverse cultural orientations. They may try to identify with and follow both cultures. This tends to be especially true in families where ethnic identity is extremely important to both parents. In other families, one culture may be dominant. In this case, young people may feel turmoil about the role each cultural group plays in who they are and how they identify themselves. The parent who spends the most time with children may impart her/his cultural orientation. An excellent example of the mother's impact on the children in a multiethnic Asian American family is the novelist Gail Tsukiyama. Her father is Japanese American from Hawai'i and her mother is a Chinese immigrant. Tsukiyama explained that her cultural identity is predominantly shaped by Chinese culture due to the influence of her mother. In her novels, Tsukiyama has demonstrated her ability to negotiate both her Chinese and Japanese heritages, and describe both the similarities and differences between traditional Japanese and Chinese cultures. For example, her novel *The Samurai's Garden* (St. Martin's Press, 1996) is about a Chinese young man who goes to live in Japan for a year during the Japanese invasion of China during the late 1930s. Tsukiyama presented both the beauty and ethnocentrism of the Japanese culture, while discussing the strong family ties of the Chinese protagonist.

Third, historical animosities are often a major aspect of cultural conflicts in diverse Asian communities: these differences should be addressed and not ignored. Many Asian ethnic groups hold old country hostilities and impart them to their children. For example, because of past wars and political conflicts, a child who is both Cambodian and Vietnamese may feel unaccepted in both Vietnamese and Cambodian communities. This can lead to confusion, negative self-image, or even self-hate. To address this, multiethnic Asian American young people should be encouraged to learn about the history of each group so they know how the animosities began and understand that these differences do not have to define their feelings and identities today.

Finally, teachers and service providers need to understand that ethnic identity may be a portion of how a person identifies

who she/he is.[10] A person's sense of self may also include one's education, career interests, hobbies, social class, neighborhood, religious affiliation, sexual orientation, and family culture. Ethnic identity is usually integrated into a comprehensive self-image that can include many other aspects such as physical self-concept, career self-concept, and academic self-concept.

Conclusion: How Can the Multiethnic Identity of Asian Pacific American Young People be Affirmed?

Our society needs well-adjusted, joyful people who know who they are, and accept and can work with others. Teachers, counselors, social workers, parents, and service providers should be aware that they can assist multiethnic young people in developing a positive, integrated ethnic identity. Youth need role models in their lives who will listen to and discuss their insecurities and confusions. Adults can provide a caring, trusting, and accepting environment so youth feel safe while they sort through issues of identity development. Students can be directed to read literature written about the journey other Asian Americans have taken in their quest to define who they are, perhaps including some of Tsukiyama's work. It takes a village to raise a child, and in the Asian American community that village is a diverse one. If youth have the opportunity to reflect upon and clarify who they are, when someone asks a multiethnic young person, "What are you?" they will respond confidently and with a strong understanding of the richness that a multiethnic identity provides them.

Did you know?

Here are some well-known people who have a multiethnic Asian heritage:

Lou Diamond Phillips (Actor)
Tiger Woods (Golfer)

Notes

1 We regard race as a political construct. As such we believe the racial labels Asian, Black, Latino, Native American, and White are problematic and are used to isolate or exclude individuals and/or groups of people. We believe that "ethnicity" is a more accurate expression.

2 V. O. Pang and L. L. Cheng, *Struggling To Be Heard: The Unmet Needs of Asian Pacific American Children* (New York: State University of New York Press, 1998).

3 C. Chun and S. Sue, "Mental Health Issues Concerning Asian Pacific American Children," in *Struggling To Be Heard: The Unmet Needs of Asian Pacific American Children*, eds. V. O. Pang and L. L. Cheng (New York: SUNY Press, 1998), 75-87.

4 U.S. Census Bureau: "Special Tabulations (Table) 4. The Asian Population: 2000" (Feb. 2002).

5 Other Asian Pacific Islander and Native Hawaiian communities included in the U.S. Census were Samoan, Tahitian, Tokelauan, Singaporean, Sri Lanken, Thai, Pakistani, Okinawan, I-Kiribati, Yapese, Chuukese, Pohnpeian, Kosraean, Carolinian, Palauan, Mariana Islander, Guamanian or Chamorro, Maldivian, Malaysian, Melanesian, Ni-vanuaatu, Papua New Guinean, Laotian, Iwo Jiman, Indonesian, Indo Chinese Hmong, Cambodian, Burmese, Bhutanese, and Bangladeshi.

6 U.S. Census Bureau: "The Native Hawaiian and Other Pacific Islander Population: 2000 (Table 4)" 2001.

7 U.S. Census Bureau: "Special Tabulations (Table) 4. The Asian Population: 2000." 2002.

8 V.O. Pang and L. L. Cheng, *Struggling To Be Heard* (1998).

9 T. Williams-Leon and C. Nakashima, eds., *The Sum of our Parts: Mixed-Heritage Asian Americans* (Philadelphia: Temple University, 2001).

10 Ibid.

Jake
Mexican + Italian +
Native American

Kimi
Japanese? + ? + Adopted

Brittany
Chinese + Japanese

Muhtarat Agoro
Age: 20
Racial/Ethnic Heritage: Nigerian and African American

My name is Muhtarat Agoro and I am 20 years old. My dad is Nigerian, born and raised in Nigeria, and my mom is African American, from the U.S. I identify racially as Black and ethnically as a Nigerian. Jokingly, I think of myself as a true African American, but that hyphenated term already addresses American descendents of slavery.

While growing up, I was most comfortable at home—my father taught me about Nigeria, mainly cultural things, but I didn't really begin to learn about the history until I was older. My mom was involved in this learning process, too, and learned to cook the food. Outside of the home was where I had issues. As a child, when students heard my name they would say things like, "Go back to Africa." Back then I thought they were just dumb, but now I'd say their ignorance was passed on to them by their parents.

Home, family, and friends were my comfort zone.

I stuck out even more in Nigerian communities because I didn't understand Yoruba, my father's dialect, and had an African American mother. My father didn't teach my sisters and I Yoruba because he wanted his children to learn English, and because my mom didn't speak it. I embraced Nigerian culture more when I started going to a church with more Nigerian people. Some Nigerians had issues with my father for marrying someone who wasn't Nigerian. But overall, my church was where I was able to really have a sense of community with Nigerians and to become a more spiritual and loving person.

My parents did not really talk to me about being multiethnic—instead they just protected us. Back then, there weren't really words to deal with this subject and America wasn't really concerned about multiethnic people. At the time I didn't know it, but looking back I wonder if I needed authenticity and validation.

I met other multiethnic people in school, but I didn't think about it at the time. The majority of my teachers were White, and I think that my teachers could have done more to make sure that they didn't exclude people. In junior high, our discussions about race and multiculturalism were limited to Black/White issues. It was never discussed what happens if you can't tell what someone's race is. In my case, we never discussed that people can't seem to see beyond the fact that individuals of the same race still have differences, especially when from different countries.

I never really had a conversation about multiethnic issues until I got to college and found organizations that support multiracial and multiethnic people. I began to see that when differences in the Black community (and those of other racial groups) are acknowledged, they reveal how unique we are. Growing up, it would have helped to have had access to organizations that dealt with mixed race issues. In the new millennium, the world is becoming much smaller and people of different races and ethnicities are living as one. If we begin to really communicate and learn about other cultures, and not just go to one another's cultural events, even though we can start there, Americans will begin to cherish differences and one another. We'll begin to finally learn more about multiracial and multiethnic populations who will soon be a very large population of the world.

Testimonial

Bernardo Carlos Reyes
Age: 18
Racial/Ethnic Heritage: Mexican and Colombian

Growing up in a diverse community of Latinos, Filipinos, and African Americans in Los Angeles, being bi-Latino was not uncommon. My father was born in Jalisco, Méjico, and my mother was born in Medellín, Colombia. I have three brothers: Leo, 25; Andrés, 21; and Alejandro, 16. Though we are Americans, we have always asserted and celebrated ourselves as "Méjicanos-Colombianos."

My father and mother met in their teens, and married early. Like any relationship, they faced differences and disagreements, but some can be attributed to their cultural differences. At an early age, I noticed these differences but never found them jarring. Each year, we would celebrate Christmas reflecting both cultures. Going to my *Abuela's* we would regularly enjoy *un conversación con mis abuelos, tomando café con leche y comiendo almohabanas y buñuelos.* Going to my Mama Nina's every Sunday we would enjoy a warm bowl of *menudo*, usually after church, and later, the family would get together for a *carne asada.* Not only was the food indicative of each culture's uniqueness, but the customs and endearing colloquialisms reflect each pace of life, values, perceptions, beliefs, warmth, and personality.

My parents did not segregate the cultures nor their families. They encouraged us to practice both Mexican and Colombian Spanish dialects and customs, while affirming a Catholic and English education. Being Méjicano-Colombiano was nurtured and supported because my parents united and celebrated both cultures in our household. Despite this, I grew up feeling like something was missing. With my mother's passing when I was nine, I moved to Culver City where I grew up primarily in a large Mexican family and

community. Despite my parents' best efforts to encourage both cultures, it was not until her passing that I began to fully assert my Colombian blood, along with my Mexican spirit.

Attending a predominantly African American and Latino high school, I was exposed to various minorities as well as a small mixed race population. One of my best friends, Milagro, is also bi-Latina, of El Salvadoreña and Chilena descent. I have always been enchanted by multiethnic people not only because I can relate, but for the fact that I enjoy the beautiful influence of different cultures.

My Mexican culture is especially emphasized in my artistic ventures. Reflecting on the struggles and successes of my family, and my Los Angeles roots, I attempt to portray *el jardinero*, the *cholo*, *la abuela*, and other themes like death, family, gang violence, sacrifice, justice, labor, education, religion, and hope through the visual arts. Recently, I have ventured into writing poetry in Spanish. Next, I plan to explore social taboos in the Latino culture, such as interfaith and mixed race marriages and homosexuality.

Recently, I co-founded hi'brid at Seattle University, a student organization dedicated to multiethnic individuals and transracial adoptees. Hi'brid lets me interact with multiethnic individuals and relate to their struggles with identity and social isolation. Additionally, hi'brid has participated in MAVIN Foundation's bone marrow drives to fight leukemia by registering more mixed race and minority donors. As leukemia took my mother's life, this allows me both the opportunity to help save the life of other minorities and come to terms with my mother's death.

Testimonial

Antonio J. Manzano-Benitez
Age: 8
Racial/Ethnic Heritage: Filipino, Honduran, Norwegian and Spanish

My son Antonio is a "typical" eight-year-old American boy. He dreams about being a baseball player. At home, his room is blue and adorned with baseball posters. *Scooby Doo* is his favorite movie, pizza is his favorite food, and *Yu-gi-oh* is his favorite cartoon. He is also an avid soccer player. He learned soccer from his cousins and likes to play with his soccer team. He likes California because it's sunny. He is also "typical" because in Seattle where we live, one in six babies born are multiracial like he is.

I, too, am multiracial, and had a wonderful experience growing up. I was exposed to different cultures, customs, and foods and feel I got the best of both worlds. I never realized until I was an adult what courage it took for my parents, a Filipino/Spanish man and a Norwegian woman to go against mainstream society and get married during the 1940s. I have to say that I'm very proud of my parents.

I think there are more multiracial people today and there will be even more in the future. Antonio is part of the next generation of multiracial kids who have parents who are also multiracial. I think this helps people be more open minded. It is more acceptable for people of different races to date and marry. Instead of making racist comments, when I tell people my race they usually say that it is different or it is a good combination. They are usually curious and want to know where my parents met. Of course, some of their questions aren't very polite. A few people have asked if my mother was a war bride. A lot of people think when a person is Asian and White, the father must be White and the mother is Asian. When I tell them that my mother is of Norwegian descent they always say "Oh!."

Antonio sometimes asks questions about his race and I tell him whatever he wants to know. He knows some Spanish words that he learned from me and his Spanish teacher. I want him to grow up with a healthy identity and feel optimistic about his future because of where we live, and because of the growing awareness about multiracial issues.

Testimonial

Chapter 30

Multirace and the Future
Velina Hasu Houston, Ph.D.

What will multiracial people look like in twenty years? Will we be more White? More brown? More indistinguishable? More political? Less political? One thing is for certain: we will be even more ethnically diverse than today. This is because interracial unions are increasingly likely to include at least one person of multiethnic heritage. In Census 2000, nearly seven million Americans declared a two-race blended identity; nearly a half million identified as being of three or more races; and there were even 823 people who identified as being of six races.1 I am of three races; my children are of four. Such data indicate that the multiracial community is growing and its members are becoming more politicized about claiming their multiracial identity—but it also may mean that the category "multiracial," which is already diverse, will become even more so. As a result, future multiracial individuals' ethnicities/races may be read as less distinct than those of first-generation (and especially immigrant-kindred) multiracial people. In other words, in the future, monoracial people may perceive multiracial individuals as not so dissimilar from themselves and, therefore, view them as not being different enough to be singled out as a separate category or community.

The notion of multiple ethnicities and the progressive multiracial community has continued to confound monoracials. Frequently they skeptically ask, "But isn't everybody multiracial?" and "What about the next generation? Will they finally just be American?" These are questions tantamount to asking "But isn't everybody a human being?" Yes, but sociopolitical characteristics and issues immediately, and profoundly, distinguish one human being from the next. The idea of "American," a nationality, replacing a multiracial individual's racial identity seems to be of particular interest to the curious. Future generations of multiracial people—particularly second- and third-generation multiracials—will still encounter these attitudes that suggest that advanced hybridity automatically means dilution of the notion of a multiracial identity; and perhaps even a full discarding of it in lieu of a sole, wholly (idealized) "American" identity that supposedly eclipses ethnicity and race.

The more ethnicities a multiracial person claims, the greater the expectation that he or she releases the specificity of a "multiracial identity." The good news for today's multiracial children is that, in all probability, such a person will be able to respond to challenges more easily because of the sheer size of the progressive multiracial community of the future. Having a larger multiracial community means having a larger sociopolitical voice and presence, which will aid the community's efforts to raise its profile, establish its legitimacy as a category of race, and reach other objectives of the multiracial community's agenda. In such a way, when today's multiracial children grow up, they may live in a significantly more welcoming society than the one that multiracial adults currently face. They also may meet fiercer challenges than those encountered by today's biracial people due to the fact of their parents, less distinct racial, ethnic, or cultural heritages (and maybe less or no differentiation in pigment as well). Perhaps future multiracial individuals will grow to be like the multiracial community in Hawai'i—referred to as "locals," they constitute nearly two-thirds of the population of that state.[1] Their blended phenotype leaves no question of doubt about multiracial heritage, except that guessing the elements of that amalgam grows more difficult with each successive generation. With regards to the community of locals in Hawai'i, they are the ethnic standard in Hawai'i and not the exception to the rule. Still, they do not succumb to that hackneyed melting pot view of identity and call themselves "American" to describe their race; they call themselves hapa when it comes to race and American when it comes to nationality.

Other U.S. ethnic communities that consider themselves monoracial and label themselves as such are understood historically to have blended racial heritages. For example, the African American community, due in large part to slavery and its consequences, may include not only the African heritage that it claims, but also Native American Indian and White ancestry that it does not so readily embrace. Similarly, the Latino community has a history of intermarriage that has incorporated indigenous Native blood, African blood, and White blood with Latin ancestries. We also must consider the White population, and its own multiracial heritage that it often decries or dismisses. "Some geneticists have said that 95 percent of 'White' Americans have widely varying degrees of Black heritage...75 percent of all African Americans have at least one White ancestor and 15 percent have predominantly White blood lines."[2] As I note in *"All Mixed Up With Nowhere To Go": Cinema, Popular Culture, and the Mythology of Multiracial Identity*:

> Are "Whites" really White? Race in the United States may be entirely fiction. Thousands of ordinary folks, including

many who assume that they are White without any doubt about their identity, would be surprised by the results of genetic testing;"[3] as the White, African American, and multiracial descendants of U.S. President Thomas Jefferson have experienced. Adrian Piper observes that the amount of time a person's family has existed in the U.S. has a direct correlation to the amount of African ancestry that the family may possess. "The proximity to the continent of Africa of the country of origin from which one's forebears emigrated, as well as the colonization of a part of Africa by that country, are two further variables that increase the probability of African ancestry"[4] in such a family. While European Americans vehemently insist that they do not have a problem with such realities, Piper's assessment may be closer to the truth: "the fact of African ancestry among [U.S.] Whites ranks up there with family incest, murder, and suicide as one of the bitterest and most difficult pills...to swallow..." with the litmus test being to look a European American in the eye and compliment her by stating that "she looks as though she might have some Black ancestry."[5]

A proclivity exists in U.S. culture to view race as a dichotomy. Feminist scholar Tania Modleski acknowledges this with her comment, "The dominant culture's tendency to collapse all racial groups into one undifferentiated mass which serves as the 'Other' of White society."[6] It is no wonder then that altering the way we think about and evaluate race in the U.S. has been a long, slow journey. The path has included a solely Anglocentric interpretation of genuine race (or "racelessness") that excluded even Germans from a definition of Whiteness, referring to them as "swarthy," and labeling Italians, Greeks, and some Eastern Europeans as Black, Negro, octoroon, quadroon, or mulatto. Then the scope grew to include concepts like Mongoloid (for people of Asian descent), Oriental, Hispanic, African American, White, Asian/Pacific Islander, Native American Indian, non-White Hispanic; and, finally, the newest category of sorts: offering the multiracial individual the opportunity to check more than one box, to check all the boxes that apply. Further change is inevitable, but probably at the same pace as race category names have shifted over the years. It is true: race is not an either/or situation and many people who confine themselves to a monoracial identity for reasons of political ease or sociopolitical advantage are indeed multiracial. As long as race exists as a governmental means of delineating and measuring a community in terms of its supposed monoracial identity, then multiracial individuals must co-exist with those narrow concepts.

The ability to check multiple racial categories in the census may serve to help build a sense of community among multiracial individuals. The probability of this occurring, however, is dependent upon whether or not the census ever actually allows a category called "multiracial." Otherwise, multiracial individuals may have to guess the traditional monoracial category that they are inserted into by the Office of Management and Budget as it calculates racial communities and the sizes of their populations. (For example, will the OMB count hapa persons (people of mixed Asian/Pacific Islander descent) as Asian Americans—a big difference in community size—or place them in the category of their other race?) True institutional recognition of multiple ethnicity will not occur until "multiracial" appears as a race on the census along with the other nomenclatures such as "African American/Black" or "Caucasian/non-Hispanic White," etc. Until such recognition is given, the multiracial community must continue to fight the perceptions and limited racial notions of monoracialism that question whether multiracial people truly constitute a legitimate community that deserves institutional recognition.

As for the future, the multiracial community faces the same challenges that other communities of color face: will there be so much intermarriage and procreation with Whites and other monoraces that the community ceases to exist? African Americans and Asian Americans—as well as Whites—often fear that intermarriage and interracial offspring will dilute their "purity." Multiracial individuals, already so ethnically diverse and varied in phenotype, also must wonder if marriage outside of their community could mean a backsliding into a more traditional racial look and identity. In Hawai'i, for instance, some multiracial people possess so much Caucasian blood that they nearly have lost their multiracial look; yet, significantly, they embrace their multiracial

This map shows the pertcentage of people per state who chose three or more races to describe themselves in Census 2000.

0.0 - 0.1
0.1 - 0.15
0.16 - 0.2
0.2 - 0.25
0.26 - 0.3
0.3 - 0.4
0.4 +

identity. If such a pattern of behavior persists in the U.S., then, in all likelihood, the multiracial community—despite evolving membership and increasingly diverse looks—will survive as a community because there appears to be a personal and political tenacity that guarantees multiracial identification.

In everyday life, multiracial individuals of three-plus heritages most probably will still possess that distinct look that evokes many cultures and countries. My daughter, Kuniko-Leilani, is a perfect example. As a second-generation multiracial, her heritages include Japanese, Blackfoot Indian, African American, English, and Irish. She has been mistaken for Eurasian (European and Asian), Greek, Iranian, Ecuadorian, Hawaiian, Indonesian, and Italian, depending on the worldliness and national origin of the beholder. She does not have to project or continually deliberate the notion of multiracialism, except that she exists in a society that remains curious about those of us who do not fit monoracial expectations of appearance. Because of that curiosity, ours is a society that still "races" people. That is to say, society expresses a need to name (with terms with which they are comfortable) the racially uncategorizable. Society is not willing or able to resist the need to clarify and identify country of origin or race. Such is human nature.

Females of indeterminate race may be approached even more

Swirl

Swirl is one of the next generation of community organizations serving the multiracial, multiethnic, and multicultural community. Started in New York City in 2000 by Jen Chau, today Swirl boasts chapters in Northern California, Southern California, Minneapolis, Philadelphia, Boston, Arkansas, and South Florida. Swirl aims to unite the mixed community by providing support to mixed families, mixed individuals, transracial adoptees and interracial/cultural couples. Through a Big Sibling/Little Sibling Program, social events, educational lectures and discussions, Swirl will be a meeting place for members for the mixed community to celebrate and explore their heritages.

Learn more:
www.swirlinc.org

than men because women tend to appear more accessible and open to inquiry. Certainly, my country of origin and race and that of my daughter are questioned more than my son's. My son, Kiyoshi, however, finds that questions about his racial identity appear to stem from political inquiry rather than personal interest. For example, after 9/11, many Whites and African Americans with whom he was not well acquainted at his high school accosted him and asked, "You're not Arab, are you?" At other times when Asian Indians or Latinos are in the news for one reason or another, classmates will verify their previous guesses of his racial identity with rhetorical questions such as: "You're Latino?" "You're South American or something, right?" "You're Asian, right?" When the interest in his identity is personal, it comes from people who identify him as a member of their own community, such as Polynesians thinking that he is Tongan or Hawaiians thinking that he is Hawaiian—a personal embrace rather than political scrutiny.

Several factors have influenced my children's strong identification with being multiracial and with being part of a multiracial community. First of all, the fact that I am an immigrant-kindred multiracial reared in Japanese traditions even while living in the U.S. has created a strong, blended cultural foundation for them in the home. Secondly, I have educated them about the rewards and challenges of possessing multiple cultures and racial heritages so that they take pride in who they are, rather than thinking that being multiracial is a disadvantage. Thirdly, their phenotype is such that onlookers rarely can guess their racial heritage. As our society becomes more savvy about the phenomenon of multiple ethnicities, I find that some people even ask my children if they are multiracial. Region is also an important factor in building my children's confidence about being multiracial. I define region broadly. My children are Southern California natives and, thus, are growing up in an environment that is culturally diverse, and in which many multiracial families reside. Part of the character of the region includes the existence of multiracial community organizations that fortify a sense of community. Our "region," however, also embraces the Pacific Rim. Frequently, I take my children to Hawai'i and to Japan to immerse them in their other cultures as part of their education—and as part of mine.

When I was growing up in Kansas, I had the good fortune of living in a community with nearly 2,000 hapa families that had Japanese, Korean, and Southeast Asian immigrant parents married to Americans of various backgrounds. That environment assured me of the normalcy and vibrancy of my own multiracial identity. I recall, however, a hapa individual who had grown up in a blink-of-an-eye Kansas town that was all White except for his family; he had a Japanese immigrant mother and a White father. Due to his environment, he had chosen to deny his Asian heritage and focus solely on his White heritage, despite the fact that his phenotype was largely Asian. When he grew up, he chose to attend college in the South. It was in that environment that he learned more about who he was racially, due to the fact that a majority of his classmates saw him as Asian rather than as White. Moreover, he experienced greater racial discrimination in the South than he had in the Midwest. His small town had either tolerated him or embraced him as a member of their community; the Southern environment only saw him as an outsider. All in all, however, he treasured the "wake-up call," as he termed it. It was the seed of his politicization as a hapa and his realization that being multiracial did make a difference in the way that people perceived him. I learned this quite early in life, which made me realize that, if we were perceived as being different, then we indeed were different—we were our own community. We had to find common, collective ground to co-exist with monoracial communities and ensure that our voices would be heard.

Curiosity as an element of human nature and an element of the nature of that beast called "race" promises that discourses about ethnicity and race shall always be contentious ground. That will not change. But on the other hand, the multiracial movement as a social phenomenon and a political reality will also continue to be as dynamic as it is today. Of course, the concept of being multiracial also depends on the way that the idea of being monoracial and the institution of race mutate over time. The notions of progressive multiracialism and a multiracial community were established only about 25 years ago. It is a young phenomenon and, therefore, a discussion of its future is one that must remain flexible and unconstrained in terms of possibilities. Thinking about being multiracial—the way to define it, the way to fortify it, the way to preserve it, the way it fits into the overall notion of race in the U.S.

or globally—is an organic, lively process in which challenges and new hypotheses will continue to emerge. In navigating the world of multiracial children, it is important to respect their view of their multiracial identity and to understand the diversity of the multiracial experience. Who is multiracial? What do they look like? What do they act like? Simply consider the established monoraces and you will have your answer: we are not monolithic; our character and state of being is as diverse and individual as Whiteness, Blackness, Asianness, etc. Most importantly, we are an ethnic community that has fought for recognition governmentally and has made some important strides that allow multiracial children to declare their allegiance to this community with confidence about its viability and potential.

Did you know?

Here are some well-known multiracial people of three or more racial heritages:

Tiger Woods (Golfer)
African American, Thai, Chinese, Caucasian, and Native American

Lou Diamond Phillips (Actor)
Scottish, Irish, Cherokee, Filipino, Hawaiian, Chinese, and Spanish

Notes

1 For additional discussion on multiracial reporting in Census 2000, please see: Jones, Nicholas A. and Amy Symens Smith. 2001. *The Two or More Races Population: 2000*. U.S. Census Bureau, Census 2000 Brief Series (C2KBR/01-6). Washington, D.C. www.census.gov/prod/2001pubs/c2kbr01-1.pdf.

2 S. T.Haizlip, *The Sweeter the Juice: A Family Memoir in Black and White* (New York: Simon & Schuster, 1994), 15.

3 F. H. Wu, "Looking Ahead: The Hapa Century?" Asian American Village at Minorities' Job Bank (17 January 2000).

4 A. Piper, "Passing for White, Passing for Black," in *Critical White Studies: Looking Behind the Mirror*, eds. R. Delgado and J. Stefancic (Philadelphia: Temple University Press, 1997), 426-429.

5 Ibid.

6 T. Modleski, *Feminism Without Women: Culture and Criticism in a "Postfeminist" Age* (New York, London: Routledge, 1991), 63-133.

Binah
Filipina +
Caucasian

Kalani
Hawaiian + Filipino + Chinese +
Spanish + English + Irish + Scottish
Portuguese + Blackfoot

Kanna
Japanese + German +
Irish + Austrian

Kota
Japanese +
German + Irish +
Austrian

Chris
Vietnamese +
Adopted

Kelly
Vietnamese + ? +
Adopted

Section 4:
Resources

Avery
Black +
Caucasian +
Native
American

Suni
Samoan + Chinese

Yasmin
Indian + African
American +
Caucasian +
Blackfoot

Mena
Korean +
Caucasian

Books

We have compiled the following list of resources to help your exploration of the mixed race experience. Please note that it is not an exhaustive list. Rather, our goal was to create a list of easily accessible MAVIN Foundation "favorites." Please accept our apologies for resources that we have seemingly overlooked.

CHILDREN

A China Adoption Story: Why Mommy Do We Look Different?
Frances M. Koh, Honolulu: East West Press, 2000

An American Face
Jan M. Czech, Washington, DC: Child Welfare League of America, 2000

The Aunt in Our House
Angela Johnson, London: Orchard Books, 1996

Black is Brown is Tan
Arnold Adoff, New York: HarperCollins Publishers, Inc., 1991

Black, White, Just Right
Marguerite Davol, Morton Grove, IL: Albert Whitman & Co., 1993

The Coffee Can Kid
Jan M. Czech, Washington, DC: Child Welfare League of America, 2002

Dounia
Natacha Karvoskaia, New York: Kane/Miller Book Publishers, 1995

Family
Isabell Monk, Minneapolis MN: Lerner Publishing Group, 2001

Families Are Different
Nina Pellegrini, New York: Holiday House, 1991

For My Family, Love Allie
Ellen B. Senisi, Morton Grove IL: Albert Whitman & Co., 1998
Senisi's book uses photographs and simple text to tell the story of Allie's participation in a family barbecue party. Like many of the most engaging books of this genre, universal themes are combined with perspectives and experiences from a particular point of view. Its simplicity and its depiction of multiracial families in an ordinary, familiar setting seems a welcome departure from depictions of interracial families as strange or remarkable.
- MAVIN #2

Ginger Brown: Too Many Houses
Sharon D. Wyeth, New York: Random House, 1996

Growing Up Biracial: Trevor's Story
Bethany Kandel, Minneapolis, MN: Lerner Publishing Group, 1997

Heart of Mine: A Story of Adoption
Elisabeth K. Dyssegaard, Dan Hojer and Lotta Hojer, Monticello, MN: R&S Books, 2001

Hope
Isabell Monk, Minneapolis, MN: Lerner Publishing Group, 1999

Horace
Holly Keller, New York: HarperCollins Children's Books, 1991

Less Than Half, More Than Whole
Michael Lacapa, Flagstaff, AZ: Northland Publishing, 1998

Rosie's Family: An Adoption Story
Lori Rosove, New York: Asia Press, 2001
Excerpt from book: "I also LOVE my family...You may be wondering why I look different from my family. It's because I was adopted. That means I was born to a mom and dad who couldn't look after me (I call them birth parents) so another mom and dad (I call them...well, just mom and dad) made me a part of their family. Mom tells me that all families are special because families are the people who will love you and take care of you no matter where you came from."

Sun Dance at Turtle Rock
Patricia C. Viglucci, Rochester, NY: Stone Pine Books-Patri Publications, 1996

Two Lands, One Heart: An American Boy's Journey to His Mother's Vietnam
Jeremy Schmidt and Ted Wood, New York: Walker & Company, 1995

Two Mrs. Gibsons
Toyomi Igus, San Francisco: Childrens Books Press, 2001
Toyomi Igus' Two Mrs. Gibsons compares the personal and cultural styles of a Black/Japanese girl's beloved African American grandmother and Japanese immigrant mother. These two very different women spend considerable time and care with our protagonist, and are similar to each other in their love of the little girl and her father.
- MAVIN #2

When You Were Born in Korea
Brian E. Boyd, St. Paul, MN: Yeong & Yeong Book Company, 1993

When You Were Born in Vietnam
Therese Bartlett, St. Paul, MN: Yeong & Yeong Book Company, 2001

The World of Daughter McGuire
Sharon Wyeth, New York: Delacorte Press, 1994

Yoshiko and the Foreigner
Mimi O. Little, New York: Farrar Straus & Giroux, 1996

You'll Be Me/I'll Be You
Pili Mandelbaum, New York: Kane/Miller Book Publishers, 1990

YOUNG ADULT
All But the Right Folks
Joan K. Nichols, Owings Mills, MD: Stemmer House Publishing, 1985

Ankiza (The Roosevelt High School Series)
Gloria Velasquez, St. Simons Island, GA: Piñata Publishing, 2001

Black Indians
W. L. Katz, New York: Simon and Schuester, 1986
Through careful research and rare antique prints and photographs this book reveals how Black and red people learned to live and work together in the Americas to oppose White oppression. Here is an American story that reveals a little-known aspect of our past and shatters some myths.
- Simon and Schuster, Inc.

Broken Bridge
Philip Pullman, New York: Random House, 1994

Claiming Place: Biracial Young Adults of the Post-Civil Rights Era
Marion Kilson, Westport, CT: Bergin & Garvey, 2001

Friendship Sees No Color: An Award-Winning Teen Writes About Growing Up Biracial and the Interracial Pen Pal Program He Founded
Brian Harris, Stamford, CT: Hannacroix Creek Books, Inc., 1998

The House You Pass on the Way
Jacqueline Woodson, New York: Bantam Books, 1997

If You Come Softly
Jacqueline Woodson, New York: Putnam Publishing Group, 1998

Interracial America
Bonnie Szumski, Ed., San Diego: Greenhaven Press, 1996

Lives of Our Own
Lorri Hewett, New York: Dutton Books, 1998

Whale Talk
Chris Crutcher, New York: HarperCollins Publishers, Inc., 2001

Who Will Tell My Brother?
Marlene Carvell, Concord, NH: Hyperion Press, 2002

The Window
Michael Dorris, Concord, NH: Hyperion Press, 1997

FICTION (Adult Level Reading)

A Bend in the River
Susan Gibbs, Sterling Heights MI: Hawkshadow Publishing Company, Inc., 2002

A Parchment of Leaves
Silas House, Chapel Hill, NC: Algonquin Books, 2002

Almost a Woman
Esmeralda Santiago, New York: Random House, 1999

Always Running
Luis J. Rodriguez, New York: Simon & Schuster Trade Paperbacks, 1994

An Empty Lap: One Couple's Journey to Parenthood
Jill Smolowe, New York: Pocket Star, 1997

Birds Without Feathers
Karen Derzack, Mike Derzack and Cynthia Sterling, New York: Soho Press, Inc., 1994

Burnt Bread and Chutney
Carmit Delman, New York: Random House, 2002

Caucasia
Danzy Senna, New York: Riverhead Books, 1998
Throughout the novel, Senna superbly illustrates the emotional toll that politics and race take on one especially gutsy young girl's development as she makes her way through the parallel limbos between Black and White, and between girl and young woman.
- *New York Times* Book Review

Chocolate Sangria
Tracy Price-Thomson, New York: Random House, 2003

Close Encounters
Sandra Kitt, Woodbridge, CT: G.K. Hall & Company, 2000

Cloud Mountain
Aimee E. Liu, New York: Warner Books, 1998

Clover
Dori Sanders, Chapel Hill, NC: Algonquin Books, 1990

The Crown of Columbus
Louise Erdrich and Michael Dorris, New York: HarperCollins Publishers, Inc., 1999

Don't the Moon Look Lonesome: A Novel in Blues and Swing
Stanley Crouch, New York: Pantheon Books, 2000

Down These Mean Streets
Piri Thomas, New York: Random House, 1967, 1997 revised edition

The End of a Primitive
Chester B. Himes, New York: W. W. Norton & Company, 1997

Face
Aimee E. Liu, New York: Warner Books, 1994

The Family Nobody Wanted
Helen G. Doss, Boston: Northeastern University Press, 2001

The Flamingo Rising
Larry Baker, London: Little, Brown & Company, 1997

For the Love of Sang
Rachel Anderson, Colorado Springs, CO: Chariot Victor Publishing, 1990

Heads By Harry
Lois-Ann Yamanaka, New York: Avon Books, 2000

The House Behind The Cedars
Charles W. Chesnutt, London: The X Press, 1900, 1998 revised edition

In the Fall
Jeffrey Lent, New York: Knopf Publishing Group, 2001

The Keepers of the House
Shirley A. Grau, Baton Rouge, LA: Louisiana State University Press, 1995

Kin: Poems
Crystal Williams, East Lansing, MI: Michigan State University Press, 2000

Lady Moses
Lucinda Roy, New York: HarperCollins Publishers, Inc., 1998

The Last Generation: Prose and Poetry
Cherrie Moraga, Cambridge, MA: South End Press, 1993

Losing Isaiah
Seth J. Margolis, Concord, NH: Hyperion Press, 1993

Meeting of the Waters
Kim McLarin, New York: William Morrow & Co., 2001

Milk in My Coffee
Eric J. Dickey, New York: E. P. Dutton, 1998

My Place
Sally Morgan, Sydney Australia: New South Wales University Press, Ltd., 2000

My Year of Meats
Ruth L. Ozeki, New York: Viking Press, 1999

Never Letting Go of Hope
Shannon Guymon, Springville, UT: Bonneville Books, 2001

On Gold Mountain
Lisa See, New York: Vintage Books, 1996

Paper Bullets
Kip Fulbeck, Seattle: University of Washington Press, 2001

Passing
Nella Larsen, New York: The Penguin Group, 1929, 1997 revised edition

The Quarry
Charles W. Chesnutt, Princeton NJ: Princeton University Press, 1928, 1999 revised edition

Quicksand
Nella Larsen, New York: The Penguin Group, 2002 revised edition

Shark Dialogues
Kiana Davenport, New York: The Penguin Group, 1995

Sky Daddy
Canaan Parker, Boston: Alyson Publishings, 1997

Sweetbitter
Reginald Gibbons, Seattle: Broken Moon Press, 1994

The Sweeter the Juice
Shirlee T. Haizlip, New York: Simon & Schuster, 1994

They Came To Stay
Ruth Gruber and Marjorie Margolies-Mezvinsky, New York: Putnam Publishing Group, 1976

The Time of Our Singing
Richard Powers, New York: Farrar Straus & Giroux, 2003

21 Sugar Street
Lynn Lauber, New York: Norton, 1993

When I Was Puerto Rican
Esmeralda Santiago, New York: Vintage Books, 1994

White Teeth
Zadie Smith, New York: Knopf, 2001

Why She Left Us
Rahna R. Rizzuto, New York: HarperCollins Publishers, Inc., 1999

INTERRACIAL MARRIAGES & RELATIONSHIPS

A Completely New Look at Interracial Sexuality: Public Opinion and Select Commentaries
Lawrence Raymond Tenzer, Ed., Manahawkin, NJ: Scholars' Publishing House, 1990

Beyond the Whiteness of Whiteness: A Memoir of a White Mother of Black Sons
Jane Lazarre, Durham, NC: Duke University Press, 1996

Chinese American Intermarriage
Betty Lee Sung, New York: Center for Migration Studies, 1989

Christmas and 33 Years Inside an Interracial Family
H. J. Belton Hamilton, Self-published, 1990

The Colour of Love: Mixed Race Relationships
Yasmin Brown and Anne Montague, London: Virago, 1992

Coping With Interracial Dating
Renea D. Nash, New York: Rosen Publishing Group, 1997

Counseling Interracial Individuals and Families
Bea Wehrly, Alexandria, VA: American Counseling Association, 1996

Counseling Multiracial Families
Kelley R. Kenney, Mark E. Kenney and Bea Wehrly, Eds., Thousand Oaks, CA: Sage Publications, 1999

Cross-Cultural Marriages and the Church: Living the Global Neighborhood
J. Lawrence Driskill, Pasadena, CA: Hope Publishing House, 1995

Cross-Cultural Marriage: Identity and Choice
Rosemary A. Breger and Rosanna Hill, Eds., London: Berg Publishing, Ltd., 1998

Crossing the Line: Interracial Couples in the South
Robert P. McNamara, New York: Greenwood Press, 1999

Different Worlds: Interracial and Cross-Cultural Dating
Janet Bode, London: Franklin Watts, Inc., 1989

Forbidden Love: The Secret History of Mixed-Race America
Gary B. Nash, New York: Henry Holt & Company, Inc., 1999

Free Indeed: The Autobiography of an Interracial Couple
Juanita Hallett, Ruth B. White and Steve White, Eds. Abbeville, SC: A Place for Us Ministries, 1990

Inside the Mixed Marriage: Accounts of Changing Attitudes, Patterns, and Perceptions of Cross-Cultural and Interracial Marriages
Michael Warren and Walter R. Johnson, Eds., Lanham, MD: University Press of America, Inc., 1994

Interracial Intimacy: The Regulation of Race and Romance
Rachel F. Moran, Chicago: University of Chicago Press, 2001

Intermarried Couples in Therapy
Man Keung Ho, Springfield, IL: Charles C. Thomas Publishing, Ltd., 1990

Interracialism: Black-White Intermarriage in American History, Literature, and Law
Werner Sollors, Ed., New York: Oxford University Press, 2000

Looking Beyond the Mask: When American Women Marry Japanese Men
Nancy B. Diggs, New York: State University of New York Press, 2001

Love in Black and White
Mark Mathabane and Gail Mathabane, New York: HarperCollins Publishers, Inc., 1992

Love's Revolution: Interracial Marriage
Maria P. P. Root, Philadelphia: Temple University Press, 2001
In the last quarter of the twentieth century, interracial relationships and marriages have steadily multiplied. Millions of people have followed their hearts, believing they would be better human beings with partners than alone. In Love's Revolution: Interracial Marriage, *more than one hundred vignettes give a contemporary view of committed interracial relationships.*
- MAVIN #6

Loving v. *Virginia*: **Interracial Marriage**
Karen Alonso, Berkeley Heights, NJ: Enslow Publishers, Inc., 2000

Making Ethnic Choices: California's Punjabi Mexican Americans
Karen I. Leonard, Philadelphia: Temple University Press, 1992

Marriage Beyond Black and White: An Interracial Family Portrait
David and Barbara Douglas, Wilmette, IL: Baha'i Publishing Trust, 2002

Marrying the Natives: Love and Interracial Marriage
Peter M. Rinaldo, Briarcliff Manor, NY: Dorpete Press, 1996

Miscegenation: Making Race in America
Elise V. Lemire, Philadelphia: University of Pennsylvania Press, 2002

Mixed Blood: Intermarriage and Ethnic Identity in Twentieth Century America
Paul R. Spickard, Madison, WI: University of Wisconsin Press, 1989

Mixed Matches: How To Create Successful Interracial, Interethnic, and Interfaith Relationships
Joel Crohn, New York: Fawcett Columbine, 1995

Mixed Messages: Responding to Interracial Marriage
Fred Prinzing and Anita Prinzing, Chicago: Moody Press, 1991

Multiracial Couples: Black and White Voices
Terri A. Karis, Richard C. Powell and Paul C. Rosenblatt, Eds., Thousand Oaks, CA: Sage Publications, 1995

Of Many Colors: Portraits of Multiracial Families
Peggy Gillespie and Gigi Kaeser, Eds., Boston: University of Massachusetts Press, 1997
This award-winning exhibit and book offers a powerful and moving vision of the growing diversity of the American family. These families clearly have much to teach everyone about the most intimate form of integration: family love. In a world where race is considered by many to be a formidable barrier between people, the families in this exhibit are celebrated as 20th Century pioneers willing to risk disapproval and misunderstanding to find richness and value in diversity.
- Family Diversity Projects, Inc.

Race Mixing: Black-White Marriage in Post-War America
Renee C. Romano, Cambridge, MA: Harvard University Press, 2003

Strange Fruit
Lillian Smith, Fort Washington, PA: Harvest Books, 1992

Swaying: Essays on Intercultural Love
Jessie Carroll Grearson and Lauren B. Smith, Eds., Iowa City, IA: University of Iowa Press, 1995

MIXED RACE IDENTITY & EXPERIENCE

Africans and Native Americans: The Language of Race and the Evolution of Red-Black Peoples
Jack D. Forbes, Urbana, IL: University of Illinois Press, 1993

American Mixed Race: The Culture of Microdiversity
Naomi Zack, Ed., London: Rowman & Littlefield Publishers, Inc., 1995

As We Are Now: Mixblood Essays on Race and Identity
William S. Penn, Ed., Berkeley and Los Angeles: University of California Press, 1997

Beyond Black: Biracial Identity in America
David L. Brunsma and Kerry Rockquemore, Thousand Oaks, CA: Sage Publications, 2001

Beyond Race: The Bhagavad-Gita in Black and White
Charles Michael Byrd, Philadelphia: Xlibris Corporation, 2002

Black and White Racial Identity: Theory, Research, and Practice
Janet E. Helms, New York: Greenwood Press, 1990

Black, Jewish, and Interracial: It's Not the Color of Your Skin, but the Race of Your Kin
Katya Gibel Azoulay, Durham, NC: Duke University Press, 1997

Black, White & Jewish: Autobiography of a Shifting Self
Rebecca Walker, New York: Riverhead Books, 2001
Rebecca Walker, daughter of celebrated African American writer, Alice Walker and Jewish civil rights attorney, Mel Leventhal, delivers a poignant look into the life of a biracial child achieving a sense of self in this coming of age autobiography. While the title of her book may suggest a focus on race, Walker shows that while being mixed race is a large part of a multiracial person's identity, myriad factors in life shift one's sense of self.
- MAVIN #6

Black, White, or Mixed Race?: Race and Racism in the Lives of Young People of Mixed Parentage
Barbara Tizard, New York: Routledge, 1993

Black, White, Other: Biracial Americans Talk About Race and Identity
Lise Funderburg, New York: William Morrow & Company, Inc., 1994
Black, White, Other shows how a mixed heritage generates a reality distinct from Black or White experience. Differences between internal and external perception are especially difficult, pressuring individuals to question what they are. Funderburg's interviewees range from no-one-would-ever-know Whites to individuals strongly Black-influenced, from those embittered or weakened by the prejudice of their parents to those whose dual heritages have given them self-assurance. The free expression of attitudes, opinions, and experiences here is lively and thought-provoking.
- Booklist

The Book of Sarahs: A Memoir of Race and Identity
Catherine E. McKinley, Washington. DC: Counterpoint, 2002
From back cover: "The Book of Sarahs traces McKinley's own time of revelations: after a five-year period marked by dead ends and disappointments, she finds her birth mother and a half-sister named Sarah, the name that was originally given to her. When she locates her birth father and meets several of his eleven other children she begins to see the whole mosaic of her parentage—African American, WASP, Jewish, Native American—and then is confronted with a final revelation that threatens to destabilize all

she has uncovered. In telling of her struggles both to fit into and to defy social conventions, McKinley challenges us to rethink our own preconceptions about race, identity, kinship, loyalty, and love."

Borderlands/La Frontera: The New Mestiza
Gloria Anzaldua, San Francisco: Spinsters/Aunt Lute, 1987

Brown: The Last Discovery of America
Richard Rodriguez, New York: The Penguin Group, 2002

Bulletproof Diva: Tales of Race, Sex, and Hair
Lisa Jones, Ed., New York: Doubleday, 1994

Check All That Apply: Finding Wholeness as a Multiracial Person
Sundee Tucker Frazier, Downers Grove, IL: InterVarsity Press, 2002

The Color Complex: The Politics of Skin Color Among African Americans
Kathy Russell, New York: Hartcourt Bruce Jovanich, 1992

The Color of Water: A Black Man's Tribute to His White Mother
James McBride, New York: Berkeley Publishing Group, 1997
Complex and moving...suffused with issues of race, religion and identity. Yet those issues, so much a part of their lives and stories, are not central. The triumph of the book—and of their lives—is that race and religion are transcended in these interwoven histories by family love, the sheer force of a mother's will and her unshakable insistence that only two things really mattered: school and church... The two stories, son's and mother's, beautifully juxtaposed, strike a graceful note at a time of racial polarization.
- New York Times Book Review

Communication, Race, and Family: Exploring Communication in Black, White, and Biracial Families
Rhunette C. Diggs and Thomas J. Socha, Mahwah, NJ: Lawrence Erlbaum & Associates, 1999

The Construction of Racial Identity in Children of Mixed Parentage: Mixed Metaphors
Ilan Katz, London: Jessica Kingsley Publishing, 1996

Coping as a Biracial/Biethnic Teen
Renea D. Nash, New York: Rosen Publishing Group, 1995

Crossbloods: Bone Courts, Bingo, and Other Reports
Gerald Vizenor, Minneapolis, MN: University of Minnesota Press, 1976, 1990 revised edition

Crossing: A White Man's Journey Into Black America
Walt Harrington, New York: HarperCollins Publishers, Inc., 1992

Crossing the Color Line: Race, Parenting, and Culture
Maureen T. Reddy, New Brunswick, NJ: Rutgers University Press, 1994

Dim Sum, Bagels, and Grits: A Sourcebook for Multicultural Families
Myra Alperson, New York: Farrar Straus & Giroux, 2001

Diversity and Citizenship Education: Global Perspectives
James A. Banks, Ed., San Francisco: Jossey Bass, 2004

Divided to the Vein: A Journey Into Race and Family
Scott Minerbrook, New York: Harcourt Brace & Company, 1996

Does Anybody Else Look Like Me?: A Parent's Guide to Raising Multiracial Children
Donna Jackson-Nakazawa, Cambridge, MA: Perseus Publishing, 2003
Drawing on psychological research and input from more than 60 multiracial families, Does Anybody Else Look Like Me? *addresses the special questions and concerns facing mixed race families today, explaining how they can best prepare their multiracial children to make their way confidently in our color-conscious world. Full of powerful stories and expert counsel, parents in mixed race families will find understanding and insight here as they strive to raise their children in a changing world.*
- Perseus Publishing

The Dust of Life: America's Children Abandoned in Vietnam
Robert S. McKelvey, Seattle: University of Washington Press, 1999

Edgewalkers: Defusing Cultural Boundaries on the New Global Frontier
Nina Boyd Krebs, New York: New Horizon Press, 1999

Everything You Need to Know About Being a Biracial/Biethnic Child
Renea D. Nash, New York: Rosen Publishing Group, 1995

From Black to Biracial: Transforming Racial Identity Among Americans
Kathleen O. Korgen, New York: Praeger Publishers, 1998

The Future Is Mestizo: Life Where Cultures Meet, Revised Edition
Virgilio Elizondo, Boulder, CO: University Press of Colorado, 2000
Quote from author: "There have been vast differences between Nordic America and Latin America—biologically and spiritually. The U.S.A. has rejected, and even prohibited by law, race mixing, while it was the natural way of Latin America. Spiritually, the U.S.A. has been basically Protestant while Latin American bas been generally Catholic. But today, these two very different 'humanities' are meeting, mixing and influencing one another at every level of human existence; thus the great border between the two Americas is becoming the cradle of a new humanity."
- MAVIN #5

Half and Half: Writers on Growing Up Biracial and Bicultural
Claudine Chiawei O'Hearn, Ed., New York: Pantheon Books, 1998
Claudine Chiawei O'Hearn's edited collection, Half and Half, *is a delightful, very well-received collection of literary-quality creative nonfiction essays written by biracial people and bicultural people who are immigrants, children of immigrants, and often themselves the parents of biracial children. Furthermore, a diversity of male and female perspectives and racial/ethnic backgrounds is represented, instead of the more usual Black/White examples of biraciality.*
- MAVIN #2

How Did You Get to be Mexican?: A White/Brown Man's Search for Identity
Kevin R. Johnson, Philadelphia: Temple University Press, 1999

Hybrid: Bisexuals, Multiracials, and Other Misfits Under American Law
Ruth Colker, New York: New York University Press, 1996

I Am Who I Am: Speaking Out About Multiracial Identity
Kathlyn Gay, New York: Franklin Watts, 1995

I'm Chocolate, You're Vanilla: Raising Healthy Black and Biracial Children in a Race-Conscious World
Marguerite Wright, San Francisco: Jossey Bass, 2000

Interracial America: Opposing Viewpoints
Mary E. Williams, Ed., San Diego: Greenhaven Press, 2001

The Interracial Experience: Growing Up Black/White Racially Mixed in the United States
Ursula M. Brown, New York: Praeger Publishers, 2000

Intersecting Circles: The Voices of Hapa Women in Poetry and Prose
Nora Okja Keller and Marie Hara, Eds., Honolulu: Bamboo Ridge Press, 1999

Jefferson's Children: The Story of One American Family
Jane Feldman and Shannon Lanier, New York: Random House, 2000

Meatless Days
Sara Suleri, Chicago: The University of Chicago Press, 1989

Memories of My Ghost Brother
Heinz I. Fenkl, New York: The Penguin Group, 1996

Miscegenation Blues: Voices of Mixed Race Women
Carol Camper, Toronto, ON: Sister Vision Press, 1994
Miscegenation Blues: Voices of Mixed Race Women *is certainly recommended reading for anyone interested in learning more about the interracial experience. It also provides a rare Canadian perspective on mixed race people, as many of the contributors were born or currently live in Canada. The book's ability to raise challenging questions and the literary and aesthetic merit of the works included make* Miscegenation Blues: Voices of Mixed Race Women *an enjoyable and informative book to read.*
- Interracial Voice

Mississippi Chinese: Between Black and White
James W. Loeweb, Cambridge, MA: Harvard University Press, 1971

Mixed Feelings: The Complex Lives of Mixed Race Britons
Yasmin Alibhai-Brown, London: Trafalgar Square, 2002

Mixed Matches: How To Create Successful Interracial, Interethnic, and Interfaith Relationships
Joel Crohn, New York: Fawcett Columbine, 1995

Mixed Race America and the Law: A Reader
Kevin R. Johnson, Ed., New York: New York University Press, 2003

Mixed Race Literature
Jonathan Brennan, Ed., Stanford, CA: Stanford University Press, 2002

Mixed Race Children: A Study of Identity
Anne Wilson, Boston: Allen & Unwin, 1987

More Than Black?: Multiracial Identity and the New Racial Order
G. Reginald Daniel, Philadelphia: Temple University Press, 2002
Even as the twenty-first century opens, a racial hierarchy still prevents people of color, including individuals of mixed race, from enjoying the same privileges as Euro-Americans. In this book, G. Reginald Daniel argues that we are at a crossroads, with members of a new multiracial movement pointing the way toward equality. More Than Black? *regards the crumbling of the old racial order as an opportunity for substantially more than an improvement in U.S. race relations; it offers no less than a radical transformation of the nation's racial consciousness and the practice of democracy.*
- Temple University Press

Mulattas and Mestizas: Representing Mixed Identities in the Americas, 1850-2000
Suzanne Bost, Athens, GA: University of Georgia Press, 2003

Multicultural Education: Issues and Perspectives
James A. Banks and C. A. M. Banks, Eds., New York: Wiley, 2003

Multicultural Encounters: Cases Narratives from a Counseling Practice
Stephen Murphy-Shigematsu, New York: Teachers College Press, 2002

The Multiracial Experience: Racial Borders As the New Frontier
Maria P. P. Root, Ed., Thousand Oaks, CA: Sage Publications, 1996
From back cover: Maria P. P. Root has masterfully assembled an engaging set of articles that insightfully explore practically every aspect of the multiracial experience. The contributors reflect a wide range of mixed racial ethnicities, which further adds to the vibrancy and relevance of the text. Root's reader may be the single best source for understanding why the U.S. Bureau of the Census is being pressured to include a new multiracial category in the next census.
- William E. Cross Jr., Psychology and African American Studies, Pennsylvania State University

Multiracial Identity: An International Perspective
Diedre L. Badejo and Mark Christian, New York: Palgrave Macmillan, 2000

Neither Black Nor White Yet Both: Thematic Explorations of Interracial Literature
Werner Sollors, Cambridge, MA: Harvard University Press, 1999

New Faces in a Changing America: Multiracial Identity in the 21st Century
Herman L. DeBose and Loretta I. Winters, Thousand Oaks, CA: Sage Publications, 2003

New People: Miscegenation and Mulattos in the United States
Joel Williamson, New York: New York University Press, 1984

New Perspectives on Racial Identity Development: A Theoretical and Practical Anthology
Charmaine L. Wijeyesinghe and B. W. Jackson, Ed., New York: New York University Press, 2001

The New Race Question: How the Census Counts Multiracial Individuals
Joel Perlmann and Mary Waters, Ed., New York: Russell Sage Foundation, 2002

Passing for Black
Wade H. Hall and Mae Street Kidd, Lexington, KY: University Press of Kentucky, 1997

Passing for White: Race, Religion, and the Healy Family
James M. O'Toole, Boston: University of Massachusetts Press, 2002

Proudly Red and Black: Stories of African and Native Americans
William S. Katz, New York: Atheneum, 1993

Psychology of the Americas: Mestizo Perspectives on Personality and Mental Health
Manuel Ramirez, III, New York: Pergamon Press, 1983

Puerto Rican Americans: The Meaning of Migration to the Mainland
Joseph P. Fitzpatrick, Englewood Cliffs, NJ: Prentice-Hall, 1971

Rabbit Proof Fence
Nugi Garimara and Doris Pilkington, St. Lucia Australia: University of Queensland Press, 1996

Race and Mixed Race
Naomi Zack, Philadelphia: Temple University Press, 1993
In the first philosophical challenge to accepted racial classifications in the United States, Naomi Zack uses philosophical methods to criticize their logic. Tracing social and historical problems related to racial identity, she discusses why race is a matter of such importance in America and examines the treatment of mixed race in law, society, and literature. Exploring the existential problems of mixed race identity, she points out how the biracial system in this country generates a special racial alienation for many Americans.
- Temple University Press

Race Traitor
Nowl Ignatiev and John Garvey, Eds., New York: Routledge, 1996

Racial and Ethnic Identity in School Practices: Aspects of Human Development
Rosa Hernandez Sheets and Etta R. Hollins, Eds., Mahwah, NJ: Lawrence Erlbaum & Associates, 1999

Racial Categorization of Multiracial Children in Schools
Jane A. Chiong, Westport, CT: Greenwood Press, 1998

Racially Mixed People in America
Maria P. P. Root, Ed., Thousand Oaks, CA: Sage Publications, 1992
Racially Mixed People in America is not just a "feel good" affirmation of mixed race people. It offers explanations of "how possibly" the constructed notions of race operate in our society through an examination of mixed race people from the "margins" of psychological and sociological studies to the center of race relations discourse. This, perhaps, is its greatest contribution.
- Amerasia Journal

Raiding the Gene Pool: The Social Construction of Mixed Race
Jill Olumide, London: Pluto Press, 2002

The Rainbow Effect: Transracial Families
Kathlyn Gay, London: Franklin Watts, Inc., 1987

Recovering History, Constructing Race: The Indian, Black, and White Roots of Mexican Americans
Martha Menchaca, Austin, TX: University of Texas Press, 2001

Rethinking "Mixed Race"
David Parker and Miri Song, Ed., London: Pluto Press, 2000

Shades of Black: Diversity in African American Identity
William E. Cross, Jr., Philadelphia: Temple University Press, 1991

The Shadow of Race: Growing Up as a Multiethnic, Multicultural, and "Multiracial" American
Teja Arboleda and Christine Clark, Mahwah, NJ: Lawrence Erlbaum & Associates, 1999

Showing Our Colors: Afro-German Women Speak Out
May Opitz, K. Oguntoye and D. Schultz, Eds., Boston: University of Massachusetts Press, 1991

Skin Color Recognition: Preference and Identification in Interracial Children
Wayne W. Gunthorpe, Lanham, MD: University Press of America, Inc., 1998

Spurious Issues: Race and Multiracial Identity Politics
Rainier Spencer, Boulder, CO: Westview Press, 1999

The Sum of Our Parts: Mixed Heritage Asian Americans
Cynthia L. Nakashima and Teresa Williams-León, Eds., Philadelphia: Temple University Press, 2001
The Sum of Our Parts *tackles the Asian American mixed race experience. Edited by Teresa Williams-León and Cynthia L. Nakashima,* Parts *begs the reader to experience some of the over-arching complexities of mixed-ness against an Asian and Pacific Islander backdrop. The anthology's 19 essays are separated into four sections, which seek to organize the diversified experiences of being mixed race and Asian American. Section One explores a historical perspective of mixed race Asian Americans; Two discusses family and identity; Three explores Asian American communities and politics, while the final section explores the Asian mixed race experience overseas.*
- MAVIN #6

Tomorrow's Children: Meeting the Needs of Multiracial and Multiethnic Children at Home, in Early Childhood Programs, and at School
Francis Wardle, Denver, CO: Center for the Study of Biracial Children, 1999

Tripping on the Color Line: Black-White Multiracial Families in a Racially Divided World
Heather M. Dalmage, Piscataway, NJ: Rutgers University Press, 2000

The Unwanted
Kien Nguyen, New York: Little, Brown & Co., 2001
Nguyen's book is an unforgettable chronicle of the horrors of war. It is also a memorable account of the cruelties that countless Amerasians have endured in their own countries. Nguyen observes, "It's estimated that more than fifty thousand Amerasian children shared my fate, or worse...I kept writing in hopes that these innocent victims' lost childhoods might finally be mourned, and their buried secrets at last revealed."
- MAVIN #6

The Voices of Amerasians: Ethnicity, Identity, and Empowerment in Interracial Japanese Americans
Stephen L. H. Murry-Shigematsu, Dissertation.com, 1999

Two Worlds Walking: Short Stories, Essays, and Poetry by Writers with Mixed Heritages
C. W. Truesdale and Diane Glancy, Eds., New York: New Rivers Press, 1994

We Are a People: Narrative and Multiplicity in Constructing Ethnic Identity
W. Jeffrey Burroughs and Paul R. Spickard, Philadelphia: Temple University Press, 2000

What Are You?: Voices of Mixed-Race Young People
Pearl F. Gaskins, Ed., New York: Henry Holt & Company, Inc., 1999

White Man Falling: Race, Gender, and White Supremacy
Abby L. Ferber, Lanham, MD: Rowman & Littlefield Publishers, Inc., 1998

White Women, Race Matters: The Social Construction of Whiteness
Ruth Frankenberg, Minneapolis, MN: University of Minnesota Press, 1993

Who Is Black? One Nation's Definition
F. James Davis, University Park, PA: Pennsylvania State University Press, 1991

TRANSRACIAL ADOPTION

Adoption Across Borders
Howard Altstein and Rita J. Simon, London: Rowman & Littlefield Publishers, Inc., 2000

Adoption and Ethics: The Role of Race, Culture, and National Origin in Adoption
Madelyn Freundlich, Washington, DC: Child Welfare League of America, 2000

Adoption Nation
Adam Pertman, New York: Basic Books, 2001

Adoption of Black Children: Counteracting Institutional Discrimination
Dawn Day, Lanham, MD: Lexington Books, 1979

Adoption, Race, and Identity: From Infancy through Adolescence
Howard Altstein and Rita J. Simon, New York: Praeger Publishers, 1992

"Are Those Kids Yours?": American Families with Children Adopted from Other Countries
Cheri Register, New York: Free Press, 1991

Birthmarks: Transracial Adoption in Contemporary America
Sandra Patton, New York: New York University Press, 2000

Butterflies in the Wind: Spanish/Indian Children with White Parents
Jean Nelson and Heino R. Erichsen, Los Niños International, 1992

The Case for Transracial Adoption
Howard Altstein, Marygold S. Melli and Rita J. Simon, Washington, DC: The American University Press, 1994
From back cover: Simon, Altstein, and Melli have focused the sometimes shrill political debate over transracial adoption to what really counts—the best interest of the child. The literature review and the original research of the authors discussed in The Case for Transracial Adoption *provide evidence that transracial adoption provides for the most fundamental developmental needs of children—*

their need for stability, security, and a loving family.
- Mary Beth Seader, National Council for Adoption

The Children: A Personal Record for the Use of Adoptive Parents
Jan De Hartog, Princeton, NJ: Scribner, 1969

Children of Special Value: Interracial Adoption in America
David C. Anderson, New York: St. Martin's Press, 1971

Colour of Difference: Journeys in Transracial Adoption
Sarah Armstrong and Petrina Slaytor, Eds., Annandale, Australia: Federation Press, 2001

The Ethics of Transracial Adoption
Hawley Fogg-Davis, Ithaca, NY: Cornell University Press, 2002

Far From the Reservation: The Transracial Adoption of American Indian Children
David Fanshel, Lanham, MD: Scarecrow Press, 1972

Flight of the Stork
Anne C. Bernstein, Perspectives Press, 1994 revised edition

Gift Children: A Story of Race, Family, and Adoption in a Divided America
J. Douglas Dates, New York: Ticknor & Fields, 1993

In the Best Interests of the Child: Culture, Identity and Transracial Adoption
Jane Aldridge and Ivor Gaber, Eds., London: Free Association Books, 1995

In Their Own Voices: Transracial Adoptees Tell Their Stories
Rhonda M. Roorda and Rita J. Simon, Eds., New York: Columbia University Press, 2000
From back cover: In Their Own Voices *sheds light on a very complex and controversial debate. The debate would be richer and wiser if those who seek to defend or condemn transracial adoption read this book first. It should be required reading for anyone who is thinking of adopting or has adopted a child from another race.*
- Barbara Davidson, civil rights advocate and adoptive mother

Inside Transracial Adoption
Beth Hallinan and Gail Steinberg, Fort Wayne, IN: Perspectives Press, 2000

The International Adoption Handbook: How To Make an Overseas Adoption Work For You
Myra Alperson, New York: Henry Holt & Company, Inc., 1997

International and Transracial Adoptions: A Mental Health Perspective
Christopher Bagley, Hants, UK: Avebury Publishing, 1993

Looking for Lost Bird: A Jewish Woman Discovers Her Navajo Roots
Yvette Melanson and Claire Safran, New York: Bard/Avon Books, 1999
Looking for Lost Bird *is a book-length, journalist's narrative of the complex life of a woman raised by her adoptive Jewish parents in New York in the 1960s and 1970s. She, upon her (biological) family's invitation, relocates herself, her husband and daughters to the Navajo Nation in order to reconnect with her birth family and community. Melanson's book contains some important contextual information about the history of the adoption of Native Americans, about the selling of children through illegal adoption networks and about the contemporary life and concerns of a Navajo family.*
- MAVIN #3

Loving Across the Color Line: A White Adoptive Mother Learns About Race
Sharon Rush, London: Rowman & Littlefield Publishers, Inc., 2000

The Mulberry Bird: Story of an Adoption
Anne B. Brodzinsky, Fort Wayne, IN: Perspectives Press, 1986

Seeds From a Silent Tree: An Anthology By Korean Adoptees
Jo Rankin and Tonya Bishoff, Eds., San Diego: Pandal Press, 1997

Secret Thoughts of an Adoptive Mother
Jana Wolff, Kansas City, MO: Andrews McMeel Publishing, 1997

Transracial Adoptees and Their Families: A Study of Identity and Commitment
Rita J. Simon, New York: Praeger Publishers, 1987

Transracial Adoption and Foster Care: Practice Issues for Professionals
Joseph Crumbley, Washington, DC: Child Welfare League of America, 1999

Transracial Adoption: Children and Parents Speak
Kathy Harris and Constance Pohl, Eds., Self-published, 1992

Voices From Another Place
Susan Soon-Keum Cox, Ed., St. Paul, MN: Yeong & Yeong Book Company, 1999
Voices From Another Place*, edited by Susan Soon-keum Cox, is filled with emotionally charged testimonials, beautiful artwork and moving poems. Together, they create a comprehensive look at the Korean adoptee experience.*
- MAVIN #6

West Meets East: Americans Adopt Chinese Children
Gail Gamache, Richard C. Tessler & Liming Liu, Westport, CT: Bergin & Garvey, 1999

Films

This list was adapted from Rose Adams' research and was originally used by Stanford University's Green Library.

DOCUMENTARIES

An American Love Story (1999) 600 min. (VHS)
This ambitious 10-part PBS documentary by Jennifer Fox chronicles the lives of an interracial family (Black father, White mother, and their two biracial daughters).

Banana Split (1991) 37 min. (VHS)
In this film, hapa director Kip Fulbeck interweaves narratives, stories, and media clips to focus on biracial ethnicity exploration and Asian self-identity. He examines the relationship between his father who is Caucasian and his mother who is Chinese and also explores ethnic dating patterns and media stereotypes of Asian American men.

Cunanan's Conundrum (1998) 10 min. (VHS)
Stuart Gaffney's intriguing film demystifies the stereotype of Andrew Cunanan, the queer, biracial suspected killer of fashion designer Gianni Versaci. Through images gathered solely from media footage, Gaffney's film explores how Cunanan's racial ambiguity confused and intrigued the media.

Days of Waiting (1990) 28 min. (VHS)
A documentary about artist Estelle Peck Ishigo's internment with her Japanese American husband during World War II and the difficulties of readjustment at war's end.

Do 2 Halves Really Make a Whole? (1993) 30 min. (VHS)
Features the diverse viewpoints of people with multiracial Asian heritages. African and Japanese American poet and playwright Velina Hasu Houston lives an "amalgamated existence" and encourages others to take pride in all that they are. Performance artist Dan Kwong constantly struggles with two strong and often conflicting Asian heritages: Japanese and Chinese American. Chinese Japanese Chicana Scots storyteller, actress, and performance artist Brenda Wong Aoki uses her unique ethnic mix to intersect social circles.

Doubles: Japan and America's Intercultural Children (1995) 58 min. (English version), 85 min. (Japanese version) (VHS)
This film by Regge Life is the first in-depth look at the lives of intercultural children of Japanese and Americans from inside America as well as inside Japan.

En Ryo Identity (1991) 23 min. (VHS)
This film addresses the complexities of establishing and asserting a biracial identity. Director Mayeda Berges also looks at mainstream media constructions of Asian American identity juxtaposed with Hollywood representations of Asians and interviews his Japanese American grandmother about her internment camp experiences.

First Person Plural (2000) 56 min. (VHS)

Deann Borshay Liem was adopted from Korea by a White American family in 1966. Her memory of her birth family was almost forgotten until dreams inspired her to look at her past and try to unite her adoptive and biological families.

Mixed Blood (1992) 20 min. (VHS)

Mixed blood takes a personal view of interracial relationships between Asian Americans and non-Asian Americans. Valerie Soe, the director combines interviews with over 30 concerned individuals, text and clips from scientific films and classic miscegenation dramas. This video explores the complexities of cross-cultural intimacy and whether such choices have public and political implications.

Mixed Feelings (1998) 45 min. (VHS)

Through interviews with five University of California, Berkeley students, producer and director Mikko Jokela examines what it is like to grow up of mixed Asian heritage in American society in this experimental documentary.

Outside Looking In: Transracial Adoption in America (2001) 57 min. (VHS)

Phil Bertelsen provides a unique perspective as both an adoptee and filmmaker in his exploration of transracial adoption and identity through three families located in three different regions of the country.

Quiet Passages: the Japanese American War Bride Experience (1991) 26 min. (VHS)

Through a combination of archival photographs and interviews, this film records the journey by several Japanese American war brides to the Midwest where they settled and raised their families.

Tanto Tiempo (1992) 26 min. (35mm)

This is Cheryl Quintana Leader's award-winning story of Mia and her Mexican mother, who have adapted an Anglo lifestyle. Mia rediscovers her Aztec heritage and incorporates both it and her mother back into her life.

Unforgettable Face (1993) 13 min. (VHS)

George Oiye, one of the Japanese American soldiers who liberated people from Dachau in 1945, and Yanina Cywinska, then a 16-year-old prisoner in the death camp, reunite some forty years after World War II.

Unlocking the Heart of Adoption (2003) 56 min. (VHS)

This film chronicles the journey of birthmother and filmmaker, Sheila Ganz, and compelling first person stories of adoptees, birthparents and adoptive parents in both same race and transracial adoptions.

FEATURE FILMS / SHORT STORIES

Catfish in Black Bean Sauce (2000) 119 min. (VHS)

This comedy directed by, produced by, and starring Chi Muoi Lo centers on the marriage proposal and birth mother discovery of two adult Vietnamese Americans adopted by an African American couple after the fall of Saigon.

Come See the Paradise (1990) 135 min. (VHS)

Set against the background of a controversial period in American history, the internment of Japanese Americans during World War II, *Come See The Paradise* is the love story of an Irish American man and a Japanese American woman.

Guess Who's Coming to Dinner (1967) 108 min. (VHS)

When the daughter of a White liberal newspaper publisher and the son of a Black retired postal worker want to get married, they face opposition from both their families.

Jungle Fever (1991) 131 min. (VHS)

A Black architect begins an affair with his working class Italian secretary. Their relationship causes them to be scrutinized by their friends, cast out from their families, and shunned by their neighbors in this view of inner-city life.

Losing Isaiah (1995) 106 min. (VHS)

Directed by Stephen Gyllenhaal and starring Jessica Lange and Halle Berry, this movie centers on a Black birth mother's struggle to regain custody of her abandoned son from his White adoptive mother.

Mississippi Masala (1992) 118 min. (VHS)

In this erotic interracial love story, an African American businessman falls for a beautiful Indian immigrant, only to encounter shock and outrage from both families.

Multi-Facial (1994) 20 min.

Vin Diesel wrote, directed, starred in, and financed this debut short film about a struggling multiracial actor.

Othello
There are several versions of this play. This famous play of love turned bad by unfounded jealousy is one of Shakespeare's four great tragedies.

Secrets and Lies (1996) 142 min. (VHS)
After her adoptive parents die, a young Black woman seeks out her natural birth mother and discovers that her mother is White. When her mother springs her newfound daughter on the rest of the family, the resulting chaos reveals a series of secrets and lies.

Web sites

NATIONAL/INTERNATIONAL MULTIRACIAL ORGANIZATIONS

Association of MultiEthnic Americans (AMEA) {www.ameasite.org}
AMEA aims to educate and advocate on behalf of multiethnic individuals and families by collaborating with others to eradicate all forms of discrimination.

Center for the Study of Biracial Children {www.csbc.cncfamily.com}
The Center for the Study of Biracial Children provides advocacy, training, and consulting. Its primary mission is to advocate for the rights of interracial families and multiracial people.

Intermix {www.intermix.org.uk}
Intermix offers friendship, support, information, and advice to mixed race individuals, racially mixed couples and transracial adoptees in the United Kingdom.

Hapa Issues Forum (HIF) {www.hapaissuesforum.org}
HIF is California-based nonprofit dedicated to enriching the lives of Asian/Pacific Islanders of mixed heritage and developing communities that value true diversity.

MAVIN Foundation {www.mavinfoundation.org}
MAVIN is the nation's leading organization that is redefining diversity through innovative projects celebrating mixed race youth and families.

Swirl, Inc. {www.swirlinc.org}
Swirl is a New York-based nonprofit that offers social support for the mixed community, with several chapters across the nation.

LOCAL MULTIRACIAL ORGANIZATIONS

Getting Interracial Families Together (GIFT) {http://members.aol.com/njgift}
This New Jersey-based organization has resource links to other multiracial Web sites, publications, and events.

Interracial Family Alliance of Houston {www.ifahouston.org}
IFA of Houston is an organization that serves interracial families and multiracial individuals in the Houston metropolitan area.

Interracial/Intercultural Pride (I-Pride) {www.i-pride.org}
I-Pride is a San Francisco Bay Area organization that strives to educate our selves, our children, and our community about the facts of interculturalism and interracial identity.

Multiracial Americans of Southern California (MASC)
{www.multiculti.org}
MASC's mission is to address the social, cultural, and educational interests of racially and culturally mixed individuals, couples, and families in Southern California.

Multiracial Family Circle (MFC) {www.cdiversity.com/mfc}
MFC of Kansas City seeks to educate both the public and policy-makers on issues surrounding transracial/multiracial people and families.

Multiracial Interracial eXperience (MIX)
{www.mavinfoundation.org/mix.html}
MIX is the Seattle, Washington area's support organization for multiracial youth and families, interracial couples, and transracial adoptees.

Oregon Council on Multiracial Affairs (OCMA)
{www.ocma-multiracial.org}
Based in Portland, OCMA's mission is to broaden awareness of the multiracial and multicultural experience in Oregon.

MULTIRACIAL WEB SITES OF INTEREST
Eurasian Nation {www.eurasiannation.com}
This Web site is the premier online resource for people of mixed European and Asian descent. It aims to provide quality content on Eurasian issues and to act as a discussion forum for Eurasians.

Great Owl Books {www.viconet.com/greatowlbooks/}
Great Owl Books "...offers books which will help you explore ideas, affirm your vision or enrich your sense of self." Geared towards the mixed race community.

The Half Korean Page {www.halfkorean.com}
This is a groundbreaking Web page for half-Koreans of all backgrounds. Created by David Lee Sanders.

Hapas.com {www.hapas.com}
Hapas.com is an online forum and community all about being Eurasian, biracial, mixed, multiracial, Amerasian, Blasian, half Asian, or what many call "hapa."

Mixedfolks.com {www.mixedfolks.com}
This Web site boasts a huge database of famous mixed race people. Many pictures, links, and bios are included.

Polly Wanna Cracka? {www.pollywannacracka.com}
Description from Web site: "Polly Wanna Cracka? is devoted to presenting quality links and resources regarding interracial, and multicultural families, relationships, organizations, and topics."

Yahoo! Directory for Biracial & Multiracial Resources
{dir.yahoo.com/Society_and_Culture/Cultures_and_Groups/Biracial_and_Multiracial/}
Yahoo categorical listing of various biracial and multiracial Web sites.

POLITICAL MULTIRACIAL WEB SITES
Interracial Voice {www.interracialvoice.com}
Interracial Voice defines itself as a "voice of conscience in the worldwide interracial/mixed race community."

The Multiracial Activist {www.multiracial.com}
This group is a libertarian-oriented activist journal covering social and civil liberties issues of interest to individuals who perceive themselves to be biracial or multiracial. Interracial couples/families and transracial adoptee issues are also pursued.

Project RACE {www.projectrace.com}
Description from Web site: "A national organization leading the movement for a multiracial classification."

ADOPTION/TRANSRACIAL ADOPTION WEB SITES
Adoption Advocates International {www.adoptionadvocates.org}
Description from Web site: "AAI is an experienced international adoption agency focusing on children from Haiti, China, Thailand, and Ethiopia. We are committed to processing each adoption with respect for the welfare of the child while providing emotional support and guidance for the adopting parents."

Adoptive Families Magazine
{www.adoptivefamiliesmagazine.com}
Adoptive Families Magazine is an award-winning national adoption magazine. Provides information, contacts, and resources for prospective and existing adoptive parents.

Adoptive Families Together (AFT) {www.adoptivefamilies.org}
Founded in Massachusetts, AFT is a network of families who embrace the benefits of peer support among other adoptive families.

Asian Adult Adoptees of Washington (AAAW) {www.aaaw.org}
AAAW provides support for Asian adult adoptees in Washington State and administers a teen mentorship program.

Also Known As (AKA) {www.alsoknownas.org/splash.html}
A 501(c)(3) non profit organization, AKA seeks to serve all people who are or have ties to transracial adoptees. It opens the possibility of intercountry and interracial adoptions for future generations.

Children's Hope International {www.childrenshopeint.org}
Children's Hope International is a nationwide non profit international adoption agency.

Holt International Children's Services {www.holtintl.org}
Holt International Children's Services is dedicated to finding every child a permanent and loving home through family preservation, and both domestic and international adoption.

International Concerns for Children {www.iccadopt.org}
International Concerns for Children is a publication and resource for information on international adoption agencies.

Joint Council on International Children's Services {www.jcics.org}
Description from Web site: "Joint Council on International Children's Services advocates on behalf of children in need of permanent families by promoting ethical practices in intercountry adoption."

Korean American Adoptee Adoptive Family Network (KAAN) {www.kaanet.com}
KAAN's mission is to network groups and individuals related to Korean adoptions. The network facilitates dialogue, promotes resource sharing, and disseminates information.

Medina Children's Services {www.medinachild.org}
Medina Children's Services is a Seattle-based non profit benefiting abused and at-risk children. This organization sees to it that they grow up in stable and nurturing family environments.

National Adoption Information Clearinghouse (NAIC) {www.calib.com/naic}
NAIC is a national resource for information on all aspects of adoption for professionals, policymakers, and the general public.

National Council for Adoption {www.ncfa-usa.org/home.html}
The National Council for Adoption is 501(c)(3) charity that assists children in finding permanent homes in the United States.

North American Council on Adoptable Children {www.nacac.org}
This organization supports adoptive families and finds homes for thousands of foster children in need.

Northwest Adoption Exchange (NWAE) {www.nwae.org}
NWAE helps recruit prospective adoptive parents throughout the United States. It provides consultation, training, and technical assistance to adoption agencies, social workers, and adoptive parent support groups.

Oregon Alliance of Children's Programs {www.oregonalliance.org}
By providing quality programs and services, the Oregon Alliance of Children's Programs is committed to the well being of Oregon's disenfranchised children, youth, and families.

The Pearl S. Buck Foundation {www.pearl-s-buck.org/psbi/}
Description from Web site: "Pearl S. Buck International (PSBI) is a non-sectarian development and humanitarian assistance organization dedicated to improving the quality of life and expanding opportunities for children, who, as a result of the circumstances of their birth, have been denied access to educational, social, economic and civil rights. The foundation has a particular emphasis on programs in Asia."

Vietnamese Adoptee Network (VAN) {www.van-online.org}
VAN is a national support organization for Vietnamese adoptees and their families

World Association for Children and Parents (WACAP) {www.wacap.org}
WACAP is one of the largest and most experienced international non profit adoption and child assistance agencies in the United States. Founded in 1976 by a group of adoptive parents, WACAP places children with adoptive families and provides medical, educational, and financial aid to children in need.

BONE MARROW WEB SITES

National Marrow Donor Program (NMDP) {www.marrow.org}
The NMDP is the international leader in facilitating unrelated marrow and blood stem cell transplantation.

Matchmaker Bone Marrow Project
{www.mavinfoundation.org/matchmaker.html}
MAVIN Foundation's Matchmaker Bone Marrow Project is the only national bone marrow program dedicated to mixed race donor recruitment and education.

GRANT-MAKING FOUNDATIONS

K & F Baxter Family Foundation
{www. kfbaxterfoundation.org}
Since 1997, the K & F Baxter Family Foundation has made nearly $750,000 in grants to support the multiracial community.

Contributor Bios

Devon Alisa Abdallah, a native of the Pacific Northwest, is of Lebanese and European descent. Devon is a community activist and a founding member of the Arab American Community Coalition, an alliance of organizations and individuals in the Greater Seattle area. Currently, she works as a Program Coordinator at International Community Health Services, a clinic that serves Asian and Pacific Islander communities. Devon holds a graduate degree from the London School of Economics and has traveled extensively.

James A. Banks is Russell F. Stark University Professor and Director of the Center for Multicultural Education at the University of Washington, Seattle. His books include *Teaching Strategies for Ethnic Studies*, *Educating Citizens in a Multicultural Society*, the *Handbook of Research on Multicultural Education*, and *Diversity and Citizenship Education: Global Perspectives*. Professor Banks is a member of the Board on Children, Youth, and Families of the National Research Council, the Institute of Medicine of the National Academy of Sciences, and of the National Academy of Education.

Lillian Comas-Díaz, the senior editor of *Women of Color: Integrating Ethnicity and Gender in Psychotherapy* (Guilford) and of *Clinical Guidelines in Cross-Cultural Mental Health* (Wiley), has written extensively on culture, race, ethnicity, and gender. A practicing clinical psychologist, writer, and scholar, Lillian explores the relationship of oppression, resilience, and liberation. A mixed race Puerto Rican, she lives with her Danish-American-Cherokee husband in Washington, D.C.

Susan Soon-keum Cox, adopted from Korea in 1956, has been an adoption professional since 1978. She has directed heritage camps, motherland tours to Korea, and was founder of the International Gathering of Korean Adoptees. Ms. Cox is a member of The Hague Special Commission on Intercountry Adoption, and was appointed to the first White House Commission on Asian and Pacific Islanders. She is a nationally recognized presenter and editor of *Voices from Another Place*.

Sheila Chung is Director of the Bay Area Immigrant Rights Coalition, and former Executive Director of Hapa Issues Forum. She graduated from the University of California at Berkeley, where she received a B.A. with high honors in International Politics and first got involved in the multiracial movement. Currently, Sheila is a board member of the Japantown Task Force, and a fellow in Emerge, a political training program for Bay Area women Democrats. Sheila is the daughter of Korean and Argentine immigrants.

Heather Dalmage, Associate Professor of Sociology and Director of the Mansfield Institute for Social Justice at Roosevelt University in Chicago, is the author of *Tripping on the Color Line: Black-White Multiracial Families in a Racially Divided World* (Rutgers University Press, 2000), and editor of *The Politics of Multiracialism: Rethinking Race in the U.S.* (SUNY Press, forthcoming). She has published numerous articles including, "Factors of Integration: The Guatemalan Experience in Chicago," "Teaching Cultural Capital as Rules and Resistance," and, "Mama Are You Brown: Multiracial Families and the Color Line."

Wei Ming Dariotis is Assistant Professor of Asian American Studies at San Francisco State University. She specializes in Asian Americans of mixed heritage, and is the Facilitator of the SF Chapter of Hapa Issues Forum, and Faculty Advisor to SFSU's Hapa Club and Women's Center. She is working on several projects relating to mixed heritage identity, including an anthology (co-edited with Erin O'Brien), *Bi Bi Grrrls: Bisexual/Biracial Women Speak Out*; a video project (with Daniel Morii Schwinn), "American Hapa: A New GenerAsian;" a book on Hapa artists, titled, *Hapa Culture: Creating Community*; and a novel featuring a Bisexual Hapa vampire protagonist, *Lydia: Hapa Vampyre*.

Juanita Dimas is a licensed clinical/community psychologist, with a specialization in working with diverse populations, and in researching cultural factors related to health and mental health. Her dissertation was the first multivariate, empirical model of children of inter-ethnic families, and the largest empirical sample of such a population. Dr. Dimas earned her Ph.D. in Clinical Psychology from the University of California, Berkeley, and served her clinical internship and postdoctoral fellowship at the University of California, San Francisco, Public Service and Minority Cluster, based at San Francisco General Hospital. She is a Chicana and Irish American mix.

Ramona E. Douglass has been a civil rights activist for nearly three decades. As a multiracial adult of Italian, Native American/Lakota, and mixed African American heritage, she has been a part of the multiracial movement in America since its inception. As a U.S. Department of Commerce federal appointee to the 2000 Census Advisory Committee in Washington, D.C., since 1995 she has consistently represented multiracial community interests before Congress, the national media, and the Executive Office of the President. She has been a part of the Association of MultiEthnic Americans (AMEA) board of directors since its founding in 1988, serving in the capacities of vice president (1988-1994), president (1994-1999), and currently director of media and public relations. Currently, she is a senior sales manager and corporate trainer for a medical manufacturing company in the San Fernando Valley.

Peony Fhagen Smith is a multiracial (European American and something other than European American) monocultural (Jewish American) mother of two young children (three years and 16 months) who resides in Needham, Massachusetts with her husband. She recently received her doctorate in Developmental Psychology in August 2002 and has taught college level psychology courses for the past three years at Simmons College and Wellesley College. She has just recently decided to leave academia in pursuit of a nonacademic career.

Pearl Fuyo Gaskins is a journalist and the author of *What Are You? Voices of Mixed-Race Young People* (Henry Holt, 1999). The book was named an American Library Association Best Book for Young Adults, a Booklist Editors' Choice, a Notable Social Studies Trade Book for Young People, and a Bank Street College of Education Best Children's Book. Ms. Gaskins' mother is Japanese American and her late father was European American.

Christine C. Iijima Hall received her Ph.D. in social psychology from UCLA. Currently, she is the Director of Employee Services for the Maricopa Community College District. Prior to this, she was with Arizona State University and the American Psychological Association. Dr. Hall has authored numerous book chapters and journal articles on multiracial identity, ethnic women and body image. Her dissertation research was one of the first studies done on biracial identity in the United States.

Velina Hasu Houston is an internationally acclaimed multi-genre author of plays, film and television, poetry, and cultural criticism. Producers of her plays (12 commissions) include Pittsburgh Public Theatre, The Globe Theatres, Manhattan Theatre Club, Sacramento Theatre Company, George Street Playhouse, Japan Society, Negro Ensemble Company, and others. For film and TV, she has written for Columbia Pictures, Sidney Poitier, PBS, and others. Her honors include: Japan Foundation fellow, Rockefeller Foundation fellow (twice), James Zumberge Research and Innovation Fund fellow (thrice), Remy Martin Screenwriting Award, National Japanese American Historical Society Woman of Merit, and others. She is associate professor, director of playwriting, and resident playwright at USC's School of Theatre. For over a decade, she taught the legendary Advanced 434 Screenwriting Workshop at UCLA's School of Theater, Film, and Television.

Donna Jackson's book, *Does Anybody Else Look Like Me? A Parent's Guide to Raising Multiracial Children*, about parenting children in mixed race families from pre-school through college will be published by Perseus Publishing in 2003. She is also the author of *How to Make the World a Better Place for Women* (Hyperion, 1992), and has written on psychology/family life issues for national magazines including *My Generation*, *Modern Maturity*, *Redbook*, *Baby Talk*, *New Woman*, and *Working Mother*. She is a graduate of Duke University and the Radcliffe Publishing Procedures program, and resides with her Japanese American husband and two biracial children in Maryland.

Nicholas A. Jones is a Sociology Ph.D. student at the University of Michigan and a research analyst at the U.S. Census Bureau. Nicholas' research focuses on the identities and experiences of children and young adults of racially mixed parentage. Currently, he is analyzing race reporting patterns and demographic characteristics of multiracial children and interracial families from Census 2000 to shed light on the complexities and challenges associated with identifying the multiracial population in the United States.

Matt Kelley is the founder, president, and CEO of MAVIN Foundation, the nation's leading organization dedicated to multiracial youth and families. In 1998, as a 19-year-old freshman at Wesleyan University, he founded *MAVIN* magazine, the only internationally acclaimed magazine celebrating multiracial and transracially adopted young people. For his unique approach to race and diversity issues, he has been featured in over 300 print and television features, and is the recipient of numerous awards. He also serves as vice president of the Association of MultiEthnic Americans (AMEA). Matt lives in Seattle.

Robin A. LaDue is a clinical psychologist in private practice in Renton, Washington. She is also affiliated with the Dept. of Psychiatry and Behavioral Sciences and the Native American Center for Excellence at the University of Washington. She has been involved in research, clinical services, and community education in the field of Fetal Alcohol Syndrome for the past 20 years. Her work in this area has included longitudinal studies of adolescents and adults with FAS as well as forensic consultation, evaluations, therapy, and expert testimony. Dr. Ladue has lectured extensively on an international basis in the areas of FAS and Native American mental health issues. She specializes in treating emotional trauma and recovery from addictions along with working in the field of Community Protection. She is the author of the award winning video/book series *Journey Through the Healing Circle* and is enrolled with the Cowlitz Indian tribe of Washington. She resides in Seattle, Washington with her husband, Bruce Harmon, and her three cats, Mo, Gracie, and Bug.

Kevin Maillard is a member of the Seminole Nation of Oklahoma. He received his B. A. from Duke University, a M. A. degree in Philosophy from the University of Michigan, J.D. from the University of Pennsylvania, and his Ph.D. from the University of Michigan. His research interests include Federal Indian Law, family law, racial classification and identity in American Indians, transracial adoption, and law and literature. He has worked at Hughes Hubbard & Reed, NY, NY as a summer associate and at the Lawrenceville School, NJ, as a Master of English and Ethics.

Gina E. Miranda is a faculty member in the School of Social Service Administration at the University of Chicago and an affiliate of the Center for the Study of Race, Politics, and Culture. Her areas of interest for teaching and research include race and child welfare, transracial adoption, multiracial identity, interpretive methodology, and culturally relevant social work practice and education. She has practiced social work in the areas of child welfare and child protective services, and is currently compiling a series of interviews with mixed race transracial adoptees to explore factors that affect the identity work among this population. She is herself both transracially adopted and of Black-White mixed heritage.

Mary Murchison-Edwords, an African American, has been interracially married for 23 years and is the mother of two mixed race teenage daughters. She is the former director of the Interracial Club of Buffalo, a support group and social organization for interracial couples, mixed race people, and families who have adopted transracially and/or internationally. A film buff, she has done extensive research for her upcoming book *Reel Color: A History of Interracial, Intercultural, and Interethnic Relationships in Movies and Television.* She has an M.A. degree in psychology from the United States International University.

Jennifer Mariko Pang is a Seattle native who currently works at the Fred Hutchinson Cancer Research Center as a Research Technician. She received her B.A. in biochemistry at Occidental College in Los Angeles where she participated in immunology research and sang in the college glee club.

Matthew Akio Pang is a student at Tulane University in New Orleans and an Electrical Engineering major. Pang was undergraduate Student Body President at Tulane from 2002-2003. He plans on going to law school.

Valerie Ooka Pang is a professor of Teacher Education at San Diego State University. Her research interests are caring-centered multicultural education, teacher prejudice reduction, ethnic identity development, and social studies. She has published in journals like *Harvard Educational Review*, *The Journal of Teacher Education*, and *The Kappan*.

Maria P. P. Root is a psychologist in a private practice and a leading scholar on multiracial identity. She has edited two award-winning books, *Racially Mixed in America* (1992) and *The Multiracial Experience: Racial Borders as the New Frontier* (1996). She has also published a widely distributed "Bill of Rights for Racially Mixed People" as well as her newest book, *Love's Revolution: Interracial Marriage* (2001).

Rosa Hernández Sheets is an Associate Professor at Texas Tech University. She is co-editor of *Starting Small: Teaching Tolerance in Preschool and the Early Grades* (Teaching Tolerance Project, 1997) and senior editor of *Racial and Ethnic Identity in School Practices: Aspects of Human Development* (Erlbaum, 1999). Her current research examines effective preparation of teachers of color and explores the ways successful teachers recognize, interpret, and respond to children's cultural displays of competency resulting from their cultural socialization process.

Karen Suyemoto is an Assistant Professor in Psychology and Asian American Studies at the University of Massachusetts, Boston, where she teaches classes related to psychology and race, culture, and gender. She has presented and published on multiracial identity and issues, particularly identity in multiracial Japanese European Americans. Her current interests include racial and ethnic identities in multiracial and Asian American individuals and groups, and the psychological and educational needs of Asian American urban students.

Amy Symens Smith is a research analyst at the U.S. Census Bureau in Washington, D.C., and a Sociology Ph.D. student at Bowling Green State University, Bowling Green, Ohio. Amy produces annual population estimates by age, sex, race, and Hispanic origin for the U.S. Her research focuses on the two or more races population and their demographic characteristics. She is particularly interested in the race reporting patterns for children and parents in interracial families.

Cathy Tashiro is an assistant professor in the nursing program of the University of Washington, Tacoma campus. In addition to her degrees in the health sciences, she has a B.A. in Oriental studies from Columbia University and a doctorate in sociology from the University of California, San Francisco. Cathy's doctoral dissertation examined dimensions of identity for older mixed African Americans and Asian Americans, and she has published on health and people of mixed race.

Suni Tolton received a B. A. in sociology and certificate in criminology and corrections from the University of Utah and a MSW from the University of Washington in Seattle. She has enjoyed working with recent immigrant Asian, Pacific Islander, African American, and East African youth in community-based settings and is interested in health and acculturation issues. Suni was born in Christchurch, New Zealand and raised in Anchorage, Alaska.

Shelly Tomishima is a licensed psychologist. She received her B.A. and M.A. from San José State University in psychology and her Ph.D. from the University of Utah in counseling psychology. She clinically works with children and is interested in working with autistic and abused children. She is also interested in racism, multicultural counseling, and biracial identity. She teaches at the University of Phoenix, Hawai'i Campus. Her father is Japanese and her mother is Irish.

Kendra Wallace's research and publications explore topics of diversity, schooling, and issues related to identity and culture in teaching and learning. She teaches courses at both the undergraduate and graduate level on the social foundations of education, qualitative research methods, racial, ethnic, and gender diversity in schools, and sociocultural approaches to human learning and cognition.

Charmaine Leitzau Wijeyesinghe has consulted in social justice and organizational development since 1985. Her professional background includes 13 years in higher education administration, and program development for the National Conference of Community and Justice, based in NYC. She has taught undergraduate and graduate education courses at the University of Massachusetts in Amherst. She writes and presents conference seminars on multiracial identity and the application of racial identity theory in conflict resolution strategies.

Melissa Wolfe has worked in the child welfare field for six years. She is pursuing a M. A. degree in technical communication from the University of Washington and has completed academic programs in journalism, photography, and Web development. She is currently creating a Web-based resource for teenagers transitioning out of foster care in the King County, Washington region. She also serves with the Asian American Journalists Association Seattle chapter and volunteers to support at-risk youth and children affected by HIV/AIDS.

References

A Conceptual Framework of Identity Formation in a Society of Multiple Cultures: Applying Theory to Practice. Seattle: Casey Family Programs, 2000.

Abadio-Clottey, A. and K. Clottey. *Beyond Fear: Twelve Spiritual Keys to Racial Healing*. Tiburon, CA: H. J. Kramer, 1998.

Alba, R. D. *Ethnic Identity: The Transformation of White America*. New Haven, CT: Yale University Press, 1990.

Algarín, M. and M. Piñero, ed. *Nuyorican Poetry: An Anthology of Puerto Rican Words and Feelings*. New York: William Morrow & Co., 1975.

"All Mixed Up." Salon.com. 14 February 2000. "http://dir.salon.com/news/feature/2000/02/14/mixed_race/index.html"

Allman, K. M. "(Un)Natural Boundaries: Mixed Race, Gender, and Sexuality" *The Multiracial Experience: Racial Borders as the New Frontier*. Ed. M. P. P. Root. Thousand Oaks, CA: Sage Publications, 1996. 277-290.

Almeida, Personal Interview. 1993.

Anthony, E. J. and B. J. Cohler, ed. *The Invulnerable Child*. New York: The Guilford Press, 1987.

"Ancestry: Religious Affiliations of Arab Americans." *Arab American Institute*. 2002. "http://www.aaiusa.org"

Arab American Institute Website. 2002. *Arab American Institute*. "http://www.aaiusa.org"

Arce, C. H., E. Murguia, and W. P. Frisbie. "Phenotype and Life Chances Among Chicanos." *Hispanic Journal of Behavioral Sciences* 9 (1987): 19-32.

Augenbraum, H. and I. Stavens. *Growing Up Latino: Memoirs and Stories*. New York: Houghton Mifflin Co, 1993.

Baker, A., D. Olson and C. Mincer. *The WAY to Work: An Independent Living/Aftercare Program for High-Risk Youth*. Washington, DC: CWLA Press, 2000.

Ball, E. *Slaves in the Family*. New York: Farrar, Straus, & Giroux, 1998.

Banks, J. A. *Diversity and Citizenship Education: Global Perspectives*. San Fransisco: JosseyBass, 2004.

Barbell, K. and M. Freundlich. "Foster Care Today." *Casey Family Programs National Center for Resource Family Support*. Washington, DC, 2001. "http://www.casey.org/cnc/policy_issues/foster_care_today_info.htm"

Barbujani, G., A. Magggini, E. Minch, and L. L. Cavalli-Sforza. "An Apportionment of Human DNA Diversity." *Proceedings of the National Academy of Sciences of the United States of America* 94-9 (1997): 4516-4519.

Begg, E. *The Cult of the Black Virgin*. London: Arkana/Penguin Books, 1985.

Bernal, M. E. and G. P. Knight, ed. *Ethnic Identity: Formation and Transmission Among Hispanics and Other Minorities*. New York: State University of New York Press, 1993.

Bernal, M. E., G. P. Knight, C. A. Garza, K. A. Ocampo, and M. K. Cota. "The Development of Ethnic Identity in Mexican-American Children." *Hispanic Journal of Behavioral Sciences* 12 (1990): 3-24.

Blome, W. "What Happens to Foster Kids: Educational Experiences of a Random Sample of Foster Care Youth and a Match Group of Non-Foster Care Youth." *Child and Adolescent Social Work Journal* 4(1) (1997). 41-53.

Borrero, A. M. "Honor our African Roots." *Hispanic Magazine*. April 2000. "http://www.hispaniconline.com/magazine/2000/apr/Forum/index.html"

Bowman, J. E. and R. F. Murray. *Genetic Variation and Disorders in Peoples of African Origin*. Baltimore: The Johns Hopkins University Press, 1990.

Boykin, A. W. and F. D. Toms. "Black Child Socialization: a Conceptual Framework." *Black Children: Social, Educational and Parental Environments*. Eds. H. P. McAdoo and J. L. McAdoo. Newbury, CA: Sage, 1985. 33-51.

Brandell, J. B. "Treatment of the Biracial Child: Theoretical and Clinical Issues." *Journal of Multicultural Counseling and Development* 16(4) (1988): 176-187.

Brooks, D., A. Bussiere, R. P. Barth and G. Patterson. *Adoption and Race: Implementing the Multiethnic Placement Act of 1994 and the Interethnic Adoption Provisions*. San Francisco: Stuart Foundations, 1997.

Brooks, J., ed. *Confounding the Color Line*. Lincoln, NE: University of Nebraska Press, 2002.

Brown, N. G. and R. E. Douglass. "Making the Invisible Visible: The Growth of Community Network Organizations." *The Multiracial Experience: Racial Borders as the New Frontier*. Ed. M. P. P. Root. Thousand Oaks, CA: Sage, 1996. 323-340.

Brown, P. M. "Biracial Identity and Social Marginality." *Child and Social Work Journal* 7(4) (1990): 319-337.

Bugawan, T. L., J. D. Chang, W. Klitz, and H. A. Erlich. "PCR/Oligonucleotide Probe Typing of HLA Class II Alleles in a Filipino Population Reveals an Unusual Distribution of HLA Haplotypes." *American Journal of Human Genetics* 54(2) (1994): 331-340.

Buriel, R. "Integration with Traditional Mexican-American Culture and Sociocultural Adjustment." Chicano Psychology. Ed. Martinez. Littleton, CO: Academic Press, Inc., 1984.

Carey, M., (2002). Interview. *The Larry King Show*. CNN, 19 December 2002.

Castillo, A. *Massacre of the Dreamers: Essays on Xicanisma*. New York: Penguin, 1995.

Castillo, A., ed. *Goddess of the Americas/La Diosa de las Américas: Writings on the Virgin of Guadalupe.* New York: Riverhead Books, 1996.

Chun, C. and S. Sue. "Mental Health Issues Concerning Asian Pacific American Children." *Struggling To Be Heard: The Unmet Needs of Asian Pacific American Children.* Eds. V. O. Pang and L. L. Cheng. New York: SUNY Press, 1998. 75-87.

Chung, C. Personal Interview. 23 May 2002.

Collins, J. W. and R. J. David. "Race and Birthweight in Biracial Infants." *American Journal of Public Health,* 83(8) (1993): 1125-1129.

Comas-Díaz, L. "Puerto Rican Women's Cross Cultural Transitions: Developmental and Clinical Implications." *The Psychosocial Development of Puerto Rican Women.* Eds. C. G. Coll and M. L. Mattei. New York: Praeger, 1989. 166-199.

Comas-Díaz, L. "LatiNegra: Mental Health Needs of African Latinas." *Journal of Feminist Family Therapy* 5 (1994): 35-74.

Comas-Díaz, L. "The Black Madonna: The Psychospiritual Feminism of Guadalupe, Kali and Monserrat." *Feminist Family: Empowerment and Social Location.* Eds. L. Silvestein and T. J. Goodrich. Washington, DC: American Psychological Association, in press.

Comas-Díaz, L., A. Arroyo and J. C. Lovelace, "Enriching Self-Concept Through a Puerto Rican Cultural Awareness Program." *Personnel and Guidance Journal* 60(5) (1982): 306-308.

Comas-Díaz, L. and M. A. Jansen. "Global Conflict and Violence Against Women." *Peace and Conflict: Journal of Peace Psychology* 1 (1995): 315-331.

Comas-Díaz, L., M. B. Lykes and R. Alarcón. "Ethnic Conflict and Psychology of Liberation in Guatemala, Perú and Puerto Rico." *American Psychologist* 53(7) (1998): 778-792.

Cross, W. E. "Discovering the Black Referent: The Psychology of Black Liberation." *Beyond Black and White: An Alternative America.* Eds. V. J. Dixon and B. G. Foster. Boston: Little Brown, 1971. 96-110.

Cross, W. E. *Shades of Black: Diversity in African American Identity.* Philadelphia: Temple University Press, 1991.

Crumbley, J. *Transracial Adoption and Foster Care: Practice Issues for Professionals.* Washington, DC: CWLA Press, 1999.

Curtis, P. A., G. Dale Jr. and J. C. Kendall, ed. *The Foster Care Crisis: Translating Research into Policy and Practice.* Lincoln, NE: University of Nebraska Press, 1999. 84.

Dalmage, H. *Tripping on the Color Line: Black-White Multiracial Families in a Racially Divided World.* New Brunswick, NJ: Rutgers University Press, 2000.

Daniel, G. R. "Passers and Pluralists: Subverting the Racial Divide." *Racially Mixed People in America.* Ed. Maria P. P. Root. Newbury Park, CA: Sage, 1992. 304-321.

Davis, F. J. *Who is Black? One Nation's Definition.* University Park, PA: Pennsylvania State University Press, 1991.

Day, D. *The Adoption of Black Children.* Lanham, MA: Lexington Books, 1979.

Deloria, V. *Custer Died for Your Sins.* Norman, OK: University of Oklahoma Press, 1988.

Del Valle, M. Personal Interview, 1993.

Del Valle, M. "Acculturation, Sex Roles and Racial Definitions of Puerto Rican College Students in Puerto Rico and the United States." Diss. University of Massachusetts, 1989.

Derman-Sparks, L., C. T. Higa and B. Sparks. "Children, Race and Racism: How Race Awareness Develops." *Bulletin* 11(3 & 4) (1980): 8.

Dimas, J. M. "Cultural Behavior and Ethnic Identity in Children of Interethnic Families: A Structural Family Model." In press.

Durazo, C. Personal Interview, 13 May 2002.

Dyson, M. E. "Essentialism and the Complexities of Racial Identity." *Multiculturalism: A Critical Reader.* Ed. D. T. Goldberg. Cambridge, MA: Blackwell Press, 1994.

Curtis, P. A., G. Dale, Jr. and J. C. Kendall, ed. *The Foster Care Crisis: Translating Research into Policy and Practice.* Lincoln, NE: University of Nebraska Press, 1999.

Erikson, E. H. "Identity and the Life Cycle: Selected Papers." *Psychological Issues Monograph Series* 1(1) (1959).

Evans, B. *Youth in Foster Care: The Shortcomings of Child Protection Services.* New York: Garland Publishing Inc., 1997.

Favor, J. M. *Authentic Blackness.* Durham, NC: Duke University Press, 1999.

Fears, D. "People of Color Who Never Felt They Were Black: Racial Label Surprises Many Latino Immigrants." *The Washington Post* 26 December 2002: sec A01.

Ferrante, J. *Sociology in a Global Perspective* (4th ed.). Belmont, CA: Wadsworth Publishing, 2001.

Firestein, B. A. ed. *Bisexuality: The Psychology and Politics of an Invisible Minority.* Thousand Oaks, CA: Sage Publications, 1996.

Flavell, J. H., P. H. Miller and S. A. Miller. *Cognitive Development* (3rd ed.). Englewood Cliffs, NJ: Prentice Hall, 1993.

Flores, C. Personal Interview, 5 May 2002.

Fogg-Davis, H. *The Ethics of Transracial Adoption.* Ithaca, NY: Cornell University Press, 2002.

Folaron, G. and P. M. Hess. "Placement Considerations for Children of Mixed African American and Caucasian Parentage." *Child Welfare* 72(2) (1993): 113-125.

Fong, R. and N. Mokuau. "Not Simply 'Asian Americans': Periodical Literature Review on Asians and Pacific Islanders." *Social Work* 39 (1994): 298-305.

Frank, R. "The Misuse of Biology in Demographic Research on Racial/Ethnic Differences: A Reply to Van Den Oord and Rowe." *Demography* 38(4) (2001): 563-567.

Franklin, A. J. and N. Boyd-Franklin. "A Psychoeducational Perspective on Black Parenting." *Black Children.* Eds. H. McAdoo and J. McAdoo. Beverly Hills, CA: Sage, 1985.

Frisby, M. K. "Black, White, Other." *Emerge* 7(3) (1996): 48-57.

Fulbeck, K. *Paper Bullets: A Fictional Autobiography.* Seattle: University of Washington Press, 2001.

Galland, C. *Longing for Darkness: Tara and the Black Madonna.* New York: Compass/Penguin Press, 1990.

Garmezy, N. "Children Under Stress: Perspectives or Antecedents and Correlates of Vulnerability and Resistance to Psychopathology." *Further Explorations in Personality.* Eds. A. Robin, J. Arnoff, A. Barclay, and R. Zucker. New York: Wiley, 1980.

Gaskins, P. *What Are You? Voices of Mixed-Race Young People.* New York: Henry Holt and Company, 1999.

Gee, J. P. *Social Linguistics and Literacies: Ideologies in Discourses.* New York: Falmer, 1990. 142.

Gee, J. P. *The Social Mind: Language, Ideology and Social Practice.* New York: Bergin and Garvey, 1992.

Geng, L. et. al. "Determination of HLA Class II Alleles by Genotyping in a Manchu Population in the Northern Part of China and its Relationship with Han and Japanese Populations." *Tissue Antigens* 46(2) (1995): 111-116.

Gibb, J. T. "Identity and Marginality: Issues in the Treatment of Biracial Adolescents." *American Orthopsychiatric Association* 57(2) (1987): 265-278.

Gilles, T. and J. Kroll. *Barriers to Same Race Placement.* North American Council on Adoptable Children, April 1991. http://www.nysccc.org/T-Rarts/Barriers.html

Gill, O. and B. Jackson. *Adoption and Race: Black, Asian, and Mixed Race Children in Families.* New York: St. Martin's Press, 1983.

Ginorio, A. B. "A Study of Racial Perception in Puerto Rico." Diss. University of Puerto Rico, 1971.

Goldberg, D. *Racial Subjects: Writing on Race in America.* New York: Routledge, 1997.

Gonzalez-Wippler, M. *Santería: The Religion.* New York: Harmony Books, 1989.

Gordon-Reed, A. *Thomas Jefferson and Sally Hemings: An American Controversy.* Charlottesville, VA: University Press of Virginia, 1997.

Gotanda, N. "A Critique of 'Our Constitution is Color-Blind.'" *Critical Race Theory.* Eds. K. Crenshaw et. al. New York: New York University Press, 1995.

Graham, S. Personal Interviews. 1994.

Graves, J. L. *The Emperor's New Clothes: Biological Theories of Race at the Millennium.* New Brunswick, NJ: Rutgers University Press, 2001.

Greene, B. "Human Diversity in Clinical Psychology: Lesbians and Gay Sexual Orientations." *The Clinical Psychologist* 46 (1993): 74-82.

Greene, B. "Still Here: A Perspective on Psychotherapy with African American Women." *New Directions in Feminist Psychology: Practice, Theory and Research.* Eds. J. Chrisler and D. Howard. New York: Springer, 1992. 13-25.

Greene, B. "What Has Gone Before: The Legacy of Racism and Sexism in the Lives of Black Mothers and Daughters." *Women & Therapy* 9 (1990): 207-230.

Grieco, E. M. and R. C. Cassidy. U.S. Census Bureau: "Overview of Race and Hispanic Origin: 2000." Census Brief Series C2KBR/01-1, March 2001. "www.census.gov/prod/2001pubs/c2kbr01-1.pdf"

Grow, L. J., and D. Shapiro. "Black Children-White Parents: A Study of Transracial Adoption." Washington, DC: Child Welfare League of America, 1974.

Haizlip, S. T. *The Sweeter the Juice: A Family Memoir in Black and White.* New York: Simon and Schuster, 1994.

Hall, C. C. I. "Asian Eyes, Body Image and Eating Disorders of Asian and Asian American Women." *Eating Disorders* 8(17) (1995).

Hall, C. "The Ethnic Identity of Racially Mixed People: A Study of Black-Japanese." Diss. University of California, Los Angeles, 1980.

Hall, C. C. I. and T. C. Turner. "The Diversity of Biracial Individuals: Asian-White and Asian-Minority Biracial Identity." *The Sum of Our Parts: Mixed Heritage Asian Americans.* Eds. T. Williams- León and C. L. Nakashima. Philadelphia: Temple University Press, 2001.

Hanna, J. M. "Migration and Acculturation Among Samoans: Some Sources of Stress and Support." *Social Science Medicine* 46(10) (1998): 1325-1336.

Hardiman, R. W. "Identity Development: A Process Oriented Model for Describing the Racial Consciousness of White Americans." Diss. University of Massachusetts, Amherst, 1982.

Hardiman, R. and B. W. Jackson. "Racial Identity Development: Understanding Racial Dynamics in College Classrooms and on Campus." *Promoting Diversity in College Classrooms: Innovative Responses for the Curriculum, Faculty, and Iinstitutions.* Ed. M. Adams. San Francisco: Jossey-Bass, 1992.

Harlow, C. W. "Profile of Jail Inmates 1996." Washington, DC: U.S. Department of Justice, Bureau of Justice Statistics, 1998.

Harrison, A. O. et. al. "Family Ecologies of Ethnic Minority Children." *Child Development* 61 (1990): 347-362.

Harter, S. "The Development of Self-Representations." *Handbook of Child Psychology: Vol. 3. Social, Emotional, and Personality Development.* Eds. W. Damon and N. Eisenberg. New York: Wiley, 1998. 553-617.

Hartup, W. W. "The Company They Keep: Friendships and Their Developmental Significance." *Child Development* 67 (1996): 1-13.

Heath, S. B. and M. W. McLaughlin, ed. *Identity and Inner-City Youth: Beyond Ethnicity and Gender.* New York: Teachers College Press, 1993.

Heck, K. E., J. D. Parker, C. J. McKendry and K. C. Schoendorf. "Multiple-Race Mothers on the California Birth Certificate, 2000." *Ethnicity & Disease* 11(4) (2001): 626-632.

Helms, J. E. *Black and White Racial Identity: Theory, Research, and Practice.* New York: Greenwood Press, 1990.

Hurtado, S., J. Milem, A. Clayton-Pederson and W. Allen. "Enhancing Campus Climates for Racial/Ethnic Diversity: Educational Policy and Practice." *The Review of Higher Education* 21(3) (1998): 279-302.

Ignatiev, N. *How the Irish Became White.* New York: Routledge, 1995.

"It's My Life: Summary of a Framework for Youth Transitioning from Foster Care to Successful Adulthood." Seattle: Casey Family Programs, 2001.

Jackson, B. W. *The Function of a Theory of Black Identity Development in Achieving Relevance in Education for Black Students.* Diss. University of Massachusetts, Amherst, 1976.

Jacobs, J. H. "Identity Development in Biracial Children." *Racially Mixed People in America.* Ed. Maria P. P. Root. Thousand Oaks, CA.: Sage Publications, 1992. 190-206.

Jacobson, M. F. *Whiteness of a Different Color: European Immigrants and the Alchemy of Race.* Cambridge, MA: Harvard University Press, 1998.

Jaimes, M. A., "Some Kind of Indian: On Race, Eugenics and Mixed-Bloods." *American Mixed Race.* Ed. N. Zack. Lanham, MD: Rowman and Littlefield, 1990.

Jaret, C. and D. C. Reitzes. "The Importance of Racial-Ethnic Identity and Social Setting for Blacks, Whites, and Multiracials." *Sociological Perspectives* 42(4) (1999).

Jaworowski, S. "Hawaiian Demographic Data: 'Ehia Kanaka Maoli?'" Legislative Reference Bureau Report. 1998. "http://www.hawaii.gov/lrb/study.html"

John, J. *Black Baby White Hands: A View From the Crib.* Silver Spring, MD: Soul Water Publishing, 2002.

Johnson, R. C. "Offspring of Cross-Race and Cross-Ethnic Marriages in Hawai'i." *Racially Mixed People in America.* Ed. M. P. P. Root. Newbury Park, CA: Sage, 1992. 239-249.

Jones, N. A. and A. S. Smith. U. S. Census Bureau: "The Two or More Races Population: 2000." Census 2000 Brief Series C2KBR/01-6, 2001. "http://www.census.gov/prod/2001pubs/c2kbr01-6.pdf"

Jones, R. S. "The End of Africanity?: The Bi-racial Assault on Blackness." *The Western Journal of Black Studies* 18(4) (1994): 201-210.

Jones, V. E. "A Rich Sense of Self." *The Boston Globe* 29 February 2000: A1, A7.

Jorge, A. "The Black Puerto Rican Woman in Contemporary American Society." *The Puerto Rican Woman.* Ed. E. Acosta-Belén. New York: Praeger, 1979. 134-141.

Kanuha, V. "Compounding the Triple Jeopardy: Battering in Lesbian of Color Relationships." *Therapy & Women* 9 (1990): 169-184.

Katz, W. *Black Indians: A Hidden Heritage.* New York: Atheneum, 1986.

Kerwin, C., J. G. Ponterotto, B. L. Jackson and A. Harris. "Racial Identity in Biracial Children: A Qualitative Investigation." *Journal of Counseling Psychology* 40(2) (1993): 221-231.

Kich, G. "The Developmental Process of Asserting a Biracial, Bicultural Identity." *Racially Mixed People in America.* Ed. M. P. P. Root. Newbury Park, CA: Sage, 1992. 304-321.

King, Jr., M. L. *Letter From the Birmingham Jail.* New York: HarperCollins, 1962/1994: Original work published 1963.

Klor de Alva, J. J. "The Invention of Ethnic Origins and the Negotiation of Latino Identity, 1969-1981." *Challenging Fronteras: Structuring Latina and Latino Lives in the U.S.* Eds. M. Romero, P. Hondagneu-Sotelo, and V. Ortiz. New York: Routledge, 1997. 55-74.

Knipe, J. and J. Warren. *Youth Work Resources: Foster Youth Share Their Ideas for Change.* Washington, DC: CWLA Press, 1999.

Krieger, N. "Shades of Difference: Theoretical Underpinnings of the Medical Controversy on Black/White Differences in the United States, 1830-1870." *International Journal of Health Services* 17(2) (1987): 259-278.

Ladner, J. A. *Mixed Families.* Garden City, NY: Anchor Press, 1977.

Lave, J. and E. Wenger. *Situated Learning: Legitimate Peripheral Participation.* Cambridge, UK: Cambridge University Press, 1990.

Leadership Challenges and Opportunities: Asian American and Pacific Islander Woman's Lens. Online: Asian Pacific American Women's Leadership Institute. 2003. "http://www.apawli.org/report2/5_yr_report_layout.pdf"

Lee, E. and N. Mokuau. "Meeting the Mental Health Needs of Asian and Pacific Islander Americans." *Cultural Diversity Series.* Alexandria, VA: National Technical Assistance Center for State Mental Health Planning, 2002.

Leon, N. *Las Castas de Mexico Colonial o Nueva España. (The Castes from Colonial Mexico or New Spain).* Mexico City: Departamento de Antropología Anatómica. Talleres Gráficos del Museo Nacional de Arqueología, Historia y Etnografía, 1924.

Leonard, K. "California's Punjabi Mexican Americans: Ethnic Choices Made by the Descendants of Punjabi Pioneers and their Mexican Wives." *The World & I* 4(5), May 1989.

Lindelof, B. "In Yuba City, Traces Remain of Fading Mexican-Hindu Culture. *Sacramento Bee* 11 November 1991.

Longres, J. F. "Racism and its Effects on Puerto Rican Continentals." *Social Casework* 55 (1974): 67-75.

Lundbom, A. Personal Interview. 5 November 2002.

Lyles, M. R., A. Yancey, C. Grace and J. H. Carter. "Racial Identity and Self-Esteem: Problems Peculiar to Biracial Children." *Journal of the American Academy of Child Psychiatry* 24(2) (1985): 150-153.

Lynch, E. W. and M. J. Hanson. *Developing Cross-Cultural Competence."* Baltimore, MD: Paul H. Brookes Publishing Co., 1998.

Martinez, C. "Mexican Americans." *Clinical Guidelines in Cross Cultural Mental Health.* Eds. L. Comas-Díaz and E. H. Griffith. New York: Wiley, 1988.

Mass, A. "Interracial Japanese Americans: The Best of Both Worlds or the End of the Japanese Community?" *Racially Mixed People in America.* Ed. M. P. P. Root. Newbury Park, CA: Sage, 1992. 265-279.

McGoldrick, M. and R.Gerson. *Genograms in Family Assessment.* New York: Norton, 1985.

McRoy, R. G. and H. Grape. "Skin Color in Transracial and Inracial Adoptive Placements: Implications for Special Needs Adoptions." *Child Welfare* 78(5) (1983): 673-689.

McRoy, R. G. and L. A. Zurcher. *Transracial and Inracial Adoptees: The Adolescent Years.* Springfield, IL: Charles C. Thomas, 1983.

Miller, R. "The Human Ecology of Multiracial Identity." *Racially Mixed People in America.* Ed. M. P. P. Root. Newbury Park, CA: Sage, 1992.

Miranda, G. E. "Mixed Feelings: Stories of Race, Kinship, and Identity Among Biracial Adoptees." Diss. University of Wisconsin, Madison, 2002.

Mizio, E. "The Impact of Macro Systems on Puerto Rican Families." *The Psychosocial Development of Minority Group Children.* Ed. G. J. Powell. New York: Brunner/Mazel, 1983.

Modleski, T. *Feminism Without Women: Culture and Criticism in a "Postfeminist" Age.* New York: Routledge, 1991.

Montagu, A. *Man's Most Dangerous Myth: The Fallacy of Race.* 6th ed. Walnut Creek, CA: AltaMira Press, 1997.

Morrison, T. *Playing in the Dark: Whiteness and the Literary Imagination.* Cambridge, MD: Harvard University Press, 1992.

Nakashira, C. "An Invisible Monster: The Creation and Denial of Mixed Race People in America." *Racially Mixed People in America.* Ed. M. P. P. Root. Newbury Park, CA: Sage, 1992.

Nash, G. *Forbidden Love: The Secret History of Mixed Race America.* New York: Henry Holt and Co., 1999.

National Multicultural Interpreter Project. (2000). Asian/Pacific Islander Curriculum: Cultural Knowledge and Sensitivity-Lecture Notes. December 2002. "http://www.colorado.edu/slhs/tiem.online/NMIP/5B.pdf"

Normant, L. *Who's Black and Who's Not?: New Ethnicity Raises Provocative Questions About Racial Identity. Ebony* 45(5) (1990).

O'Hearn, C. C., ed. *Half and Half: Writers on Growing up Biracial and Bicultural.* New York: Random House Books, 1998.

Omi, M. and H. Winant. *Racial Formation in the United States: from the 1960s to the 1980s.* New York: Routledge, 1986.

Ota, P. S. Personal Interview. 5 May 2002.

Pact, An Adoption Alliance. *Trainers Guide for Transracial Adoption.* Richmond, CA: Pact Press, 2000.

Pang, V. O. and L. L. Cheng. *Struggling To Be Heard: The Unmet Needs of Asian Pacific American Children.* New York: State University of New York Press, 1998.

Parham, T. A. and J. E. Helms, "Relation of Racial Identity Attitudes to Self-Actualization and Affective States of Black Students." *Journal of Counseling Psychology* 32 (1985), 431-40.

Patton, S. *Birthmarks: Transracial Adoption in Contemporary America.* New York: New York University Press, 2000.

Perez y Mena, A. *Speaking with the Dead: Development of Afro-Latin Religion Among Puerto Ricans in the United States.* New York: AMS Press, 1991.

Perez, C. "The Color Issue: The Apparent Favoritism of Lighter Skin Reverberates Within the Latino Community." *LatinoLA* 26 June 2000. "http://www.latinola.com/story.php?story=127"

Perez v. Sharp (October 1, 1948) 32 Cal.2d 711, 198 P.2d 17.

Phinney, J. S., B. T. Lochner, and R. Murphy. "Ethnic Identity Development and Psychological Adjustment in Adolescence." *Ethnic Issues in Adolescent Mental Health.* Eds. A. R. Stiffman and L. E. Davis. Newbury Park, CA: Sage, 1990. 53-72.

Piaget, J. *The Origins of Intelligence in Children.* M. Cook, Trans. New York: International Universities Press, 1952.

Piper, A. "Passing for White, Passing for Black." *Critical White Studies: Looking Behind the Mirror.* Eds. R. Delgado and J. Stefancic. Philadelphia: Temple University Press, 1997. 426-429.

President's Advisory Commission on Asian American and Pacific Islanders. "Asian Americans and Pacific Islanders: A People Looking Forward. Action for Access and Partnerships in the 21st Century." *Interim Report to the President and the Nation*, 2001.

Ramos Rosado, M. "La Mujer Puertorriqueña Negra: La Otra Cara de la Historia" (The Black Puerto Rican Woman)." *Homines* 10(2) (1986): 491-497.

Rankin, S. *Foster Care in the "Coloured" Community of Durban.* Institute for Social and Economic Research: University of Durban-Westville, 1983.

"Revision to the Standards for the Classification of Federal Data on Race and Ethnicity." *Federal Register* (30 October 1997). "http://www.census.gov/population/www/socdemo/race/Ombdir15.html"

Rhodes, P., ed. *Racial Matching in Fostering: the Challenge to Social Work Practice.* London, England: Avebury Press, 1992.

Rivera, E. *Family Installments: Memories of Growing Up Hispanic.* New York: William Morrow & Co, 1982.

Rodriguez, J. "Guadalupe: The Feminine Face of God." *Goddess of the Americas/La Diosa de las Américas: Writings on the Virgin of Guadalupe.* Ed. A. Castillo. New York: Riverhead Books, 1997.

Roman, N. P. and P. B. Wolfe. "Web of Failure: The Relationship Between Foster Care and Homelessness." *Public Welfare* 55(1995). 4-11.

Romy, C. R. Personal Interview. 12 May 2002.

Root, M. P. P. "A Bill of Rights for Racially Mixed People." *The Multiracial Experience: Racial Borders as the New Frontier.* Ed. M. P. P. Root. Newbury Park, CA: Sage, 1996.

Root, M. P. P. "Experiences and Processes Affecting Racial Identity Development: Preliminary Results from the Biracial Sibling Project." *Cultural Diversity and Mental Health,* 4(3) (1998): 237-247.

Root, M. P. P. "From Exotic to a Dime a Dozen." *Women and Therapy.* Eds. A. Gillem and C. Thompson. New York: Haworth Press, 2003.

Root, M. P. P. *Love's Revolution: Interracial Marriage.* Philadelphia: Temple University Press, 2001.

Root, M. P. P., ed. *The Multiracial Experience, Racial Borders as the New Frontier.* Newbury Park, CA: Sage, 1996.

Root, M. P. P., ed. *Racially Mixed People in America*. Newbury Park, CA: Sage, 1992.

Root, M. P. P. "Resolving 'Other' Status: Identity Development of Biracial Individuals." *Diversity and Complexity in Feminist Therapy*. Ed. L. S. Brown and M. P. P. Root. New York: Haworth, 1990. 185-205.

Ross, H. "Serving Pacific Islanders in Southern California." *Closing the Gap,* June/July 2000: 14.

Russell, K. E., M. Wilson and R. Hall. *The Color Complex: The Politics of Skin Color Among African Americans*. New York: Doubleday, 1992.

Saman, H. H. "Who Are Arab Americans?" *Groliers Multimedia Encyclopedia*. CD-ROM. New York: Grolier Electronic Publishing, 2001.

Schaffer, D. R. *Social and Personality Development* (3rd ed.). Pacific Grove, CA: Brooks/Cole, 1994.

Schmitt, E. "For 7 Million People in Census, One Race Category Isn't Enough." *The New York Times* 13 March 2001: sec A1, A14.

Schofield, J. W. "The Colorblind Perspective in School: Causes and Consequences." *Multicultural Education: Issues and Perspectives*. Eds. J. A. Banks and C. A. Mcgee-Banks. San Francisco: JosseyBass, 2002.

Seda B. E. *Requiem Por Una Cultura* (Requiem for a Culture). Río Piedras, Puerto Rico: Editorial Edil, 1970.

Setia, S. et. al. "Neonatal Jaundice in Asian, White, and Mixed Race Infants." *Archives of Pediatric and Adolescent Medicine* 156(3) (2002): 276-279.

Sheets, R. H. "Friendship and Multiracial Identity Formation: Can Friendship Cross Colors?" *Working with Mixed Heritage Students, PreK-12: Connecting Development with Practice*. Ed. K. Wallace. Westport, CT: Greenwood Publishing, in press.

Simon, R. J., H. Alstein, and M. S. Melli. *The Case for Transracial Adoption*. Washington, DC: American University Press, 1994.

Simon, R. J., and R. Roorda, *In Their Own Voices*. New York, NY: Columbia University Press, 2000.

Sklaroff, S. "E-mail Nation." *U. S. News Online* 22 March 1999. "www.usnews.com/usnews/search/magazine_search.htm"

Spickard, P. R. *Mixed Blood: Intermarriage and Ethnic Identity in Twentieth-Century America*. Madison, WI: University of Wisconsin Press, 1989.

Spindler, G. and L. Spindler. "Do Anthropologists Need Learning Theory?" *Education and Cultural Process*. Ed. G. D. Spindler. Prospect Heights, IL: Waveland Press, 1987. 53-69.

Stephan, C. W. "Intergroup Anxiety and Intergroup Interaction, 'Prejudice, Polemic or Progress.'" *Cultural Diversity and the Schools*. Eds. J. Lynch, C. Modgil and S. Modgil. London: The Falmer Press, 1992.

Stephan, W. *Reducing Prejudice and Stereotyping in Schools*. New York: Teachers College Press, 1999.

Stephen, C. "Ethnic Identity Among Mixed-Heritage People in Hawaii." *Symbolic Interaction* 14 (1991): 261-277.

Stevenson, H. C. "Theoretical Considerations in Measuring Racial Identity and Socialization: Extending the Self Further." *African American Identity Development*. Ed. R. L. Jones. Hampton, VA: Cobb & Henry, 1998.

Takeuchi D. T., N. Mokuau and C. Chun. "Mental Health Services for Asian Americans and Pacific Islanders." *Journal of Mental Health Administration* 19(3) (1992): 237-245.

Tashiro, C. "Mixed But Not Matched: Multiracial People and the Organization of Health Knowledge." *The Sum of Our Parts: Mixed Heritage Asian Americans.* Eds. T. Williams-Leon and C. L. Nakashima. Philadelphia: Temple University Press, 2001. 173-182.

Teish, L. *Jambalaya: The Natural Woman's Book of Personal Charms and Practical Rituals.* San Francisco: Harper & Row, 1988.

"The Story of 'Ala-ed-Din and the Wonderful Lamp.'" *Stories from the Thousand and One Nights.* Ed. C. W. Eliot. New York: P.F. Collier & Son, 2001.

Thomas, P. *Down These Mean Streets.* New York: New American Library, 1967.

Thornton, M. "A Social History of a Multiethnic Identity: The Case of Black-Japanese Americans." Diss. University of Michigan, 1983.

Tomishima, S. A. "Factors and Experiences in Biracial and Biethnic Identity Development." Diss. University of Utah, 2000.

Tsukiyama, G. *The Samurai's Garden.* New York: St. Martin's Griffin, 1994.

Twine, F. W. "Heterosexual Alliances: The Romantic Management of Racial Identity." *The Multiracial Experience: Racial Borders as the New Frontier.* Ed. M. P. P. Root. Thousand Oaks, CA: Sage Publications, 1996. 291-304.

U.S. Census Bureau: Census 2000." "http://www.census.gov/main/www/cen2000.html"

U.S. Census Bureau: "Special Tabulations (Table) 4. The Asian Population: 2000." Feb. 2002. "http://www.census.gov/population/een2000/phc-t08/tab05.pdf"

U.S. Census Bureau: "The Native Hawaiian and Other Pacific Islander Population: 2000 (Table) 4." 2001. "http://www.census.gov/prod/2001pubs/c2kbr01-14.pdf"

U.S. Census Bureau: "Ranking Tables for Counties by Race Alone, Race Alone or in Combination, and Two or More Races Populations." Summary File 1, PHC-T-14. 2000.

U.S. Census Bureau: "Overview of Race and Hispanic Origin." Origin 2001. "http://www.census.gov/prod/2001pubs/c2kbr01-1.pdf"

U.S. Department of Health and Human Services. "http:/www.acf.dhhs.gov/programs/cb/dis/afcars"

Van den Oord, E. and D. Rowe. "Racial Differences in Birth Health Risk: A Quantitative Approach." *Demography* 37(3) (2000): 285-298.

Vasconcelos, J. *The Cosmic Race* (La Raza Cósmica). Trans. D. T. Jaén. Baltimore, MD: Johns Hopkins University, 1997.

Vroegh, K. *Transracial Adoption: How Is It 17 Years Later?* Chicago: Chicago Child Care Society, 1997.

Wardle, F. "Children of Mixed Parentage: How Can Professionals Respond?" *Children Today* 18(4) (1989): 10-13.

Wardle, F. "Interracial Children and their Families: How School Social Workers Should Respond." *Social Work in Education* 13(4) (1991): 215-223.

Wardle, F. *Tomorrow's Children: Meeting the Needs of Multiracial and Multiethnic Children at Home, in Early Childhood Programs, and at School.* Denver, CO: Center for the Study of Biracial Children, 1999.

Wehrly, B., K. R. Kenney and M. E. Kenney. *Counseling Multiracial Families.* Thousand Oaks, CA: Sage Publications, 1999.

Wijeyesinghe, C. "Towards an Understanding of the Racial Identity of Biracial People: The Experience of Racial Self-identification of African-American/Euro-American Adults and the Factors Affecting their Choices of Racial Identity." Diss. University of Massachusetts, Amherst, 1992.

Wijeyesinghe, C. L. "Racial Identity in Multiracial People: An Alternative Paradigm." *New Perspectives on Racial Identity Development: A Theoretical and Practical Anthology.* Eds. C. L. Wijeyesinghe and B. W. Jackson. New York: New York University Press, 2001.

Williams, T. K. "Prism Lives: Identity of Binational Amerasians." *Racially Mixed People in America,* Ed. M. P. P. Root. Thousand Oaks, CA: Sage Publications, 1992. 280-303.

Williams-León , T. and C. Nakashima, ed. *The Sum of Our Parts: Mixed-Heritage Asian Americans.* Philadephia: Temple University, 2001.

Wolcott, H. F. "The Anthropology of Learning." *Education and Cultural Process.* Ed. G. D. Spindler. Prospect Heights, IL: Waveland Press, 1987. 26-52.

Wu, F. H. "Looking Ahead: The Hapa Century?" *Asian American Village @ Minorities' Job Bank,* 17 January 2000. "http://www.imdiversity.com/villages/asian/article_detail.asp?Article_ID=3548"

Zack, N. *Race and Mixed Race.* Philadelphia: Temple University Press, 1993.

Zastrow, C. *Outcome of Black Children/White Parents: Transracial* Adoption. San Francisco: R & E Research Associates, Inc., 1977.

Zea, M. C., M. Mason and A. Murguia. "Psychotherapy with Members of Latino/Latina Religions and Spiritual Traditions." *Handbook of Psychotherapy and Religious Diversity.* Eds. P. S. Richards and A. E. Bergin. Washington, DC: American Psychological Association, 2000. 397-419.

Zenón Cruz, I. *Narciso Descubre Su Trasero* (Narcissus Discovers His Buttocks). Humacao, Puerto Rico: Editorial Furidi, 1975.

Zimmerman, B. J., and D. H. Schunk, ed. *Self-Regulated Learning and Academic Achievement: Theoretical Perspectives.* Mahwah, NJ: Erlbaum, 2001.